EUROPEAN CASES
OF THE
REINCARNATION TYPE

European Cases of the Reincarnation Type

Ian Stevenson, M.D.

McFarland & Company, Inc., Publishers

Jefferson, North Carolina, and London

ALSO BY IAN STEVENSON

Children Who Remember Previous Lives:
A Question of Reincarnation
(McFarland, 2001)

The present work is a reprint of the illustrated casebound edition of
European Cases of the Reincarnation Type, *first published in 2003*
by McFarland.

LIBRARY OF CONGRESS CATALOGUING-IN-PUBLICATION DATA

Stevenson, Ian.
European cases of the reincarnation type / Ian Stevenson.
p.   cm.
Includes bibliographical references and index.

ISBN 978-0-7864-4249-2
softcover : 50# alkaline paper ∞

1. Reincarnation — Europe — Case studies.   I. Title.
BL518.S73   2008   133.9'01'35094 — dc21   2003001320

British Library cataloguing data are available

On the cover: Painting by Henriette Roos in 1936, rapidly and in the
dark (courtesy of Henriette Roos)

Manufactured in the United States of America

McFarland & Company, Inc., Publishers
Box 611, Jefferson, North Carolina 28640
www.mcfarlandpub.com

Acknowledgments

I must first express my gratitude to the subjects and other informants of the cases for their willingness to share information with me and allow it to be published here.

Next I thank other persons who referred cases to me. For this I wish to mention: the late Zoe Alacevich, Rita Castrén, Francisco Coelho, Dr. Erlendur Haraldsson, the late Dr. Karl Müller, and the late Dr. Winifred Rushforth.

Dr. Nicholas McClean-Rice conducted the first interviews for three cases. Dr. Erlendur Haraldsson in Iceland, Rita Castrén in Finland, and Bernadete Martins in Portugal assisted me as interpreters.

Several historians gave me advice and opinions about details in the case of Edward Ryall. For this assistance I thank Patricia Croot, Robert Dunning, Peter Earle, John Fowles, Derek Shorrocks, and W. M. Wigfield.

For the case of John East I received assistance from Dr. Alan Gauld, the late Guy Lambert, and Colonel W. L. Vale.

For similar assistance in my study of the case of Traude von Hutten I wish to thank Dr. Günter Stein and Dr. Heinrich Wendt.

Edith Turner made helpful comments on the case of Gedeon Haich. Also for the same case, I thank Verlag Eduard Fankhauser for permission to cite passages from *Einweihung* by Elisabeth Haich.

Angelika Neidhart gave permission for the citation of passages from the booklet by her father, Georg Neidhart, in which he described his experiences. I thank her also for permission to reproduce the sketch of a castle that figured in her father's experience.

Colonel I. C. Taylor sent me details about the soldiers on both sides of the Battle of Culloden, relevant to the case of Jenny McLeod.

Officials of the War Archives section of the Austrian Department of Archives in Vienna kindly answered my inquiries relevant to the case of Helmut Kraus.

Dawn Hunt showed unusual expertise in locating and often borrowing from libraries many obscure sources of information. She also assisted in the analysis of the features of European cases.

The staffs of numerous libraries have greatly assisted me. In particular I thank those of the British Library, the University Library of Cambridge University, the Alderman Library of the University of Virginia, the Staatsbibliothek of Munich, the Municipal Library of Hadleigh, Essex, and the Biblioteca Bozzano-DeBoni in Bologna. I could not use the last named library myself and therefore appreciate greatly the assistance through the mails of Silvio Ravaldini and Orfeo Fiocchi.

Dr. Mario Varvoglis, Director of the Institut Métapsychique International, gave permission for a translation of the report of a case first published in *Revue métapsychique*.

For the reproduction of photographs which they took or for which they have rights I thank Erlendur Haraldsson, Daniela Meissner, Mirror Syndication International, and the National Museums of Scotland.

Dr. Jean-Pierre Schnetzler and Madeleine Rous directed me to sources of information about the belief in reincarnation among modern Europeans.

James Matlock and Dr. Emily Williams Kelly carefully read the entire book and improved it in numerous ways. So did Patricia Estes, who also skillfully processed it through many revisions.

Contents

Preface

In writing this book I have had three purposes. First, I wanted to show that cases suggestive of reincarnation occur in Europe. By presenting reports of some much older cases—ones that I did not investigate myself—I am also able to show that cases of this type occurred in the first half of the 20th century. Nearly all the cases that I have studied and reported in previous publications occurred in Asia, West Africa, and among the tribes of northwest North America; and nearly all the inhabitants of these areas believe in reincarnation. Only a minority of Europeans do so. Although I can show that cases occur in Europe, they seem to be proportionately rarer there than in the other regions just mentioned, where I have found an abundance of cases ever since I began investigating them. In fact, we do not know whether the cases occur less often in Europe than in Asia or are only reported less often in Europe; both these possibilities may be true.

Second, I think some of the cases here reported show features similar to those of cases that I have previously investigated in Asia. These are principally: a very young age of the child's first speaking about a previous life; a forgetting of the claimed memories in middle childhood; a high incidence of violent death in the lives seemingly remembered; and frequently a reference to the mode of death in the subject's statements. Similarly, the European subjects often show behavior that is unusual for their family and that accords with the subject's statements about the previous life.

Third, I believe that at least some of the cases of this volume provide evidence of a paranormal process. By this I mean that we cannot explain some of the subject's statements or unusual behavior by normal means of communication. For these, reincarnation becomes a plausible interpretation, although—as I have never ceased to assert—it is not the only one.

The dates on the drafts of some of the case reports show that I have been writing this book—intermittently—for some 30 years. For many years I neglected European cases, including the effort to ascertain more cases, while I concentrated on the cases, largely found in Asia, whose subjects had relevant birthmarks and birth defects. My associates and I are now again becoming active in the search for European cases, which I hope the publication of this book will facilitate.

Notes for the Guidance of Readers

The personal names used in this book are a mix of real names and pseudonyms. In a few cases I have changed names of places in order better to conceal an identity.

In many places I have omitted qualifying words like *claimed*, *apparent*, and *seeming* before nouns, such as *memories*, that describe features of the cases. I have done this for ease of reading without intending to beg the principal question of the cases, which is that of whether these features include some paranormal process. By *paranormal* I mean not explicable by currently accepted knowledge of sensory processes.

In a further effort to assist readers I have in some cases referred to the subject only by his or her first name. This usage suggests a development of friendship between myself and the subject or a member of the subject's family. I have had this pleasure with some families, but not in all the cases in which I have adopted this familiar style.

Because I want to show when I can resemblances between the features of European cases and those of other areas of the world, I have sometimes mentioned parallel features in cases that occurred outside Europe.

I will explain or clarify several terms that my colleagues and I have adopted. First, we use the term *previous personality* for the deceased person — actual or presumed — to whom the subject's statements refer. In some cases informants identify a previous personality on the basis of predictions, dreams, or birthmarks before the subject has made any relevant statements about a previous life. When we satisfy ourselves that the child's statements and perhaps other features of the case correspond correctly to the life of a particular person, we describe the case as *solved*. Cases for which we fail to identify such a person we call *unsolved*. We refer to cases in which the subject and previous personality belong to the same family (sometimes an extended family) as *same-family cases*. We refer to cases in which the subject speaks about a previous life as a member of the opposite sex as *sex-change cases*.

The Appendix provides references to reports of all cases referred to in this book.

3

Part I

European Beliefs About Reincarnation

This book reports cases suggestive of reincarnation in Europe. The cases provide evidence of varying strengths. Prior beliefs influence judgments about evidence; and they influence even more the primary observations that furnish the evidence. This makes knowledge about the belief in reincarnation important for the appraisal of the cases. I begin the book, therefore, with a brief review of the belief in reincarnation among Europeans.

Some philosophers of ancient Greece believed in reincarnation and taught it to their students. Of these the earliest is Pythagoras (c. 582–500 B.C.) (Diogenes Laertius, c. 250/1925; Dodds, 1951; Iamblichus c. 310/1965). (Pythagoras was said to have remembered previous lives [Burkert, 1972, Diogenes Laertius c. 250/1925], but I am not concerned with that claim here.) The best known of the ancient Greek advocates of reincarnation, Plato, expounded the concept in numerous works, such as *Phaedo, Phaedrus, Meno*, (Plato, 1936) and *The Republic*, (Plato, 1935). Apollonius, a Greek born in Tyana and a sage and philosopher of the 1st century A.D., made reincarnation a central tenet of his teaching (Philostratus, 1912). Two centuries later, Plotinus (c. 205–270) and succeeding Neoplatonists taught reincarnation (Inge, 1941; Wallis, 1972). Plotinus himself had an ethicized concept of reincarnation, one not dissimilar to that then developing in India and conceivably influenced by Indian thought. He wrote: "Such things ... as happen to the good without justice, as punishments, or poverty, or disease, may be said to take place through offences committed in a former life" (Plotinus, 1909, p. 229).

We could extend the list of European philosophers who taught reincarnation within the Roman dominions before the development of formal Christianity, but this would tell us little about their influence on ordinary people. I think it was slight. Julius Caesar indicated this when he thought the belief in reincarnation, which he found among the Druids of Gaul and Britain, worthy of comment in *The Gallic War*

(Caesar, 1917).* Elsewhere, outside of Roman influence, the belief had some currency. Some writings of northern Europeans (Norsemen) before the Christianization of their lands suggest that the belief in reincarnation occurred among them (Davidson, 1964; Ker, 1904); but we do not know how widespread it then was.

The New Testament records incidents in the life of Jesus from which we can conclude not that Jesus taught reincarnation,† but that the concept was known to the people around him and considered discussable. This does not mean, however, that all the early Christians believed in reincarnation; probably most did not. Some of those in early Christianity who did believe in reincarnation called themselves, or were called, Gnostics. They formed a current of spiritual thought rather than a formal group. Some of their writings endorse the idea of terrestrial reincarnations (Mead, 1921). Christian Gnostics almost certainly drew on ideas familiar to Greek philosophers and perhaps Indian ones also (Eliade, 1982).

Christian theologians of the first few centuries after the life of Jesus frequently engaged themselves with the doctrines of Pythagoras and Plato, which, as I mentioned, Neoplatonists still expounded (Scheffczyk, 1985). One Christian Apologist, Tertullian (c. 160–c.225), opposed the Neoplatonists with unusual vigor (Tertullian, 1950; Scheffczyk, 1985). In the following passage he ridiculed the idea that an old man could die and later be reborn as an infant.

> At their birth, all men are imbued with the souls of infants; but how comes it that a man who dies in old age returns to life as an infant? … At least the soul ought to come back at the age it had when it departed, so as to resume life where it left off.
> If they did return as precisely the same souls, even though they might acquire different bodies and totally different fates in life, they ought to bring back with them the same characters, desires, and emotions they had before, since we should hardly have the right to pronounce them the same if they were lacking in precisely the characteristics which might prove their identity [Tertullian, 1950, p. 251].

Beginning as a persecuted minority, Christians needed to codify their beliefs. The codification brought formal declarations both of what was believed and of what was not to be believed. Regarding reincarnation the developing Christian orthodoxy focused on the teachings of Origen (c. 185–c. 254), a saintly scholar who undertook a consolidation of Christian doctrine in *On First Principles*. Like his near contemporary Plotinus, Origen concerned himself with undeserved suffering, the problem of theodicy. He suggested that conduct in a life or lives before birth might explain

---

The belief in reincarnation persisted among the Celts long after they became formally Christians. At the beginning of the 20th century Evans-Wentz (1911) recorded the belief among the Celtic inhabitants of Scotland, Wales, and Ireland.

†*Most translators, up to the 19th century and sometimes beyond, used the word* metempsychosis, *but some referred to the concept as* palingenesis; *others used* transmigration. *Inge (1941) rejected* metempsychosis, *preferring instead to use* metensomatosis, *because the bodies, not the souls, are changed at rebirth. The word* reincarnation *has currency now, and I will use it throughout this work. Buddhists prefer the word* rebirth, *which helps them to distinguish their concept of* anatta *(no soul) from that of Hinduism and most other beliefs in reincarnation, which include the idea of a persisting soul attached to successive physical bodies. In modern writings the word* metempsychosis *emphasizes the possibility of humans being reborn in the bodies of nonhuman animals.*

inequities at birth (Origen, 1973). At first considered harmless, Origen's concept of preexistence gradually aroused increasing opposition. Some historians have asserted that the Second Council of Constantinople in 553 anathematized Origen's teachings; but this seems doubtful. The Council condemned other heresies besides those of Origen; his name barely figures in its transactions (Murphy and Sherwood, 1973). Nevertheless, some scholars have come to regard this Council as decisive in the church's turning away from the idea of reincarnation. It seems important to note, therefore, that the pope, Vigilius, refused to attend the Council, which, packed by the emperor Justinian, tamely decreed what he instructed it to do (Browning, 1971). Furthermore, the decrees of the Council of Constantinople did not abruptly extinguish the belief in reincarnation among Christians. The question remained undecided until the time of Gregory the Great (c. 540–604), half a century later (Bigg, 1913).

Responsible scholars have differed about whether Origen believed and taught that reincarnation occurs (Butterworth, 1973; Daniélou, 1955; Krüger, 1996; Mac-Gregor, 1978; Prat, 1907). Reincarnation entails preexistence, but preexistence does not entail reincarnation. Nevertheless, theologians concerned about orthodoxy confused the two. They considered the teaching of either of these ideas a dangerous return to those of Pythagoras and Plato and therefore beyond the limits of tolerable dissent.

For centuries afterward little was thought and even less spoken about reincarnation in Europe. Exceptions occurred and were condemned or repressed. At the time of the Byzantine Renaissance a pupil of Michael Psellus "was excommunicated in 1082 for teaching pagan doctrines, including, it was alleged, transmigration" (Wallis, 1972, p. 162).* St. Thomas Aquinas (1225–1274) found Platonic ideas incompatible with Christianity and expressly opposed the idea of reincarnation (George, 1996; Thomas Aquinas, c. 1269/1984). In the meantime, however, heretical beliefs, including that in reincarnation, spread in Europe, especially in France and Italy. In the 13th century the Cathars (or Albigenses) of southwestern France came near to a complete secession from the Roman Catholic Church. The church only recovered this territory when the pope, Innocent III, authorized soldiers from northern France to conquer and subdue the rebellious regions of the southwest. The northerners, with the utmost cruelty, stamped out Catharism and all its teachings (Johnson, 1976; Le Roy Ladurie, 1975; Madaule, 1961; Runciman, 1969).

The extirpation of Catharism as a practiced religion could not prevent occasional philosophers from aberrantly endorsing the concept of reincarnation. In the late 15th century the Roman Catholic Church condemned the teachings of the Florentine Platonist Pico della Mirandola (1463–1494), which included reincarnation. A little more than a century later, in 1600, the Inquisition sentenced Giordano Bruno to be burned at the stake for, among other heresies, teaching reincarnation (Singer, 1950).

---

*The teachings of persons and communities accused of heresies, from Psellus to Giordano Bruno, included other unacceptable ideas besides that of reincarnation. Sometimes they offered an amalgam of concepts derived not only from Plato but also, for example, from Manicheism or from independent thinking.

In the several centuries following the judicial murder of Bruno, the idea of reincarnation caused no trouble to the Christian churches, whether Roman Catholic, Orthodox, or Protestant. Yet the idea persisted in the minds of many Europeans. Numerous poets, essayists, and philosophers alluded to it. To give one example only, Shakespeare could assume that theater-goers of the late 16th century would understand his allusions to Pythagoras in *Twelfth Night, As You Like It,* and *The Merchant of Venice.**

In the late 18th century translations of the texts of Asian religions began to reach Europeans. They became better acquainted with Asia and its religions than they had been. In the 19th century, however, the German philosopher Schopenhauer noted the isolation, as it were, of Europe from the belief in reincarnation that the majority of the world's population then held. In 1851 he wrote

> Were an Asiatic to ask me for a definition of Europe I should be forced to answer him: It is that part of the world completely dominated by the outrageous and incredible delusion that a man's birth is his beginning and that he is created out of nothing [p. 395; my translation].

The immense popular success of Sir Edwin Arnold's poem *The Light of Asia,* first published in 1879, reflected as well as caused a greater interest among Europeans in Buddhism, which the poem expounded.† We may say the same of Theosophy and its stepsibling, Anthroposophy. Both of these increased popular understanding of Hinduism and Buddhism, including the idea of reincarnation; but they built upon and elaborated, not always wisely, the work of translating scholars such as T. W. Rhys Davids, who founded the Pali Text Society in 1881, and Max Müller. These scholars had already made it possible for Thomas Henry Huxley (a biologist not an orientalist) to present, in the Romanes lecture of 1893, a knowledgeable and sympathetic summary of Hinduism and Buddhism with allusions to reincarnation (Huxley, 1905).

Bergunder (1994), in a study of the belief in the reincarnation of ancestors throughout the world, mentioned that modern European parents sometimes believe that a deceased child may reincarnate as a later-born baby in the same family. As examples he cited the case of Bianca Battista, of which I include the report (from 1911) in this book, and that of the Spanish surrealist painter Salvador Dalí. The first-born son of the painter's parents, called Salvador, died at the age of 21 months on August 1, 1903. Their second son, the painter, was born a bare 9 months later, on May 11, 1904, and given the name of his deceased brother (Secrest, 1986). Salvador Dalí seems never to have claimed memories of his deceased brother's life. His parents, particularly his father, however, believed that their deceased son had reincarnated.

---

*Head and Cranston (1977) and MacGregor (1978) cited numerous references to reincarnation or endorsements of the belief by European authors.

†In the preface to his poem, Arnold wrote: "A generation ago little or nothing was known in Europe of this great faith of Asia, which had nevertheless existed during twenty-four centuries, and at this day surpasses, in the number of its followers and the area of its prevalence, any other form of creed" (Arnold, 1879/1911, p. vii).

In the middle of the 19th century the Roman Catholic Church refused to recognize the newly unified state of Italy. In France the anticlericalism that developed later in that century led to the legislative separation, in 1905, of the Roman Catholic Church and the state. Some deplored these developments as opening the way to materialism, but freedom to think for oneself may lead to other beliefs, such as that in reincarnation. Somehow, in the century after Schopenhauer's definition of Europe, his dictum no longer became as true as it had been. And so we come to the surveys of the belief among modern Europeans.

The first survey known to me occurred in 1947. The persons interviewed were few, only 500, and they lived in a small area (a borough of London, England). Only about 4% of the persons interviewed spontaneously expressed a belief in reincarnation. These were, however, 10% of all those professing belief in some kind of survival after death (Mass-Observation, 1947).

In the 1960s surveys about religious beliefs were conducted in other (European) countries. In 1968 one was carried out in eight countries of West Europe. By that time an average of 18% of the respondents believed in reincarnation. The proportion of positive respondents showed a range between 10% in Netherlands and 25% in (West) Germany. In France 23% of respondents believed in reincarnation and in Great Britain 18% did so (Gallup Opinion Index, 1969).

Later surveys have shown a further increase in the proportion of (West) Europeans who believe in reincarnation. In a survey of ten European countries reported in 1986, the average of respondents who believed in reincarnation had increased to 21%, but this increase seems mainly due to a large number of positive responses in Great Britain. The figures for (West) Germany and France remained unchanged (Harding, Phillips, and Fogarty, 1986). Surveys of the early 1990s showed further increases in the belief in reincarnation. At this time 26% of respondents in Germany believed in reincarnation as did 28% of those in France and 29% of those in Great Britain and in Austria (Inglehart, Basañez, and Moreno, 1998).*

Surveys in France have shown a marked decline in adherence to the Roman Catholic Church. In 1966 80% of respondents counted themselves as Roman Catholics; in a survey of 1990 only 58% of the respondents did so (Lambert, 1994). In the same survey 38% of the respondents declared themselves "without any religion," and 39% of this group believed in reincarnation. Not all French persons expressing belief in reincarnation, however, were irreligious. On the contrary, 34% of persons who considered themselves practicing Catholics believed in reincarnation. It nevertheless appears that in France at least, an increased belief in reincarnation accompanied both a decline in attachment to the country's dominant religion and an increase in detachment from all religions.

A similar development to that in France appears to have occurred in England, where the state religion is the Anglican Church. Many persons continue to belong to a Christian Church, whether Anglican or other, while not believing everything there taught (Davie, 1990). Of these, many have come to believe in reincarnation, although

---

*No overall figures for West Europe can be calculated from the data for the early 1990s.

not necessarily attaching themselves to any New Age Group (Waterhouse, 1999). In short, they have privatized their religion (Walter and Waterhouse, 1999).

Europeans who believe in reincarnation have rarely grouped themselves in organized sects. (An exception occurred in the spiritist followers of Allan Kardec [1804–1869], who taught reincarnation in France.) The vocabulary of popular writings on reincarnation in Europe often shows obvious borrowings from Hinduism and Buddhism, for example, in the widespread use of words like *karma*, *astral body*, and *akashic record*. No strictly European scriptural system embodying the belief in reincarnation exists (Bochinger, 1996).

The increase in the numbers of Europeans who believe in reincarnation has not gone unremarked by those charged with maintaining Christian orthodoxy. They will accept no syncretic admission of the idea of reincarnation within Christianity, for which nevertheless some devout Catholics have wished (Stanley, 1989). Important theologians in France have railed against the belief in reincarnation (Stanley, 1998). The official catechism of the Roman Catholic Church in France states categorically that "There is no reincarnation after death" (Catéchisme de l'église Catholique, 1992, p. 217).*

The heads of the Roman Catholic Church in England must find dismaying that large numbers of formal Roman Catholics believe in reincarnation. A survey of Roman Catholics in England and Wales, conducted in 1978, found that 27% of respondents believed in reincarnation (Hornsby-Smith and Lee, 1979). The Rev. Joseph Crehan, S. J., believed himself obliged to publish a booklet inveighing against the belief in reincarnation (Crehan, 1978).

In Germany also, Roman Catholic theologians have responded polemically to the increased belief in reincarnation among Europeans (Kaspar, 1990; Schönborn, 1990).

Although the surveys I have cited show a substantial increase in the belief in reincarnation — even within the several decades of their being conducted — they do not explain why so many persons in Europe have adopted this belief. I think they cannot have done so on the basis of publicly available evidence for reincarnation. As I shall show in Part II, a small number of European cases of the reincarnation type were published during the first half of the 20th century; but few persons without a special interest in the subject would have read these reports. More abundant evidence from larger numbers of cases only became available in the last third of the century and could not have stimulated the earlier increase in the belief that the surveys demonstrated.

In the absence of other obvious answers I permit myself the following conjecture about why church attendance has declined and the belief in reincarnation has increased during the last hundred years or more. The achievements of the scientific

---

*The catechism is universally valid for Roman Catholics wherever they are in the world. I compared the French text of the negative assertion about reincarnation with that of the English language edition, Catechism of the Catholic Church, published in 1994. The wording is precisely the same. The authority cited is the passage in St. Paul's epistle to the Hebrews: "And as it is appointed unto men once to die, but after this the judgment" (Heb. 9:27 KJV).

method during the past 4 centuries have brought two important refutations of formal Christian doctrine: I refer to cosmology before Copernicus, Kepler, and Galileo and to biology before Lamarck and Darwin. The decline in the membership of Christian churches reflects a general loss of confidence in authoritative statements by representatives of the churches.

"Beware of the man with a single book." So runs an Arabian proverb. It is a strange saying to come from Arabia. Yet Arabs are not the only peoples to vest their faith in one book. Some Christians have shown this failing also. Now, however, increasing numbers of them have found the Bible to contain much truth, but not all of it. In the 20th century several philosophers discussed the idea of reincarnation sympathetically, and even positively (Almeder, 1992, 1997; Broad, 1962; Ducasse, 1961; Lund, 1985; McTaggart, 1906; Paterson, 1995). Few scientists have done so.

The writings of most modern scientists offer no solution to the seeming injustice of birth defects and other inequalities at birth. Instead they depict an exclusively material existence ending in extinction at death. Unsatisfied with this, many human beings— perhaps especially in modern Europe —continue to search for some meaning to life that transcends their own present existence. Reincarnation offers hope of a life after death; and it offers a possibility of our eventually understanding the causes of our suffering. These offerings do not make it true; only evidence can show whether it is or is not true. They may, however, account for the increasing attractiveness of the belief in reincarnation.

Part II

Uninvestigated Cases from the First Third of the 20th Century

In this chapter I describe eight older cases. They all occurred in the first third of the 20th century. We do not have precise dates for the occurrence of some of the cases, but I have presented them here in what I believe was their chronological order.

None of the cases of this chapter received an outside investigation, by which I mean that of someone not immediately concerned as the subject or an informant for the case. We may ask ourselves what an investigator contributes to the report of a case. First, he or she must make, or have made, an accurate record of the details of a case. No one can accomplish this without the cooperation of firsthand witnesses. We have these witnesses for the eight cases included in this section. The first reports of them were written, with one exception, either by the subject himself or by the father, other relative, employer, or an acquaintance of the subject. In the exceptional case (not previously published) the subject narrated his experience to a respected landowner of his region.

Second, an investigator asks informants about details omitted from spontaneous narratives. Among other details, dates can become important. The cases of this chapter show wide variations in the supply of this detail. For the case of Alessandrina Samonà the subject's father furnished precise dates for some events in the development of the case and sufficiently close dates for other events. In contrast, Giuseppe Costa, who wrote autobiographically about his experiences, furnished no dates whatever for their various phases.

Third, we expect an investigator to appraise the reliability of the informants for a case. To do this the investigator should, when feasible, interview the informants. I could not do that for these eight cases, with the exception of that of Georg Neidhart, whom I met on two occasions. If an investigator cannot interview the informants, some other means of probing their reliability may assist. Reports that include errors of verifiable details evoke diminished confidence compared with ones not having such defects. So do reports that show the reporter eager to persuade readers to agree with the reporter's interpretations. Those that contain sufficient detail, as I think most in this chapter do, enable readers to evaluate a case, even when they cannot interview the informants for it.

The few older cases presented in this chapter do not permit any kind of quantitative comparison between them and more recent cases. We can, nevertheless, note the occurrence of one feature of some older cases that we do not find in more recent ones. For example, apparitional experiences occurred in three of the earlier cases, but in none of the later ones. Also, in three of the older cases, but only one of the later ones, the participants reported mediumistic communications with deceased persons. In other features the older cases resemble the later ones.

Some of the writers have provided initials, but not full names for the subject or other persons concerned in a case. To make their reports easier to read I have supplied complete names, which are pseudonyms.

The reports of three of the cases include references to past events about which we can consult contemporary records or historians' citations of these. I have included references to these sources.

Readers who believe that the strength of evidence evaporates with the passage of time* and those who think earlier observers less careful than we are will find these older cases unconvincing. I do not belong in their group. If a reader asks why we should find these cases credible, I ask why we should not.

CASE REPORTS

GIUSEPPE COSTA

The subject himself reported this case in a book entitled *Di là dalla vita*, which could be translated into English — although the book never has been — by *From the Beyond to This Life* (Costa, 1923). The author was Giuseppe Costa, and he devoted some 50 pages — about one-quarter — of the book to an account of personal experiences that convinced him that he had lived before. The remainder of the book offers a popular summary of psychical research.

The report lacks dates for events. Costa's book was published in 1923. A number of years later Ernesto Bozzano, who was then the leading investigator of psychical

---

To readers doubtful of the accuracy of memories for these experiences over a period of years (before the making of a written record) I recommend studies and discussions of this question that my colleagues and I have published (Cook, Greyson, and Stevenson, 1998; Stevenson and Keil, 2000).

phenomena in Italy, met Costa and became interested in his case. In 1940 Bozzano published a chapter in a book that was partly an account of his interview with Costa and partly a summary of the section in Costa's book in which Costa described his claimed memories of a previous life (Bozzano, 1940). The chapter was later reprinted in *Luce e Ombra* (Bozzano, 1994). Bozzano did not give a date for his meeting with Costa. He stated that Costa's book had been published "a good many years ago," so we can suppose that he met Costa around 1935. In his book Costa did not mention when he was born. Bozzano stated that he seemed to be in his 50s when they met. If we build on this flimsy evidence, we can suppose that Costa was born around 1880. He would have been in his 40s in 1923, when he published his book. In it he refers to the culminating events of his experiences as having occurred "many years earlier" than his time of writing. One important event of his experiences (that I shall describe) occurred just before the final examinations of his years at college, which would perhaps have been around 1904. Costa trained and worked as an engineer. The later experiences that led to their verification occurred, we can believe, before he was 30 years old, let us say in about 1910.

I base my account of the case on Bozzano (1940/1994), but I have also consulted Costa's book, the text of which sometimes differs from Bozzano's in unimportant ways. Dr. Karl Müller, from whom I first learned of the case, gave me a brief summary of it in English; he had prepared this from Brazzini (1952), who, however, had summarized Bozzano's report.

Costa's experiences developed, as I have estimated, from early childhood until his early 30s. We can identify several distinct phases in their occurrence.

The first phase began in early childhood, but Costa did not mention a particular age. His family had a painting hanging on the wall of their living room that depicted an oriental scene: a city with towers and golden domes on the banks of a body of water. (He learned later that the painting was of Constantinople and the Bosporus.) This picture aroused in him a series of images that jumbled around in his mind: scenes of large numbers of armed men, ships sailing, banners flying, the noise of a battle, mountains, the sea stretching to the horizon, hills covered with flowers. When the young Costa tried to order these images into some rational sequence, he found them intractable. Yet their vividness impressed him, and even as a young child he believed he had somehow lived through the scenes arising in his mind.

Costa did not say where he was born, but he passed his infancy and childhood in the small town of Gonzaga, near Mantua. He attended the lyceum in Mantua. These places are in the valley of the river Po, where the countryside is flat and the sea about 100 kilometers away. Costa asserted that, whatever the origin of those childhood images, they had no basis in any of his surroundings at that time of his life.

The next phase of his experiences occurred when, at the age of 10, his father took him for the first time to Venice. As soon as he arrived there he had a sense of familiarity with the city, as if he had been there before, long ago. That same night he had a vivid dream. In it all the disparate, seemingly unrelated images that he had earlier experienced became ordered in a chronological sequence, as follows:

After a long journey in boats, through rivers and canals, we arrived in Venice. We traveled in barques filled with armed soldiers in the clothing of the Middle Ages. I seemed to be about 30 years old and had some kind of command. After a stay in Venice we embarked in galleys on which two banners waved: a blue one with the image of the Virgin Mary among golden stars, and that of Savoy, red with a white cross.* On the larger† galley, which was more painted and decorated [than the other], there was someone to whom everyone showed great respect and who spoke to me with great friendliness. Then came the sea, seemingly endless, stretching beyond the horizon. Then we disembarked in a sunny land with a clear sky of cobalt blue. Then the army embarked again and landed at a different place. There the troops were coordinated; there were tents full of soldiers, beneath a city with old towers bristling with armaments. Then came our assault, a battle of tremendous violence ending when we broke into the city. Then finally came the march of our splendid army into the city with its domes of gold on the wonderful bay. This was the magnificent city, Constantinople, depicted in the painting of [our house in] Gonzaga, as I learned later [Bozzano, 1940, pp. 317–18; my translation].

Costa emphasized that the images of his dream reproduced those of his earlier childhood, but the dream assembled them into a rational order that strengthened his belief in having lived through the scenes of the earlier images and the dream.§

From his early youth Costa had a keen interest in arms, fencing, gymnastics, and horseback riding. He engaged in these activities to the point of neglecting the assigned classical studies — Latin and Greek — of his high school. He volunteered to join the army and was appointed a second lieutenant in the Royal Cavalry of Piedmont. He was then stationed in Vercelli, which is about halfway between Milan and Turin. Here he delighted in the military life. It all seemed entirely natural to him, as if he had resumed a previous occupation.

In Vercelli he had another of his unusual experiences. One day he was passing the church of Saint Andrea, when the sounds of some sacred music impelled him to enter the church. As he entered, however, he experienced an unpleasant feeling of some kind of repentance carried over from the past. He did not know what to make of this, but conjectured that perhaps he had participated in some ceremony at this church that had burdened his mind.

After this episode, Costa became involved in responsibilities toward his family. His apparent memories of a previous life lost their importance. He was essentially a materialist and might have forgotten all about the earlier unusual experiences if he had not had another one that completely reversed his convictions.

This experience occurred as he was preparing for the final examinations for his

---

*One may question whether a schoolboy of the 1890s, as I have supposed Costa to have been, would recognize the flag of the medieval County of Savoy. This seems less implausible when we remember that Italy became united in the 1860s under the house of Savoy, which before that time had been rulers of Piedmont and Sardinia. The blue flag showing the Virgin surrounded by golden stars would be a less accessible detail.

†Costa used the Italian word maggiore (larger), which implies that there were only two galleys.

§In the case of Georg Neidhart (included later in this Part) the subject also had disordered images in childhood that became coherently assembled in his early adulthood. Ruprecht Schulz, whose case I describe in Part III of this work, had in childhood what I call a behavioral memory; but he had no images of a previous life until his middle adulthood.

degree.* He studied so long and so intensely that he worked himself into a state of near-exhaustion, could not stay awake any more, and collapsed onto his bed. As he turned over in the ensuing sleep, he struck and upset an oil lamp that was burning in his bedroom. The lamp then emitted noxious fumes that quickly filled the bedroom. He awakened, but then found himself above his physical body and looking down on it. He sensed that his life was in danger, and in this extremity he somehow called for help to his mother, who was sleeping in the next room. He became aware that he could see through the wall into his mother's bedroom. He saw her awaken with a start, go to the window of her room, which she opened, and then run to his room, where she opened a window to dispel the fumes there. In his opinion later, this action saved his life. Costa was particularly impressed when, knowing that he could not physically have seen through the wall to his mother's bedroom, he asked her whether she had opened the window of her own room before coming to help him, and she replied that she had done this. He felt liberated by the experience and never doubted again that body and mind are separable.†

The last of Costa's unusual experiences, including the culminating one, occurred when he and two friends made a tour in the valley of Aosta§ and visited several of its castles. Costa recorded his reactions on visiting three of them: Ussel, Fénis, and Verrès. At Ussel he felt a sense of sadness and oppression. As I shall explain later, he subsequently attributed this malaise to events in the previous life of which he later obtained some verification. At Fénis he had no unusual experience.

In contrast, at Verrès, he was profoundly moved. He described himself as filled with strong emotions of somewhat mixed quality: love and regrets. (He did not describe any recurrence of images at this stage.) He found the ruined castle so moving that he decided to return to it at the time of sunset. When he got back to the castle later, a great storm came up, and he had to spend the night in the castle. It seems not to have been inhabited at this time, but he found an old bed on which he could sleep. Despite the raging storm he felt serene and soon fell asleep. After some time he awoke and noticed a light that he described as phosphorescent. The light expanded until it developed the form of a human being and then discernibly that of a woman. The figure beckoned Costa to follow her, and he did this. At first briefly frightened by the phantasm, he then became fascinated, and as he came closer to the figure he experienced a feeling of the deepest love. Then he heard the figure speak: "Ibleto! I wanted to see you again once more before divine death unites us once more.... Read near the tower of Albenga an account of one of your past lives.... Remember me and that I am waiting for you until the time comes."

---

*This must have been for his qualification as an engineer. Costa does not say so explicitly, but one can infer that he resigned from the army and trained as an engineer. Alternatively, he may have continued to be active in the cavalry part-time, the service being similar to that in the National Guard of the United States.

†Costa's report includes three features of experiences near death, which, my colleagues and I have proposed, suggest survival of human personality after death when they occur together. These are: unusual clarity of consciousness, seeing the physical body from a different position in space, and paranormal perception (Cook, Greyson, and Stevenson, 1998).

§Aosta is about 80 kilometers north and slightly west of Turin. It is the principal town of a long and (in the Middle Ages) strategically important valley, close to the present border between Italy and France.

Costa had learned at the time he visited the castle of Verrès that a man called Ibleto di Challant had built it in 1380. He probably also learned that Ibleto di Challant was a trusted counselor of Amadeus VI, count of Savoy. He decided, however, to study whatever he could find "near the tower of Albenga."* He soon learned that there are (or were at that time) several towers in Albenga. Which was the one he wanted? From inquiring around he learned that the owner of one of them was a descendant of the family of di Challant. He then introduced himself to the proprietor, Marquis Del Carretto di Balestrina, and on the pretext of studying medieval history, he asked to be allowed to examine whatever records were available concerning Ibleto di Challant. The marquis obligingly made available to Costa a number of family documents about the di Challant family that he had inherited. Among these Costa found a biography of Ibleto di Challant written by Boniface II, lord of Fénis, which was one of the castles that Costa had visited. This work was an unpublished manuscript, written in French.†

Costa's Summary of Boniface's Biography of Ibleto di Challant

Ibleto di Challant was born in 1330, the son of Giovanni di Challant. He eventually inherited half a dozen substantial properties including Verrès and Montjovet. From his youth on, he was at the court of the count of Savoy, Amadeus VI (1334–1383), who was known as the "Green Count" because of his wearing clothes of that color at tourneys. Ibleto di Challant became an advisor and military companion to Amadeus VI.

At the court of Amadeus VI, Ibleto fell in love with the count's sister, Blanche of Savoy. He wished to marry her, but for reasons of state Amadeus arranged for her to marry Galeazzo Visconti, lord of Milan. With some reluctance, Ibleto married a woman, Giacometta di Chatillon, designated by his father.

In 1366 Ibleto accompanied Amadeus VI during a kind of belated crusade against the Turks near Constantinople. The expedition embarked from Venice, stopped somewhere in Morea (southern Greece) for regrouping, and went to Gallipoli (which the Turks had taken from the declining Byzantine Empire in 1354). After capturing Gallipoli the Italians went on to Constantinople. Amadeus then found the emperor, John, ineffective and unhelpful in repelling the Turks. Becoming discouraged about prospects of success, Amadeus returned to Italy and thereafter played an important part in its affairs until his death in 1383. Ibleto di Challant then became an advisor of his son, Amadeus VII, who was known as the "Red Count," so named because of his favorite color. Amadeus VII died at the age of 29, under somewhat mysterious circumstances. He fell from his horse and thereafter had a wound in his leg that did

---

*Albenga is on the coast of Italy at the Ligurian Sea. It is about 70 kilometers southwest of Genoa.

†Costa supposed that Boniface's biography of Ibleto di Challant had been written around 1450. This was in the period of Middle French. Costa described the language as "tortuous, contorted ... and almost incomprehensible." I am surprised that he could read it, and I have asked myself whether the work was written at a later date.

not heal. He may have died of tetanus. Boniface stated that he died in the arms of Ibleto di Challant. After the premature death of Amadeus VII in 1391, Ibleto di Challant continued for a time in the service of Bona di Borbone, the regent for her son, Amadeus VIII, who was then an 8-year-old boy. Toward the end of the century, tired of intrigues and warfare, he retired to the castle of Verrès, where he died in 1409.

In 1377 Amadeus VI freed the city of Biella (northeast of Turin) from the control of the bishop of Vercelli. He captured the bishop, who was held prisoner for almost a year at Ibleto di Challant's castle of Montjovet. For this offence, the pope, Gregory XI, excommunicated Ibleto. In 1378 Gregory XI died, and his successor at Rome (it was the time of the Great Schism in the Papacy), Urban VI, released Ibleto from the sentence of excommunication with the condition that he ceremonially express his repentance to the bishop of Vercelli in the church of St. Andrea. Ibleto did this. Costa believed a subliminal memory of this humiliation accounted for the oppressive feeling he had when, as a young man, he had gone into the church of St. Andrea in Vercelli.

Costa also found an explanation for the unpleasant feeling he had experienced at Ussel, when he learned (from the documents at Albenga) that two members of the di Challant family, who held the castle of Ussel, had robbed and plundered the people of the valley. The count of Savoy levied a fine on them, but this did not cancel the damage they had done to the family name.

Information About Ibleto di Challant from Other Sources

It seemed to me important to learn about the life of Ibleto di Challant from sources other than the (presumably still unpublished) manuscript biography by Boniface.

The history of the counts of Savoy in the 14th century has not much interested Anglo-Saxon historians. A fairly detailed history of Venice refers in two lines to the expedition of the count of Savoy against the Turks in 1366 (Norwich, 1982). This work mentions that Venice grudgingly contributed two galleys to the expedition. In a history of Venice in the late Middle Ages (Hodgson, 1910) I found the following footnote:

> The count of Savoy (Amadeus VI, surnamed "The Green") sailed from Venice in 1366, took Gallipoli and entered Constantinople, where he found that the Emperor John V was a prisoner of the King of Bulgaria at Widdin. He pressed on and released the Emperor and brought him back to his capital … [p. 489].

What seems an obscure corner of history to me in the early 21st century may not have been unknown to a schoolboy of Italy in the late 19th century. I found some information about Ibleto di Challant in a biography of Count Amadeus VI of Savoy (Cognasso, 1926). This work gives several pages to Amadeus's crusade against the Turks in 1366. It describes the departure from Venice, a landing at Morea, then the taking of Gallipoli and entry into Constantinople. The description of the crusade contains no reference to participation by Ibleto di Challant. Cognasso does not refer to him until he describes the events of 1374, when Ibleto di Challant was "captain general of the Piedmontese forces." In 1378, Cognasso wrote, Ibleto di Challant suppressed a rebellion at Biella (northeast of Vercelli) and kept the bishop a prisoner in his (di Challant's) castle of Montjovet; but Cognasso did not mention the pope's excommunicating Ibleto di Challant for this offence. Ibleto di Challant's name occurs from time to time in Cognasso's narrations of the later years of Amadeus's reign and the much shorter reign of his son, Amadeus VII (Cognasso, 1926, 1931). Carbonelli (1912) mentions Ibleto di Challant's service to the Regent of the boy Amadeus VIII after the death of Amadeus VII.

Two later biographies of Amadeus VI mention Ibleto di Challant more than a few times (Cox, 1967; Savoia, 1956); but neither of them refers to Ibleto di Challant's participation in Amadeus's crusade of 1366. An earlier work, a detailed history of the di Challant family, mentioned Ibleto di Challant's participation in that crusade (Vaccarone, 1893). This work also mentions the pope's excommunication of Ibleto di Challant for having imprisoned the bishop of Vercelli in his castle at Montjovet; but it does not mention a penance later performed by Ibleto di Challant in the Church of Saint Andrea at Vercelli.

No source I have consulted confirmed that Amadeus VII died "in the arms" of Ibleto di Challant. He may, however, have been present when Amadeus died, and he was among those suspected unjustly of having poisoned Amadeus.

In three details Costa's account (based solely on Boniface's biography) differs from information other sources provide. He wrote that Amadeus took 10,000 soldiers on his expedition to Constantinople in 1366; but Cognasso estimated that he could have had no more than 2,000 men, of cavalry and infantry together. This discrepancy may have derived from an error on the part of Boniface. A second discrepancy occurred in Costa's description of the fighting in Turkey. He implied that a battle was fought at Constantinople. The only battle of the campaign was in fact fought before Gallipoli. The Turks then surrendered that town, and from there the Savoyards marched easily to Constantinople. The third discrepancy seems the most important. As I mentioned, Costa learned from Boniface that Ibleto di Challant wished to marry Blanche, the sister of Amadeus VI. Instead, Amadeus arranged for her to marry Galeazzo Visconti of Milan, which she did on September 28, 1350 (Mesquita, 1941). Costa conjectured that Ibleto di Challant's unhappiness over his thwarted love for Blanche became a factor in his joining Amadeus's crusade. The expedition to Constantinople, however, did not occur until 1366, and it seems unlikely, although not impossible, that Ibleto di Challant's thwarted love for Blanche could have been a factor, more than 15 years later, in his joining the crusade.

Costa's Identification of the Apparitional Figure at Verrès

Costa did not clearly identify the apparitional figure who spoke to him during the night he spent in the castle of Verrès. He conjectured that she might have been

Blanche of Savoy, with whom Ibleto di Challant had been in love. He also thought she might have been Giacometta di Chatillon, whom Ibleto had married.

Giacometta must have died before Ibleto di Challant, because he married, as his second wife, Giovanna di Nus (Vaccarone, 1893). Costa did not mention her.

Physical Resemblances Between Costa and Ibleto di Challant

Costa found (probably at Albenga) a portrait of Ibleto di Challant, which he reproduced in his book. Bozzano believed that the faces of Ibleto (as depicted in the portrait) and that of Costa were so similar that one might have been mistaken for the other. Ibleto had been a large man, almost a giant among his contemporaries. Costa himself was a large person whose great size and martial bearing much impressed Bozzano.

Costa's Conviction About the Paranormal Features of His Experiences

Costa believed that the documents (including the biography of Ibleto) that he found at Albenga had verified the details in the dream he had had as a 10 year-old child when he first went to Venice. He found particularly impressive the direction the apparitional figure had given him to study relevant documents at Albenga. These documents, he learned, had descended in the family for centuries. Like a ball falling in a pinball machine, however, the documents might have gone to other descendants. The name of di Challant was not part of the name of the Marquis Del Carretto di Balestrina. Costa thought that few persons outside the marquis's immediate family would have known that he (the marquis) was a descendant of a di Challant.

Comment

Costa did not state any date for the painting of Constantinople that hung in his family's living room and that had stimulated his first images of a previous life when he was a young child. Presumably, however, it would have depicted Constantinople as it was in the 19th century. This must have differed much from the appearance of the city in the 14th century. Yet perhaps not everything had changed. The emperor Justinian had the present building of the Haghia Sophia erected in 532. (The Turks converted it into a mosque after they conquered Constantinople in 1453; it is now a museum.) The cover of Runciman's account of the siege of Constantinople in 1453 reproduces a depiction of the siege painted in 1499 (Runciman, 1965). It shows the walls and many towers, although no golden domes. Given these features and the city's location on a large body of water, the Bosporus, the painting on the wall of the

Costa house in Gonzaga may well have aroused memories of a previous age in Constantinople.

Costa was 10 when he first went to Venice with his father. A boy of that age would almost certainly have learned something of the history of the counts and dukes of Savoy. The king of Italy in 1890 was Humbert I, a descendant of Amadeus VI. We can ask, however, whether a boy so young could have learned about the futile crusade that Amadeus undertook in 1366. If he had, he might have known that a man called Ibleto di Challant had an important role in that expedition.

Normal explanations that take us this far, however, seem powerless to explain how Costa learned about the verifying documents he found at Albenga. Bozzano obviously brooded about this case after he had listened to Costa. Trying the fit of other explanations, he came to believe that Costa had grounds for thinking he had remembered a previous life.

BIANCA BATTISTA

A report of this case appeared first in the Italian magazine *Ultra* in 1911 (Battista, 1911). The report consisted of a letter written by the subject's father, Florinda Battista, who was a captain in the Italian army. Delanne (1924) reprinted the letter in French. I made the following translation into English.

The Report

In August 1905 my wife was three months pregnant when, lying in bed and fully awake, she had an apparitional experience that profoundly affected her. Our little daughter, who had died three years earlier, unexpectedly appeared to her with childlike joyousness and quietly said the following words: "Mama. I am coming back." Before my wife could recover from her surprise, the figure disappeared.

When I returned home and my wife, still much moved by her experience, told me about it, I thought at first that she had had a hallucination. At the same time I did not wish to deprive her of the conviction she had of having received some kind of communication from Heaven; and so I agreed immediately to her request that we give the baby that was to be born the name of the older deceased sister: Bianca. At that time I had no knowledge of what I learned much later of Theosophy, and I would have considered quite mad anyone who spoke to me about reincarnation. I was quite convinced that a person dies once and does not come back.

Six months later, in February 1906, my wife gave birth to a baby girl who resembled in every particular her older sister. She had the same large dark eyes and thick, curly hair. These features did not affect my materialistic stance; but my wife, delighted with the favor she had received, believed that a miracle had occurred and that she had given birth to the same child twice. This child is now about six years old and has, like her deceased sister, developed precociously both emotionally and intellectually. Both these girls could clearly pronounce the word "Mama" when they were seven months old, whereas our other daughters, although they were no less intelligent, could not say this word until they were twelve months old.

For the better understanding of what I am going to describe next, I should mention here that during the lifetime of the first Bianca we had a Swiss servant called Mary, who spoke only French. She had brought from her native mountains a sort of *cantilena*, a kind of lullaby. It acted as if it came from the head of Morpheus, such was its soporific effect when she sang it to our little daughter. After that child's death Mary returned to her country, and we shut out all memory of the lullaby, which tended to remind us of our lost child. Nine years passed away and we had completely forgotten about the lullaby; then an extraordinary event revived our memory of it. A week ago, I was with my wife in my study, adjoining the bedroom, when we both distinctly heard the lullaby, like a distant echo. The sound came from the bedroom near us. At first, both moved and puzzled, we did not recognize the song as coming from our child. Looking into the bedroom, however, we saw our daughter, the second Bianca, sitting up on the bed and singing the lullaby with the most perfect French accent. We had certainly never taught it to her. My wife — trying not to show any surprise — asked her what she was singing. Bianca said that it was a French song. She did not know a word of French apart from a few her sisters had taught her. Then I asked her: "Who taught you this song?" Bianca replied: "No one. I just know it by myself." Then she continued singing it like someone who had never sung anything else in her life.

From the facts that I have carefully reported, readers may choose whatever interpretation they wish. As for me, I have reached the following conclusion: The dead come back.

ALESSANDRINA SAMONÀ

The father of the subject of this case published the first report of it (Samonà, 1911). He was also the father of the older daughter of whom he believed his younger daughter was the reincarnation. The report generated some discussion among those who read it because of the short interval — about 8 months— between the death of the older daughter and the subject's birth. Carmelo Samonà published further information about the case when the subject was about 2 years old (Samonà, 1913a). He also replied to criticism concerning the short interval between the death and presumed rebirth (Samonà, 1913b, 1914). Subsequently, he sent a report about the subject's further development to Charles Lancelin, who later included this information in a book (Lancelin, 1922). This book contained an account of the only imaged memory the subject had expressed in words.

The Report

Both the children principally concerned in this case were called Alessandrina, and for easier distinction between them I will call them Alessandrina I and Alessandrina II. Their parents were Carmelo Samonà, a physician of Palermo, Italy, and his wife, Adele. They also had three sons.

Alessandrina I died of meningitis at the age of about 5, on March 15, 1910. Three days after the child's death her grief-stricken mother dreamed of her dead daughter, who said to her: "Mother, do not cry. I have not left you, only withdrawn. Look! I am going to become small like this." As she said this, she gestured to show the small size of a baby. Then she added: "You will have to suffer again for me." Three days later Adele Samonà had the same dream.* One of her friends suggested that the dream foretold the reincarnation of Alessandrina I. At this point Adele knew nothing about reincarnation and even after reading a book on the subject that her friend brought to her she remained unpersuaded of its possibility. She had had a miscarriage in 1909 and a related surgical operation; subsequently, she still had some uterine bleeding. These events made her doubtful that she could ever become pregnant again.

Some days after the two dreams when Carmelo Samonà was trying to comfort his inconsolable wife they heard three loud knocks as if someone was at the front door. Their three sons, who were with them at the time, also heard the knocks. They thought their aunt Caterina (Carmelo Samonà's sister), who often visited at this hour, had arrived, and they opened the door expecting to see her. No one was there.

The episode of the knocks stimulated the Samonàs to undertake amateur mediumistic seances.† (Samonà's report does not state how they went about this or which one of several family members who participated was regarded as the responsible medium.) They received communications appearing to come from Alessandrina I and also from a deceased sister of Carmelo Samonà called Giannina, who had died many years before at the age of 15. In these communications the purported Alessandrina I said that she had made the knocks the family had heard earlier in order to draw attention to herself. She continued to reassure her mother that she would be returning and said that this would be before Christmas. She wanted all her family and friends to know about her returning. She repeated this so often that Carmelo Samonà began to find the mediumistic sessions tedious. He believed that the Alessandrina communicator had become monoideistic with her concern that everyone should be told about her coming back.

On April 10 Adele Samonà became aware that she was pregnant. (The report does not say how she knew this.) At a mediumistic session on May 4, the Alessandrina I communicator said, somewhat confusedly, that there was someone else around her mother. The Samonàs did not understand this until the other communicator, Giannina, explained that there was a second being who wished to be reborn as their child. At later sessions the Alessandrina I communicator said she was to be born along with a sister; and the Giannina communicator told the Samonàs that the reborn Alessandrina would closely resemble Alessandrina I.

After a time the mediumistic communications ceased. The Alessandrina I communicator had previously explained that there could be no communications from

---

*I have called dreams of this type "announcing dreams." They occur often among cases in Asia, especially among those in Myanmar (Burma) and Turkey. They also occur frequently among the cases of the Tlingit of southeastern Alaska (Stevenson, 1987/2001).

†Carmelo Samonà had earlier published a book on psychical research, which, according to Lancelin (1922), competent investigators had much praised. I have not seen this book myself.

her after the 3rd month of pregnancy, because she (the Alessandrina I communicator) would after that time "be more and more attached to 'matter' and sleeping."

In August an obstetrician examined Adele and found that she was pregnant with twins. The remainder of her pregnancy was not free of troublesome symptoms, but these ceased and, on November 22, 1910, she gave birth to twin girls. Immediately, one of the babies was seen to have a remarkable physical similarity to Alessandrina I, and she was given the same name, thus becoming Alessandrina II. Her sister was called Maria Pace. Carmela Samonà concluded his first report of the case by describing three physical features in which Alessandrina II resembled Alessandrina I and differed from Maria Pace: hyperemia of the left eye, seborrhea of the right ear, and a slight asymmetry of the face.

In support of his statements Samonà published (as a supplement to his report) several letters from members of his family and friends who testified that they had learned before the twins were born about Adele's dreams, the three knocks, and the subsequent mediumistic sessions, including the prediction of the birth of twin girls before Christmas. Of these corroborations that of Samonà's sister Caterina has the greatest value, because she visited her brother and sister-in-law almost daily and would have learned quickly of each development in the case.

In the summer of 1913 Alessandrina II and Maria Pace were 2½ years old. Carmelo Samonà then published a second report in which he emphasized the behavioral similarities between the two Alessandrinas (Samonà, 1913a). Both Alessandrinas were generally quiet, and they would sit contentedly in their mother's lap; Maria Pace, although no less affectionate toward their mother, was somewhat restless and would come to her mother and soon go off again to play with her toys. The Alessandrinas had little interest in toys, but liked to play with other children. Both the Alessandrinas had phobias of loud noises and of barbers, and they both disliked cheese in any form. Maria Pace did not have these traits. The Alessandrinas both enjoyed folding and smoothing clothing or other cloth, such as sheets and towels. They also liked to play with shoes and sometimes played at putting on shoes that were obviously too large for them. Maria Pace did not engage in these kinds of plays.

Both Alessandrinas sometimes spoke about themselves in the third person. They would say, for example, "Alessandrina is afraid." They also had a habit of playfully modifying names, for example by calling their Aunt Caterina, "Caterana." Maria Pace did not show such verbal oddities.

In 1913 the physical similarities between the two Alessandrinas had become more obvious than they had been when the twins were born. In his second report Carmelo Samonà published photographs of Alessandrina I at the age of 3 years and 8 months and of the twins at 2 years of age (Samonà, 1913a). The photographs show the facial asymmetry of the Alessandrinas. In both of them the left eye is appreciably closer to the midline than the right eye and the left labial commissure is shorter than the right one. Maria Pace did not have these asymmetries of the face.* Carmelo Samonà con-

*The facial asymmetries of the two Alessandrinas impressed me also, and I published Samonà's photographs of the two Alessandrina's in a brief report of the case (Stevenson, 1997).

sidered that Alessandrina II resembled Alessandrina I "perfectly," except that she was a little fairer than her deceased older sister. Both Alessandrinas were left-handed; but Maria Pace and all other members of the family were right-handed.

The reports of this case received some attention in Europe, at least among readers of spiritualist literature. Among these was Charles Lancelin, who corresponded with Carmelo Samonà about the case of his twins. Lancelin reproduced in a book a letter he had received from Carmelo Samonà that was dated March 20, 1921 (Lancelin, 1922). This letter referred to the continuing differences between the twins and the persistent resemblance of Alessandrina II to Alessandrina I. Alessandrina II had in the meantime developed an interest in "spiritual matters" and sometimes meditated; she had little interest in domestic affairs. In contrast, Maria Pace liked to play with her dolls and was interested in housekeeping.

Carmelo Samonà included in his letter a report of the only occasion in which Alessandrina II had mentioned any event in the previous life. I quote the relevant paragraphs from the letter (which I have translated from the French):

> Two years ago [when the twins would have been 8–9 years old] we were discussing with the twins taking them on an excursion to Monreale [a town 10 kilometers southwest of Palermo]. As you know, Monreale has the most magnificent Norman church in the world. My wife told our girls "when you go to Monreale, you will see some sights you have never seen before." Alessandrina [II] replied: "But mama, I know Monreale. I have already seen it." My wife then told her that she had never been to Monreale. Alessandrina [II] replied: "Yes, I have. I have been there. Don't you remember that there is a great church there with a huge man on the roof with his arms spread out." (Here she gestured with her own arms spread apart.) "And do you not remember how we went there with a lady who had horns, and we met some small priests who wore red?"
>
> We had absolutely no memory of ever having spoken to the twins about Monreale; Maria Pace knew nothing about the place. Nevertheless, we thought that some other member of the family could have spoken about its great church with its statue of Jesus on the portal; but we could not at first make any sense of the "lady with horns" and "the priests in red." Then suddenly my wife remembered that we had gone to Monreale and taken Alessandrina [I] with us. This was a few months before our daughter died. We had also taken a friend of ours who lived elsewhere and who had come to Palermo to consult the doctors here about some excrescences on her forehead. Also, just as we were going into the church we happened to meet some Orthodox priests who were wearing blue robes ornamented with red. We then further remembered that these details had much impressed Alessandrina [I].
>
> Even if we suppose that one of us had spoken to Alessandrina [II] about the church at Monreale, it is not believable that such a person would have mentioned the "lady with horns" or "the priests dressed in red," because these were features of no interest to us.

Comment

As I mentioned, contemporary commentators on this case faulted it for the short interval — 8 months — between the death of Alessandrina I and the birth of Alessandrina II. The critics noted that Adele Samonà only became aware that she was pregnant on April 10, 1910, which, assuming she had become pregnant a week or so before, would make the duration of the pregnancy perhaps not much more than 7 months. A gestation of that length, however, is not incompatible with survival of twin babies. In one of his replies to critics who asserted that the presumed gestation was too short, Samonà quoted several texts of obstetrics which mentioned the common occurrence of prematurity in twin pregnancies (Samonà, 1914). A recently published monograph on twins has affirmed this (Segal, 1999).

Commentators on the case also suggested that it might have developed from a maternal impression* on the part of Adele Samonà acting on her gestating daughter who, to satisfy her intense grief, she identified as the reincarnation of Alessandrina I.† This explanation will take us some distance, but seems insufficient to explain the detailed knowledge that Alessandrina II had of the visit by Alessandrina I to Monreale.§

BLANCHE COURTAIN

This case was first published in 1911 in *Le Messager de Liège*, a spiritualist publication. The author of the article derived his information from the subject's father, P. Courtain, who was then a retired mechanic, formerly employed in the state railway system of Belgium. The family lived at Pont-à-Celles, which is a village in the area of Charleroi, about 40 kilometers south of Brussels.

Delanne (1924) reprinted the report and I have translated the following from his work:

The Report

The family concerned in this case knew absolutely nothing about spiritualism when the case I am reporting occurred. They became convinced of its truth by the events I shall describe. This family are entirely reliable people. Among their children they had two daughters who were then aged 7 and 5. The younger daughter was called Blanche. She had delicate health. From time to time she told her parents that she was seeing "spirits." She described her maternal and paternal grandparents who had all died about 15 years before Blanche was born. Blanche's parents thought her visions were perhaps a symptom of an illness, and they took her to see a doctor in Gouy-lez-Piétons. The

---

*I have published elsewhere further information, reports of illustrative cases, and extensive references to other publications about maternal impressions (Stevenson, 1992, 1997).

†In Part I I referred to the belief among some Europeans that a later-born child is the reincarnation of a deceased sibling.

§In other, more recent cases of the reincarnation type, the interval between the previous personality's death and the subject's birth has been less than 9 months. Examples occurred in the cases of Ravi Shankar Gupta, Sujith Lakmal Jayaratne, and Cemil Fahrici.

doctor questioned Blanche, examined her, and then gave her parents some medicine to give her. The visit and medicine cost 7½ francs.

The next day....Blanche said to her parents in a determined way: "I won't take that medicine the doctor prescribed for me." "Why is that?" said her father. "Do you mean to throw away 7½ francs? You should take the medicine." "No," said Blanche. "I won't take it. There is someone near me who tells me he will get me well without that medicine. Besides, I know what to do myself. I was a pharmacist." "You were a pharmacist?" her parents said. They were stunned and asked themselves whether Blanche had become mad. "Yes," said Blanche. "I was a pharmacist in Brussels." She then gave the street and number of the pharmacy. "If you don't believe me, go and see for yourselves. There is still a pharmacy there and the door of the place is completely white."

Blanche's parents did not know what to say or do about her statements and for some time they did not talk about the matter. One day, about two years later, Blanche's older sister was to go into Brussels, and her parents suggested that Blanche also go. "Yes," said Blanche, "I will go and take my sister to the place I told you about." "But you don't know Brussels," her parents said. To this Blanche replied: "That makes no difference. Once I am there I will show my sister the way."

The journey was made as planned. When the two sisters reached the railway station at Brussels, the older one said to Blanche: "Now show me the way." "All right," said Blanche, "Come on. It is this way." They walked for some time and then Blanche said: "This is the street. Look! There is the house and you can see that it is a pharmacy." Her sister, amazed, found that everything Blanche had said — the street, the number of the house, and the color of the door — were exactly as Blanche had described. No detail was incorrect.

Comment

In the 19th and 20th centuries spiritualists of the European continent generally believed in reincarnation. (Those of Great Britain did not.) The reporter of this case saw no need to include additional details in his account and probably never asked for any.

A reader of this report thought it improbable that children only 9 and 7 years old would be allowed to travel by themselves in a railway train to Brussels. The reporter of the case said nothing about this. The journey would have lasted an hour or less, and I can suppose that the children's father asked the train's conductor to give the children help, if they needed it. Apparently they did not.

LAURE RAYNAUD

A report of this case was first published in *Psychic Magazine* in its issue of January 1914. The author was Dr. Gaston Durville, a physician of Paris. (I have not seen this first report.) Subsequently, Lancelin (1922) and Delanne (1924) published extracts from Durville's report. On comparing the two later reports, which cite long extracts from the earlier one of Durville, I found that, although they agree on the essentials, each contains some details omitted in the other. I have therefore drawn on both in what follows.

The Report

Laure Raynaud was born in the village of Aumont, near Amiens, France, in 1868. Her mother later told Durville that Laure even as a young child rebelled against the teachings of the Roman Catholic Church. She rejected the ideas of heaven, hell, and purgatory, saying that after death one returns to earth in another body. Her parents had to force her to attend Mass. The parish priest used to visit and listen to her fascinated, but then he went away nonplussed and annoyed. For her part, Laure Raynaud found it prudent to stop challenging conventional beliefs.

At the age of 17 she decided to become a healer and practiced as such for a time in Amiens. Later, she moved to Paris where she first learned "magnetism" (a precursor of hypnosis) in the school of Hector Durville. (I think Hector was a relative, perhaps a brother, of Gaston Durville.) She then continued to work as a healer. For the last 2 years of her life (1911–13) Gaston Durville employed her in his clinic in Paris. She had married in 1904. Durville's report does not suggest that Laure Raynaud spoke about specific memories of a previous life when she was a child. Her husband told Durville that Laure had spoken to him about such memories from the time of their first acquaintance. By the time she began working for Durville she was speaking freely about the memories to anyone who would listen. Durville, although skeptical, did listen.

Laure Raynaud stated the following details of what she asserted were memories of a previous life.

1. She had lived in a sunny climate, somewhere in the south, perhaps Egypt or Italy. (She thought the country was more probably Italy.)
2. She lived in a large house, much larger than ordinary houses.
3. The house had many large windows.
4. The tops of the windows were arched.
5. There was a large terrace at the house.
6. The house had two stories.
7. At the top of the house there was another terrace.
8. The house was located in a large park with old trees in it.
9. The ground sloped down in front of the house and sloped upwards behind it.
10. She had some serious "chest disease" and coughed much.
11. Near the large house there was a cluster of small houses where workers lived.
12. She was about 25 years old.
13. This life had occurred about a century earlier.

The images of this life seemed entirely clear to Laure Raynaud. She particularly dwelt on scenes of walking up and down on the large terrace and wandering in the park, all the time feeling unwell. She experienced herself as being depressed and irritable, perhaps embittered by her illness, and afraid of impending death.

Laure Raynaud remembered no name of the previous life — either of persons or of specific places. She was sure, however, that she could recognize the house where she had lived if she ever saw it.

In March 1913 one of Durville's wealthy patients, who lived in Genoa, asked him to come there to examine and treat her. He was too busy to leave Paris then and instead asked Laure Raynaud to go to Genoa and do what she could for the patient. Laure Raynaud agreed and left by train for Italy. Upon arrival in Turin she began to have a sense of familiarity with the countryside through which the train passed; and this feeling became stronger when she reached Genoa. At Genoa she mentioned to the persons with whom she was staying her belief that she had had a previous life in this region. She spoke of her wish to find the house she described. One of her hosts, Piero Carlotti, said that he knew a house in the outskirts of Genoa that seemed to correspond to her description, and he offered to take her there. She accepted and they drove to this house in an automobile. Laure Raynaud said this particular house was not the one she remembered, but that one, she thought, was nearby. So they drove on and came to a large mansion that Laure Raynaud recognized as "hers." It belonged to a well-known Genoese family, the Spontinis. The house corresponded closely to Laure Raynaud's description. Its dominant feature was a large number of unusually tall windows whose upper ends were arched. There was a broad terrace around the lower level of the house and a small terrace at its top. Figure 1 reproduces a photograph of the house, which was originally published by Lancelin (1922). It shows these features. One detail does not seem to correspond.

The photograph of the house shows that it had three stories, although it is possible, given the sloping ground, that one story may have been a kind of basement. The photograph does not illustrate the park and its trees or show the slopes in front of the house and behind it. Lancelin, however, described these slopes as according with Laure Raynaud's description.*

Satisfied that they had located the house of Laure Raynaud's previous life, she and Piero Carlotti returned to Genoa. Back there Laure Raynaud seemingly retrieved another memory she had not had before. She said that she was certain that in the previous life her body was buried not in the cemetery, but in the church itself. Piero Carlotti reported this item to Gaston Durville, who initiated a search of the records of the parish where the Spontini family lived. A correspondent in Genoa found the following record and sent it to Durville:

> October 23, 1809. Giovanna Spontini, widow of Benjamino Spontini, who lived for
> several years in her home, who was chronically ill and whose state of health recently

---

*Delanne's text differs from Lancelin in this detail. Delanne mentioned only one slope, that at the back of the house, which he said, contrary to Laure Raynaud's statement, was downward.

Figure 1. House of Giovanna Spontini near Genoa, Italy, recognized by Laure Raynaud. (From Lancelin, 1922.)

gave rise to much concern after she caught a severe chill, died on the 21st of this month. She had been strengthened by all the offices of the church and today with our written permission and that of the mayor her body was brought with a private ceremony into the church of Notre-Dame-du-Mont.

Laure Raynaud died a few months after she returned from Genoa to Paris, toward the end of 1913.

Gaston Durville concluded his report of Laure Raynaud's claimed memories with the following statement: "So, is this then a case of reincarnation? I have to say that I know nothing about the subject, but I believe the reincarnationist hypothesis is no more absurd than any other" (Lancelin, 1922, p. 373; Delanne, 1924, p. 297).

Comment

Laura Raynaud's failure to state specifying names obliges us to consider the likelihood of chance in the correspondence between her statements and the details obtained about the life of Giovanna Spontini and the house in which she lived near Genoa. The details of Laure Raynaud's description of the house are all, save one, correct for the one she identified. Yet they are not independent of each other, and all could probably be found in other Italian mansions of the Renaissance style. If, however, we add to these details those of a chronically ill proprietress whose dead body was placed inside a church instead of in a cemetery, the likelihood of coincidence diminishes substantially.

Georg Neidhart

In 1924 the subject of this case, then 26 years old, became depressed and during this condition experienced a series of images that he believed derived from a previous life in the Bavarian Forest during the 12th century. He spent several years, first in trying to find the location of this life, and then in efforts to verify some of the details in his images. He believed that he had succeeded in this. He thought that he had lived a life at the castle of Weissenstein, near Regen, Bavaria. For some time he told no one else about his experience and his conclusions concerning it; but eventually he began to tell other persons about them. Later, he published a booklet about reincarnation in which he included a detailed report of his own experience and his efforts at verifying it (Neidhart, 1957).

In the meantime, he had read extensively in the literature of psychical research and spiritualism. He founded a small society to discuss paranormal and spiritual experiences and participated in sittings with mediums. He sometimes gave lectures about his experiences.

In 1927 he married his second wife, Anneliese, and in 1936 their only child, Angelika, was born.

I learned of this case in the early 1960s and met Georg Neidhart together with his wife (Anneliese) and daughter (Angelika) at their home in Munich, first in May 1964 and again in October 1965. Georg Neidhart died in 1966.

Subsequently, I visited Anneliese and Angelika Neidhart from time to time when I was in Munich, where, among other researches, I used the Staatsbibliothek to study relevant sources of information for this case.

In April 1971 I went to Regen, accompanied by Anneliese Neidhart. The mayor's office kindly arranged for Alfons Schubert, an expert on Regen, the castle of Weissenstein, and the surrounding area, to give us an extensive guided tour. As I shall explain later, the castle, except for the tower, was only a ruin, and I do not claim to have learned anything new by visiting it.

The Report

I shall present here my translation of Georg Neidhart's own account of his experience in having the memories of a previous life.

My life began in May 1898. It did not differ in essential matters from that of millions of other people. It was defined by the circumstances into which I was born, mainly the economic condition of my parents and the general political situation of the time. Since my parents were Roman Catholics, I was raised in this faith. During my time at secondary school, my religious training was made deeper and more enduring by an extraordinarily good, unforgettable instructor in religion. And while my excellent mother lovingly attended to the welfare of my soul, my rather stern father held me to conscientious punctuality and a sense of responsibility. Altogether during childhood I had few unmet needs.

After attending secondary school, I began to learn my father's trade [that of a copper-smith]. At the outbreak of the First World War, however, I had to give up my apprenticeship. I was still under 19 when called up for service in the [German] Imperial Navy. With this change in outer circumstances my spiritual life also took a turn of fundamental importance.

In the Navy I was trained to be a radio operator and then assigned on fishing steamers and on various "suicide patrols" in the Baltic Sea. After not quite 2 years of war service full of many changes and dangers, I was demobilized on January 1, 1919.

Upon returning to Munich, my native city, I found a completely changed situation. The political barometers pointed to storms. A revolution was going on and bullets whipped the air. Dead bodies, including some of children, mostly innocent victims, lay around the street and offered a gruesome spectacle. And then the inflation that soon set in ruined every plan. As a consequence I had to abandon the idea of becoming an engineer. Then came my journeyman's examination, my [first] marriage, the birth of a daughter, and the death of my wife — all within less than 2 years. When these were over, I was still under 25 years old.*

These were terrible blows that Destiny had struck me in such a brief time. Joy and suffering — the eternal, changing opposites of man's existence had seemed to unite during these days. And naturally these fateful years were not without effects. The belief in an impersonal, incomprehensible but just Creator had become fundamentally shattered. Doubts rose up and became stronger than the previous belief. I could see no way to reach the perfect love and mercy of God. My opposition to God had grown so great that my prayers were more a struggle with the question of the basic justice of God than a petition offered meekly.

In this state of spiritual conflict I tried more and more to forget my own particular blows of fate which, however, I still thought of as being unjust knocks. Nevertheless, and despite my efforts, the whole question of a Divine justice and love kept coming back to me. It would not be suppressed and absorbed me completely. My confessor of those days thought he understood my trouble, and his well-meant admonitions and encouragements directed me to turn back toward an earnest petitioning and even imploring of almighty God.

While this struggle went on inside me, I had completely changed the outer conditions of my life. I had no place of my own to live in, and a friend let me live with him. My life began to resemble that of a hermit more than one of a businessman or artisan. In a circle of friends which I joined we talked about Christian mysticism and other religious problems. We also sang religious songs eagerly. We very rarely met without singing at least one or more religious songs. We also started a library for ourselves. It

---

*Georg Neidhart's chronology seems slightly off here. He was 25 years old in May 1923. The appalling inflation in Germany to which he referred lasted from the last months of 1922 to December 1923.

consisted, however, chiefly of the Bible, books on Christian mysticism, other religious writings, and song books.

During this period I underwent an experience which affected me deeply and totally transformed me. I completely forgot all my suffering and abandoned my quarrel with Fate. I was remade into another, completely different person — a man who now understood why Fate had struck him so hard.

The experience began on a spring morning, a clear, serene day that will remain in my memory forever. On this day I had an inner experience that was utterly new for me. In an unusual manner I had similar experiences at particular times over the ensuing years and even decades.

I have even now an excellent ability to recover memories. Only names give me some difficulty. Since that spring morning I have known that it is possible to remember, that one can cross the threshold of birth and experience visual and even auditory images of events lying in another time period centuries ago. I was definitely not dreaming. I enjoy sound, deep and always dreamless sleep. And the night before this particular first experience was completely dreamless also. The day itself began like any other. I had had my breakfast, and I was in no way disturbed in my thoughts. My senses and thoughts were clear. Nothing gave any indication of anything unusual, such as what occurred during the ensuing hours.

In this completely unprepared state there arose into my mind an absolutely astonishing mixture of images from a time period of centuries earlier. The whole experience was so peculiar and so overwhelming that I determined to make a record of it in writing. I did not expect, however that this decision [to make a written record] would have any particular consequence. Ten days, including however some periods of sleeplessness at night, went by before I finished the sequence and came to the end [of the images].

What I had by that time written down gave the main events of a former life — in various scenes and images — with some of the associated principal and secondary people involved. The details of dates, names, and places gave the whole series a degree of plausibility. I felt completely identified with the scenes experienced. I was living, weeping, laughing, and fighting as the principal figure of the whole picture. It was no event from outside that was somehow affecting or influencing me. Instead, it was something which rose up from the deepest layers inside me. When I reflect now on the whole experience, I cannot understand it in any other way.

Later on, I read and studied well anything I could find written in books or articles on parapsychology, mysticism, the scientific study of religion, and similar philosophical problems. And today I still read everything that I find printed on these subjects.

The intensive study of such books and articles gave me the idea not only of the possibility of definitely verifying my experience, but that of advancing knowledge in this field beyond where it was. That idea helped me also because it was only in this way [through my efforts to verify the experience] that I arrived at the firm conclusion that I had not fallen into a delusional state on the days when I had had these unusual experiences.

My misfortunes had taught me that one must always finish things by oneself. This led me to decide to find out the truth of my experience by myself.

As I have already indicated, I had the definite feeling that these inner visions referred to a previous existence of myself. And in relation to that life the question of divine justice seemed to be answered, and I decided that earthly existences have a sort of guilt-penance course that extends over several earthly existences. In fact, I believe one can even go further. It seems to me that I have ties at present with persons who were living then [in the days of the inner visions] and are living again now and somehow fatefully tied into my present life. That belief, however, does not by itself lead to a detailed and precise understanding. And so now, in the spirit of science, I shall go into more detail. From the notes that I made at the time of the experience I shall now present an account of those portions [of the experience] that have seemed to me valid and susceptible of confirmation.

We have to start with the year [A.D.] 1150 because this actually appears in my notes and I believe that this year provides the starting point for my investigations. It certainly is no small matter that we are considering an interval of 775 years.* We have to take into account that almost no—or very few—persons of historical importance are figures in the events related [to the inner visions]. Similarly the whole region [where the events took place] was very little known [elsewhere] at the time, a fact which made investigation particularly difficult.

My memories begin with the description of the castle around the year 1150 as it is shown in my sketch.† It stands on a mountain on top of jagged rocks and has a trapezoid shape made necessary by the rock formation. Entrance to the castle is provided only by a wooden drawbridge which crosses an extremely deep moat that winds around the mountain. One reaches the courtyard of the castle through a gate with a portcullis. Inside, on the right and on the small side of the castle area, a strong four-sided tower rises up above the steep rocky cliff. Its flat upper level surface, surrounded with battlements offers a wide view of the surrounding territory. On the two long sides of the rugged and almost vertically steep cliffs the living quarters [of the castle] rise up. They are large, multi-storied buildings which are strongly built into the depths [of the cliffs] as well as above them. A double-sided outside staircase leads to the upper portions of one [of these buildings]. Opposite the outside staircase is a wooden draw-well with a stone border wall. The plan and building of the castle reveal a definite boldness which unquestionably give an impression of something quite extraordinary if not unique.

My "inner visions" take me from Munich, where I was living, in a northeasterly direction, across the Danube into an area that was lonely, undeveloped, mountainous and covered with primeval forest. The mountains seem all thickly forested. Not far from the castle, a small river winds through the country and eventually, after a very circuitous course, finally reaches the Danube. On the north side of the Danube a chain of tall hills dominates the castle. If one approaches it from the west it is difficult to find.

I did not get the name of the castle in the "inner visions." I only got the impression that it was near a highway that was much traveled in 1150. There were also two other roads that crossed each other near the castle. But they were unimportant and could be considered mere paths.

In my "inner vision" I stand on a high four-cornered tower and look at the surrounding area of country. One sees only mountains and forests. The tower is erected on top of jagged rocks which are overgrown with ferns. The side of the mountain is covered with huge spruces and firs which block the view. In the distance on the other side of a rather dark shining river I can see another, similar tower. Otherwise there is nothing else to see. There are no houses or anything else in the way of human habitation. When I look from the tower into the courtyard, I can see on the right side of the wooden bridge the entrance to a secret passageway cut into the rocks.

Next in the experience the following events occurred. In the castle courtyard, sur-

---

*Georg Neidhart here means the interval between A.D. 1150 and 1924 when he had his experience and made his notes, not 1957, when his account was first written out fully and published.

†In his booklet Georg Neidhart reproduced a sketch of the castle that he seemed to see during his experience. The sketch has written on it the initials GN and the date of 1924. Figure 2 reproduces the sketch.

rounded by men and women, two men dressed in the costume of the early Middle Ages and armed were quarreling. The quarrel was about freedom and justice. Harsh and in fact insulting words are exchanged. And it becomes unmistakable from their increasingly menacing attitudes that the two quarreling men have in fact been feuding for a long time. One of these quarrelers, evidently the aggressor, is called Kühneberg, and the other is called von Falkenstein. I feel myself living now everything that happened to Kühneberg in 1150. I live what happens to him and what provokes him to anger.

Kühneberg is a battler for freedom and justice. In the quarrel, which takes a dangerous turn, he calls von Falkenstein a "foreigner" and a "vassal." He reproaches him with being a mere compliant "footstool" of the clerical power, and accuses him of viciously trying to win the favor of the woman he has chosen for a wife. The bystanders are unable to check the heated dispute and bring the two "fighting cocks" back to reason. Finally the two men draw their swords. A fierce duel ensues in which von Falkenstein is beaten and left to die of his wounds where he falls. The death of the official von Falkenstein shapes the later life of Kühneberg. As experienced in the later parts of the "inner visions," Kühneberg is a determined opponent of the arrogance and encroachments of episcopal vassals, and he carries on his struggle with every means at his disposal.

Through his marriage and a clever maneuver against his drunkard father-in-law, he is able to increase the strength of his position considerably. The leader of the men now united to him by marriage [i.e., Kühneberg's father-in-law], however, disapproved of the roughness and immoderation of Kühneberg's methods. Kühneberg's hate knew no limits. The "civic regulations" that were coming into force, the springing up of monasteries and towns, and antagonism toward unjust taxes increased his hatred beyond all bounds.

So he decides to make the few roads that approached the surrounding settlements unsafe by carrying out raids on them. He hopes in this way to provoke his enemy [the bishop] to attack him, knowing that he is unassailable in his castle and can easily resist any attack there. In short, Kühneberg becomes with his followers an outlaw and brigand. In order to bind his followers closely to him he promises them liberal shares of the booty. His wife and some of the sensible people around him try to hold him back from the increasingly violent expressions of his rage. Their efforts are fruitless. He considers that his methods are the only correct ones. Gradually the conduct of the castle's inhabitants becomes more uncontrolled and savage. This is specially the case with his close adherents. Finally a rebellion breaks out within the castle. Even his own wife joins the opposition to him. A small group of her trusted followers led by [a man called] Arnet take a definite position against her husband. Kühneberg crushes this rebellion. In doing so he wins over his wife's trusted confidante, who develops a passionate attachment to him.

It is a dry year, and a shortage of water develops inside the castle. Its enemies approach and finally besiege the castle. Kühneberg's wife [Wulfhilde] dies under mysterious circumstances. Discontent spreads among the besieged people and discord increases. The obscure death of Wulfhilde, Kühneberg's wife, deepens the division within his followers even more. The split [between the groups] steadily increases and finally threatens their survival. In desperation from the emergency Kühneberg resolves to attempt a sortie from the castle. He throws himself at his enemies and in fierce combat meets his death.

In the "inner visions" the names of the persons whose lives were entwined in the Fate of the fierce lord of the castle came into consciousness. The principal protagonists, as already mentioned, were von Falkenstein and Kühneberg. Kühneberg's father-in-law was called Höchting and his daughter was called Wulfhilde. Eva was Wulfhilde's confidante, and Arnet was the chief of the men joined to Kühneberg by his marriage.

The men in these events lived largely in the saddle. As I have also already indicated, the forests around the castle were still untouched by man, generally quite impenetrable and inhabited by bears and wolves. In addition the customs and manners of the time as well as the objects and other details of the scenes, which I included in my notes, harmonized with the date mentioned [1150] and offered clues for a reliable verification.

Figure 2. Sketch of castle made by Georg Neidhart in 1924. From *Werden Wir Wiedergeboren?* (Courtesy of Angelika Neidhart.)

Within just a few weeks of making my notes about my experience, I set off to visit the Bavarian Forest. It was the first time I had ever been in the area. I remained there for 6 weeks. That length of time, however, was still insufficient. I had to return to the Forest several more times. Research into events that took place almost 800 years ago is not simple, as I soon discovered. New difficulties seemed always to be cropping up.

The Bavarian Forest was in those days [1924] not much opened up, largely trackless, and therefore visited very little. It could happen to a traveler that the road he was traveling along suddenly stopped and became just an ill-defined path. It could even happen that such a path itself could lead into an absolutely impenetrable forest, or a swamp, and just end.

So it seemed that if these "memories" were not delusional, but contained elements of real experiences, then perhaps I could find the place of the previous life by following my intuition. From inquiries I had learned that in the neighborhood of Regen* there was a considerably decayed ruin of a castle. So I decided to start out from the railway station at Regen by myself, without asking anyone where the castle ruins were. I thought this might be a test of just how accurate my seeming memories were.

There was a torrential rain falling as I set out from Regen on this adventure. I did not stay on any road, but listened to an inner guidance for direction. Soon I was climbing up a narrow path which led up a steep mountain through a thick almost impenetrable forest. It was a rather tiring journey. Giant tree trunks were all around. I had to go around or climb over huge rocks, and ferns as tall as a man slapped my face. Finally I came out into the open on the peak of a mountain. I was standing in front of the

---

*Regen is a small town in northeastern Bavaria near the border of the Czech Republic (formerly Bohemia). It is about 140 kilometers northeast of Munich.

ruins of the once proud castle which had been erected on high, much fissured quartz rocks, standing defiantly above the surrounding region. Of the castle only the tower remained standing. It, however, had been considerably restored. By means of a somewhat unfirm wooden staircase, I climbed to the top of the tower to see the view of the surrounding area. Of the two high main buildings of the castle [seen in the vision; see Figure 2] I could only make out definitely the parts of them attached to the tower. However, from the shape of the peculiar and extremely hard rock cliffs, it was really impossible for the building complex to have had any other shape than a trapezoid one, as I had outlined it in the sketch I made at the time of having my memories. And if this was the case, then the secret passageway (about which I had also made a note) must be located near the main gate.* I found it quickly and was able to proceed, in a stooped position, about 80 to 100 meters along it. Farther penetration was prevented by a general caving in of the tunnel. (When I went to visit the ruins again in 1957, even the part that had previously been open had been filled with rubbish.)

According to information given me by some residents of Regen, this secret passageway descended in a steep course from the castle, then went underground for several kilometers and actually under the river bed† until it finally came out on a thickly wooded mountain peak at the other side of the river. Formerly, inhabitants of the area—long since dead—supposedly knew the course of the secret tunnel. As it became caved in, however, traversing the tunnel was forbidden.

In looking around from the top of the tower my attention was particularly focused on the present-day town of Regen. I was especially fascinated by the unusual, massive four-cornered tower of the main church because this tower did not seem to fit into the rest of the building of the church. In the notes I made, as I have mentioned earlier, I had included mention of a tower similar to that of the castle which stood on the other side of the river from it. Understandably this unusual and evidently extremely high church tower left me eager to have more information about it. No one in the area, however, was able to give me information about the origin of this church tower.§ Neither the ministers nor teachers seemed informed about it. I was advised to apply to the office of the archbishop in Passau [the nearest large town and seat of an archbishop].

At the archbishop's office I was received with politeness and helpfulness, and my story was listened to. However, here also I could learn nothing further about the relevant history of the period around 1150. I was told that all the old records and documents or other sources which could have given definite information about this period had been lost in a fire. I was told nevertheless to apply to the Archives in Trausnitz Castle. [Trausnitz is about 60 kilometers north and slightly west of Regen.]

The curator of the archives of Trausnitz Castle was a friendly and obliging official who readily listened to my story, that of a man who thought he had lived at Castle Weissenstein around 1150. Quietly and calmly he followed my account. He did not laugh at me or contradict me. In fact he seemed to be listening with interest. His face only showed puzzlement and even amazement. I shall never forget the words with which he responded to me: "You cannot know all these things, since research on this district is just now getting under way." Then he told me how difficult and troublesome it had been to put together from scanty family documents even a general impression of

---

*Georg Neidhart had mentioned this passageway earlier in his report.
†If Georg Neidhart meant that the passageway went under the River Regen, the distance would have been a little more than 2 kilometers. There are, however, other smaller streams in the area of Weissenstein.
§This tower in Regen, which was later incorporated in a church, dates from the 12th century.

the period around 1150. He was particularly impressed by my understanding of the political situation of that period.

Further Information Brought Out in Interviews with Georg Neidhart

In discussing his experience with me, Georg Neidhart emphasized that the memories came to him like a complete reliving with all attendant emotions. He did not experience the events as if he were watching a motion picture show.

The life of Kühneberg was unfolded in the scenes of the "inner visions" in a chronological sequence without any repetition.

When Georg Neidhart was a small child between 5 and 7 years old, he had then had what he later took to be memories of previous lives. They seemed rather mixed up, and he thought memories from different lives were mingled. There was not the orderly sequence he experienced when he was 25 years old during the 10 days of imaged memories he then had.* Prominent in these childhood memories was a scene with a large four-poster bed of old style and a scene of his own beheading. This last was part of a previous life in France that he thought he later remembered in more detail. He astounded his father by narrating the account of the beheading to him.

In his report cited above Georg Neidhart mentioned that he had discerned some connections between the persons participating in the events of his memories and persons known to him. He had not, however, inferred any precise conclusions about causal connections between the events in the 12th-century life and his present life. Specifically, he did not interpret the death of his first wife, which had preceded the depressed and skeptical condition in which the memories came to him, as being somehow connected with the 12th-century life. (His restraint in drawing conclusions about such connections impressed me favorably.) He did, however, emerge from the experience with a different view of life and death, and it seems to have been this new view rather than any precise interpretations of the meaning of his memories for the present life that led him to speak of himself as an altered man after the experience.

Despite his firm conviction that he had lived a previous life, he remained a devout Roman Catholic all his life.

Independent Verifications of Details in Georg Neidhart's Experience

I consulted several sources of information about the history of eastern Bavaria where Castle Weissenstein is located, but I learned little that could verify the details of Georg Neidhart's experience.

---

*The case of Giuseppe Costa provides another example of a child having scattered images, apparently of a previous life, that later became organized into a coherent sequence.

The records from the Middle Ages of what is now the Bavarian Forest are meager. As Georg Neidhart wrote, the region was little settled and still mainly covered in woods during the 12th century. It was then largely within the domain of the bishopric of Passau. A monastery was found at Rinchnach early in the 12th century. Records first mention the name of Regen in 1149 (Oswald, 1952).

The castle of Weissenstein (2 kilometers from Regen) was almost certainly built in the 12th century, but no one knows by whom. A primitively developed trade route between Bavaria and Bohemia, which passed by Weissenstein, seems to have been considerably used; and it probably provided the reason for the erection of a castle to protect travelers. We can plausibly suppose, therefore, that the holder of Castle Weissenstein, if he turned outlaw, could find ample plunder from users of the trade route.

A large fortified tower was erected on the northern side of the River Regen possibly in the 12th century or even earlier (Oswald, 1952). The river now runs through the town of Regen. The fortified tower had no connection with the first church built at Regen. In the late 15th century the tower was incorporated in a newly built parish church.

Of the several names that came to Georg Neidhart during his "inner visions" only one figures in contemporary records. Von Müller cited a document according to which Konrad von Falkenstein had illegally seized control of a group of communities within the bishopric of Passau (von Müller, 1924). The bishopric comprised a large area, and the document gave no more specifying details. A note suggests that this Konrad von Falkenstein lived in the 13th century, not the 12th, which was the one that Georg Neidhart thought correct. In another source of contemporary records, the name of "Kienberch" occurs in 1130, and later, as probably modified, this is spelled "Kienberger" in the 13th century (Monumenta Boica, 1765). I am unwilling to count these names as verifying the existence of Georg Neidhart's "Kühneberg," although they may be.

As I neared completion of this book I thought that research later than the 1920s, when Georg Neidhart had made his inquiries, might have yielded more information about the early history of Castle Weissenstein. This proved wrong. In April 2001 I wrote to the Stattsarchiv of Landshut at Castle Trausnitz, where Georg Neidhart had sought confirmation almost 60 years earlier. The senior archivist replied that the castle was generally thought to have been built by the Counts of Bogen who were hereditary administrators of the district, but this was conjecture. The lines of the Counts of Bogen died out in 1242, and the castle then came under the direct control of the Dukes of Bavaria. These assumptions—they can hardly be called facts—make it unlikely that the castle would have been the site for "robber barons" in the 12th century. This, the archivist wrote me, was more likely in the later Middle Ages.

The ruins of Castle Weissenstein, in the 1920s and later, offer no additional verifications. Barring archeological investigation we cannot now reconstruct how the buildings were originally laid out. The four-sided tower is an exception (See Figure 3). Nevertheless, an engraving of the castle as it appeared in 1726 definitely indicates a trapezoid shape (Hackl, 1950). (See Figure 4.)

Almost every castle of the period when Weissenstein was built had many of the

Top: Figure 3. The ruins of Weissenstein Castle as they appeared in 2001. (Photograph by Daniela Meissner.) *Bottom:* Figure 4. The castle of Weissenstein as it appeared in 1726. The buildings had a trapezoid form. (Courtesy of the Municipality of Regen.)

features Georg Neidhart mentioned, such as a wooden drawbridge, a moat, a portcullis, and a draw-well. (A visitor to the castle in 1633, cited by Oswald [1952] crossed over a wooden bridge, dangerously swaying above the moat, in order to reach the castle. This bridge may have replaced an earlier drawbridge, but we do not know that. One important detail possibly confirmed was the existence in the 12th century of a four-sided tower, similar to that of Weissenstein, on the opposite side of the River Regen.

In sum, although the sources that Georg Neidhart (and later I) consulted could verify little about the details in his experience, they also furnished no evidence to negate them. His description of life in a castle of the Bavarian Forest during the Middle Ages seems plausible. If this life occurred at Castle Weissenstein, the events he seemed to remember so clearly may have taken place later than he thought.

CHRISTOPHE ALBRET

The report of this case (Delarrey, 1955) did not include the full name or even a pseudonym for the subject; so I have given him a complete name. The case consists of a mediumistic prediction of the reincarnation of a person known to the author's wife who was to be recognized by a malformation of his right ear similar to one the communicating person had had.

In translating the report I have completed other names in places where Delarrey had only furnished initials.

The case occurred in 1924. It was first published in 1948 in *La revue spirite*, a spiritualist magazine. A note from the editor of *Revue métapsychique* explains that Dr. Maurice Delarrey, the author of the report, delayed its publication because it had occurred in a family totally opposed to any endeavors to communicate with deceased persons.

The Report

At a time when I was still somewhat skeptical about the idea of reincarnation my wife and I engaged in experiments with a kind of ouija board or planchette. I gradually became convinced of the objective reality of the communications we received.

One day the planchette, in the hand of my wife, spelled out slowly and with difficulty the letters of the name: *Felix*. In response to our questions we could not obtain anything further from this communicator at this session. The next day, however, the same name was spelled out and this time the name of the family, *Fresnel*, was also given.

I could not remember ever knowing anyone by this name, but my wife recalled that her father at one time had had a servant with this name; the man was with him for about 10 years. I therefore asked the presumed communicator: "Were you at one time employed by the Boileau family in the village of Renage?" This evoked a definite affirmation.

At this point my wife, searching through old memories, recalled the unusual detail that Felix Fresnel had a malformation of his right ear the pinna of which stuck out and forward, somewhat like the ear of a bat. In this it differed from his left ear.

It was only at our fourth session that this "spirit" succeeded in communicating more easily so that we could have a kind of conversation. I conjecture that, 20 years after this person's death, this was perhaps the first time he had tried to communicate with living persons.... At any rate, at each session his responses became more rapid and clearer.

At the sixth session, the following exchange occurred between this *Felix* and ourselves, after he had given his name.

Q: What do you wish now?

R: I want to say that I am coming back among you soon.

Q: Say that again? Among *us*?

R: Yes. At last. In your family.

Q: But our family is large and scattered around here and there. Could you at least say in what region you will be born?

R: Yes, it will be at Peyron. (Here he gave precise details about the location; readers will understand later why I do not provide the real names.)

Q: You mean it will be in the family of our young relative Yves?

R: Yes, he already has two daughters.

Q: Do you know their names and ages?

R: Yes (and he correctly gave their names and exact ages).

Q: And do you now know the date of your birth?

R: Yes, September 24, in the morning.

Q: Fair enough! But if a birth does take place on this precise date this could be just because you can predict it in advance. What will prove to us that the baby really is yourself Felix who is born then and there?

R: Miss Jeanne will easily recognize me — by my ear.

Here I should note that my wife's name is Jeanne, but at the time Felix Fresnel died we were not married; in fact, we did not even know each other then.

After this last session we had no further communication from this personality. I carefully noted, however, the date he had indicated. It was May then, and we were unaware that our young relative was pregnant.

On September 24, 1924 at 8 o'clock in the morning I received a telephone call from our relative's husband, who announced the birth of his son. I had no intention of telling him that we had news of this event 4 months earlier. Given his outlook, he would have thought I had links with diabolic and infernal sources. I also had no intention of doing anything to challenge his sincere beliefs in the teaching of the Roman Catholic Church.

It happened that 3 months after the birth of this boy, my wife and I were invited to a family reunion at the home where our *Felix* had been born with a new name. There was a fair-sized crowd there and the young mother (our relative) was happily showing off her baby son. Having already given birth to two girls, she had had some fear that she might have a third girl. Greeting us, she said: "Come and see our fine boy. He is not, however, accustomed to such a crowd. He is not in a good humor today, which is unlike him. Every time he sees someone new he starts crying and won't stop. We cannot comfort him."

We went into the room where the baby was. As soon as my wife came near the crib, the baby began to smile, even while tears were still running down his cheeks; and he stretched out his two little hands to my wife, who took him in her arms. He seemed joyous and trying — as much as such a young baby could — to mumble something. Seeing this, the young mother said: "Look at that! One might have thought he knew you."

After the usual compliments I said to our young relative: "What is that bandage on his head for? Does he have some kind of wound?" "Oh no," she said. "It is nothing. The poor thing must have been in a bad position in my body. He was born with his right ear sticking out. The doctor tells us that with this covering the ear will develop normally. Within a few months there will be nothing abnormal to see."

Additional Information

In order to avoid interrupting Delarrey's account of how the case developed chronologically, I omitted earlier his statement about his wife's use of the ouija board. He wrote:

> I should note here that when my wife uses a ouija board, she is entirely unaware of what she is spelling out, even though she does not appear to be in any way in a trance. While her hand is moving with the planchette she can carry on a conversation with other people present on any topic [Delarrey, 1955, p. 41].

Comment

Predictions of congenital anomalies made by mediums supposedly communicating with a discarnate person to be reborn do not occur often. The only other instance that I can now remember is that in the case of Huriye Bugay (Stevenson, 1997).

JAMES FRASER

This case consists of a recurrent vivid dream. I first learned about it from a brief account included in a book on the highland clans of Scotland (Moncreiffe and Hicks, 1967). I wrote to the senior author of this book, Sir Iain Moncreiffe of that Ilk, and asked whether I could learn more details of the case. He obligingly sent me copies of correspondence he had had with Major Charles Ian Fraser, to whom the dreamer, James Fraser, had given an account of the dream in the late 1920s. Charles Ian Fraser was a prominent landowner of the area, the local laird. He did not make a written record of the dream until he described it in a letter to Iain Moncreiffe dated August 14, 1962. Iain Moncreiffe sent me copies of four letters Charles Ian Fraser had written to him about the dream. He also added additional information about the background of the case in subsequent correspondence with me. Charles Ian Fraser died in 1963, before I had learned of the case.

The Report

James Fraser was born in 1870, probably in Beauly, Inverness-shire, Scotland. He was educated through primary school, but not beyond. In adulthood he worked as a wheelwright. Charles Ian Fraser described James Fraser as "just literate." Nevertheless, he had some interest in the history of Scotland, including his region of it. He was an omnivorous reader of books, especially about the Scottish highlands. He attended meetings of the Beauly Mutual Improvement Association, where lecturers from time to time spoke on local history. Charles Ian Fraser gave such a lecture. In his lecture he alluded to a celebrated battle of the 16th century between two Scottish clans. This battle occurred on July 3, 1544, near Loch Lochy and was known (in Gaelic) as Blar-na-Leine, which in English means "the swampy place." The Clanranalds (a sept of the MacDonalds) and their allies fought against the Frasers of Lovat and killed, among others, the 3rd Lord Lovat and his son. Few combatants on either side survived the battle. It was said that only four Frasers survived (Fraser, 1905). The clan might have been exterminated, but a large number of the Fraser wives were pregnant and gave birth to sons.*

About a week after the lecture James Fraser called on Charles Ian Fraser and said he would like to tell him privately about a dream he had had. He had found that "people would laugh at him," if he spoke about his dream to other persons.

James Fraser described his dream in a state of some excitement, and he became impatient when Charles Ian Fraser interrupted him to ask for more details.

The Content of the Dream

James Fraser first described† an awareness in the dream that

his father and relatives and friends seemed to be present but looked quite different in features and build. Yet something told him their identity…. Their clothing was quite different and so was the appearance of the countryside [compared with the area around Beauly]. But he knew he was in Mac Shimi's§ country [that of the Frasers of Lovat] and that his family and neighbors had received a summons to arms…. Most of them wore "garments of stuff" and some had leather or sheepskin about them. The better-to-do were riding on "shaggy horses" and had "chain-mail armor" with conical headgear and two-handed swords. Most of the men had bows and arrows and many had "battle-axes." All had some form of dirk….

He and his comrades went "down the Great Glen" [the long valley in Inverness-shire in which lie Loch Ness and Loch Lochy] until [they reached] Fort Augustus [not

*This epidemiological detail is not unique. An increase in the ratio of male to female births has been recorded during and after several wars, including both World Wars. I have given sources of these data elsewhere (Stevenson, 1974a).

†In the quotation from Charles Ian Fraser's report I have made a few insertions to facilitate reading or explain geographical features.

§Mac Shimi is Gaelic for "son of Simon." The chiefs of the Frasers of Lovat are descendants of an important ancestor, Sir Simon Fraser, who chased the English after the Battle of Bannockburn in 1314.

then known by that name.] They were joined by many others of Mac Shimi's clansmen from Stratherrick [south of Loch Ness]. These men were similarly clothed and armed.... They were to fight a battle against the Clanranald MacDonalds. In a very little while, by the shores of Loch Lochy, they did. [The battle began with] "showers of arrows".... All the mounted men dismounted and led the vanguard on foot with their two-handed swords. And suddenly [he] heard a cry for help, and near him on the ground his father was struggling in the grip of someone who was not a MacDonald, but who was that day fighting in their array. He saw a battle-axe lying on the ground beside his father, picked it up, hit his father's assailant on the head with it, and killed him.

Then he saw a big tall man in trousers and a coat of chain-mail protecting a number of wounded Frasers who had crawled into an angle formed by two turf or dry-stone dykes; the big man was swinging his two-handed sword around him. This man was the Laird of Foyers. He fought until he fell wounded from an arrow.

Features of the Dream

James Fraser said that he had the dream "many times; it was always the same." The images seemed somewhat disconnected, as if he "was just getting glimpses of something from the past."

Charles Ian Fraser did not ask James Fraser whether he had noticed any circumstance that seemed to instigate the dream. Nor did he learn how old James Fraser had been when he first had the dream.

When Charles Ian Fraser asked James Fraser how he could tell in the dream that it was of the battle of Blar-na-Leine and how he could tell that a man in the dream was the laird of Foyers, he replied that he "just knew."

James Fraser showed strong emotion during his narration of the dream. He seemed to experience the "terror of the arrows" as he narrated this opening scene of the battle.

Charles Ian Fraser's Appraisal of the Dream

James Fraser's accurate description of the clothing and arms of the combatants particularly impressed Charles Ian Fraser. Completely absent from the details were the conventional romantic features of warfare in the Scottish highlands: tartans, balmoral caps, one-handed swords with basket hilts, and target shields.

Charles Ian Fraser, who had known James Fraser, but not well, before James Fraser visited him and narrated his dream, learned that he was well regarded in the community, although reputed to be somewhat "fanciful," especially if in liquor. He might have earned the reputation for being "fanciful" by narrating his dream to other persons.* James Fraser died at the age of 72 on July 9, 1942.

---

*In Part I, I cited Evans-Wentz (1911), who found traces of a belief in reincarnation in the Scottish highlands during the first decade of the last century. Among the cases that I investigated, and describe later in this work (Part III), that of Jenny McLeod occurred in a community of Inverness-shire within 25 kilometers of Beauly, where James Fraser lived.

Charles Ian Fraser had no doubt that James Fraser had read at least some of the published accounts of the battle of Blar-na-Leine. Yet he did not think such reading or other normally acquired knowledge could adequately account for the dream. He found that James Fraser did not enrich the dream when questioned. For example, when asked whether, in the dream, he and his father had been killed in the battle, James Fraser said "I do not know." Charles Ian Fraser concluded one of his letters to Iain Moncreiffe (dated August 19, 1962) by writing: "I remain convinced that whatever James Fraser did or did not read a good part of his narrative to me was wholly personal and genuine." He considered reincarnation a possible interpretation of the dream.

Normal Sources of Information
About the Battle of "Blar-na-Leine"

The battle of Blar-na-Leine does not figure in popular histories of Scotland. It is not, however, obscure to persons with a deeper interest in the history of the Scottish highlands. On the contrary, several books readily available in the region of Inverness describe the battle. They name the combating clans and mention the chain-mail worn and the weapons used: bows and arrows and two-handed swords (Fraser, 1905; Keltie, 1875; Macdonald, 1934). In a chapter on the Frasers of Foyers, Mackenzie (1896) described the death of the laird of Foyers from wounds received in the battle.

Comment

Charles Ian Fraser, both in his original record of the dream and in his subsequent correspondence with Iain Moncreiffe, carefully considered the possibility of normal sources of information for the content of James Fraser's recurrent dream. James Fraser certainly had access to some published sources of information about the battle of Blar-na-Leine. It seemed to Charles Ian Fraser, however, and it seems to me also, that the correspondence between the content of the dream and known facts about the battle does not explain the personal quality of the experience that James Fraser had in his recurrent dream. He seemed to be living the events of the dream.

Moncreiffe in his brief summary of the case speculates that because the Frasers were much inbred James Fraser could well have been descended from a participant in the battle of Blar-na-Leine. He thought "ancestral memory" a plausible explanation for the dream. I have elsewhere summarized the case of an American subject (Mary Magruder) who from childhood on had nightmares that might be explained by "ancestral memory," in her case inherited from an 18th-century forebear. Our present knowledge of genetics, however, does not accommodate the idea of a physical transmission of detailed imagery, such as occurs in dreams of previous lives, from one generation to later ones.

CONCLUDING REMARKS
ABOUT THE OLDER CASES

My closing remark in introducing these eight older cases asserted their credibility. I hope the reports that followed adequately showed why I believe this. Here I will review some of the features of the cases that I have found persuasive.

None of the persons concerned in these cases endeavored to exploit them or even to publicize them substantially. One subject wrote a book and another a booklet about his experiences; but these had little sale and seem quickly to have gone out of print. Contrary to a common myth about persons who remember previous lives, none of the persons whose lives were remembered (or whose rebirth was predicted) had any important celebrity. Giuseppe Costa remembered the life of a person of some renown in his own time and a little later; but Ibleto di Challant had no enduring fame except to historians of medieval Italy.

With one exception the philosophical and religious stances of the persons concerned did not prepare them for the case about which they testified. Two of the subjects (Costa and Neidhart) were avowed materialists at the time of their experiences. The informants for two other cases (Battista and Albret) emphasized their skepticism until the case they reported developed. The family involved in a fifth case (Courtain) had no prior knowledge of spiritualism (which entailed reincarnation in continental Europe of the time). In a sixth case (Fraser) the subject's experience baffled him, seems to have been rejected by his peers, and led him to seek a sympathetic or at least open-minded listener.

In the two remaining cases (Samonà and Raynaud) the person (or persons) concerned had had some knowledge of spiritualism and the idea of reincarnation. In the case of Allessandrina Samonà, however, her parents had no prior expectation that Adele Samonà could have another pregnancy let alone that their deceased daughter would be reborn among them. The case of Laure Raynaud provides the single instance of a subject — in her case apparently from childhood — with a previous firm belief in reincarnation and in the reality of memories of a previous life that she had.

The unpreparedness of the subjects (or informants) in seven of the eight cases that developed does not confirm reincarnation as the best interpretation for them. It does, however, contribute to their authenticity,* a condition we require before we consider reincarnation as a contender explanation of them.

---

*By authenticity *I mean the accuracy of the reports of a case that we receive from informants for it (or investigators of it). The reports should correspond to the "events that actually happened." In practice we can rarely know "what actually happened" and so our judgment about authenticity depends on our detection of carelessness, inconsistencies, and motives to suppress or embellish facts.*

Authenticity does not entail paranormality *in a judgment of which we invoke means of communication not explicable by accepted knowledge of communication or physical movement.*

Part III

Investigated Cases from the Second Half of the 20th Century

During the years between 1961 and 1988 I traveled frequently to Asia to investigate cases suggestive of reincarnation there. I sometimes stopped in Europe and investigated cases there that came to my attention. In 1963-64 I spent a sabbatical leave in Zurich and then had the opportunity of studying European cases without long journeys. Altogether I obtained some information on more than 250 European cases. From these I selected 32 cases for inclusion in this volume.

To readers who ask why I culled so many cases, I offer several reasons. For cases beginning in childhood I required that I be able to interview at least one older relative, usually a parent or sibling, who testified about what the subject had said and done in early childhood. This rule eliminated numerous cases of persons who said and believed that they had, as children, remembered a previous life; but I could not meet an older person who would corroborate this claim. Moreover, the adults I required needed to remember at least some details of what the subject had said. The subject of one case that seemed promising referred me to her mother; however, when the mother wrote that she remembered her daughter having spoken about a previous life in childhood, but could give no details, I stopped our inquiries in the case. I also required that I myself meet the subject of the case; and I followed this rule with five exceptions.

I also rejected numerous cases of dreams that the dreamer said were set in a previous time and other place; but I included 7 cases of such dreams, and these have a range of evidence that shows both the possibility that at least some of them derive from previous lives and the equal or greater possibility of wrongly attributing them to such lives.

I omitted some cases because they had insufficient detail; nevertheless, I included some other cases with meager data, because they had some unusual feature. I also had to omit some cases that initially showed value but could not be fully investigated, either because the families concerned would not cooperate or because they had moved away from the last address I had for them.

The lack of corroborating older persons (if the subject is already an adult when we first learn about a case) tells us that we could probably find and study more cases if we could improve our ability to learn about them earlier, that is, when the subject is still under 5 or 6 years old. I became more certain of this when I reviewed, as I shall next describe, how I learned about the cases selected for this book.

Three persons referred 9 (almost one third) of the cases to me. They were the late Dr. Karl Müller, of Zurich; Dr. Erlendur Haraldsson, of Reykjavik, and Rita Castrén, of Helsinki. European psychiatrists familiar with my research referred 2 cases to me. Other persons familiar with this research referred 5 other cases. In 7 cases the subject or a subject's parent wrote to me about the case. I learned of the remaining 10 cases by reading an account of the case in a newspaper or magazine, after which I wrote to the correspondent to initiate a detailed investigation. Six of these 10 cases emerged, one might say, in response to solicitations by newspapers who invited their readers to send them accounts of claimed memories of previous lives. In some instances the newspapers published reports of the "winners," that is, cases the editors judged most worthy of being taken seriously.

I conclude from the foregoing analysis that we can learn about more European cases when willing informants for them are invited to submit reports for (possibly anonymous) publication or when they learn the name and address of qualified investigators. Even so, I believe cases occur less frequently in Europe than in many parts of Asia, in West Africa, and in northwest North America.*

Interviews were the principal and indeed almost the only means I used for investigating the European cases. Difficulties of language rarely occurred. During my stay in Zurich I improved my knowledge of French and began to learn German. These languages were helpful in France, Germany, and Austria. Gifted interpreters assisted me in Finland, Iceland, and Portugal.

My interviews were rarely brief, and I usually preceded and followed them with letters inquiring about details. I was able to learn about the subject's further development in more than half the cases that began in early childhood. I could do this because either I arranged to have follow-up interviews when the children had grown up or I met the subject first when he or she was already an adult.

This discussion of cases in Europe would remain incomplete without some reference to cases occurring with hypnosis. I cannot forget that two of the cases of responsive xenoglossy that I investigated emerged during hypnosis (Stevenson, 1974b;

---

*I cannot prove this assertion, because there has been only one systematic survey of the prevalence of cases. This showed that about 1 person in 500 of a district of northern India had claimed to remember a previous life (Barker and Pasricha, 1979). We have ascertained cases as easily in Lebanon, Nigeria, and British Columbia as in India. If cases were as frequent in Europe as they seem to be in the countries I have named I think that we would have learned of more than we have.

1984); and this has led me never to condemn research with hypnosis. That said, however, I must add that I think all but a very few cases of claimed previous lives induced by hypnosis are worthless. Even in age regression to earlier events in this life, subjects mingle confabulated details with accurate memories (Orne, 1951). Purported regressions to previous lives nearly always generate "previous personalities" whose existence cannot be traced.* Investigations have sometimes shown the exact or probable origin of the details of a claimed previous life in a publication or other normal source available to the hypnotized person (Björkhem, 1961; Harris, 1986; Kampman, 1973, 1975; Kampman and Hirvenoja, 1978; Venn, 1986; and Wilson, 1981.)

It nevertheless proves difficult to show that an apparently remembered previous life could not have occurred, especially if the life was that of an obscure person living remote in time from ourselves. Rivas (1991) succeeded in one case, and I have included two examples in this work. The obstacles to a demonstration of nonexistence has provided some market for novels purportedly based on memories of previous lives (Grant, 1939; Hawkes, 1981).

CASE REPORTS: CHILDREN

GLADYS DEACON

Summary of the Case and Its Investigation

Gladys Deacon was born in Market Harborough, Leicestershire, England, on January 25, 1900. Her parents were Benjamin Deacon and his wife, Emma. Benjamin Deacon was a carpenter. They were Roman Catholics. Gladys had one sister, younger by 2 years, and a brother.

When she was a young child, Gladys Deacon had a fear of falling that amounted to a phobia. She also had a special fondness for the name "Margaret." She later learned that her parents had considered calling her Margaret, but decided against this because her mother did not like names that could be shortened. She had no imaged memories of a previous life until the age of 11.

When she was 11 years old, Gladys Deacon was taken on a trip to Dorset, and while there she had a strong sense of familiarity with a place near Yeovil that she and her mother passed in the train. She then had a sudden upwelling of seeming memories of a previous life as a young girl who had fallen and injured her leg while running down a hill. She thought her name then had been Margaret.

Although the modern interest in hypnotic regression to previous lives dates from the publication of The Search for Bridey Murphy *(Bernstein, 1956/1965), experiments in hypnotic regression of this type were first undertaken in Europe in the middle of the 19th century (Delanne, 1924). They attained some popularity through the endeavors and publications of Rochas (1911/1924) in the early 20th century.*

Her mother scolded her for making such statements, and she apparently thought little about the matter until, at the age of 28 (in 1928) she was again in Dorset and unexpectedly verified her memories, which corresponded to events in the life and death of a child called Margaret Kempthorne.

A few years later, the (London) *Sunday Express* invited its readers to submit true accounts of apparent memories of previous lives. Gladys Deacon wrote out an account of her experience and sent it to the newspaper, which published it on June 2, 1935, along with some others. It thus came to my attention, although not for many years. I cannot now remember when I first learned about the case, but in the early 1960s I decided to try to meet Gladys Deacon, if she were still living.

At the end of her letter to the *Sunday Express*, Gladys Deacon had given her name and what I took to be her address in the town of Lutterworth, which is in southern Leicestershire. When I went to this address, I learned that the house belonged to Gladys Deacon's sister. (Gladys Deacon had been living there when she wrote her letter to the *Sunday Express* and had therefore given that address.) Her sister directed me to the nearby town of Stoke Albany, which is close to Market Harborough, where Gladys Deacon was then living. On August 9, 1963, I called on her and found her cordially agreeable to my interviewing her about her experience. During the interview I learned a few more details about the experience and about other events in her life. Subsequently, she answered some additional questions in correspondence.

Later, in the 1970s, I attempted to trace records of Margaret Kempthorne, but as will be seen, I did not succeed.

Gladys Deacon's mother died when she was 18 years old. The woman with whom Gladys Deacon was traveling in 1928 (who would have been a potential witness of the verification of her statements) died some years before I began my inquiries for the case. The case therefore rests entirely on the statements of Gladys Deacon.

Gladys Deacon's Account in 1935 of Her Experience and Its Verification

When I met Gladys Deacon in 1963, I showed her (and she read) a copy of the account of her experience published by the *Sunday Express*. She said that it had been printed accurately, and I shall quote it in full:

> As a girl of eleven I was taken with my brother from our home in Northants [Northamptonshire] to spend Christmas with relatives in Weymouth [Dorset].
> After leaving Yeovil our train stopped for some time, and to my surprise I found the country quite familiar to me, especially a hilly field opposite.
> I said to my brother, "When I was quite a little girl I lived in a house near here. I remember running down a hill in that field with two grown-ups holding my hands, and we all fell down and I hurt my leg badly."
> Here my mother broke in to scold me for telling deliberate untruths. I had never been that way before and certainly never lived there. I insisted that I had, and that when I ran down the hill I was wearing a white frock down to my ankles with little

green leaves on it, and the persons holding my hands were wearing blue-and-white checked frocks.

I said, "My name was Margaret then."

This was too much for my mother. I was forbidden to speak again till we reached Weymouth. I knew afterwards I could not have run down that hill, but the memory still remained as clear as any real memory of childhood.

The sequel came seventeen years later.

I was motoring [in 1928] with my then employer through Dorset. While having a tire changed we went to a cottage not far from Poole where a young woman got us tea.

While waiting for it, I saw an old portrait on glass, and to my amazement I saw it was of myself as I was then, running down that hill, a child of five with a plain, serious face, in a long white dress sprigged with green.

I exclaimed, "Why that is me," and of course both my employer and the woman laughed. The woman said, "Well, that child died years ago, but I guess you were just like her when you were small," and my employer agreed.

Seeing I was interested, the woman called her mother to tell me the story of the child.

She said the child was a Margaret Kempthorne, the only child of a farmer. The mother of the story-teller at that time was employed at the farm as a dairy-maid.

When Margaret was about five she was running down a hill with this dairymaid and another, when one of the grown-ups caught her foot in a rabbit-hole, and they all fell, with the child undermost.

Her leg was very badly broken. She never recovered and died two months after, though, as the old lady told me, with rather morbid relish, "My mother said that for such a wee girl she fought hard to live, and died just after calling out, 'I won't die'."

She did not know where the farm was, but the market town was Yeovil. I asked when this happened and in answer she took the portrait down and on the back was gummed a slip of paper.

I read there, "Margaret Kempthorne, born January 25th, 1830, died October 11, 1835," and on that day when Margaret died my father's mother was born, miles away in Northants, and my own birthday is on January 25th.

Additional Information Obtained in 1963

At the time of my interview with Gladys Deacon, her memory for the hill at Yeovil where she remembered falling remained as clear as when she had been a child. Her memory for the scene in the cottage when she found the picture on glass of Margaret Kempthorne had faded somewhat.

Gladys Deacon's mother came from Weymouth, but left Dorset as a young girl of 18 and did not return except during vacations. Gladys Deacon was sure that her mother did not know anything about the girl who fell down the hill. If she had recognized her daughter's account as relating to events within her knowledge, she would surely have corrected the child for attributing to herself something that had happened to another child. Instead, Emma Deacon behaved as if she thought Gladys was inventing the story totally.

I learned that Gladys Deacon had visited Weymouth when she was 2 years old.

She had almost certainly traveled at that time along the railway line between Yeovil and Weymouth. If so, this might have contributed to her sense of familiarity with the area near Yeovil when she again visited it at the age of 11.

As I mentioned, Gladys Deacon's parents had considered calling her Margaret, but decided against this. Gladys Deacon liked the name Margaret. (She did not, however, say that she had asked her parents to change her name.) She thought it likely that her parents had told her as a child that they had considered calling her Margaret.

Gladys Deacon had no memory of a previous life (which she could recall in 1963) prior to the second visit to Yeovil when she was 11. At that time the sense of familiarity with the hill near Yeovil was immediately followed by the memories of the run down the hill and the fall and injured leg. Following this experience of a sudden upwelling of memories, no additional details came into her consciousness. She had nothing to add to the earlier written account of the original experience and had not elaborated it in any way.

She regretted that she had not offered to purchase the painting of Margaret Kempthorne on glass, but she had felt diffident about making such an offer to the owner.

Gladys Deacon was a Roman Catholic and had definite reservations about "what she should believe" concerning reincarnation while remaining orthodox in her religion. Yet she said that she could not forget or deny her original experience of the apparent memory.

Unsuccessful Efforts to Verify Independently the Life and Death of Margaret Kempthorne

National registration of births and deaths did not begin in England until 1837. The dates of Margaret Kempthorne's birth and death came before registration began, which meant that parish records of baptisms and burials would provide almost the only pertinent records, especially given that Margaret Kempthorne died as a young child.

Gladys Deacon had not learned the name of the village where Margaret Kempthorne had lived. The possibilities were restricted somewhat by knowing that the village lay along the railway line between Yeovil and Weymouth, but Gladys Deacon had not stated how far from Yeovil the train had traveled when it had halted and she had had her experience of suddenly remembering a previous life.

Yetminster, a village about 10 kilometers south of Yeovil and on the railway line going toward Weymouth, seemed to meet the requirements. Accordingly, I wrote to the vicar of the church there. He forwarded my letter to the County Record Office in Dorchester. (The baptismal and burial records of Yetminster for the 1830s had been deposited in the central archives of the county in Dorchester.) An assistant archivist at the Record Office made a thorough search of the baptismal and burial records of Yetminster, but found no trace of Margaret Kempthorne. She also searched for the name Kempthorne in a few other records, such as an index of wills and a record of marriages, but found the name not mentioned.

I could not have asked this obliging archivist to search the records of the many other possible parishes. The office of the mayor of Yeovil wrote me that there are 100 parish churches within a 10-mile radius of Yeovil. I was unwilling to pay for a professional record searcher to examine all the records that might have to be examined before the correct one, if it existed, was found.

Gladys Deacon's Phobia of Falling

Gladys Deacon told me that she had always been especially afraid of falling. As a young child, she did not slide like other children, and she seemed to be particularly careful to avoid falls. She had no important fall in childhood, although she had fallen in adulthood.

I talked briefly with Gladys Deacon's younger sister, and she could not recall Gladys's fear of falling.

Comment

The visit that Gladys paid with her mother to Dorset when she was 2, including the probable journey along the railway line between Yeovil and Weymouth, could account for her sense of familiarity with the area around Yeovil that Gladys had when she was 11 years old. It could not, however, explain all the other details of seeming memories that came into her consciousness during the second visit.

The case includes some feature found in other cases of the reincarnation type. The preoccupation of Gladys Deacon's parents with the name Margaret and her own fondness for this name resemble other cases in which parents have been impressed to call a child by a particular name that has later been found to be the name of the previous personality claimed by the child.

The sudden onset of memories during stimulation by a scene of a previous life resembles similar arousals of memories in the cases of Norman Despers in Alaska and of Mallika Aroumougam in India. As I shall explain later, reincarnation may explain some instances of the experience of déjà vu.

JENNY MCLEOD

The subject of this case had two relevant experiences, of different types. As a child of about 2 years old, Jenny McLeod made about six accurate statements concerning the life of her great-grandmother who had died in 1948. A few years later, when Jenny was between 7 and 8 years old, she began to have a series of frequent, recurrent dreams that she related to the Battle of Culloden in 1746. I will report the experience of early childhood here and that of the recurrent dreams in a later section with other examples of such dreams.

Summary of the Case and Its Investigation

Jenny McLeod was born in Aberdeen, Scotland, on November 7, 1949. Her parents were Hamish McLeod and his wife, Margaret. Jenny was the third of their four children (all daughters). When Jenny was born, her family was living in Kingussie, and when she was about 5 years old, they moved (in 1954) to the small town of Tore, which is 25 kilometers northwest of Inverness. They were still living there when I first investigated the case in 1967.

Jenny began to speak coherently when she was about 1 year old. When she was about 2, she made half a dozen statements about a previous life that matched details in the life of her great-grandmother, Bessie Gordon, who had died in February 1948.

The case came to the attention of the McLeod's minister, the Reverend H. W. S. Muir. In May 1967, he wrote a short summary of the case, which he sent to a friend of mine who was a psychiatrist in Edinburgh, and she forwarded the summary to me. I corresponded with the Reverend Muir and then, later in 1967, went to Tore, where I interviewed Jenny's mother, Margaret, on October 11. The next day I met and interviewed Jenny herself at the University of St. Andrews. Jenny's father was away at the time of my visit to Tore, and I never met him. Jenny's grandmother to whom Jenny had directly addressed her statements (at the age of 2) had died in 1961. Margaret McLeod, however, had been a witness of what Jenny had said to her grandmother.

In the years following my meeting with Jenny in 1967, she and I corresponded from time to time, and I had hoped to meet her again on some occasion when I was in the United Kingdom. Unfortunately, this was not feasible until September 1992. In that month I met her again and had a long talk with her about her later life. She was then almost 43 years old.

In 1992 I went to Portree and visited the area of it known as The Lump and Bayfield Road, where Jenny's grandmother had lived. I was advised to consult Roger Miket, the Portree Museum's Officer and a local historian. He was away at the time I was in Portree, but he answered some of my questions in correspondence.

Jenny's Statements About a Previous Life Made When an Infant

Jenny was about 2 years old when she made her few remarks about the previous life. One day, in the early afternoon she was sitting on her grandmother's knee, and her grandmother was feeding her. Her mother was in the same room. Jenny unexpectedly said: "Do you remember when I used to feed you, Grannie?" Apparently led on by an association, Jenny then mentioned a hill called The Lump at Portree. She spoke about the house there, which had a little pier of its own. She referred to some steps which provided a shorter way of reaching the house than going around the road by The Lump. She talked about the "nice little dogs" that she had had. (The McLeods had no dogs of their own, large or small.)

The Reverend H. W. S. Muir, in his brief summary of the case, said that Jenny had made additional statements, giving the names of other places and streets in Portree. Margaret McLeod — speaking to me 5 months later — said that Jenny "did not say much more" than I have recorded above. She said that Jenny became sleepy after having her lunch and that ended the conversation about Portree. She never spoke about it again.

The Accuracy and Specificity of Jenny's Statements About the Previous Life

Jenny's mother told me that Jenny's statements were correct for aspects of the life of her (Jenny's) maternal great-grandmother, Bessie Gordon. She (Bessie Gordon) had been born in Portree of the Isle of Skye in 1865 and lived all her life there. Her house was close to the sea and also near the hill called The Lump. It was the only house of that area with its own pier. Jenny's knowledge about steps to the house was also correct.

When I was in Portree, I went to The Lump and also walked along the road near The Lump whose name, as well as that of the house in question, Margaret McLeod had given me. The road ran along the rim of the harbor. There were no longer any piers in front of the houses. Roger Miket wrote me, however, in a letter dated October 28, 1992, and confirmed some of the details. The house identified by Margaret McLeod had indeed been that of Bessie Gordon, and it had been the only one of the houses along this road that had had a pier or jetty in front of it. (The pier did not actually belong to the house, but to an adjacent Salmon Station.) There had also been near the house and pier "steps or rather stepping stones leading over to Seafield on the bay opposite."

Bessie Gordon married and had nine children, three sons and six daughters of whom one was Mary Gordon, Jenny's grandmother, to whom Jenny made her few statements about Portree. She bred West Highland Terriers. She remained agile and fully alert into her 80s, dying in Portree at the age of 83 in 1948. Her death was attributed to "old age"; she was in bed for only 2 days before her death.

Margaret McLeod remembered her grandmother well and thought her distinctive in her cheerfulness, the excellence of her voice, and her great fondness for books and reading.

Bessie Gordon appears to have been particularly fond of Margaret McLeod. She once gave her son a ring that she especially valued; but later she took it back and gave it to Margaret McLeod.

Lack of Opportunities for Jenny to Have Learned Normally About Portree

Up to the age of 2 — when she spoke about the previous life — Jenny's mother was constantly with her. Jenny slept with her at night. Margaret McLeod was familiar with Portree herself, but she was positive that no one had ever mentioned Portree to or in front of Jenny up to the time she spoke about it.

Resemblance in Physique Between Jenny and Bessie Gordon

Margaret McLeod said that Jenny resembled her great-grandmother in her "build." She thought that their distinctive physique was unusual among the members of the family. This feature evidently impressed Margaret McLeod greatly, because she had mentioned it earlier to the Reverend H. W. S. Muir, who included it in his brief summary of the case.

Comment. In 1967 I was still learning to give attention to birthmarks and birth defects in these cases, and it had not yet occurred to me that the subject of a case might resemble in physique the person whose life the subject seemed to remember. I thus lost many opportunities, such as the one in this case, to obtain additional data of potential importance; and the chapter on physique is one of the shortest in my work on the cases whose subjects have birthmarks or birth defects (Stevenson, 1997).

Resemblances in Behavior Between Jenny and Bessie Gordon

The Reverend H. W. S. Muir, in his summary of the case, noted that Margaret McLeod believed that Jenny resembled her great-grandmother, not only in build, but also "in her ways and speaking and in her manner of going about things."

To me, Margaret McLeod mentioned several traits in which Jenny resembled her great-grandmother, such as a fondness for home-made soup and for highland dancing. She said, however, that her other daughters shared these tastes. There remained, however, two traits in which Jenny differed from her sisters and resembled her great-grandmother. They were both unusually fond of reading and both had good singing voices.

Additional Information

Margaret McLeod believed in reincarnation. Furthermore, she believed in transmigration (metempsychosis), that is, that nonhuman animals may reincarnate as humans and vice-versa. She told me that she believed that her enormous ginger cat, who slept on his personal cushion throughout most of my visit to the McLeod residence, was the reincarnation of some human, she was unsure who. The cat had a special affinity for Margaret McLeod.

I did not learn the origin of Margaret McLeod's belief in reincarnation. Her mother tongue was Gaelic, and it was her first language. In Part I, I mentioned that Evans-Wentz (1911) found evidence that the belief in reincarnation persisted among the

Highlanders of Scotland into the second decade of the 20th century, and it may have lasted longer in pockets. Margaret McLeod was born in 1922, barely a decade after the publication of Evans-Wentz's book.

Jenny's Later Development

When I met Jenny in September 1992, she was successfully employed in a business. Her mother had died in 1991 and her father a few years before that. Margaret McLeod did not discuss Jenny's experiences as a child with Jenny, which was possibly due to the attitude of her husband, who had been and remained uninterested.

Jenny believed that she could still remember the occasion when she sat on her grandmother's knee and asked her whether she (the grandmother) remembered being fed by Jenny.

Jenny showed herself keenly interested in reincarnation and asked me many questions about other cases of children who claim to remember previous lives. She expressed an interest in reading the Reverend Muir's original letters about her case, and I showed them to her.

CATHERINE WALLIS

I include this case with some hesitation. This does not arise from the failure to verify the subject's statements, because I have published other unverified cases and this book includes several others. Nor does it arise because regrettably I have not met the subject; for four other cases of this volume I have not met the subjects. Instead, my doubts come partly because the subject was older (about 5 years of age) when she first referred to a previous life than are most children who talk about previous lives. They mainly derive, however, from the acknowledged skill of the subject in conceiving "stories" that she knew were fantasies and in the telling of which her father encouraged her. I was led to set aside this objection by the subject's firm insistence that she could tell the difference between her made-up "stories" and the memories she claims to have had of a real previous life. In addition, although her account of the previous life has had some accretions (stimulated, I believe, by questioning on the part of adults), the central core of her statements remained remarkably stable over the several years between the time when she first had the apparent memories and the time when she could no longer recall them.

Summary of the Case and Its Investigation

Catherine Wallis was born in Portsmouth, England, on March 27, 1975. Her parents were Christopher Wallis and his wife, Crystal. I believe Catherine was their only child. They separated when Catherine was about 3 years old. Thereafter Catherine lived with her father. He was a sculptor and teacher.

Catherine began to speak coherently when she was about 2 years old. I learned of nothing unusual about her early years—apart from her parents' divorce. At that time she moved with her father to Edinburgh. They later returned to the south of England and were living on his mother's farm in Wiltshire when Catherine spoke about a previous life.

Catherine and her father—living together alone—developed a close relationship. They fell into the habit of making up and telling each other stories for amusement. They had been doing this one evening—as they were bathing before Catherine went to bed—when it suddenly occurred to Christopher Wallis to ask Catherine: "Who do you think you were before you were you?" This evoked Catherine's account of what she then and later believed was a real previous life. Catherine was then about 5 years old and therefore spoke first about the previous life in about 1980.

Christopher Wallis had made a habit of writing down Catherine's stories, and he similarly recorded her account of her claimed previous life. He had kept his notes and, as will be seen, he used them in writing his first letter to me.

Early in 1982 I was interviewed about cases suggestive of reincarnation for a program broadcast from London by the British Broadcasting Corporation. The BBC forwarded letters sent to them for me. Christopher Wallis decided to write out for me an account of what Catherine had said about a previous life and the circumstances in which she had spoken. His letter was postmarked July 21, 1982, and I quote from it below.

Subsequently, I corresponded with Christopher Wallis about questions that occurred to me concerning Catherine's statements. During the next 10 years I wished and expected to meet him and Catherine, but was not able to do so. I did, however, refer them back to the BBC, which wished to interview children like Catherine. Accordingly, she was interviewed for a BBC program on February 21, 1983, by June Knox-Mawer. Two months later, a colleague then working with me, Dr. Nicholas McClean-Rice, was in England, and he visited Christopher and Catherine Wallis at their home in Wiltshire. Both the interview for the BBC and that of Dr. McClean-Rice were tape-recorded and transcribed. I have made use of them in this report. Catherine was not quite 8 when June Knox-Mawer interviewed her and just over 8 when Dr. McClean-Rice did. Christopher Wallis was present at both these interviews, and I shall occasionally refer to his statements during them in what follows.

After more than 10 years of correspondence I succeeded in meeting Christopher Wallis. We met in the National Gallery, London, on June 11, 1993. Although we talked for more than 2 hours, I learned of nothing new that would assist in understanding the source of Catherine's statements about a previous life. I missed meeting Catherine, who by this time was living with her mother in Eire.

In the following year, I corresponded with Christopher Wallis about Catherine's willingness to undergo hypnosis. He wrote that Catherine was agreeable to this, but the psychologist in London who had expressed interest in this project never communicated with Catherine or her father.

Statements Made by Catherine

Catherine's Statements at the Age of About 5. The following account of Catherine's statements derives from Christopher Wallis's letter to me of July 21, 1982.

I am her [Catherine's] father and when she was about five and a half we had been living together alone for about two years. In that time we had built a very close relationship. As do a lot of parents, I made up stories for her and she for me. We often played mental games seeing what things we could find in our minds and following lines of thought back by various means. One day we had been soaking in the bath together for a very long time as we had got deeply involved in a game of imagining you were in a room and what could you see in that room? On the other side there was always a door and what was through that door? My rooms tended to be rather ordinary and full of things like tables, chairs, knives, and forks, etc., and her rooms were sumptuously beautiful, full of jewels, gold, carpets and bright windows. The game went on for ages through passages, down stairways.

Finally, we got out of the bath and as we were drying I asked her: "Who do think you were before you were you?"

She started to talk straight away in a very self possessed way and without hesitation. It may have been fifteen minutes to half an hour before she had finished and afterwards I went to write it down as accurately as I could. I am afraid that a lot of the detail is missing as her story came out in such a flow but I think I managed to record the most relevant parts.

Here it is straight from my notebook.

Drying ourselves I asked her "who were you before you were you?"

"Rosy" she said as if I ought to have known; in a way reminding me of something she had already told me.

"Rose who?" I asked

"Rosy Abelisk (Abelisque?)

"What was your mother's name?"

"Mary Ann Abelisk" she went straight on "we lived in a little white wooden house, just by a zebra crossing — it was a farm house and on one side of the road there were chickens and in the morning she used to take me in the pram [perambulator: baby carriage] to feed the chickens and the chickens would make a terrible noise. When I was two I was bored because I couldn't get out of the pram, but then when I was three I used to help my mummy to collect the eggs and once I dropped one but it was alright because it landed on the hay."

"What was the pram like?" I asked wondering if it might give a clue to the date or time when this might be happening.

"It was made like a basket" she said "with hooks around the side."

"What was your mummy like?"

"She had golden hair which was long but she always wore it up in a bun on her head."

"Was your daddy there?"

"No, he wasn't there. He was a long way away in England — I think — I remember when I was six we planned to go to England to see him but I didn't speak English."

"What did you speak?"

"French, I think, we were in America but I spoke French. It was the best time for me because it was very exciting. We had to go on a long journey and when we got

there I jumped off the train into his arms. Then we came back and after that everything was just ordinary.

We were quite poor, a wood cutter lived in the house and he used to make money
by selling his wood."

"Can you remember what the name of the school was at all?" It was something
like: "ecco missi" she said, really testing the words "eccoo missre." I repeated it once or
twice. "École missive" I finally persuaded myself. The mission school? It would fit very
well into the story. Was "École missive" the French for mission school? She remembered the name but couldn't remember any more about it.

Here there was some discussion about death or dying — I wrote down "How were
you killed though?'

"When one day I was just crossing the road to collect the eggs and because it was
a crossing I didn't look and just as I stepped out a Coca-Cola lorry [truck] hit me and
I was rolled over and over. Then I went to hospital and I had two broken legs and I
was all sore around my neck."

"Can you remember were you in pain?"

"No. No pain. I just remember the soreness."

"How long were you in there?"

"Five fortnights and then I just died.

"Thank you, Rosy, for telling me the story" I said tucking her up in bed.

"It's not a story," she said. "It's true."

Statements Made by Catherine at the Age of About 7½. After receiving Christopher Wallis's letter of July 21, 1982, I replied, in September 1982, offering a few comments and asking him to write again if Catherine made any further statements related
to the presumed previous life. After some delay, he replied in a letter dated February 8, 1983. In it, he mentioned that he had "tried very gently" to obtain more details
from Catherine soon after he had received my letter of the preceding September. I
take the following from his reply of February 8, 1983.

When your last letter came I tried very gently to lead her back into talking about
Rosy's life to see if she could remember the name of a town.

She described buildings, people and even the sign board outside the school but
not the words on it and she also talked about the nearby town with "department
stores" which is not an English expression. We tend to call even large shops, "shops!"

One curious point (which she has mentioned since) is that her mother was an assid-
uous collector of scraps of material and made a lot of her clothes out of patchwork —
when she went to school everyone laughed at her because of her patchwork clothes.

She describes the school teachers as being very strict, mostly men, and wearing
black suits with waistcoats and blue shirts and the building as being white or stone
with a spire on the top.

I did not press her further and we just talk about it very casually as I am a little
bit afraid that she may become self conscious or start inventing things. However, at the
moment she seems to be able to walk around in her memory and see things clearly.

I asked her if she felt the same as when she was making up a story and she replied
that it was different and that she could see herself doing things.

Statements Made by Catherine at the Age of About 8. During Catherine's interviews with June Knox-Mawer and Dr. McClean-Rice (early in 1983), the interviewers

asked her many questions, in the hope that they could elicit more details about the presumed previous life.

In some instances Catherine appears to have achieved an amplification of some detail that she had mentioned 3 years earlier at the time of her first statements to her father. For example, asked about how Rosy brought the wood she had cut back to the house, Catherine told June Knox-Mawer: "There was a basket and it had sort of wheels on it, and I always used to bring that with the wood on it, like a wheelbarrow but a wicker basket."

Catherine also filled in details for June Knox-Mawer about how she had been struck and injured by the Coca-Cola lorry. Ordinarily, she said, there was little traffic on the road she crossed to go to school and to collect the eggs. She was about halfway across the road when the lorry suddenly appeared, and she could not escape. She said she was 10 years old when she was injured and died.

In other instances, Catherine introduced completely new details that had not figured at all in her first statements. For example, she talked at considerable length to Dr. McClean-Rice about a neighboring farmer called Nox. She had said nothing about him earlier. She first mentioned him to her father the day before Dr. McClean-Rice's visit, when she and her father had been talking about the life of Rosy. She also introduced other persons she had not previously mentioned, such as Mrs. Nox (the wife of Mr. Nox) and Rosy's best friend at school. In addition to introducing new persons and objects, Catherine changed one detail, that of the hair of Rosy's mother. In her first statement to her father Catherine had described her mother's hair as golden. In talking with Dr. McClean-Rice, she said it was "dark."

To both June Knox-Mawer and Dr. McClean-Rice, Catherine said with evident firmness that she could tell the difference between stories she made up and the details of the life as Rosy. For example, the following exchange occurred between Catherine and June Knox-Mawer:

> KNOX-MAWER: ...When you tell your father about these things, Catherine, is it as if you're there still or is it as if you're telling....
> CATHERINE: It is ... it is ... it's as if I was there and I was telling somebody about my life.
> KNOX-MAWER: Trying really hard to explain.... It must be very hard ... to explain.
> CATHERINE: I could hear it all in my head, and it was like I was there telling somebody about my life.

During the interview with Dr. McClean-Rice, Christopher Wallis and Catherine talked about the reality to Catherine of her seeming memories of a previous life, and the following exchange is taken from the transcript of this interview:

> C. WALLIS: What's the difference like when, when you're making up a story about Mrs. Churchville or something —
> CATHERINE: It's very different.
> C. WALLIS: It feels different, is it? Describe — what's the difference between like making up a story and ... do you remember?
> CATHERINE: It's, it's a different thing altogether then.

June Knox-Mawer asked Catherine whether she had any memories of the previous life before she had first spoken about them to her father at the age of about 5. Catherine said that the night before that occasion she had dreamed the scene of meeting Rosy's father and jumping into his arms. She later described this dream to Dr. McClean-Rice as "too real." She said: "It wasn't just a dream. It was true." She said that the other parts of the memories came to her the next day as she was in the bath with her father.

Catherine knew when she talked with June Knox-Mawer that she was 7 (not quite 8) years old and that she was claiming to remember the life of a girl who had died at the age of 10. About this experience the following exchange occurred:

> CATHERINE: …sometimes I feel … sometimes when I'm in bed I feel like going backwards to when I was ten and then going forward to when I'm 7.
> KNOX-MAWER: Because you're 7 now.
> CATHERINE: Different lives….
> KNOX-MAWER: Say that again. Different what?
> CATHERINE: When … sometimes when I'm in bed it feels like I'm … I'm … I feel like going … keep going back to when my other life and it keeps going back to this life.
> KNOX-MAWER: Is that confusing for you?
> CATHERINE: Very confusing.

June Knox-Mawer also interviewed Catherine's mother, Crystal, for the BBC program, and I have read the transcript of this interview. Crystal had not been present when Catherine first spoke about the previous life to her father, and she could add nothing to what he had written and said about the details of Catherine's memories. She did describe Catherine as having been an unusually sensitive child, who was mature beyond her years.

The Consistency of the Core Statements Made by Catherine. Although I have drawn attention to additional details that Catherine stated when questioned by her father and other interviewers when she was 7 and 8 years old, these additional details were not inconsistent with what she had said earlier. All of her statements are unverifiable and all may be fictions. Or the first account she gave at the age of about 5 may derive from a real previous life and the later additions could be fictional additions. We can say, however, that Catherine never varied the core of her statements (except for the detail about the color of the hair of Rosy's mother).

Comparing the tape-recordings of the later interviews with Christopher Wallis's first account of Catherine's statements, I agree with a statement he made to June Knox-Mawer. Referring to his own reluctance to press Catherine with questions, he said:

> I didn't like to sort of bring it [the previous life memories] up again because children who are making up stories all the time can easily elaborate on it, and so I just left it as something that I wrote down and it wasn't discussed at all. But when it did come up the things she told me were quite consistent with the original … the original story.

Conjectures About a Possible Location of the Previous Life

Catherine's statements furnish almost no basis for conjectures about where the previous life she believed she had lived might have occurred. The details of speaking French in America suggest Quebec or a French-speaking enclave in New England. A stone building with a spire suggests a typical Roman Catholic Church in a village of French Canada. Another possibility is a place in the French-speaking parts of Louisiana, especially the Acadian (Cajun) country around Lafayette.

Coca-Cola was first produced in 1886 and sold in bottles soon afterward (Watters, 1978). It was not distributed in motorized trucks before the 1910s and not widely distributed in them until the 1920s (Stevens, 1986). Such distribution had to await the development of both trucks and adequate highways.

Beyond these fragmentary clues, we have nothing that could take us further: Catherine never mentioned the name of a town or village.

Christopher Wallis's suggestion that "école missive" could be French for "mission school" is not strictly correct. The French word *missive* means a message or communication. A missionary school would be called in French "une école missionnaire." In fact, Catherine came close to this with the phrase "eccoo missre."

Other Relevant Information

The Wallises had no connection whatever with France or French Canada. Christopher Wallis could think of only one possible source for an item in Catherine's statements. His wife had had a patchwork skirt, which Catherine would have seen when she was very young.

One element in Catherine's statements had a parallel in a susceptibility that she showed as a child. She did not like being mocked. The situation of being mocked occurred in Catherine's statements about how the wealthier school children who had better clothes derided the patchwork clothes that Rosy wore.

Catherine had no phobia of vehicles.

Catherine's Maturity Compared with Other Children of Her Age

Although I have never met Catherine, her father's letters gave me the impression that she was an unusually intelligent child and mature beyond her years. Her father's first letter to me showed that he thought she had a more creative imagination than he had. Beyond that, however, she spoke seriously about matters that do not ordinarily concern a young child. She talked easily about what we could call creation myths and spoke comfortably about the soul, using that word herself. June Knox-Mawer evidently also believed that Catherine was mature beyond her years. In this connection I cite an exchange between her and Christopher Wallis during the BBC interview of February 21, 1983. (Catherine was not present during this part of the recording.)

KNOX-MAWER: Do you yourself have a slightly uncanny feeling with Catherine sometimes, that she is in fact telling you the kind of odd things that most children don't seem to have access to, something odd....

C. WALLIS: Yes, that sort of feeling that I actually couldn't believe some of the things she was saying. I thought am I really hearing this, you know, this actually come out ... out of her. And it certainly didn't seem to be the sort of things that children talk about. It was odd ... it was very odd.... Some creation myth stories which were very ... were very ... and her manner seemed ... at one time to be very much older than she actually is ... I think she always has been aware of ... people's feelings and much more mature in her approach ... and it ... well it is slightly disconcerting.*

Catherine's Birthmark

Catherine was born with a birthmark described by her father as "a bright red birthmark at the base of the skull on the left hand side — it has faded completely over the years, but a trace of it may be visible under the hair — I have not looked for a long time."

Because Catherine had described "a soreness around my neck" after the Coca-Cola truck struck Rosy, Christopher Wallis thought her birthmark might derive from the injury to Rosy to which Catherine had referred.

It happens, however, that at least 3% of children are born with birthmarks at the site of Catherine's (Corson, 1934). These are areas of erythema, a type of nevus flammeus, sometimes called "salmon patches" and, popularly, "stork's bites." In some series the incidence of such nuchal birthmarks has been found to be much higher than 3%. Most of them fade and disappear as the child grows, but they persist into later childhood and beyond in 5% of cases (Hodgman, Freeman, and Levan, 1971). Catherine's birthmark had in fact remained until 1983, when it was prominent enough for Dr. McClean-Rice to photograph it.

In a few verified cases that I have investigated there have been grounds for believing that a birthmark at this location might derive from a previous life (Stevenson, 1997). Given the frequency of such birthmarks in children who do *not* remember previous lives, however, I do not think we should attribute Catherine's birthmark to a previous life she believed she remembered.

Catherine's Later Development

During the late 1980s I did not correspond with Christopher Wallis. Then in 1990 I wrote him about the possible participation of Catherine in a documentary film that the BBC was to produce. He replied cordially and also gave some information about Catherine's later development.

In about 1985 Catherine had told him one night

I have discussed this feature of "adult attitude" elsewhere (Stevenson 1987/2001). Subjects who showed it include Suleyman Andary, Kumkum Verma, Bongkuch Promsin, Thiang San Kla, Maung Htay Win, Chanai Choomalaiwong, and the Ven. Chaokhun Rajsuthajarn.

that she felt "rocky" swinging backwards and forwards between two identities. She was very uncomfortable about it for a while, but shortly after this she started to go outdoors to play a lot more than she had done previously (about age 10). Quite recently [1990] she has told me that up to that age she was very frightened of dying (till she was ten years old). [Catherine had said that Rosy was 10 when she had died.]

From the foregoing it appears that Catherine continued to have some memories of the previous life until she was about 10. As of 1990, Christopher Wallis wrote (in the letter of August 6, 1990): "She says that she now has only a memory of her previous memories. She remembers remembering."

Comment

I cannot reach any firm conclusion about whether Catherine had memories of a previous life that was actually lived. (We have to say the same about all unsolved cases.)

Catherine's comparatively late age of beginning to remember the previous life points away from a paranormal interpretation; but she was not unique in that respect because a few subjects of some verified cases, such as Suleyman Andary, have not begun to speak about a previous life until they were older than 5 years.

Catherine also did not express her memories spontaneously, but only in response to her father's question. (And this came after he and she had been telling each other fictional stories.) Yet there are parallel cases with this feature also, most notably perhaps that of Dolon Champa Mitra.

The stability of the original core of Catherine's memories speaks slightly in favor of a paranormal interpretation of them. And yet the most palpably absurd fantasies have sometimes shown remarkable stability over many years. The case of Hélène Smith (Flournoy, 1899) offers an excellent example of this.

In the introduction to this report I mentioned that Catherine's confidence in her ability to distinguish memories from fantasies had tilted me toward including the case in this volume. Nevertheless, I have to say now that I consider this the least important feature when we try to find the right interpretation for the case. I wish I could share Catherine's confidence (which I certainly respect as her honest conviction); but a widely acknowledged fact about memory is that confidence in its accuracy has no correlation with its accuracy. This is at least well attested with regard to testimony of eye-witnesses (Wells and Murray, 1984), and it seems likely to be true of other kinds of memory also.

CARL EDON

This case is unsolved. Its value comes from the subject's claim to remember a previous life as a person of another country and the unusual behavior, according with his statements, that the subject showed as a young child.

Summary of the Case and Its Investigation

Carl Edon was born in Middlesbrough, England, on December 29, 1972. His parents were James Edon and his wife, Valerie. Carl was the third of their three children. He had a sister 5 years older and a brother 11 years older. James Edon was a bus driver.

Carl was able to speak coherently when he was about 2 years old. Almost immediately he began to say: "I crashed a plane through a window." He repeated this often and gradually added further details about a previous life that he seemed to remember. He said that he was on a bombing mission over England when he crashed. From additional details that Carl added to his narration his parents concluded that he was talking about the life of a German Air Force pilot who had been killed during World War II.

Carl added to the evidence for this when, as he became able to draw, he made sketches with swastikas and eagles on them and, a little later, drew a sketch of the panel of a pilot's cockpit. He also showed a fondness for Germany and some behavior that could be considered "German."

A brief report of this case was published in an article in the magazine *Woman's Own* on August 7, 1982. Through the editor of the magazine I was able to learn the address of the Edons. In January 1984, Dr. Nicholas McClean-Rice went to Middlesbrough, where he interviewed Carl's parents and spoke also with Carl. Carl was then just over 11 years of age. In the meantime, the case had received additional publicity, including much attention in the regional newspapers. A German journalist went to Middlesbrough and interviewed Carl and his parents; his report appeared in *Morgenpost* (a newspaper of Berlin) on July 17, 1983.

After Dr. McClean-Rice's meeting with the Edons, I neglected the case for 10 years before deciding that we could and should learn more about it. I therefore resumed the correspondence with the Edons and, on June 13, 1993, I went to Middlesbrough and had a long meeting with Carl and his parents. In the following years I heard from them in correspondence from time to time. On October 15, 1998, I returned to Middlesbrough and had another long interview with James and Valerie Edon. (By this time, as I shall explain later, Carl had died.) I asked for this meeting in order to review some details of the case. The Edons' two other children came to their parents' house toward the end of my interviews, but I found that they could add no additional information.

Statements Made by Carl

Carl's first statement about the previous life, which he afterwards repeated often, was: "I crashed a plane through a window." He later added that the airplane he had crashed was a bomber and a Messerschmitt. (Valerie Edon recalled that Carl had given a number, 101 or 104, for the type of Messerschmitt, but she no longer remembered [in 1983] which number he had given.* He said he was on a bombing mission when he crashed.) He also added the detail that in the crash he had lost his right leg.

Carl said that his name was Robert and his father's name was Fritz; he had a brother called Peter. He did not remember the name of the previous mother, but described her as being dark and wearing glasses. He said that she was bossy. He also said that he was 23 years old when he died and that he had a fiancée who was 19 years old; she was blond and thin.

Comment. In 1993 I learned of numerous additional statements that Carl had made, but by that time 18–19 years had passed since he had first spoken about the previous life, and I believe it appropriate to confine the list of his statements to those that his parents stated in 1983. I am sure this entails loss of additional details, but it avoids erroneously listing items that Carl may have added, either to please questioners or from normally acquired knowledge.

Carl's Sketches

Carl began to make sketches and drawings as early as between 2 and 3 years of age. He drew airplanes, badges, and insignias. His parents remembered his drawing an airplane and putting a swastika on it. (They noted that the swastika was reversed.) He also drew an eagle, which his parents later identified as "the German eagle." At the age of 6 he drew the panel of an airplane's cockpit and described the function of the gauges. He mentioned at this time that the bomber he flew had a red pedal which was pressed to release the bombs. One of his other drawings was apparently of an insignia with wings laterally and an eagle in the center.

Carl's initial drawings were crude, although what he was attempting to draw seemed obvious enough to his parents. As he became older, he continued to draw badges and insignia, but with increasing skill.

Carl's Behavior Related to the Previous Life

Circumstances and Manner of Carl's Speaking About the Previous Life. Carl's early statements were spontaneous and had no identified stimulus. When he became old enough to watch television programs about Germany, he would sometimes comment on some details of an actor's costume. He would say, for example, that the actor did not have the badge on his uniform in the right place.

On another occasion Carl was watching a documentary film about the Holocaust that showed a scene at a concentration camp. (His parents later believed they

---

Persons poorly informed about the German military aircraft used in World War II (of which I was one) believed that Messerschmitt aircraft were exclusively fighters. This is broadly true, but the Messerschmitt 262, an early jet-propelled airplane, was "employed as a fighter, as a ground-attack or low-level bomber, and for reconnaissance duties" (United States Government Printing Office, 1945).

remembered this to have been Auschwitz, but were unsure; it might have been another camp.) The scene stimulated Carl to say that his camp, that is, the airplane base from which his bomber flew, was near this concentration camp.

Friends of the family would sometimes ask Carl for details, for example, of what he wore in the previous life; and he would then tell them. They might also ask him to make a sketch of some object from the previous life, and he would do that. (His parents let the friends take these sketches home and keep them. They themselves preserved none that Carl made spontaneously.)

Carl's Preferences for Food

Carl differed from other members of his family in preferring coffee to tea, and in liking to eat thick soups and sausages.

Carl's Posture, Gait, and Gestures

When he was first talking about the previous life, Carl spontaneously demonstrated the characteristic Nazi salute with the right arm raised and straight. He also demonstrated the goose-step march of German soldiers. When standing up he always stood erect with his hands at his sides.

Carl's Fondness for Germany

Carl expressed a wish to go to Germany and live there. Once a play being performed at his school had a part for a German, and Carl insisted on acting this part in the play.

Other Relevant Behavior of Carl

Compared with the other children of the family, Carl was unusually clean and almost compulsively tidy. He liked to dress well. He seems to have been somewhat rebellious and naughtier than the usual young child.

Carl's Physical Appearance

Carl was extremely blond. His hair was straw colored and his eyebrows and eyelashes were also blond. His eyes were blue. In his comparative lack of pigmentation of his hair Carl differed markedly from the other members of his immediate family who all had brown hair. His mother had blue eyes.

The Attitudes of Carl's Parents and Schoolmates Toward His Memories

Carl's parents were members of the Church of England. They knew little about reincarnation and were initially baffled by Carl's statements, sketches, and behavior. His father at first believed Carl was describing a childish fantasy. They never suppressed his talking about the previous life. His father indeed perhaps indirectly encouraged it. He would ask Carl questions about some detail and then check Carl's answer in a book. Carl's parents also encouraged visitors to invite him to make sketches of objects, such as insignias, from the previous life. After some years of listening to Carl, they became more or less convinced that he was referring to a real life that he certainly believed he had lived. They were undogmatic and continued to think the case a mystery.

Carl's schoolmates, on the other hand, teased him cruelly. They mockingly imitated his goose-step walking and called him a German and a Nazi. This contributed to Carl's stopping to speak about the previous life when he was about 10 or 11 years old. For a time, Carl tried to avoid going to school because he found the teasing there so unpleasant.

Possibilities for Carl's Normal Acquisition of Information About the Theme of the Previous Life

James Edon was born in 1947. Valerie Edon was born in 1946. Her father had fought in the British Army during World War II. In the fighting in north Africa he had witnessed the deaths of some of his comrades. He hated Germans and sometimes said so after the war. He died in 1968, 4 years before Carl was born.

Carl was speaking about the previous life abundantly in 1974–76. By that time, 30 years had elapsed since the end of World War II, and it was little discussed. James Edon was confident that in those days Carl was in bed before the time in the evening when any of the rare films about the war were shown on television. He was sure such films could not have been a source of Carl's interest in the German Air Force and his knowledge of airplanes and German insignias and badges.

Carl continued referring to the previous life until he was 10 or 11 years old. In the later years of childhood he would have had opportunities to see occasional films about World War II on television. (I mentioned above his recognition of a concentration camp.)

The family had few books and none about World War II. James Edon said that when he asked Carl a question about some detail in the previous life to which Carl was referring he had to borrow a book from a local library in order to learn that Carl had been correct.

Carl's Birthmark

Carl was born with a prominent elevated hyperpigmented nevus in his right groin. It increased in size as he grew, and it eventually protruded so that he caught his clothes in it. When he was a young adult, it was about 2.5 centimeters in diameter. A physician removed it under a local anesthetic early in 1993. When (in 1993) I examined the area where it had been, stitch marks were still visible; the scar was pink.

Carl never complained of pain in the area of the nevus, and he never limped when walking.

His parents conjectured a connection between the nevus and Carl's statement that he had lost his right leg when the airplane of the previous life crashed; Carl himself never made that connection.

Conjectures About a Deceased Person Whose Life Carl Seemed to Remember

James Edon's brother married a German woman whose father had been a German Air Force pilot killed in action during World War II. This knowledge stimulated speculation that Carl might be remembering the life of this pilot. Unfortunately, the (German) wife of the pilot had remarried and, although her second husband was English and she had moved to England, she was unforthcoming about details of her past. The Edons were unable to elicit any helpful information from her about her first (German) husband. She knew of Carl's statements about a previous life, and the Edons learned that she "did not believe in it." Her (also German) daughter, James Edon's sister-in-law, experienced difficulty in completing pregnancies. She had a stillborn child and a miscarriage in the years before Carl was born. She later gave birth to two live babies of whom the older was 8 months older than Carl.

A second line of conjecture about the identity of the person to whose life Carl referred derived from the crash near Middlesbrough of a German bomber.

On January 15, 1942, a German Dornier 217E attacked coastal defenses near the mouth of the River Tees, then struck the cable of a barrage balloon and crashed. It came down at South Bank, a community almost adjoining Middlesbrough, where Carl was born 30 years later. The bodies of three of its crew were quickly recovered and duly buried. The wreckage of the crashed bomber was gradually covered over and forgotten until, in November 1997, excavations for new pipelines led to its being unearthed and to the discovery of the remains of a fourth crew member. The insignia associated with this body showed that it was that of Hans Maneke, the bomber's radio operator. The bodies of three other crewmen, Joachim Lehnis (pilot), Heinrich Richter (bombardier), and Rudolph Matern (navigator), had been earlier identified and buried in 1942. I learned about the unearthing of the Dornier's wreckage and the discovery of Hans Maneke's body during my visit to Middlesbrough in October 1998. James and Valerie Edon gave me numerous newspaper clippings about these events.

Comment. The first of these speculations suggests that the deceased German Air Force pilot was trying to be reborn as his daughter's child and mistakenly came into the nearby Edons' family. Several cases that I have published make this suggestion at least plausible. Examples occurred in the cases of B. B. Saxena, Bir Sahai, and Lalitha Abeyawardena.

The second speculation suggests that Carl was remembering the life of the Dornier's pilot, Joachim Lehnis. This would make the case similar to those of several blond children in Burma (Myanmar) who claimed to remember the previous lives of American and British airmen killed in Burma during World War II. Maung Zaw Win Aung and Ma Par are subjects of such cases. Carl's detail that he crashed his airplane into a building is not compatible with the history of the Dornier, which crashed after being cut by the cable of a barrage balloon; nor is the name Robert that he gave for himself that of the pilot of the Dornier.

Carl's Later Development

As I mentioned, Carl stopped speaking about the previous life around the age of 10 or 11, largely because of the merciless teasing of which he had been a victim after his case received publicity in local newspapers. After this he seemed to lose interest in what he had been saying earlier.

In 1983 he told Dr. McClean-Rice that he was not remembering details "very well." He was then just over 11 years old.

At the age of 16 Carl left school and became employed as a coupler by British Rail. He developed a close companionship with a girl to whom he was more or less affianced. They had one child.

When I met him in June 1993, Carl seemed to have forgotten all memories of the previous life, but he did not say this explicitly.

In August 1995, James and Valerie Edon wrote me with the distressing news that Carl had been murdered a few days earlier. His murderer was identified, arrested, tried, and sent to prison for life. Carl's girlfriend gave birth to a second child later that year.

Comment

This case, perhaps more than any other I have studied, shows the great importance of reaching a case when the subject is young and still talking about a previous life. It shows no less the importance of completing the investigation as soon as possible, even when an investigator reaches its scene after the usual age when the children speak most about a previous life. The two delays—first in our learning about the case and second in not pursuing its investigation—may have caused the loss of much valuable detail. I particularly regret the loss of the sketches that Carl Edon made when he was between the ages of 2 and 4.

Despite the loss of some — perhaps many — details, enough remained for our investigation to warrant my saying that we cannot explain the case by present knowledge of genetics or environmental influences. Therefore, I believe reincarnation is at least a plausible explanation for it.

WILFRED ROBERTSON

No case of this work has fewer details than this one. That, however, is an important reason for reporting it. It adds to the evidence that cases of this type exhibit a wide range in the amount of detail seemingly remembered by the subjects. The cases of Swarnlata Mishra, Marta Lorenz, and Suzanne Ghanem are perhaps at the extreme end in richness of details; and the present case, the next one, and that of Graham Le-Gros are near the extreme other end.

Summary of the Case and Its Investigation

Wilfred Robertson was born in London, England, on November 3, 1955. His parents were Herbert Robertson and his wife, Audrey. Wilfred was their third child. Their oldest son, Thomas, had died about 2½ years before Wilfred's birth. A third brother, Geoffrey, was born in October 1948. The family were Christians, and I believe they were members of the Church of England.

When Wilfred was a young child, he made four statements about the life of his older deceased brother, Thomas. These statements suggested to the children's parents that Wilfred was the reincarnation of Thomas.

The case was brought to my attention in 1968 by Margaret Thayer, who was a member of a group of Anthroposophists* in London. She had become acquainted with Audrey Robertson after Thomas's death when Audrey was in a state of extreme grief combined with a burden of guilt over her care of Thomas before he died. Margaret Thayer encouraged Audrey to believe that Thomas might be reborn as another child to Audrey.

Margaret Thayer wrote me about the few statements that Wilfred had made and that were suggestive of memories of Thomas's life.

On March 1, 1970, I met Herbert and Audrey Robertson in London. Wilfred was then about 14½ years old, and I did not meet him. They were able to confirm what Margaret Thayer had already communicated to me about the case, but remembered no additional statements Wilfred had made that could have been allusions to Thomas's life.

---

*Rudolf Steiner (1861–1925), born a Roman Catholic in (then) Austrian Croatia, developed a teaching that sought to combine science, Christianity, and elements of Theosophy (to which group Steiner had for a time belonged). He called his teachings Anthroposophy, and reincarnation was an important concept in them.

In 1980 I corresponded again with Audrey Robertson, when she wrote me to inform me of the death of Margaret Thayer. I was in London in August 1980 and talked with Audrey Robertson on the telephone, but did not meet her. There had been no further developments in the case since 1970.

I derived some of the details of events during the last illness of Thomas Robertson from Margaret Thayer, who was therefore a secondhand informant for them. She did not meet the Robertsons until after Thomas's death.

The Life and Death of Thomas Robertson

Thomas Robertson, the oldest son of Herbert and Audrey Robertson, was born in London on July 2, 1946. He was an unhealthy child. He was affectionate and also wanted other persons to show affection toward him. Audrey Robertson said that he was a whiner and that she "got out of patience with his whining." She was unsure of herself as a mother (with her first child). She said: "I went to pieces when anything went wrong." Thomas, she believed, needed a placid mother, which she was not.

During the night of April 3, 1953, Audrey Robertson dreamed that she was with a figure wearing a dark cloak. In the dream she knew that Thomas was dead. The next day Thomas became ill with a sore throat, but she minimized this, because he had been inclined to have sore throats. At this time her second son, Geoffrey, was also ill, and he seemed to need more attention than Thomas. Audrey thought Thomas was jealous of the attention she was giving to Geoffrey, and she became impatient with Thomas. Too late, she realized that Thomas was in fact much more seriously ill than Geoffrey. After only a week of illness, Thomas died on April 11, 1953. He was not quite 7 years old. His death was attributed to polioencephalitis.

Audrey Robertson's grief over the death of Thomas combined with a heavy sense of guilt about her attitude toward him during his brief final illness. She had not neglected him in any way, but nevertheless reproached herself for her attitude toward him and came to believe herself responsible for his death. Margaret Thayer, who came to know her soon afterward, said that Audrey was then in a state of "almost suicidal despair."

A mutual friend introduced her to Margaret Thayer, who, in turn told her about the idea of reincarnation as taught in Anthroposophy. The Robertsons at this time had "been inclined to believe in reincarnation before, but had not given it much study." Margaret Thayer stimulated Audrey to consider the possibility that Thomas might be reborn in their family. She found this idea solacing, and when she later became pregnant with Wilfred she hoped, perhaps more than she expected, that her baby would be Thomas reborn.

Statements Made by Wilfred

Wilfred made four statements suggesting he had memories of Thomas's life. He saw a book that had been "lying around" and said that it was his. The book had belonged to Thomas and had his name written inside the cover. Audrey said that Wilfred was "very tiny" when he made this statement. He was not yet able to read.

When Wilfred was between 5 and 7 years old, his mother was putting him to bed one night when he said he remembered going to the "little school." Wilfred himself was then going to a large school with between 20 and 30 teachers. He had never gone to a little school, nor had he ever seen the one that Thomas had attended. When the family lived in another community, Thomas had attended a "little school" that had only two teachers.

Audrey once overheard Wilfred say to his older brother, Geoffrey, that he had once seen him in his pram. This was correct for Thomas, who had been 2 years older than Geoffrey. I do not know how old Wilfred was when he made this statement.

Margaret Thayer wrote to me that Audrey had told her that Wilfred had said of a photograph of Thomas that it was of himself. Audrey did not remember this statement in 1970, but in 1980 she said that she "vaguely remembered that Wilfred had commented on a photograph of Thomas." She was sure that Margaret Thayer would not have mentioned the item to me if she (Audrey) had not told it to her.

Wilfred's Behavior Related to the Previous Life

Circumstances and Manner of Wilfred's Speaking About the Previous Life. Wilfred's four allusions to Thomas's life did not occur in any noticeable circumstances. Audrey Robertson noted that she could not pursue with him a topic that he mentioned. When he referred to going to the "little school," she asked him who the teacher was. He did not answer, but turned to another subject.

Wilfred's Attitude of Being an Older Person. Wilfred behaved toward his older brother Geoffrey as if he (Geoffrey) were younger to him (as Geoffrey had been to Thomas). Audrey Robertson said that Wilfred was "quite bossy toward Geoffrey." Geoffrey found Wilfred's superior attitude toward him annoying.

One of Wilfred's schoolteachers noted that he was somewhat reserved and mentioned this to the Robertsons. When they spoke to Wilfred about the matter, he replied: "The trouble is she does not realize how much I know."

Other Behavior of Wilfred

Herbert and Audrey Robertson said that Wilfred had a different relationship with them than that of Thomas. Whereas Thomas had been affectionate and had sought affection, Wilfred was inclined to be aloof and reserved, not just with them but with other persons also. Audrey Robertson believed that Wilfred was even antagonistic toward her and that his attitude derived from her mismanagement of Thomas's whining behavior and her impatience with Thomas when he was mortally ill. Herbert

Robertson thought Audrey exaggerated Wilfred's "antagonism" as specially focused on her; to him Wilfred showed a reserve toward all other persons, not just his mother.

The Attitude of Wilfred's Mother Toward the Possibility That He Was Thomas Reborn

Audrey Robertson said in 1970 that she had not made up her mind as to whether Wilfred was or was not Thomas reborn. She still thought of Thomas as a separate person, and she meditated about all three of her children.

As I mentioned, she blamed herself for Thomas's death almost as if she had murdered him. She wanted to make some kind of reparation to him. She wanted *his* forgiveness; what the church thought about her did not matter. In this situation, Wilfred's inability to return her affection for him had the effect of prolonging her guilt toward Thomas.

In a letter that she wrote in August 1980, Audrey Robertson seemed to have backed away from any commitment to reincarnation as the best interpretation of Wilfred's statements and behavior. She wrote:

> It was Margaret Thayer who always thought there was a strong possibility of Thomas having come back as Wilfred and, of course, wishful thinking on my part in those early years.

Wilfred's Later Development

My last information about Wilfred came in the mentioned letter from Audrey Robertson in August 1980. Wilfred was then 25 years old. He had never made any further statements suggestive of memories of the life of Thomas. After completing high school, he earned a degree in chemical engineering at a British university and then obtained a job as a consultant.

Audrey Robertson remained impressed by the differences in the personalities of Thomas and Wilfred. She remembered Thomas as being affectionate and somewhat dependent. Wilfred, she wrote, was kind but independent and aloof.

Comment

Like all other cases in which the two persons concerned belong to the same family, this one has an important weakness, which is the hope of having a deceased loved member of the family return to them. This can lead to attaching unwarranted meanings to chance remarks or similarities of behavior between the two persons concerned. Although such misinterpretation may have occurred in this case, I found no evidence that it did. My notes of 1970 state that Audrey Robertson "seemed eager not to exaggerate any feature of the case."

GILLIAN CUNNINGHAM

This is another case in which the subject made only a few statements about a previous life. It is unsolved.

Summary of the Case and Its Investigation

Gillian Cunningham was born in Ilford, Essex, England, on October 19, 1958. Her parents were Leonard Cunningham and his wife, Lillian. Gillian was their third and youngest child.

When Gillian was 2 years old, she made several statements suggesting memories of a previous life. She never spoke about the possible previous life again, and what she said then was insufficiently specific to permit any verification of her statements.

This case came to my attention when Gillian herself responded to a request by the London *Sun* for readers to send it accounts of memories suggestive of reincarnation. Gillian wrote the briefest possible summary of her experience, and it was published in the newspaper on March 10, 1972. I wrote to her, in care of the newspaper, and the newspaper forwarded my letter to her. Her mother, Lillian Cunningham, replied with information about what Gillian had said concerning a previous life when she was 2 years old.

In October 1972, I was in London and telephoned Lillian Cunningham at her home in Essex. We had a conversation about Gillian's experience, but did not meet then. During our conversation I broached the possibility of hypnotizing Gillian to learn whether under hypnosis she might bring into consciousness additional details about the presumed previous life — details that might permit verification of what she had said when 2 years old. Lillian Cunningham seemed doubtful about asking Gillian to undergo hypnosis, and I did not press my suggestion on her.

A few years later, Gillian herself, who was by this time 16 years old, wrote to me and said that she would like to be hypnotized. In order to be sure that her mother approved of this and that it was otherwise appropriate, I decided that I should meet Gillian and her mother. I therefore met them in London on March 2, 1976. At our meeting I clarified some details about what Gillian had said when she was 2 years old; and I also discussed the plan for a trial of hypnosis.

Subsequently, I wrote about Gillian to Dr. Leonard Wilder, a dentist with competence in hypnosis and an interest in hypnotic regression to possible previous lives. He agreed to hypnotize her. He did so on three occasions in 1976 and sent me a report of the results in a letter dated December 6, 1976. Gillian was a good hypnotic subject. Under hypnosis, however, although she added a few details to what she had said when 2 years old, none of these provided verifiable information, even when added to what she had said spontaneously 18 years earlier. Instead, Gillian evoked two other "previous lives." One was of a woman called Lydia Johnson who had supposedly lived in Suffolk during the 17th century. The other was of a woman called Sarah O'Shea who had supposedly lived in Dublin during the late 19th century and the first part of the 20th century. She did not give enough information about either of these personalities to warrant attempts at verification.

Statements Made by Gillian

I will next cite Lillian Cunningham's letter to me dated August 1, 1972, in which she described Gillian's statements. (As with similar citations, I have made a few minor editorial adjustments to the text without changing its meaning.)

> It was in the evening about 6:30 when I was bathing her [Gillian] before putting her to bed. As mothers talk to their children I was saying that when she grew up she could be anything she wanted but it is then that she started to talk adultly.
>
> She insisted that *when* she was a lady she was a farmer's wife.
>
> I said no when you grow up you *can* be a farmer's wife but no she again said when I was a farmer's wife, I had four sons and she went on to name them. One son's name was Nicholas, this name only do I remember as it was my grandfather's name (which was only found out when he was in his seventies).
>
> I then tried to trick her and said: "What kind of farm? She answered "Dairy." Again I tried: What do you keep on a dairy farm?" She answered "cows of course!" And then she reverted to baby talk again.
>
> I have tried many times since to get her to try and remember her old life but I have never succeeded.

A False Trail Toward Verification of Gillian's Statements

Lillian Cunningham's letter referred to her (paternal) grandfather, one of whose names was Nicholas. When I met her in March 1976, I obtained information from her for a complete family tree back to Nicholas's mother. Lillian Cunningham had thought, for a time, that Gillian had remembered the life of this great-grandmother, and Gillian had said this in her letter to the *Sun*. The first difficulty with this attribution arose because Lillian Cunningham's grandfather had never been known to his family, during most of his lifetime, as anything but George. That he had a second name, Nicholas, only emerged in his old age, perhaps at the time he applied for a pension and had to furnish authorities with a complete name. In addition, Lillian Cunningham had made some inquiries herself since we had first corresponded, and she had learned that her paternal grandfather's mother (whose name she did not learn), who would have been the mother of Nicholas, had grown up on a farm, but did not live herself on a farm after her marriage. Her husband, in fact was a fisherman, not a farmer.

The conjecture that Gillian had referred to the life of her paternal great-grandmother therefore proved groundless, and her statements remain unverified.

Gillian's Later Development

I remained intermittently in touch with Gillian and her mother in the years after our first meeting. I last heard from Gillian in a letter dated October 30, 1992, when she was 34 years old. She had trained as a nurse and became a specialist in pediatric nursing. She had had no further apparent memories of a previous life, but remained keenly interested in the subject.

Comment

The sudden, brief assumption by Gillian of an adult attitude when, at the age of 2, she spoke about a previous life has occurred in other cases. Informants have sometimes noted transient changes of behavior in other children who speak about previous lives; at one moment they may seem grave and mature and at the next moment run off and play like other children of their age. Other subjects show an "adult attitude" over a much longer period than did Gillian. Examples of this adult behavior occurred in the cases of Mounzer Haïdar, Erkan Kılıç, Nasır Toksöz, Suleyman Andary, and Semih Tutuşmuş. The footnote on page 66 lists other examples.

DAVID LLEWELYN

The subject of this case never made any explicit statement in which he claimed to remember a previous life. Instead, he showed unusual behavior, not attributable to any environmental influence, and knowledge about Jewish customs that he does not appear to have acquired normally. In addition, he suffered greatly from nightmares and phobias that accord with his unusual behavior.

Summary of the Case and Its Investigation

David Llewelyn was born on September 1, 1970, in Chester, England. His official parents were Jeffrey Llewelyn and his wife, Susan. In fact, David's father was another man, Solomon Rosenberg, with whom Susan Llewelyn had an affair lasting about 2 years. She managed to conceal from her husband the real paternity of David, although she thought that at times he had suspicions about David's illegitimacy. Susan and Jeffrey Llewelyn later divorced.

Solomon Rosenberg was a Jew and, Susan said, "very true to his faith." He attended a synagogue and patronized a shop in Chester that specialized in Jewish items. She herself was Welsh. Solomon Rosenberg saw David a few times and remarked that he resembled members of his family.

When David was only a few years old, he began to awaken in the night in a state of extreme fear; he would be shaking. He then began to show unusual behavior, such as writing and reading from right to left. He showed a knowledge of Jewish customs that his mother was sure he could not have learned normally. He described places and events that seemed like memories of concentration camps and the killing of Jews during the Holocaust of the 1940s.

Throughout his childhood David seemed to want to talk about the scenes that troubled him; and yet talking about them gave him no relief from the fear the memories — as they seemed to be — gave him.

As I mentioned in the report of Catherine Wallis's case, I was interviewed in the summer of 1982 on a program concerned with reincarnation that was broadcast by the British Broadcasting Corporation. Susan heard the program and asked the BBC for my address. She then wrote me a long letter (on September 14, 1982) in which she described David's unusual behavior and unusual knowledge of Jewish customs. I replied to her letter and asked for some more details, which Susan then furnished in a letter of November 20, 1982.

Susan agreed to be interviewed for a program of the British Broadcasting Corporation, and June Knox-Mawer interviewed her and David on February 8, 1983.

At this point it seemed appropriate for me or a colleague to meet Susan and David. Susan, however, would not agree to our meeting David. She said the interview for the BBC program had disturbed him greatly, and she did not want him troubled by a further discussion of his apparent memories of a previous life. Susan had not told David before they went on the BBC program that the subject of his nightmares and fears would be discussed; and this lack of preparation for the topics June Knox-Mawer brought up, and even to some extent pressed on him, probably increased his discomfort with the interview.

Ten years later I decided to write to Susan with the thought that David would have forgotten the apparent memories of the previous life and be willing to meet me. He and Susan were then willing to meet me, even though he had not forgotten the apparent memories; indeed he had continued to talk about them throughout the lengthy period when we were not in contact.

Finally, on October 16, 1998, I was able to meet both Susan and David at Chester. Although I had a long interview with Susan and a short one with David I learned of only one important detail of the case that Susan and David had not earlier communicated, either in correspondence with me or during the interview for the BBC program.

Susan had two daughters. I had hoped that one or both might be willing to meet me and discuss any observations they had made of David's unusual behavior. Susan, however, said that one of her daughters would not agree to say anything and that the husband of the second one, who might herself have been willing to meet me, would have opposed her doing so.

I had also hoped to meet and talk with Solomon Rosenberg. In particular, I wished to learn whether any member of his family had died in the Holocaust. He still lived in Chester and Susan knew this; but he took no interest in David, and he had never accepted any financial responsibility toward him. When I asked Susan how she knew that he was "very true to his faith," she mentioned his habit of wearing head caps and his keeping a Bible in his automobile.

David's Nightmares

David described his nightmares as scenes of large dark holes, which were deep, and he was afraid he would fall into one. He could see bodies in the hole. He was not sure if he was a boy (young child) looking at the bodies in the hole. There were people with guns. He could smell the stench of dead bodies.

Sometimes David would come to his mother crying and describe camps, guns, and people dying.

David also complained of an unusual odor in his bedroom. On one occasion he and Susan visited one of his aunts who cooked with gas. (Susan had an electric stove and her house had no connection with gas for heating or cooking.) David became aware of the odor of the cooking gas and said that it "was like the smell in my room at night, it's going to smother me."

David's Waking Images

Although nightmares seemed the dominant mode of David's imagery, he also had some waking images that troubled him. He mentioned some of these to June Knox-Mawer during the interview for the BBC. The images included people "walking around. Prisoner of war things." He said the people lived in wooden huts. In response to leading questions for June Knox-Mawer, David also said that the people in his images were aware they were prisoners and that he thought they were Jewish people.

I mention below some other images that David described in connection with his general fear of camps.

David's Unusual Behavior

In early childhood David did not like sleeping in a small room. He compulsively kept the door to his room open and with equal regularity he shut the window of the room and drew the curtains tightly closed. He put a small chest in front of the window.

When David first began to read and write, he read and also wrote from right to left. After a time he learned to read and write from left to right, but occasionally relapsed to reading and writing from right to left up to the age of 11.

When he drew, he always included a star. At the same time he seems to have had a phobia of stars. Once, when he and his mother were in a shop, he suddenly began to cry and ran out of the shop. Susan ran after him and asked him what the trouble was. David said: "It's that necklace I saw. I am afraid of it." Susan asked him to which necklace he was referring and he said: "The one with the star sign. It was beckoning to me." The necklace had a Star of David attached to it. Susan tried to tell him that the necklace was beautiful and even spoke of buying it for him; but David told her not to do that. He talked about the necklace and its star for some time afterwards. David was about 12 at the time of this episode.

In addition to his preoccupation with the Jewish star, David also had a strong dislike for the color yellow. Susan said that he had a "hatred" of the color yellow.

David also had a marked fear of camps. When he was 6, Susan once proposed that they have a vacation at a holiday camp. David resisted this vehemently. Susan explained that people can have pleasant vacations at such camps. David replied: "No. There is no happiness there. People are caged in and cold, hungry, and frightened. They'll never get out."

David never described to Susan what the people in the camps wore. He said they were like skeletons. They were bald and had no food. They were sitting around, doing nothing. In the interview for the BBC, however, David said the people in the camps wore "stripey things." In connection with the camps David often said: "I'm worried for the other people. Why did it have to happen? Why did it have to happen?"

David's Unexpected Knowledge of Jewish Customs

When still a young child David surprised his mother by asking her whether some food she was serving had blood in it.

When David was about 9 he and his parents visited another city, where David noticed a building that looked somewhat like a church. David remarked: "They wear caps there." To his mother's surprise her husband said that the building was a synagogue. David said that he would like to go in. At the time of this remark there were no persons going into or coming out of the synagogue.

David's Lack of Explicit Statements About a Previous Life

Despite the vividness of the scenes he described and the intense emotion that accompanied his narration of them, David never stated that he himself lived in the scenes he described. He did not even respond positively on this when June Knox-Mawer (for the BBC program) asked him directly whether he seemed to be present in the scenes he described.

The Attitudes of Other Persons to David's Unusual Behavior

Susan made no attempt to suppress David's statements and unusual behavior. On the contrary, she tried to comfort him and assure him that he was now in a good family and safe among loving persons. At the same time, she told him to forget about the scenes he was seemingly remembering. This had no effect on David, who continued perturbed. His older sister gave him similar advice, equally futile. Asked whether he had told anyone else besides his mother and sister about his apparent memories, David said that he had not done so because he was too afraid. He had not even confided in Jeffrey Llewelyn. Asked why he had not talked about his images with persons outside his family, David said he was afraid to do so. He said members of his family would shout at him when he tried to describe the images. (The shouting was apparently part of the effort to suppress him from talking and thinking about the images.) Susan conjectured that David was afraid other persons would laugh at him.

The Accuracy of David's Description of German Concentration Camps During World War II

David's description of camps corresponds closely to features of German concentration camps, of which the best known were Treblinka (Donat, 1979) and Auschwitz (Freeman, 1996; Frankl, 1947; Kraus and Kulka, 1966; Lengyel, 1947; Nyiszli, 1993) (both of which were in Poland). There were numerous other concentration camps equal in horror to those of Treblinka and Auschwitz (Donat, 1963; Smith, 1995). The principal victims of the death camps were Jews.

The prisoners could not escape from these camps; they were sometimes idle and talking among themselves; many had their hair cut or even shaved off; many wore striped uniforms; they were underfed to the point of severe emaciation. Sometimes pits were dug and prisoners were shot and pushed into the pits or their bodies were burned in them; a pervasive and unpleasant odor of burning or decaying human flesh was almost always present. (In concentration camps where prisoners were killed with gas [either hydrogen cyanide or carbon monoxide from engine exhausts] the prisoners would sense the odors of these gases.) The cooking gas of David's aunt might have evoked memories of the odor of one of these gases.

In the death camps of the Holocaust, children were rapidly "selected" for death if they were unfit for work, which meant being 14 years old or under. At Treblinka, for example, children were thrown into a ditch, sometimes still alive, where they were consumed by a fire. Alternatively, they could be thrown into a "regular mass grave" (Donat, 1979, pp. 37–38).

David's Opportunities for Normal Acquisition of Information Concerning Jewish Customs and Concentration Camps

Susan expressed confidence that David showed his unusual behavior related to Jewish customs and his knowledge of concentration camps before he could have had any exposure to relevant information on television. She was sure that nothing discussed in the family could have stimulated his behavior or furnished information for it.

Later, when David did watch television, he disliked programs about war and asked to have the channel changed from such programs.

David's Later Development

Unlike most of the subjects in the cases that begin in early childhood, David's memories and especially the strong emotions that accompanied them persisted into adulthood. In 1998 when I met David, he was 28 years old. At this time he was training to become a nurse.

Susan told me that he showed fear and anger when he saw Germans on television programs. He had such emotions when he encountered live Germans, for example, when he saw them in Corfu during an excursion that he and Susan took to that island.

David told me that he then remembered little of the previous life. (He had by this time come to believe that his images derived from a previous life.) He said he did remember — here I quote from my notes— "being put in a pit as a young boy and looking up to the top of the pit where he saw another boy looking at him. He thought the other boy was a companion who might save him. There were other bodies in the pit." David said this scene recurred to him sometimes, especially if he saw Germans in films or in reality. He also remembered the terrible odor of the camp and his fear of going to sleep.

David also told me he remembered occasions— which must have happened when he was a child — when his mother met Solomon Rosenberg. He then had a strong liking for Solomon Rosenberg and somehow felt close to him as he never did to his official father, Jeffrey.

In 1998 David seemed to me serious but not troubled. In correspondence with Susan during 2000, however, I learned from her that nightmares of the life in a concentration camp still troubled David. He had conceived the idea that he might "get this out of his system" if he want to Auschwitz. (He had not in childhood stated the name of Auschwitz, but had learned later and normally about this, the most notorious of the Nazi death camps.)

Comment

Even supposing that David, at an extremely early age, had learned normally about concentration camps in which millions of Jews and other persons were killed in the early 1940s, we should still need to account for the intense and prolonged effect such knowledge had on him. I believe this case inexplicable by environmental influences and inheritance. Even the most ardent geneticist would not suggest that genes would transmit the habit of reading and writing from right to left, concern about whether the food had blood in it, and images of a concentration camp.

Teuvo Koivisto, the subject of a case in Finland, also had memories of life and presumably death in a concentration camp of the Holocaust. I include a report of his case later in this Part.

GRAHAM LE-GROS

This case is one of the shortest included in this volume. It consists of a few statements and a recognition.

Summary of the Case and Its Investigation

Graham Le-Gros was born in London, England, on October 31, 1984. His parents were Alan Le-Gros and his wife, Denise. Graham was their fifth child. The Le-Gros family belonged to the middle class. His next oldest sibling, a brother, was 4 years older than he. Denise Le-Gros was a Roman Catholic; Alan Le-Gros had been baptized in the Church of England.

When Graham was still a toddler and barely able to speak, he was with his mother in an automobile when he suddenly said that he had lived before and had died in a fire on an airship. He sometimes repeated these statements over the next 8–9 years. When he was 9 he saw on television a film about the disastrous fire on the airship *Hindenburg* and spontaneously said that this scene was his "dream."

After the episode of Graham's seeming to recognize the *Hindenburg*, Denise Le-Gros, who had learned of my investigations, wrote to ask me for my opinion of Graham's statements, which she described in a letter of February 17, 1994. I asked her for additional information, and she then sent me a tape recording she made in March 1994 of a conversation she had with Graham about his experience. This added some new information. On August 28, 1994 I was in London and interviewed Graham and his mother at my hotel there. I obtained some further information from Denise Le-Gros in subsequent correspondence.

This seemed to me like a case for which a trial of hypnosis might be appropriate. Despite earlier disappointments, including that with Gillian Cunningham (Stevenson, 1987/2001), I thought it possible that Graham might furnish verifiable details during hypnosis. Graham was interested in hypnosis, and his mother approved of it. Unfortunately, I was unable to find a hypnotist in the area of London who had sufficient interest and competence in hypnosis.

Statements and a Recognition Made by Graham

Denise Le-Gros said that Graham's first statements about a previous life were that: he had been grown up and had been in an airship; there was a fire on the airship and people were screaming; they had flames coming from them; he fell down to the ground, along with other people; then he suddenly shot upwards.

When Graham was 9 years old, Denise Le-Gros, watching television one day, saw a film about the fire that destroyed the German airship *Hindenburg*. She called Graham to come into the room where the television set was on without telling him why she wanted him to come. She wrote me (in her letter of February 17, 1994) that Graham "ran in, took one look at the screen, and said: 'That's my dream, that's what *I* see; that's my dream.'" Denise Le-Gros was therefore somewhat surprised to find that Graham still preserved a memory of the previous life at the age of about 9.

During his tape-recorded conversation with his mother in March 1994, Graham seemed to remember and tell his mother additional details about his memories of the previous life. He said the airship had large letters in red on it. (This was the name of the airship, but he could not remember the name.) Graham said that he could remember paper on fire and falling off the airship and people jumping out of a hole. Some of the people spoke in a different language, but some of them were English. He thought he was about 16 years old in the previous life.

During my meeting with Graham and his mother, later in 1994, Graham mentioned two further details. He said that he remembered "walking along outside" before he saw the fire in the airship. He added: "Then it [presumably the airship] started like shaking and I fell off. That's all."

When I asked him what he had been called in the previous life, he replied: "Probably Graham." When Graham (the subject of the case) told me that his name in the previous life was "probably Graham," I turned to his mother and asked her how she and her husband had chosen the name *Graham* for their son. She replied: "I wanted him to be called Kieran and my husband wanted a more English kind of manly name. So we compromised on Graham." I asked whether Graham was a family name and she said it was not.

Graham's memories of the previous life were fading by the time I met him and his mother in 1994. He was then not quite 10 years old.

Circumstances and Manner of Graham's Speaking About the Previous Life

When Graham made his first statements about the previous life, at the age of 14 months, his vocabulary was small. In his statement about the previous life, however, he used words that he had not used earlier. The vocabulary of his statement surprised his mother as much as its content. She said that up to that age he had spoken only single words or brief phrases and had not put together whole sentences as he did on this occasion.

Denise Le-Gros told other persons about what Graham had said, and they from time to time would ask him to repeat what he had said earlier. He would then repeat to them what he had said to his mother, adding and subtracting nothing. (We have seen, however, that a little more information emerged in 1994.) The stability of his narration convinced Denise Le-Gros that he was "obviously not making it up."

When Graham spoke about the previous life, he showed no strong emotion; but Denise Le-Gros said that he was "animated." .

After Graham said that the scene of the fire of the *Hindenburg* was like his "dream," Denise Le-Gros asked him whether he had experienced his seeming memories during sleep, as a dream. He said that this had happened once in a dream.

Between his statements at the age of 14 months and his reaction to the film about the *Hindenburg*, he had never spoken spontaneously about the memories, but only when a member of the family or neighbors asked him about them.

Relevant Behavior on the Part of Graham

Graham had no phobias: not of fire, airplanes, or airships. He also had no unusual dietary likes or dislikes that could suggest a previous life as a German.

The Correspondence of Graham's Statements with Known Disasters to Airships

In the several decades (1910–1940) when airships, using the lift of hydrogen or helium, appeared to be superior to airplanes in carrying power, if not in speed, several of them crashed. In two instances an immense fire quickly consumed the airship and with it many of the crew and passengers.

The R.101 was the first of these airships to crash. It came down, during its maiden voyage from Cardington, England, to India on October 4, 1930. Apparently it had been given insufficient trial runs before being committed too hastily to the flight to India. It had never undergone a trial at full speed. The airship, unable to surmount the buffeting of a rainstorm after it crossed the English Channel, lost altitude and crashed near Beauvais, France. A fire broke out immediately, and soon nothing remained of the airship except the metal framework. There were 54 persons (officers, crew, and passengers) on board the R.101 when it crashed; all but 6 perished (Toland, 1972).

One of the stewards on the R.101 was Eric A. Graham (Leasor, 1957). He was the cook of the airship. He was so happy about being able to make the trip to India on the R.101 that he declined an offer of £50 from an acquaintance to change places with him for the journey. As cook on the airship he must have been a mature adult, which accords with Graham's statement at 14 months that he had been "grown up," and not with his later statement that he had been "about 16" years old. I have not been able to learn more about Eric Graham of the R.101.

The second airship to be consumed in a fire was the German *Hindenburg*. On May 6, 1937, it burst into flames just as it was about to "land," that is, tie up at its dock, in Lakehurst, New Jersey. On its flight from Frankfurt, Germany, to the United

States it had carried 36 passengers of whom 13 died on the scene or soon afterward in hospitals. Of the 61 crew members, 22 died. The crew and most of the passengers were German, but there were a few Americans among them (Mooney, 1972). The word *Hindenburg* was printed in large letters on the side of the airship, in red (Archbold, 1994).

Comment

When Denise Le-Gros watched the film about fire on an airship and called Graham into the room, she did not know that the film depicted the fire on the *Hindenburg*. She only learned this later, from consulting the printed television program. It is nevertheless conceivable that Graham saw the name *Hindenburg* in large letters near the bow of the airship. The fire began at the rear of the airship and photographs of the burning airship, which was being winched down toward the ground, might have shown the name. Photographs of 1937 would not, however, have shown that the letters of the airship's name were red. This detail therefore speaks in favor of a correspondence between Graham's statements and the *Hindenburg*. So does that of persons speaking a foreign language as well as English.

In the case of the R.101 I think we can be certain that everyone on board it spoke English. Almost immediately after it crashed, however, French peasants and then rescue workers were at the scene of the crash, and their voices could have been heard by the passengers and crew of the airship as they burned or fell out of the airship.

The most important specifying detail related to the R.101 is the name of the cook, Eric Graham. Because of it and because the other details are consistent with the disaster of the R.101, I believe that Eric Graham, the cook of that airship, is a plausible candidate to be the person whose life Graham remembered.

The occurrence of different details pointing to different airships increased both my wish to learn whether hypnosis might help to solve the case and my disappointment that we could not implement a trial of hypnosis.

GILLIAN AND JENNIFER POLLOCK

This book would be incomplete without mention of the case of Gillian and Jennifer Pollock. I have, however, published a detailed account of their case (Stevenson, 1997) and also a shorter account (Stevenson, 1987/2001). I will, therefore, here describe only its most important features.

Gillian and Jennifer Pollock were born in Hexham, Northumberland, England, on October 4, 1958. Their parents were John Pollock and his wife, Florence. Gillian was 10 minutes older than Jennifer. Analyses of blood groups and subgroups showed that they were monozygotic.

John and Florence Pollock had other children, and two of these, Joanna and

Jacqueline, were killed when a crazed driver ran her automobile onto the pavement where the girls were walking with a friend. They died instantly. This tragedy occurred on May 5, 1957. Joanna was 11 years old and Jacqueline 6 when they died. John and Florence Pollock were Christians, at least formally. In 1957 Florence had no interest in reincarnation and did not believe it could happen. John, on the other hand, had had a strong belief in reincarnation for many years. After the deaths of the girls he became convinced that they would be reborn in the family, and as twins. When Gillian and Jennifer were born as twins, other persons were surprised, but he was not.

Statements and Recognitions Made by Gillian and Jennifer

When the twins became able to speak, they made — between the ages of 3 and 7 — a small number of statements about the lives of Joanna and Jacqueline. Gillian remembered the life of Joanna and Jennifer that of Jacqueline. Their parents also credited them with recognizing several places and objects known to the deceased girls but not familiar to the twins. In my detailed report of the case I listed 6 statements and 5 recognitions with which their parents credited them. John and Florence Pollock also overheard the twins talking to each other about the accident in which Joanna and Jacqueline had died; but they did not mention any unusual details occurring in their talk to each other.

Some readers may think that John Pollock's somewhat fervent belief in reincarnation disqualified him as an objective observer of what the twins said and did relating to the lives of Joanna and Jacqueline. On one occasion a skeptical journalist voiced this complaint to John Pollock. To this he correctly rejoined that if he had not believed in reincarnation, he would have paid no attention to the memories the twins seemed to have had of their deceased sisters' lives.

Physical Differences Between Gillian and Jennifer

Gillian and Jennifer had closely similar faces. I believe that anyone seeing only their faces would conclude that they were monozygotic, as they were. Their physiques, however, to some extent corresponded with those of Joanna and Jacqueline. Joanna had been somewhat slender and so was Gillian; Jacqueline was somewhat stocky and so was Jennifer.

Jennifer had two birthmarks, whereas Gillian had none. A birthmark on Jennifer's forehead, near the root of her nose, corresponded to the scar of an injury (requiring three stitches) that Jacqueline incurred when she fell on a bucket at the age of 3. Jennifer also had a hyperpigmented nevus on her left waist (Figure 5). It corresponded to a nevus Jacqueline had had at the same site. No other member of the family had a nevus at this place.

Joanna had a splay-footed gait and so had Gillian. Jacqueline and Jennifer had ordinary gaits.

As I mentioned, Joanna had been 11 years old when she died, and she could write well. Jacqueline, however, was only 6 and had not learned to hold a writing implement properly. She grasped it in her fist instead of between her thumb and forefinger; and, despite efforts by her teacher to show her how to hold a pencil correctly, she continued doing this until she died. When the twins first began to write, at the age of about 4½, Gillian immediately held a pencil properly, whereas Jennifer held it in her fist as Jacqueline had done (Figure 6). She persisted in writing in this manner, at least sometimes, until the age of 23 (when I last had information about the habit).

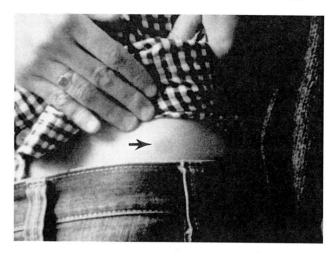

Figure 5. Nevus on left waist of Jennifer Pollock.

Behavior Shown by Both Gillian and Jennifer

Both twins had a phobia of vehicles. Both tended to look toward their maternal grandmother (instead of their mother) for maternal care and guidance. This seemed to be a reflection of the situation Joanna and Jacqueline had been in; during their lives Florence Pollock had been working and could spend little time with her daughters, who were largely cared for by their grandmother. At the time of the childhood of Gillian and Jennifer, however, the domestic circumstances had changed. Florence was no longer working and had plenty of time to spend with the twins.

Joanna and Jacqueline had both enjoyed combing the hair of other persons and so did Gillian and Jennifer.

Behavior in Which Gillian and Jennifer Differed

Because Joanna was 5 years older than Jacqueline, the younger sister tended to follow the lead of her older sister. For her part, Joanna tended to "mother" Jacqueline. Gillian and Jennifer had a similar hierarchical relationship; Jennifer looked for guidance and advice from Gillian, who showed a kind of maternal solicitude for Jennifer.

Gillian was more mature and more independent than Jennifer, which accorded with Joanna's greater age and maturity than those of her younger sister.

Joanna had been fond of other children, not just of Jacqueline. Gillian showed more interest in other children than Jennifer did.

Figure 6. Gillian (left) and Jennifer Pollock (right) at the age of about 4½ when they were learning to write. (Mirror Syndication International.)

Joanna was a notably generous young person, who readily shared what she had with others. Jacqueline was perhaps too young to have developed this trait. Be that as it may, Gillian was more generous than Jennifer.

Joanna had liked to wear costumes and to act in little plays that she herself wrote. Gillian also showed an interest in playing at acting with costumes. Jennifer had initially no interest in such play, although she entered into it with Gillian.

Comment

I would be willing, with the critical journalist, to discount much or even all of what John and Florence Pollock reported of the statements and recognitions of the twins. Although I think Florence did not, John might have let his expectation influence his observations and reporting of them.

The differences between the twins in physical features and behavior, however, seem to me inescapably important. Their monozygosity excludes a genetic factor in accounting for these differences. No postnatal factor can explain their physical differences, particularly the two birthmarks on Jennifer alone that closely corresponded to a scar and a nevus on Jacqueline. I also find it inconceivable that John and Florence, no matter how much they wanted their dead daughters back, could have so molded the behaviors of the twins that they imitated in several respects those of the older sisters. This case together with the parallel one of Indika and Kakshappa Ishwara, another pair of monozygotic twins who differed markedly, both physically and behaviorally, provide some of the strongest evidence known to me in favor of reincarnation.

NADÈGE JEGOU

The subject of this case made few statements about a previous life. Most of these occurred scattered in isolated instances during the period when she was between 2 and 4 years old; two occurred at later ages. In addition, the subject also made a small number of pertinent recognitions and showed some behavior corresponding to the life of the person to whom her statements referred. This was her mother's younger brother.

Summary of the Case and Its Investigation

This case really begins with the death of the young man, Lionel Ennuyer, to whom the subject's statements later referred. His accidental death put his mother, Yvonne Ennuyer, into a state of inconsolable grief. She believed in reincarnation, and she obtained some relief from her sorrow by hoping and to some extent expecting that her son would be reborn as a child of her daughter, Viviane Jegou.

Nadège Jegou was born at Neuilly-sur-Marne, France, on December 30, 1974. Her parents were Patrick Jegou and his wife Viviane, née Ennuyer. They had been married for 5 years without having children. After Lionel's death Viviane wished to have a baby more earnestly than before, and her obstetrician attributed Nadège's birth to Viviane's strong determination to have a baby. Later, she gave birth to a boy, Joris, who was born in 1979. Patrick Jegou was an Algerian. He was not an informant for the case, and I learned little about him; he and Viviane divorced in 1989.

Nadège began to speak clearly when she was about 2 years old. Soon afterward she began making a series of statements showing knowledge of the life of her maternal uncle, Lionel Ennuyer. When Nadège was about 3 years old, Viviane Jegou returned to work, and for a period thereafter Nadège spent more time with her grandmother, Yvonne Ennuyer, than with her mother.

Yvonne Ennuyer noticed and remembered Nadège's references to events in the life of Lionel. In October 1978 she wrote to a French friend of mine, Isola Pisani, and described what she had observed up to that time that made her believe Nadège was the reincarnation of Lionel. Isola Pisani sent her letter to me, and I met Yvonne Ennuyer in Paris soon thereafter, on November 22, 1979. We had a long interview at my hotel.

Afterwards Yvonne Ennuyer and I corresponded as she sent me reports of additional observations she had made or remembered of what Nadège said and did. On March 12, 1981, I met Yvonne Ennuyer again and also her husband, Francis, and Nadège's mother, Viviane. Nadège was present, but said little. Francis also contributed little to the available information. In effect, the only informants for this case were Yvonne Ennuyer and her daughter Viviane.

Between 1981 and 1998 I continued to correspond with the Ennuyers. I met them again in 1984 and in 1993. On the latter occasion Nadège came to the restaurant where we had lunch.

In October 1998 I was again in Paris and hoped to meet Yvonne Ennuyer once more. Unfortunately, she was not well and unable to meet me. Instead I sent her later a small number of questions about details, which she answered by mail.

The Life and Death of Lionel Ennuyer

Lionel Ennuyer was born at Chelles, France, on August 22, 1953. His parents were Francis Ennuyer and his wife, Yvonne. Lionel had two older sisters, Viviane and Lydia.

Lionel's childhood was normal. He had abundant vitality that bordered on restlessness. His adventurousness and love of risk-taking made his parents think — in the middle years of his childhood — that he required the discipline of a boarding school. They sent him to one, but after 2 years they missed him so much that they brought him home to attend school as a day student. More sociable than studious, Lionel did not pass the baccalauréat examination, popularly known as the "bac," which is required in France to qualify for higher education after secondary school. Instead of entering a university, therefore, he began to train to become an electrician. At the age of 20 he was called up for his year of obligatory military service. Characteristically, he elected to serve among the Chasseurs alpins so that he could spend time in the mountains.

Lionel had many friends, and at times he preferred to be with them instead of with his family. For example, his parents offered to take him on a trip to the United States, but he chose to attend a summer camp where he could be with his friends.

Like nearly all adolescents he thrived on the mobility of vehicles. Starting with a bicycle, he advanced to mopeds and finally acquired a motorcycle.

In December 1973 he returned home from his military station for the Christmas holidays. One evening at about 9:00 p.m. he went for a ride on his motorcycle with a companion on the pillion. Some friends followed them in an automobile. He crashed, struck his head on a roadside bench, and died almost instantly. The companion on the pillion escaped with a broken arm. The only witnesses to the accident were Lionel's friends who were in the following automobile, and they gave varying accounts of what had happened. Yvonne Ennuyer believes that the youth who was driving the automobile playfully crowded Lionel on the motorcycle and forced him on to the sidewalk, where he lost control and then probably pitched forward and landed head first. He died on December 23, 1973.

Apart from his sociability, already mentioned, Lionel had two other outstanding traits: generosity and a love of sports. He had few possessions, because he would lend or give what he had, often including money, to his companions. As for sports, he seems to have enjoyed them all: skating, skiing, tennis, swimming, shooting, and cycling.

Nearly all the foregoing biography of Lionel Ennuyer is recorded in a leaflet that Yvonne Ennuyer wrote and had printed after Lionel's death. It is therefore not colored by her later conviction that Nadège was Lionel reborn.

Statements Made by Nadège and Their Circumstances

In many of my detailed case reports I have listed the subject's statements and then, in a separate section, described the circumstances and manner of their utterance. In the present case Nadège gave no connected account of the previous life but instead made a number of isolated statements about it. Accordingly, I will describe the statements and their circumstances together. Yvonne Ennuyer never stated a precise date for Nadège's statements. We were corresponding quite often, however, and she narrated the statements in her letters to me. From the dates of her letters I could determine Nadège's age at the time of the statements to within a few months.

1. Nadège spoke spontaneously about Lionel's accident as if it had happened to her. She said that her friend had pushed her and the motorcycle had fallen onto a bench. She did not say where she (Lionel) had been wounded. I did not learn at what age Nadège first referred to the accident. She recurred to the topic from time to time and always seemed then to be reliving the event.

2. Yvonne Ennuyer showed Nadège a photograph of Lionel, saying it was of Yoyo (a nickname for Lionel). To this Nadège replied "No. It is of Nana." (Nana was Nadège's own petname for herself at this time.) Nadège was about 3½ when she made this statement. She repeated this statement on another occasion when shown a photograph of Lionel.

3. Nadège was watching a television program with her grandmother one day. A particular street of Paris, Passage Jouffroy, appeared on the screen. (This is a covered area with small boutiques on either side.) Nadège then said "That is near where Mama [meaning Viviane] works." Yvonne Ennuyer discussed this statement later with her daughter and said that she (Viviane) must have told Nadège where she worked; but Viviane said she had not done so. She then reminded her mother that she and Lionel had often met at the Passage Jouffroy, which he enjoyed and which was also near the bank where Viviane worked. Nadège was about 4 years old when she made this statement.

4. Lionel had had a kind of bed that could be folded into a cupboard. After his death it was never opened again until one day Yvonne Ennuyer thought it should be aired out and she opened it up. Nadège was standing by and said: "I slept there when I was small." Yvonne Ennuyer told her that she had never slept in that bed. To this Nadège replied: "Before I became small." Nadège was 4 years old when she made this remark.

5. On another occasion Nadège remarked to her grandmother: "When I was Lionel I used to buy carembars." Then, surprised to hear herself use the word "carembars"

she asked her grandmother: "What are carembars?" They are a candy consisting of sticks of caramel. Lionel had been very fond of them. Yvonne Ennuyer had never bought any for Nadège. Nadège was about 4½ years old when she made this statement.

6. After the last remark, Nadège went on to say: "I also used to buy some black things with a white candy inside for my mama." Yvonne Ennuyer was extremely fond of liquorice and Lionel had often bought for her liquorice rolls—which would have been black—that had a white candy in their middle. Nadège herself did not care for liquorice.

7. On another occasion Nadège was playing at her grandmother's house with her two young cousins. One of these, a 6-year-old boy, happened to open a cupboard where he discovered toy monkeys made of plush. They had been Lionel's. The boy asked Yvonne Ennuyer where the toy monkeys came from and when her mother said they were Lionel's, he asked how Lionel had obtained them. Viviane explained that he had won them in a shooting contest at a fair. Nadège overheard this and said, somewhat angrily: "No. It was I who won them at the fair." Yvonne Ennuyer, who was present at this exchange, was confident that Nadège had never seen the toy monkeys before. Nadège was about 4½ when she made this statement.

8. Once Nadège said to her mother: "Before I was in your heart, I had died." She was just under 5 years old when she made this statement. Yvonne Ennuyer was a secondhand informant for it.

9. On another occasion Nadège happened to see a black and white photograph of Lionel that was taken when he was an infant. Looking at the photograph Nadège said to her grandmother: "You know, when I was Yoyo I wore this white blouse with blue embroidery." The blouse had long since disappeared, and Yvonne Ennuyer was sure it had never been mentioned in front of Nadège. She was 5 years old when she made this statement.

10. On the occasion of one of my meetings in Paris (in 1981) with Nadège and her grandmother I was staying at the Hotel de Seine in the 6th arrondissement. Yvonne Ennuyer told me later that Nadège had afterward said that she knew a restaurant in this quarter. Nadège had never been to this quarter of Paris before, but Lionel had been to a Chinese restaurant there and had come away with a plate that was then in the possession of his sister Viviane. Nadège was then 5½ years old.

11. On an occasion when Francis Ennuyer was showing slides of travel scenes to members of the family he showed one of a footbridge in a grotto near Annecy (in Savoy). Nadège cried out: "I have been there. I remember it very well." In fact, Nadège had never been to this grotto, but Francis had taken his children there. Lionel was 6 years old at the time. Nadège was not quite 9 years old when she made this statement.

12. When Nadège was about 9½ years old, she went for a summer vacation to a camp in Savoy where Lionel had also gone, but where she had never been before. When she came back, she mentioned to her grandmother that at the camp there was a little path that she had gone along before.

Nadège's Attitude Toward Life After Death. Only three of Nadège's statements referred to life after death and before birth. One was her statement about having died before she came into her mother. Patrick Jegou told his mother-in-law (Yvonne Ennuyer) that Nadège had once said to him, when they were together on a beach during a vacation: "You know, Daddy, it is warm here in the sand; but when we were both dead it was very cold in the earth."

In 1981, when she was about 7 years old, Nadège and her grandmother were watching a television program that depicted a wounded person being rushed to a hospital in an ambulance. Listening to the sound of the ambulance Nadège commented: "This is not the music you hear when you have died."

When Nadège was about 5½ years old, she spent a vacation with her paternal grandparents, and Yvonne Ennuyer later reported to me that Nadège returned "quite changed." She assertively told Yvonne Ennuyer: "When one dies, one does not return." Yvonne Ennuyer believed that Nadège had made some statements referring to the life of Lionel in front of her other grandparents, who had then laughed at her.

If Nadège had a period of skepticism in childhood, she certainly had no objection to my studying her experiences. She has several times written letters or postcards to me and readily gave her permission for the use of her real name in this report.

Nadège's Behavior Related to the Previous Life

Circumstances and Manner of Nadège's Speaking About the Previous Life. Of the 12 statements that I have listed 8 occurred when Nadège saw some object, such as a photograph or place, familiar to Lionel, that stimulated her apparent memories and led to a sudden expression of them. She rarely made any statement about the previous life without an external stimulus. In this feature the case resembles others, such as those of Mallika Aroumougam and (later in this book) Wolfgang Neurath.

Mannerisms and Other Behavior Shared by Lionel and Nadège. Lionel enjoyed making a facial grimace in which his lower lip would be put forward. He called it making a "tortoise face." Yvonne Ennuyer showed and gave me a photograph of Lionel grimacing in this way. When Nadège was about 2 years old, she spontaneously made this grimace, exactly as Lionel had done. Her mother also remembered seeing Nadège make the grimace of the "tortoise face" that Lionel had made. Yvonne Ennuyer was sure that Nadège had never seen the photograph of Lionel grimacing in this way.

Lionel had the habit of adding a tobacco pipe with a curl of smoke coming from the bowl at the end of his personal letters; the pipe was effectively a part of his signature to the letter or postcard. Yvonne Ennuyer showed and gave me two samples of this "pipe signature." Nadège had seen these letters thus signed, but no one suggested that she should imitate them. Nevertheless, she began to end her letters with a "pipe signature." Yvonne Ennuyer sent me an example of this.

Lionel was so annoyed when his older sister Viviane married that he refused to recognize her as "Mrs." Instead, when he wrote to her and her husband, he addressed the envelope to "Mr. and Miss Jegou," instead of to "Mr. and Mrs. Jegou." When Nadège was away from home and wrote to her parents, she also addressed the envelope to Mr. and Miss Jegou." Yvonne Ennuyer gave me copies of two envelopes addressed by Lionel and Nadège in this way. She (Yvonne Ennuyer) obviously regarded Nadège's fashion of addressing envelopes as spontaneous; but because she had kept at least one envelope addressed by Lionel, I cannot affirm that Nadège never saw it or another like it.

Yvonne Ennuyer told me that Lionel and Nadège were both poor at spelling. They made, she had observed, the same mistakes in spelling. She did not give me actual examples of their errors.

In his family Lionel stood out for two characteristics from other members of the family. First, he was intensely interested in all sports. Earlier in this report, I mentioned the variety of sporting activities that he enjoyed. Nadège was also enthusiastic about sports, especially swimming, diving, and skating. At the age of 2½ she began diving into water and at 3½ dived from a height of 3 meters.

I mentioned earlier Lionel's generosity toward other persons, an unselfishness that sometimes left him without funds for himself. Nadège was equally generous toward other persons.

Other Relevant Behavior of Nadège

Nadège showed no inclination to wear male clothes or to prefer boys' play and other activities over those of girls. She once expressed a preference for being a boy instead of a girl, but that is not an uncommon wish of girls and women, even in the West.

Nadège had no phobias.

The Attitude of Nadège's Family Toward Her Statements

As I mentioned earlier, the principal informant for the case was Nadège's maternal grandmother. Nadège's mother, whom I interviewed in 1981, seemed somewhat shy and inhibited with me, and I could not satisfactorily gauge her attitude toward Nadège's statements and mannerisms suggestive of Lionel. She was not negative toward them, but I could not record her as being strongly positive. She acknowledged that several of Nadège's statements had made an impression on her.

Yvonne Ennuyer, in contrast to her daughter, was far from detached regarding Nadège's statements and mannerisms. She recounted them to me in person or in letters with obvious enthusiasm. When an occasion presented itself, she intervened in radio programs to defend the concept of reincarnation and to present the merits of Nadège's case. She undoubtedly obtained solace for the loss of Lionel by believing that he had been reborn as Nadège. She liked to hear Nadège make statements about the previous life and even at times asked her to repeat what she had said before, for example, about Lionel's fatal accident. Once, when Nadège was about 5½ years old, Yvonne Ennuyer, almost reproachfully said to Nadège: "You don't any longer speak to me about Lionel." Nadège replied: "I have told you everything."

In April 1979 Yvonne Ennuyer wrote me that she had asked Nadège: "What did you do when you were Yoyo?" Nadège had replied: "I was Lionel and I did foolish things."

In April 1980, Yvonne Ennuyer wrote me that she was asking Nadège to speak about Lionel. Although she insisted that what Nadège said when she was less than 5½ years old had been completely spontaneous, by that time Yvonne Ennuyer had already been prompting her to speak for at least a year.

There were times when Yvonne Ennuyer's enthusiasm for Nadège's case led her to see similarities between her and Lionel that others would ignore or dismiss. For example, she thought it significant that both Lionel and Nadège had hemangionas, although they were not in the same location. She believed that Nadège's eyes were also asymmetrical. Yvonne Ennuyer said that Lionel's eyes were asymmetrical. I agree that in one photograph of Lionel his left palpebral fissure is distinctly narrower than the right one, but I have not observed such asymmetry in Nadège, either in photographs or when I have met her. She also thought that severe headaches from which Nadège suffered in childhood and a cyst of her neck derived somehow from the fatal head injury of Lionel.

Nadège's Later Development

Nadège suffered greatly from headaches as a young child. In 1981 she was admitted to a pediatric neurology ward where numerous tests, including an electroencephalogram, showed no important abnormality. When she was 15, her parents divorced and this event perturbed her, but I think no more than is usual with other children undergoing a similar misfortune.

When she was 18 she had a cyst on or near her thyroid gland removed surgically.

Her scholastic career developed normally. She passed the "bac" in the summer of 1993 when she was 18½ years old. She then went to a university, where she studied English.

Comment

Because Yvonne Ennuyer is almost the only witness for this case and certainly by far the most important one, readers will have to judge the effect that her keen interest in reincarnation and her longing to have her son return had on her observations of what her granddaughter said and did. It would not be difficult to argue that she spoke of Lionel in front of Nadège, unwittingly conveyed information about him to her, and gradually induced in her a degree of identification with Lionel. There is, however, little evidence that she did do this; and her letters to me contain numerous denials that Nadège was given any clues guiding her to the content of her statements about events in the life of Lionel. That Yvonne Ennuyer wished to hear Nadège speak about that life is obvious; that she furnished the material for Nadège's statements seems less likely. I think that an unbiased reader will credit her with having paid attention to and recorded statements that a child made about a previous life which most parents and grandparents in the West would have ignored or derided.

Wolfgang Neurath

This is a case of the sex-change type in which the previous personality expressed a wish to change sex before she died. The subject made few statements related to the previous life, and these were nearly all restricted to recognitions of people and places. In addition, he showed tastes and other behavior similar to those of the previous personality.

Summary of the Case and Its Investigation

Wolfgang Neurath was born in Feldkirch, Austria, on March 3, 1934. His parents were Dieter Neurath and his wife, Marlene. Between the ages of 3 and 3½ Wolfgang made several statements that showed an unexpected familiarity with the members and residence of the family of a young girl, Poldi Holzmüller, who had died 2 months before Wolfgang's birth. The Neuraths and Holzmüllers were near neighbors. Wolfgang also showed unusual behavior thought characteristic of Poldi.

This case first came to the attention of persons outside the families immediately concerned when Poldi's younger brother, Ernst, sent an account of it to Dr. Karl Müller early in 1963. (Dr. Müller, who was a Spiritualist with a keen interest in reincarnation, had solicited information about cases with an announcement in the August 1962 issue of the German magazine *Die Andere Welt*.) Dr. Müller replied and asked Ernst Holzmüller for more information about details. Ernst Holzmüller furnished further information in a second letter. Dr. Müller, whom I had met in Zurich in 1961, sent copies of the correspondence to me.

Two years later, on October 20, 1965, I went to Feldkirch and had a lengthy interview with Ernst Holzmüller and his mother, Elisabeth. (I spent half a day with them.) Subsequently, in July 1968 Ernst Holzmüller furnished some additional information to me in correspondence. In the meantime, he had published his own account of the case in the February 1968 issue of *Die Andere Welt*.

Ernst Holzmüller was born in 1921, and so was 8 years younger than Poldi. He was also therefore a teenager or young adult when the case developed and was consequently a secondhand informant for Wolfgang's statements and (to some extent) for his behavior when young. Elisabeth Holzmüller was born in 1880, and so she was in her 80s at the time of the correspondence in 1963 with Karl Müller and my interviews of 1965. Nevertheless, her memory seemed good. Ernst Holzmüller said that she dictated his first report to Karl Müller, and she actually signed his second letter to Dr. Müller, which answered some of Dr. Müller's questions and added some further details. Later, she took a leading part in my interviews in Feldkirch, and Ernst Holzmüller's contribution consisted largely of clarifying or repeating for me what his mother had said. (I was still learning German at this time, and Elisabeth Holzmüller spoke with something of a Tyrolean accent.) I think it is correct to say that we have a firsthand account from Elisabeth Holzmüller of nearly all the events of the case. There

are, in fact, three versions of her account: the first and second letters of Ernst Holzmüller to Dr. Müller, the notes of my interview with the Holzmüllers, and Ernst
Holzmüller's account of the case in *Die Andere Welt*. The accounts differ only in some
inessential details. Ernst Holzmüller's published report describes one dream of his
mother that the other two accounts do not include.

By the time of my visit to Feldkirch in 1965, Wolfgang was 31 years old, married,
and with two children of his own. He had long since forgotten the previous life, and
I made no effort to meet him. I regret, however, that I did not ask to meet Marie
Neurath, Wolfgang's mother, who had been a witness to Wolfgang's most impressive
recognition. Poldi's Aunt Anna, the person recognized in this episode, had died in
1941.

The Life, Death, and Character of Poldi Holzmüller

Poldi Holzmüller was born in Feldkirch in 1913. She was the only daughter of
her parents, who had (at least) one son, Ernst, who was born in 1921.

As a child, Poldi seems to have been unremarkable, except that she did not play
with dolls or other toys. Her favorite pastime was cutting pictures out of newspapers and saving them. Her favorite foods were noodle soup and puffed rice. She was
notably gentle and quiet.

When Poldi became older she was sociable, but showed no interest in men and
had in fact "nothing to do with men." She was unhappy with herself. Although not
directly discontented with her family, she would sometimes say that she had come into
the wrong home and should have been born as the daughter of a rich manufacturer
instead of being the child of a middle class family.

Poldi was especially fond of her Aunt Anna, who lived in South Tyrol but came
from time to time to visit the Holzmüllers in Feldkirch. Poldi and Aunt Anna were
unusually affectionate to each other with much hugging and kissing. They called each
other by pet names. For Aunt Anna, Poldi was "Poldile," and for Poldi, Aunt Anna
was "Tantele." (The German word for aunt is *Tante*, and "Tantele" would mean something like "Auntie" in English.)

When Poldi was about 19 years old, she became ill with pulmonary tuberculosis,
from which she died after 16 months of illness. For the last year of her life she was
bed-ridden. Although the Holzmüllers were Roman Catholics, Elisabeth Holzmüller
and Poldi (but not her father) had some interest in the possibilities of survival after
death and reincarnation. Poldi said that if she were to reincarnate, she would be
reborn as a boy. She also said that if she were reborn in the neighborhood of the
Holzmüllers she would give such definite indications of her identity that her family
would certainly recognize her. Elisabeth Holzmüller seems to have encouraged these
predictions; but she did ask Poldi not to try, after death, to communicate with her
through a medium.

In the summer of 1933, Marie Neurath, became pregnant. She was a near neighbor of the Holzmüllers, and she often came to visit Poldi during her illness. When

she told Poldi about the baby carriage that she had bought for the child to be born, Poldi asked whether she could go along when the baby was being pushed in the carriage. Then she added: "But you know, what I would really like would be to be in the baby carriage myself."

Poldi died in Feldkirch on January 13, 1934.

Elisabeth Holzmüller's Dreams Between Poldi's Death and Wolfgang's Birth

After Poldi's death her mother wept inconsolably; she cried her eyes out. One night she dreamed that Poldi was sitting on her bed with saddened eyes and a nightgown soaking wet. In the dream, Elisabeth Holzmüller asked Poldi why she was so damp. Poldi replied that the wetness came from her (Elisabeth). This taught Elisabeth that crying after a death is a harmful sadness.

Elisabeth Holzmüller had another dream not long before Wolfgang's birth. In this she seemed to be in the family's garden watching some swallows that were sitting on an electric power line. One of the swallows said: "Mama, don't you see me?" Elisabeth replied: "Yes, but which swallow are you?" Then she heard Poldi say: "I am here." At that, she saw one of the swallows fly into a room of Marie Neurath's house.

Statements and Recognitions Made by Wolfgang

When Wolfgang was 8 days old, Elisabeth Holzmüller went to visit Marie Neurath. Wolfgang was asleep, in the baby carriage mentioned above. When Elisabeth went over to look at the baby, Wolfgang woke up, smiled, and stretched his hands toward Elisabeth as if to greet her.*

When Wolfgang was about 3 years old, Poldi's Aunt Anna came to visit the Holzmüllers. She had not visited the family since Poldi's death. One day, when the family were getting ready for an outing, they were standing in their garden. Marie Neurath saw them and greeted Aunt Anna. As they were chatting, Wolfgang came out of the house. He saw Aunt Anna and ran joyfully to the fence, which he tried to climb over while crying: "Tantele, Tantele." He tried to embrace Aunt Anna, but could not reach her because of the fence. Aunt Anna asked him: "Child, do you know me?" Marie Neurath herself replied, saying that this was impossible, because Wolfgang was not even born when Aunt Anna had last come to Feldkirch. Aunt Anna then said that Wolfgang must have mistaken her for some other aunt. Marie Neurath said that could not be so, because Wolfgang always called his two aunts by their given names, for

---

*I believe that Elisabeth Holzmüller made a courtesy visit to Marie Neurath after her successful delivery of her baby. She did not call out Poldi's name to the little Wolfgang lying in the baby carriage. The incident nevertheless reminds me of the custom among some Tlingit women to visit a newborn baby who they think, on the basis of an announcing dream, is a particular person reborn. They may call it by that person's Tlingit name and hope that the baby will respond with a smile or other signs of pleasure.

example, "Tante Angelika." Wolfgang looked for a time at Aunt Anna, then began to cry and went back into the house.

Two further episodes occurred when Wolfgang was about 4 years old. The first happened when Elisabeth Holzmüller had been shopping·at the local grocery store. She was about to leave the store when Wolfgang saw her and said: "Wait for me until I have done my shopping. Then I will go back with you. We belong together, you know." Wolfgang did his shopping, came out of the store, and he and Elisabeth then walked toward their houses. They passed the Neurath's house, but Wolfgang did not go in there. Instead, he went on with Elisabeth Holzmüller to the gate of her house. There he said to her: "I have to go back over there now. You know I live there now."

On the second occasion Elisabeth Holzmüller was in the same grocery store, and so were Wolfgang and his mother. When Wolfgang saw Elisabeth, he left his mother, ran over to Elisabeth and said: "Mama, please buy some puffed rice for me. My mother over there won't buy me any." Elisabeth bought him some puffed rice. There were other customers in the store, and some of them wondered that Elisabeth, who was then in her late fifties, could have such a young son. Elisabeth explained that Wolfgang was a neighbor's son and had perhaps confused her with the neighbor.

When Wolfgang was about 8 years old, Elisabeth showed him a large portrait of Poldi, asking him whether he knew her. Wolfgang looked at the portrait and, after thinking for a while, he said: "I must have seen her somewhere before, but I cannot say where any more."

When Wolfgang was about 13 years old — one account said he was 12, another 14 — he was running errands for Ernst Holzmüller, who was then in business for himself. One day Ernst asked him to go back to his (the Holzmüllers') house and fetch something he needed from the attic in the house. When Wolfgang reached the house, Elisabeth Holzmüller was there, and she offered to fetch what he needed from the attic. Wolfgang replied: "I already know where it is. I know this house well." He had in fact never been in the second story of the house, from which a door led to the attic. He correctly found the door to the attic, went up to it, and brought down what Ernst Holzmüller needed. When I was in Feldkirch, I was shown the second story of the house which had six doors leading off its central hall. The doors were nearly all exactly alike. The one to the attic was slightly different from the others, but there was no indication that it led to the attic instead of opening into a room on the same floor as the other doors did.

Wolfgang's Behavior Related to the Previous Life

Wolfgang's Gender Identification. When Wolfgang was a child, he was somewhat effeminate. In a further reference to Wolfgang's gender identification Ernst Holzmüller said that he "was not very masculine. He did not run and romp the way most boys do, but was quieter and more like a girl in this respect."

Nevertheless, Wolfgang matured normally as a man, married, and by 1965 had two children.

Wolfgang's Other Behavior Related to the Previous Life. As a child Wolfgang enjoyed cutting pictures out of newspapers as Poldi had done. His favorite foods were also hers: puffed rice and noodle soup. He was notably quiet and gentle.

Wolfgang's Physical Health

On the whole, Wolfgang enjoyed good health. Up to 1965, he had not suffered from bronchial or pulmonary diseases, although he seemed more susceptible than the average person to upper respiratory infections.

The Attitude of the Holzmüllers Toward the Case

Both Elisabeth and Ernst Holzmüller believed that Wolfgang was the reincarnation of Poldi. They considered that Poldi had given clear indications of her return, particularly in the completely spontaneous recognition of "Tantele" (Aunt Anna).

Poldi had been friendly with Marie Neurath, but the families were not especially close to each other. The Holzmüllers thought that Poldi had come back to the Neurath family in order to be near the Holzmüllers. They further suggested that Poldi's wish to lie in the waiting baby carriage might have acted, somewhat like a posthypnotic suggestion, to draw her into that carriage as Marie Neurath's baby.

Comment

Wolfgang was born less than 2 months after Poldi's death. Assuming a normal length of Marie Neurath's pregnancy with Wolfgang, she must have been in the 7th month of her pregnancy when Poldi died.

This case has the weakness of all cases in which, from predictions, dreams, and (sometimes) birthmarks, adults expect a child to make statements and show behavior suggesting memories of a loved and mourned member of their family. Dr. Müller, in his reply to Ernst Holzmüller's first letter, suggested that perhaps Elisabeth Holzmüller had guided Wolfgang by asking him questions about a previous life. In his reply, Ernst Holzmüller firmly denied this. (As I mentioned, his mother co-signed this second letter.) I will not argue that this denial should satisfy all critics. It could be true, however, that if the Holzmüllers had not had a prior belief in the possibility of reincarnation they would never have paid attention to what Wolfgang did and said; and there would then have been no case to discuss. (I mentioned this defense in the report of Gillian and Jennifer Pollock.)

Wolfgang's case has some similarities with other cases that I have investigated. The meagerness of his statements and the tendency for them to be preceded by particular stimuli reminds me of the cases of Mallika Aroumougam and Nadège Jegou. The prediction by a previous personality that she, on being reborn, will give signs of that event by which she can be recognized has a parallel in the case of Marta Lorenz.

Wolfgang's case also reminds me of that of Gnanatilleka Baddewithana. In both these cases the previous personalities showed a weak identification with their sex; Tillekeratne (the previous personality in Gnanatilleka's case) was somewhat effeminate, and Poldi lacked interest in men and could therefore be considered somewhat masculine for a woman. In both cases, the previous personality expressed a wish — not quite explicit, but almost so in Tillekeratne's case — to change sex in another incarnation. In both cases also, the subjects in childhood showed weak identifications with what, for this purpose, we may call the new sex. Gnanatilleka was somewhat boyish as a child, and Wolfgang was somewhat girlish. Considered as instances of reincarnation there seemed to be behavioral memories, residues we might call them, of the sex of the previous life. The previous personality's desire to change sex did not erase these.

HELMUT KRAUS

This is another case the subject of which I could never meet. Moreover, I interviewed only one informant for it. Nevertheless, I was able to probe some details independently, and I am confident of the case's authenticity. The subject's unusual behavior corresponded to the professional vocation of the previous personality.

Summary of the Case and Its Investigation

Helmut Kraus was born in Linz, Austria, on June 1, 1931. His father was Wilhelm Kraus, a teacher of biology at a secondary school in Linz. I did not learn other details of his family.

From the age of about 4 on, Helmut spoke frequently about a previous life. He used to preface his remarks by a phrase, such as "When I was big..." Helga Ullrich, a friend of the family who regularly brought Helmut home from the kindergarten, listened to him attentively. She described him as "very talkative." One day Helmut said to her: "When I was big I lived at 9 Manfred Street." It happened that Helga Ullrich had a friend, Anna Seehofer, who lived at 9 Manfred Street. She asked Anna Seehofer about men who had lived at this address and who had died. Anna Seehofer suggested that Helmut was referring to her cousin, General Werner Seehofer. He had stayed in this house for a time after his first wife died. Other statements Helmut made fitted the life and death of General Seehofer.

Dr. Karl Müller learned about this case from Helga Ullrich in 1958. In March 1959 she sent him an account of the case in a letter; and she later wrote a second letter to him in response to his request for more information. Dr. Müller sent me a long extract of the first letter and a photocopy of the second one.

On October 14, 1965, I interviewed Helga Ullrich in Vienna. She confirmed what she had earlier written to Dr. Müller, but was able to add few additional details. In subsequent correspondence with me she gave me some information about Helmut's later development. Anna Seehofer, General Seehofer's cousin, who would have been a potentially valuable informant for the case, died in 1957.

.In 1967 I obtained relevant information about General Seehofer's life and death from the National Library and the War Archives in Vienna.

Readers can understand how eager I was to meet Helmut Kraus and his parents, but letters that I wrote to him and his father remained unanswered — even though I had their correct addresses.

The Life and Death of General Werner Seehofer

Werner Seehofer was born in Bratislava, Slovakia (then in the Austro-Hungarian Empire) on August 14, 1868. He became a commissioned officer in the Austrian Imperial Army. During one period of his life he lived in Vienna, but I did not learn the dates of his residence there. He rose steadily in rank and in 1902 was a Colonel posted to the General Staff at Linz. He remained there at least until 1907. He presumably retained a residence there, because I learned that his widow was still living in Linz in 1919. (She was his second wife.)

By January 1918, Werner Seehofer had been promoted to General and was Commander of a Division on the Italian front. He remained in this position until his death 6 months later.

On June 17, 1918, when a new offensive began, General Seehofer left his headquarters and walked toward the front line. He continued to walk forward despite warnings from troops nearer the front line of the danger from going farther. What happened thereafter was never fully ascertained, but newspapers later reported that he had been wounded and become a prisoner of the Italian Army. He died of his wounds, probably in an Italian military hospital, soon thereafter. The motive for what seemed like a suicidal walk into the enemy's fire remained unknown; it was conjectured that General Seehofer had some kind of mental disorder that impaired his judgment. A later effort by the Austrian Military Archives to obtain information about General Seehofer's death from the pertinent Italian officials elicited no further information than they already had in Austria. The Austrians were still trying to learn what had happened to General Seehofer as late as 1934.

I learned little about General Seehofer's life outside his professional soldiering. He was a "passionate rider" and "loved sports in general."

He was not quite 50 years old when he was killed.

Statements Made by Helmut

Although Helga Ullrich described Helmut as "very talkative," she made no contemporaneous notes of what he said, and she later only remembered a few of his statements.

Helmut said that he had been a "high officer in the Great War" (World War I). He never said that he had been a general or gave the name of Seehofer. No one seems to have asked him how he had died in the previous life.

His most identifying statements occurred when he mentioned addresses of places where he had lived in the previous life. For example, he said: "When I was big I lived at 9 Manfred Street." This was verified as correct for General Seehofer by Anna Seehofer to Helga Ullrich.

On another occasion, Helmut said: "When I was big I lived for many years in Vienna." He named the street and house number of a residence there. Anna Seehofer confirmed the correctness of this statement for General Seehofer. Helmut also correctly gave the address in Linz where his in-laws of the previous life had lived. Helga Ullrich did not say — perhaps did not remember in 1959–65 — what these last two addresses were.

Helmet's Behavior Related to the Previous Life

Once, when Helmut was about 4 years old, the weather in Linz was warm, and Helga Ullrich left Helmut's overcoat open as they began to walk to his home. Helmut insisted on having the coat closed, because, he said "an officer is not allowed to go with an open overcoat."

If soldiers passed by while Helga Ullrich and Helmut were on the street, Helmut would "face front" and salute them until they had passed.

Once Helmut was taken to meet General Seehofer's widow. He behaved shyly in her presence; this was interpreted as a kind of recognition, perhaps because he was ordinarily affable.

He had a marked fear of loud noises, like gunshots.

He was regarded as more serious, more proud, and more independent than other children of his age.

When he became older, he showed a keen interest in riding and in sports.

Helmut's Birthmark

Helga Ullrich said that Helmut had a birthmark on his right temple. She described it as an area of increased pigmentation about the size of the diameter of a pencil. Helmut had no headaches in early childhood, but in later boyhood he did have headaches.

Helga Ullrich said: "It was known that General Seehofer had died from a head wound." I could not confirm this from the Military Archives in Vienna. As I mentioned, their official records were not even clear about just how General Seehofer had died. The best conjecture was that he had been wounded, captured by the Italians, and died in an Italian military hospital. When I wrote to the Military Archives in Vienna, I specifically asked whether they had information about the location of the wound or wounds on General Seehofer; and they had not. (I cannot exclude that through private sources General Seehofer's family learned more details about his death, including his wound or wounds, than the official records showed.)

Helmut's Later Development

Helmut continued to talk about the previous life until the age of about 7, when he ceased.

Helmut's father was a biologist, and there were no soldiers in the family. Instead of a military life, he chose to enter the hotel industry and trained for that. He moved from Linz to Vienna, where he was living in the 1980s.

ALFONSO LOPES

This case came to my attention in January 1997, when I was in Lisbon to give a lecture at the Gulbenkian Foundation. The subject of the case and his mother came to the lecture, and my host, Francisco Coelho, introduced me to them. I had no time then to talk with them at length, but returned for interviews with them in November 1997.

Alfonso Lopes was 34 years old when I met him. The case was more than 30 years old then. Nevertheless, his mother seemed to have a good memory for its main features, and he himself still had some memories of the previous life.

The case has the additional feature of a difference in sex between the subject and the previous personality.

Summary of the Case and Its Investigation

Alfonso Lopes was born in Lisbon, Portugal, on August 23, 1962. His parents were Fernando Lopes and his wife Irma. They had already had three daughters, Marta, Angelina, and Augusta. Fernando Lopes was a businessman who at one time owned and managed three shops. The family were Roman Catholics. The family's middle daughter, Angelina, was killed in an automobile accident in 1960.

Alfonso began to speak clearly when he was about 1 year old. When he was about 1½ years old he said to his mother: "Dear Mother." This had a particular significance for Irma Lopes because her deceased daughter, Angelina, had addressed her with this phrase, but her other daughters did not.

Thereafter, between the ages of 2 and 7, Alfonso made nine references to the life of Angelina in which he referred to objects or events of which he could apparently have had no normal knowledge. He also showed some unusual behavior that seemed concordant with his statements.

When Alfonso was 17 years old, Irma Lopes wrote an account of the principal events of the case. This seems to have been lost, or at least it was not available in 1997. In the early 1990s Irma Lopes wrote another account of the case, and Francisco Coelho sent me a copy of this in 1997.

On November 6, 1997, I met Irma and Alfonso Lopes in Lisbon and interviewed them separately during about 3 hours. Bernadete Martins acted as my interpreter. Because I had already read Irma's written account of the case, in my interview with her I inquired about further details of the events she had included in her account. In talking with Alfonso I mainly wished to learn what memories he still had and how he had developed since childhood.

I had wished to meet Fernando Lopes so that he could perhaps corroborate at least some of the account of the case that his wife had given me. Unfortunately, one of the Lopes's granddaughters had just been killed, also in a vehicular accident, shortly before my visit to Lisbon in 1997. As a result, Alfonso advised me that his father would not be available to meet me.

The Life and Death of Angelina Lopes

Angelina Lopes was the second daughter of Fernando and Irma Lopes. She was born at home in Loures, Portugal, where the family then lived, on July 20, 1953. In 1963 the family moved from Loures to Lisbon.

I did not learn of any unusual events in her short life that occurred before her unexpected death. She began school at the age of 6 and had completed the first grade by the summer of 1960, when she was not quite 7 years old. At that time her older sister, Marta, who was then 10 years old, was required to take an examination in order to complete her work in primary school. Irma Lopes accompanied her to the school and decided to take her two younger daughters with her. They spent the rest of the day on a nearby beach by a river. On the way home when they were crossing a road, a car struck Angelina and killed her. She probably died at the scene of the accident, although she was taken to a hospital anyway. She died on July 9, 1960. She was not quite 7 years old.

Angelina was an unusually affectionate child. Irma Lopes said that she was more affectionate, at least to Irma Lopes, than were her other daughters. I have already mentioned her singular habit of addressing Irma as "Dear Mother." She was also unusually generous. On one occasion, Angelina had expressed a wish to be a boy.

Events Between Angelina's Death and Alfonso's Birth

Angelina's death profoundly affected Irma Lopes. She cried inconsolably. Previously she had been a devout Roman Catholic, but now she began to doubt the existence of God. Sometimes she blamed herself for having taken the children to the beach.

In her despair she asked God to help her understand how such a terrible thing — her daughter being snatched from her by death — could happen.

About 6 months after Angelina's death a friend introduced her to Francisco Marques Rodrigues. He was a Rosicrucian and a sage who was credited with unusual wisdom and some paranormal powers. Persons who knew about him consulted him about their personal difficulties and always found reassurance in what he said. He never charged a fee for any consultation. He advised Irma Lopes to have another child and said that her daughter would return in another 2 years. The idea of a deceased child being reborn had been no part of Irma's religious training, and she became confused. Nevertheless, she continued visiting Francisco Marques Rodrigues, and he continued to advise her to prepare for the return of her daughter, perhaps in a different sex.

Toward the end of 1961 Irma Lopes became pregnant again. When she next went to see Francisco Marques Rodrigues, he opened the door and, smiling, said: "I was expecting you. I was expecting the good news." Irma Lopes expressed fears about the future, but he restored her confidence, and she left with her hope restored and with great joy at the prospect of having another baby.

In the 7th month of her pregnancy Irma Lopes dreamed of Angelina, who somehow communicated to her that her baby would be a boy. When she awoke, she told her husband they would have a boy. Otherwise her pregnancy with Alfonso was uneventful.

Statements Made by Alfonso

In this section I will combine my account of Alfonso's statements with descriptions of his accompanying behavior. Irma Lopes said that she (and other persons, presumably chiefly her husband, Fernando) had sometimes talked about Angelina in Alfonso's presence. She was sure, however, that they had never mentioned in his presence any of the events or other details included in the following statements.

1. When Alfonso was about 1½ years old, he was sitting on his mother's lap watching television. A truck was shown on the screen and then a boy running across the street. Alfonso closed his eyes so as not to watch any more and began shouting: "No. No. No." Alfonso was just learning to speak at the time. He had no vocabulary to say more. He did not cry, just shouted. Irma Lopes interpreted this unexpected reaction on the part of Alfonso as being derived from Angelina's fatal accident.

2. When Alfonso was about 2, he hugged his mother tightly and, although he still could not speak well, said to her: "Dear Mama, you cried so much, you cried so much." I mentioned earlier the special significance — with regard to Angelina — of Alfonso's saying "Dear Mama."

3. When Alfonso was about 2½, Irma Lopes, from the kitchen, heard someone working her sewing machine in another room. She knew that Alfonso had been near the machine, and she was afraid he was working the machine and would hurt himself. She rushed to him and told him not to play with the machine. He asked: "Why not?" She replied: "Because you may prick yourself." Alfonso then said: "No, Mother, I won't.

I took the needle out." Irma Lopes examined the needle and found that Alfonso had indeed removed both the needle and the screw that held it. She interpreted his doing this as a memory of the life of Angelina. Her three daughters had each pricked themselves playing with the machine, and she thought a memory of this from Angelina's life had led Alfonso to remove the needle from the machine.

4. When Alfonso was about 3, he accompanied his mother to the school that one of his sisters attended. She was taking a lunch to her daughter. Irma Lopes and Alfonso were at the street near the school when a car horn was blown. Somehow Alfonso broke away from his mother and dashed across the street to his sister, who was waiting there. Irma Lopes was so frightened that she closed her eyes, afraid to watch. The car pulled up near them without touching Alfonso. Irma Lopes was agitated, but Alfonso said to her: "Don't cry, Mama. It was the car again, you know." On the way home he repeated the same statement with a variation, saying: "It was the car, dear Mama, you cried so much and you would cry a lot again."

5. When Alfonso was 4 years old, a couple who had been neighbors of the family when they had lived at Loures came to visit the Lopes family and brought their son Hernani with them. As the adults were chatting, Alfonso asked Hernani: "Have you kept the wooden horse?" Hernani asked his mother if she still kept the wooden horse. She said: "No, I gave it to Ana." Alfonso then said: "Oh, yes. To Aninhas and her little son." Angelina had played with Hernani, and they had played together with Hernani's wooden horse. Aninhas (Ana) was a servant who had worked for both the Lopes family and their neighbors. Angelina had been very fond of her.

6. When Alfonso was not quite 6 years old and had not yet started school, he came into the kitchen where his mother was preparing breakfast. He noticed a red-checked napkin on the table and said: "Look, Mama, the napkin I used to take to school with my snack. I will take it again when I go back to school, won't I?" When Angelina went to school, Irma had sometimes prepared for her a snack that she could eat in the afternoon. (She had her lunch at home.) Irma had wrapped the snack in the red-checked napkin.

7. A few days later, Alfonso did begin school. After a few months he told his mother that his teacher wished to speak with her. With some trepidation, Irma Lopes went to the school, where the teacher explained to her that Alfonso was claiming to be a girl; she advised Irma to take him to a doctor. The teacher told Irma that Alfonso in referring to himself was using feminine word forms. (Portuguese, like French, Hindi, Burmese, and some other languages, changes certain words, such as self-referring adjectives and participles, to agree with the speaker's sex.) The teacher would correct Alfonso about his usage of these word forms, saying: "You are a boy, not a girl." Alfonso persisted, saying. "No. I am a girl."* Irma Lopes consulted Francisco Marques Rodrigues about this crisis, and he advised her that Alfonso would grow out of the habit of saying he was a girl, which he did. After the teacher had complained about Alfonso's feminine word forms, Irma herself sometimes noticed Alfonso's usage of them. He stopped doing this at the age of about 7.

8. Some time later, Alfonso returned from school and asked his mother for a glass. Thinking that he wanted a drink of water, she told him that if he wanted to drink some water he could do so by himself. Alfonso said: "No. It is not for that." He then fetched a glass, put it inside a stocking, took a needle, and acted as if he were mending

---

*Other subjects of sex-change cases who have used the verbal forms of the sex of the previous personality are: Rani Saxena, Ma Htwe Win, Sanjeev Sharma, Ma Myint Myint Zaw, Ma Myint Thein, Ma Htwe Yin, and Ma Tin Yee.

a run on the stocking. As he was doing this, he said: "Oh, I have not done this for such a long time." When the family had lived in Loures, one of Irma's sisters-in-law had worked in a seamstress's shop where she mended runs in stockings. Angelina often went to be with her aunt and pretended to be working just like her.

9. When Alfonso was about 7, he repeatedly asked his mother to take him to the gypsies' river, but Irma Lopes did not know to what he was referring. At about this time, she took Alfonso and his older sister Augusta to visit one of her sisters-in-law and her children, who lived in Loures. (I mentioned earlier that the Lopes family had moved from Loures to Lisbon in 1963, when Alfonso was 1 year old.) Alfonso, Augusta, and their cousins went out of the house to play. When they returned, Augusta said that Alfonso had frightened her by crossing the street and saying that he was going to see the bridge. Irma Lopes could remember no nearby bridge. Alfonso, overhearing mention of the bridge said: "Yes, I went to see the bridge; but it is quite changed, and there are no gypsies there." Irma Lopes then remembered the river to which he had been referring. She asked him: "Is this the river that you wanted to see?" Alfonso replied: "Yes, Mama. Can you remember the gypsies that used to be there? I wanted to help them wash their clothes." To test him a little Irma Lopes asked him: "Can you remember where we used to go when we crossed the river?" Alfonso said: "No, but I remember the river, the gypsies, and the bridge. Now there is a big bridge there, completely different from the old one." Irma Lopes explained in her written record that at the time of Angelina's death there had been no church near where they lived. Accordingly, in order to attend mass, she used to walk to a church in another community. She took her children with her. To reach the church they had to cross a small river using what was then a crude rock bridge. The new bridge had been built by the time Alfonso was born.

After the incident just described Irma Lopes several times asked Alfonso about any other memories he still might have had of the life of Angelina, but he said he had none. He said that when lying in bed before going to sleep he seemed to have vague images of a distant past, but nothing clear that he could express.

10. In 1995, when Alfonso was 33 years old, Irma Lopes asked him again about memories of the previous life. He then said that he remembered the death of a dog they had had. He correctly described the dog as being small and white with black spots. He could not remember the dog's name. The dog had died about 2 months before Angelina's death. Alfonso described it correctly.

Alfonso's Statement About Rebirth. When Alfonso was 3½ years old, the following conversation took place between Alfonso and his mother:

> ALFONSO: Mama, why do we live on earth?
> IRMA: On earth, on this place?
> ALFONSO: No, Mama, why are we born on earth?
> IRMA (mumbling): Well, son, we....
> ALFONSO: Don't you know, Mama? I do.
> IRMA: All right. Then say why.
> ALFONSO: It is one time here and another time there.

This exchange startled Irma so much that she did not pursue the topic further and later regretted not having asked Alfonso what he meant by "there."

Other Behavior of Alfonso Related to the Previous Life

Alfonso's Phobia of Vehicles. I mentioned earlier Alfonso's frightened response when he saw on television a scene in which a truck might have struck a child. Apart from this incident, however, Alfonso showed no fear of vehicles when he was a young child. Nevertheless, at the age of 16 he began to be afraid of vehicles. This gradually diminished so that by 1997 (and probably earlier) he only became afraid when he heard a car stop suddenly. He learned to drive a car himself.

Alfonso's Aversion to Places Connected to Angelina. In order to see his reaction, Irma Lopes took Alfonso, when he was 5 years old, to the beach near the school where Angelina had been killed and to the cemetery where Angelina's body was buried. Alfonso showed no sign of explicitly recognizing either place. He expressed surprise at his mother bringing him to these places, became unhappy, and wished to go away from them. At the beach he even began to cry and shouted that he wanted to leave. His reaction to the cemetery was weaker.

Other Relevant Behavior of Alfonso

Apart from his use of feminine word forms and his interest in sewing (shown in Statements 3 and 8 above), Alfonso showed no behavior that we could describe as feminine. He did not wish to be clothed in girls' clothes. When he grew up, he married and by 1997 had two children.

Like Angelina, Alfonso seemed more affectionate, at least toward his mother, than his two (living) sisters. Both Angelina and Alfonso showed a special concern for their mother.

Alfonso's Persistent Memories in 1997

During my interview with Alfonso, I asked him what, if anything, he still remembered of the previous life. He said that he could still remember the following:

    1. The wooden horse. He remembered it as being made of wood, having reins, and a tail made of real hair. It was not a rocking horse, but had wheels.
    2. The dog.
    3. Being with his mother and looking down on a river where women were washing. He remembered the slope down to the river.

Alfonso said the images of these items were so vivid to him that he believed they were of events of his own early childhood. He had even thought his mother had misled him by insisting that the items derived from Angelina's life. He was sufficiently troubled by this disagreement that he decided to consult Francisco Marques Rodrigues himself. Francisco Marques Rodrigues tried to explain to Alfonso that he was really still having memories of Angelina's life.

Comment

This case has several features closely similar to some of those in the case of Nadège Jegou. In each case the family lost a young child, the child's mother became distraught with grief, longed to have the child return, and, later, observed the child closely for evidence that this had happened. Both cases also have the feature of a difference in sex between the subject and concerned deceased personality. In both cases also, the child's statements came out sporadically and usually in response to some object, event, or meeting that stimulated its memories. The cases differ in the prior beliefs about rebirth of the mothers of the deceased children. Whereas Yvonne Ennuyer had had a longstanding belief in rebirth before her son was killed, Irma Lopes came only gradually to accept this possibility.

GEDEON HAICH

This case has the unusual feature of a European child remembering the life of a dark-skinned member of a tropical tribe.

Summary of the Case and Its Investigation

Gedeon Haich was born in Budapest, Hungary, on March 7, 1921. His parents were Subo Haich and his wife, Elisabeth. He was their only child. Gedeon's parents were members of the upper middle classes. They divorced when Gedeon was about 3½ years old. For 3 or 4 years Gedeon lived with his mother, who shared a joint household with her sister. Her sister had a daughter of about Gedeon's age so that they were childhood companions. When Gedeon was 7, his father obtained formal custody of him, but although Gedeon completed his childhood in his father's household, he spent summers with his mother and had frequent contacts with her during the remainder of the year. Elisabeth Haich subsequently married again, but not until after Gedeon had spoken about a previous life.

Unlike nearly all children who remember previous lives, Gedeon did not begin to speak about one when he was between 2 and 4. An intimation of his memories occurred, however, when he was between 4 and 5. His mother noticed that when Gedeon and his cousin were drawing together, Gedeon's cousin always gave her human figures rose-colored skins, whereas Gedeon always colored his figures dark brown. When Elisabeth Haich once suggested to Gedeon that he should not make the complexions of his human figures so dark, he said nothing but continued to color them brown.

A little later, Elisabeth Haich noticed that her son resisted, struggling and screaming, when he was asked to join other members of the family in swimming in a lake where the family had a summer home.

When Gedeon was between 6 and 7 years old, he surprised his mother one day by asking her whether he might perhaps have lived before he became her son. She asked him what made him think this, and he then said he remembered being in a different country with different people. He said that he had a wife and children. When his mother asked him where he had lived this life, he took a pencil and paper and made the drawing reproduced in Figure 7. Gedeon explained details of the drawing to his mother and concluded by saying that he had been out hunting one day, threw his spear at a tiger, wounding it but not killing it. The tiger then sprang at him, and he remembered nothing after that.

After the Second World War Elisabeth Haich moved to Zurich, Switzerland, where she founded and directed a school of yoga.

Elisabeth Haich devoted several pages of her autobiographical book *Einweihung* (Initiation) to a description of Gedeon's memories and accompanying sketches. (She did not reproduce the sketches in her book, which was first published in 1960.) I spent my first sabbatical leave in Zurich in 1963-64 and purchased a copy of *Einweihung* in 1963. After reading in it the account of Gedeon's memories, I wrote to Elisabeth Haich and expressed an interest in learning more details about Gedeon's memories. She readily agreed to my meeting her. We had two long interviews on February 13 and May 7, 1964, both in Zurich.

At our meeting on May 7, 1964, Elisabeth Haich showed me a "diary" she had kept during Gedeon's childhood up to the time when he went to live with his father. He was then about 7 or 8. The diary was written in Hungarian, and I could not read it. I could see from the dates, however, that Elisabeth Haich had made frequent entries, although not one every day. (That is why I have put "diary" in quotation marks.) Elisabeth Haich also showed me the sketches that Gedeon had drawn (Figures 8–11) as well as a cut-out doll that he made at about the time he was making the sketches.

In these first two interviews and subsequent correspondence, Elisabeth Haich answered numerous— she might have thought innumerable — questions that I put to her. She answered even more questions in our subsequent correspondence after I returned to the United States. Understanding the seriousness of my plan to write a book about European children who remember previous lives, she gave me permission to reproduce five of Gedeon's drawings in my book and to cite *Einweihung* in it as liberally as I wished.

On March 22, 1972, I was again in Zurich and met Elisabeth Haich for the last time. Later that year, on November 26, 1972, I had a long interview with Gedeon Haich in Geneva, where he was then living.

Gedeon's Statements About the Previous Life

In this section I quote mostly from the German edition of *Einweihung*, in my translation. Elisabeth Haich told me of one further statement in correspondence.

When Gedeon first spoke about his memories he said:

My wife and children and the other people there [where he had lived] are not like people here; they are all black and completely naked [p. 130].

Elisabeth Haich then asked Gedeon where he had lived. Her account continues:

The boy then got some paper and a pencil and confidently drew a hut with a conical roof and a peculiar vent for the smoke, of a kind that he could never have seen in our country [Hungary] (Figure 7). In front of the hut he showed a naked woman with long, pendulous breasts. Near the hut there was a body of water with waves and palm trees* in the background.

He showed me the drawing and explained it to me: "We lived in huts like these, which we built ourselves. Also each of us made a boat for himself by hollowing out and carving the trunk of a tree. There was a large river, but one could not go into it deeply as we can in the lake here. A kind of monster lived in the water. I don't remember what kind it was, but it bit people's legs off and that's why we did not go in the water. You can see now why last year I yelled so when you wanted me to go in the water [of the lake]. I was afraid that there was something in the water that could bite my legs; and even now I get that feeling when I go in the water, even though I know there is nothing dangerous living in the water here.

And remember, Mama, how, when we bought a boat for the family I wanted to row it. You told me that I had first to learn how to row. But I knew that I can row, because I could make my treeboat move along the water just as if it were part of me. I could even sit in my boat and flip over to one side, go under the water and come up on the other side, still in the boat. And you said: 'All right. Try to row. You will find that you can't do it.' Then you were all surprised when I, taking one oar — my arms were two short to handle both oars — showed that I could row and could even maneuver the boat between other boats and between people. With my treeboat, where I lived, I could do everything. You should have seen me! The trees were not like the ones here, but like these. Here he pointed to the trees in the drawing. [He must have then made another drawing, Figure 8, because it has trees like palm trees, but Figure 7 does not.] "And there were other plants also, completely different. Look! I am standing there hunting a large bird, and that is my hat near me" [The hat is on the ground at the extreme right of Figure 8.] [pp. 130–31].

Everything he drew showed a typical tropical scene with palms and other tropical plants. The figure that apparently represented himself was that of a typical Negro. Only the hat seemed doubtful to me. It looked like a modern man's felt hat [of a European person]. I did not, however, want to disturb him or stimulate fantasies, so I asked questions cautiously. Because, however, he could never in his life have seen naked women, except perhaps in works of art, in which the women would never have pendulous breasts, I asked him: "Why did you draw your wife with such long, hanging ugly breasts." The child looked at me with astonishment that I could ask such a question. He answered immediately as if the answer were obvious: "Because that is the way they were. And they are not ugly. She was very beautiful."

Then I asked one final question. "What is the last thing you remember?" [He said:]

---

*There are no palm trees shown in Figure 7 to which this text refers. Trees like palm trees were drawn in the sketch of Figure 8.

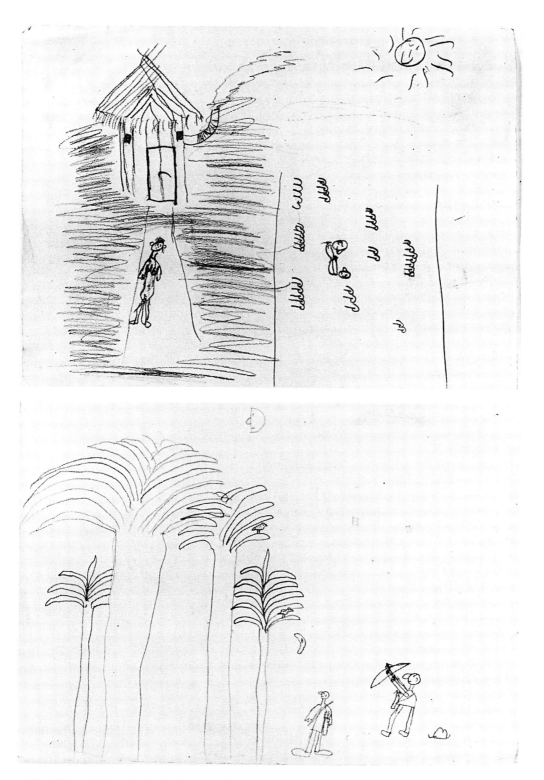

Top: Figure 7. Drawing by Gedeon Haich showing round house, woman with long breasts, and nearby water. *Bottom:* Figure 8. Drawing by Gedeon Haich showing man hunting with bow and arrow and a boomerang; the man's hat is on the ground at the right.

"I was out hunting and came upon a tiger. I threw my spear at him, but did not kill him. The tiger jumped on me with the spear still in him. I don't remember what happened then" [p. 131].

At this time, or perhaps later, Elisabeth Haich asked Gedeon to explain the curved object in the air that can be seen in Figure 8. He said it was a weapon that one threw and that returned back by itself. He said that he had made it himself. He did not use the word *boomerang*, and Elisabeth Haich did not suggest the word to him.*

The drawings reproduced in Figures 7 and 8 were made with a brown-colored pencil. They do not, however, show the brown skins of the people to which Gedeon referred. Figures 9 to 11, drawn at some other time, probably earlier, were made with other colored pencils and show the brown skins of the people sketched. Most of the drawings are not dated, but one, Figure 10, is dated November 1927; Gedeon would then have been 6½ years old.

Following the preceding statements, Gedeon talked little about the previous life. Elisabeth Haich recorded some further statements that he made during his teen years.

When he was 13, a neighbor came running to Elisabeth Haich and said that Gedeon had climbed high up in a poplar tree. The tree was, she estimated, between 20 and 25 meters high, and Gedeon could be heard but not seen because of the foliage. She ordered him to come down immediately, which he reluctantly did. She noted that he climbed down carefully, but skillfully, "like a small monkey." She asked him why he had done something so dangerous. He said that he had made a nest at the top of the tree and could eat cooked corn up there, where it tasted much better. He added: "I can see the whole area marvelously. I can look over everything." To this Elisabeth Haich replied that it was dangerous to climb so high and told him to build a nest on the ground. Gedeon looked angry, agreed, but added: "I would like to know who looked out for me when I was in the jungle and climbed trees even higher than this one to watch for animals. Where were you then?" Elisabeth Haich could not answer that question, but still insisted that Gedeon not climb trees again.

Some time later Gedeon came home from school and said with exasperation: "It's absurd. A clergyman was telling us that we only live once. I know, however, that we live many times. I know it. It is best, however, among grown-ups, not to say this but to remain quiet."

Gedeon's next statement occurred when he was 15 years old. He asked his mother to buy him a jazz drum. She agreed and they went to the biggest music shop, where Gedeon selected the largest drum. Back home, Gedeon showed an astonishing skill in playing the most complicated rhythms on the drum. He seemed to be in a kind of ecstasy, sometimes with tears in his eyes. He never said how he had learned to play the drum, but once, after playing a particularly unusual rhythm on the drum he said: "Do you see, Mama, that is the way we could send signals and messages to each other over great distances."

Elisabeth Haich did not include this detail in Einweihung, *but wrote me about it in a letter dated August 22, 1972.*

Top: Figure 9. Drawing by Gedeon Haich showing dark-skinned people. *Bottom:* Figure 10. Drawing by Gedeon Haich showing dark-skinned people.

Figure 11. Drawing by Gedeon Haich showing dark-skinned people.

The Words Used and Not Used by Gedeon. Gedeon never used the words *Negro* or *Africa*. He never specified the "monster" living in the water that could bite a person's legs. (Elisabeth Haich assumed he was referring to a crocodile.) He used a Hungarian word for the region where he lived that Elisabeth Haich translated with the German word *Urwald*, which can mean a primeval forest or, in the tropics, a jungle.

Gedeon did use the word *tiger*, but whether he meant to be specific with this word remains doubtful. In my interview with Elisabeth Haich on February 13, 1964, she said that Gedeon was using the word generically to indicate any large, ferocious beast. It could have been a tiger, or a lion, or leopard, or some other catlike animal. At our meeting on May 7, 1964, however, she remembered that Gedeon had once drawn her attention to a picture of a tiger in a book. He had also, she said, pointed to a tiger in a zoo and said that was the animal he had tried to kill with his spear and that had jumped on him.

Gedeon's Behavior Related to the Previous Life

Circumstances and Manner of Gedeon's Speaking About the Previous Life. In the summary of the case that I gave earlier I did not describe an event that appears to have stimulated Gedeon's asking his mother whether he might perhaps have lived before, after which he told her about his memories. I will now return to this beginning and quote again from *Einweihung*. When Elisabeth Haich asked Gedeon what made him think he might have lived before, he replied:

> I was in the garden and saw a large black beetle. I poked him a little with a stick. The beetle turned over on its back and lay there, absolutely motionless, as if he were dead. I was curious to see what would happen. I kept my eyes fixed on him and waited. A long time passed, maybe half an hour. Then the beetle picked himself up and ran off. That made me think that I have already lived once. It just seems as if I died and people thought that I was dead; but then I started up again, like the beetle. And so here I am, alive again. That means that I really was not dead at all. And listen, Mama, I am also asking how it is that every morning, when I wake up and my eyes are not yet open, I immediately have the feeling that I must jump out of bed and go hunting in order to find food for my wife and children. It is only when I get my eyes open and look around the room that I remember that I am a small boy and your son [pp. 129–30].

Gedeon's later statements occurred, as I have mentioned, after he had climbed high up a tree and when he was playing his jazz drum.

Comment. It would be somewhat unusual for a 7-year-old boy to remain with his eyes fixed on an object like a beetle for half an hour. Elisabeth Haich conjectured that when Gedeon did this he entered a kind of trancelike condition that facilitated the emergence of the more precise memories of a previous life that he then described to her.

Gedeon's Phobia of Water. Elisabeth Haich believed that Gedeon had gradually ceased to have the severe phobia of water that he showed when she first tried to get him to swim in the lake near their summer home in Hungary. She described him as finally becoming able to swim "like a small duck." Gedeon himself, however, told me (in 1972) that he still had some fear of water. He could swim and did so. He noticed, however, that every spring he experienced some fear before making his first dive. He did not have the fear when going into a swimming pool, only when diving into an unfamiliar river or lake. This persistent fear made him think that death in the previous life had come from drowning, an ending that differed from what he had told his mother as a young child.

Gedeon's Other Behavior Related to the Previous Life. Gedeon had no interest in reading about life among Negroes in Africa. "What is the point?" he said. "I know better how things were there and don't need to know what white men think about them. And when I do read correct descriptions I weep, even though I try not to do so." He was an adult when he made this remark. Elisabeth Haich once happened to go with Gedeon to a motion picture about Negro life, presumably in Africa. Gedeon was at that time a pilot in the air force. She could notice in the dark, however, that he was weeping, even sobbing uncontrollably during the film.

Gedeon's Skills. I have already described the unusual untaught skills that Gedeon showed in managing a boat with a single oar, climbing high up in a tree, and playing the drums. Gedeon's ability to handle a boat had particularly impressed Elisabeth Haich.

Other Relevant Behavior of Gedeon

Gedeon had no phobia of tigers, leopards, cats, or other feline animals.

Gedeon's Possible Exposure to Information About Life in the Tropics

Elisabeth Haich wrote in *Einweihung*: "I knew that he [Gedeon] had never been able to see a book about Africa. I knew every step he took and how he was occupied." Elsewhere in the book she wrote: "He had never been in a motion picture theater and had read no book about Africa." The family had no social or commercial connections with Africa or India. Gedeon had never known a Negro. In my interview with her on May 7, 1964, and again in later correspondence, she emphasized the impossibility that Gedeon could have acquired his knowledge of tropical life by normal means. Nevertheless, she must have had some doubts about this herself, because she wrote in *Einweihung* that Gedeon's praise for the long, pendulous breasts of the wife in the previous life "convinced me that he could never have heard about this."

He had, however, seen a crocodile and a tiger in a zoo.

Elisabeth Haich's Attitude Toward Gedeon's Statements and Behavior

Elisabeth Haich had a conventional Christian upbringing in Hungary. She was nevertheless open-minded about experiences that we now call paranormal. As a young woman she had experimented with "table-turning" and automatic writing. She herself had had — before Gedeon spoke about a previous life — apparent memories of two previous lives. One of these occurred in a dream and one in a kind of trancelike condition when her eyes were open. She was thus fully aware of the possibility of previous lives. Nevertheless, she listened to Gedeon without urging him to say more than he wished to say at any one time. She wrote (in *Einweihung*) that after his first exposition of his memories, when he drew the two sketches shown in Figures 7 and 8, she "took his drawings and put them in the diary that I had been keeping since his birth. I asked no more questions. I did not wish to stimulate fantasies and also did not wish him to become more deeply involved with these memories" (p. 131).

Despite Elisabeth Haich's acceptance of Gedeon's statements as deriving from a previous life, she remained dismayed that a child in a Hungarian bourgeois family of the 1920s thought he had lived a previous life in Africa. Other members of her family who learned what Gedeon had said expressed similar bafflement.

Later, Elisabeth Haich had further visions, this time of a previous life in ancient

Egypt. She believed that Gedeon had figured in this life and that she had wronged him. He had then fled from Egypt to tribes elsewhere in Africa, where he had lived, died and been reborn as a Negro. He was, however, she believed, still attracted to herself, and so he became born again as her son.

This interpretation allowed a strange statement that Gedeon had made to his mother about 6 months before he made his first statements about the previous life to fall into place. At that time Gedeon developed a serious illness with a high fever and swollen lymph glands in his neck. The doctor gave him an injection of a "serum," after which he became delirious. Elisabeth Haich stayed with him night and day for 5 days, mostly holding Gedeon in her arms. Once when she tried to change her position a little, Gedeon clung to her and cried out: "Stay! Stay! Hold me! If you just stay and hold me tight, I will forgive you everything you have done against me." Because Elisabeth Haich had, in her view, been a devoted and competent mother for Gedeon, she was nonplussed by Gedeon's remark. What, she asked Gedeon, had she done that needed forgiveness. The boy replied that he did not know, and repeated that if she would only stay and hold him tightly he would forgive her everything.

Comment. Elisabeth Haich's claimed memories of her own previous life in Egypt, and its seeming explanation of Gedeon's strange statement about forgiveness, when he was deliriously ill with fever remain unverified, and they are indeed unverifiable. The truth may lie in the reverse of Elisabeth Haich's belief. Gedeon's statement about forgiveness may have persisted in Elisabeth Haich's mind, at lower levels of awareness, until it finally generated a fantasy that seemed to explain the need for such forgiveness. I cannot now say which interpretation we should prefer.

Gedeon's Physical Appearance

Gedeon's irises were blue and his hair light brown. His hair was straight and had no suggestion of the short curls, sometimes called fuzzy hair, characteristic of African people. His lips were not thick as those of African Negroes often are. In sum, he looked like a typical European.

Gedeon's Later Development

Gedeon told me, at our meeting in 1972, that he had been abnormally short and thin during his teen years. This led him, when he was 16 or 17 years old, to practice *hatha yoga* (the kind of yoga that emphasizes exercises and postures to promote physical health). His teacher was S. R. Yesudian, who also taught yoga to his mother and subsequently became her partner in her school of yoga. The practice of yoga greatly aided Gedeon, and eventually he made teaching yoga his life's work.

During World War II Gedeon enlisted in the Hungarian Air Force, became a pilot, had his airplane shot down, and was wounded. Nevertheless, he survived the war otherwise intact. He then emigrated to Canada and for a time conducted a school teaching yoga in Vancouver. After some years in Canada he returned to Europe in 1957 and settled in Geneva, where he again conducted a school of instruction in yoga. In addition to the school he established in Geneva, he had branches of the school in Basel and Lausanne.

Gedeon was 51 years old when I met him in November 1972. He thought that he still had some memories of the previous life, but the images were not clear. I mentioned earlier his persisting fear of diving into strange waters, and this made him think that his previous life had ended in drowning. When I drew his attention to what he had said when a child about hunting a tiger, he made an attempt to remove the discrepancy by suggesting that he might have fallen into some water after throwing his spear at a beast. (He did not use the word *tiger* in speaking to me; we were speaking French, and he used the word *fauve*, which is best translated as "wild beast.")

Despite his strong commitment to yoga, Gedeon had little interest in Asian religions and had made no special study of them. He felt no attraction to India. Instead, he had a strong sense of affinity with Africa, although he had never been to that continent.

Where Could the Life Gedeon Described Have Been Lived?

With the information available from Gedeon's statements and drawings we cannot place the life he described in a particular community. The palm trees and the scanty or absent clothing tell us that the life was somewhere in the tropics. For this discussion I have set myself the modest goal not of deciding, but just that of considering whether the details fit better a life in Africa or one in South Asia, perhaps in India. I wish also to address the question of whether all the details are concordant with a life in either Africa or India.

Several of the features described or sketched by Gedeon occur among tribal people in both Africa and South Asia: dark-skinned people wearing (in some regions) little or no clothing; crocodiles in the water; palm trees; hunting with spear, bow and arrow; round huts with conical roofs and pipes to let out smoke; dugout boats.

There remain other details that may have more localizing value: boomerangs and hats shaped like the one Gedeon drew (Figure 8), and signaling with drums. Boomerangs are popularly associated with the natives of Australia. Yet they have also been used in south India and in Africa (Burton, 1987; Ruhe, 1982; Thomas, 1991). Hats shaped like the one Gedeon drew are worn by some rural people in Africa. They are made of reeds. Conceivably hats of this shape are worn elsewhere in Africa and also in parts of India. Round huts are certainly found in parts of West Africa (see Figure 12).

The detail of sending signals by beating a drum seems African to me.

Gedeon's use of the word *tiger* seemed at first discriminating to me, and I twice discussed it with Elisabeth Haich. The question I asked was: Did Gedeon use the word in a generic sense to mean any large catlike animal, or did he mean to identify the

Figure 12. Photograph of round huts in Africa. (Photograph by Ian Stevenson.)

tiger (*Felis tigris*), which is found exclusively in Asia? Unfortunately, Elisabeth Haich expressed two opinions on this matter. When I discussed it with her in February 1964, she said that Gedeon must have used the word in the generic sense; but when I reverted to the topic during my second interview with her, in May 1964, she believed that he had meant to identify the tiger that is found in Asia. She said, to illustrate her assertion, that he had once pointed to an illustration of a tiger in a book and also to a live tiger in the zoo (at Budapest, presumably) and said these were the animals that had killed him in the previous life he said he remembered. Elisabeth Haich's second statement does not necessarily settle this question. Gedeon could have recognized the photograph of a tiger and the tiger in the zoo *as like* the animal that had killed the person whose life he remembered. I am, however, far from wishing to force this opinion on my readers.

In pondering the question of a location for the life Gedeon described, we need to weigh his own conviction that it occurred in Africa, to which he felt a strong attraction. That said, however, we must explain otherwise his interest in yoga, which he eventually developed into a career as a teacher of it. Yoga derives from India and has no connection with Africa. His keen interest in yoga may have derived from — and was certainly stimulated by — his mother's interest.

I believe no single detail and also the features taken altogether do not permit us to place the life Gedeon claimed to have lived more precisely than to say that they are concordant with a life among tribal people in a tropical region of Africa or South Asia. If we decide, as I am inclined to do, that Gedeon used the word *tiger*, even when he pointed to one in a zoo, in a generic sense, then we can decide in favor of a life in Africa.

Comment

Readers will have noticed that I cannot decide which region of the tropics best fits the statements and behavior of Gedeon as a young child. I am, however, certain of one matter. We cannot explain his sketches as a young child, or his unusual behavior, by genes or the influence of his environment, alone or together.

EINAR JONSSON

The subject of this case stated no proper names of persons or places. Nevertheless, informants for the case believed his statements referred to a particular youth, who was the stepbrother of the subject's father. My study of the case has led me to the same conclusion.

Summary of the Case and Its Investigation

Einar Jonsson was born on July 25, 1969, in Reykjavik, Iceland. His parents were Jon Nielsson and Helga Haraldsdottir.* Einar was their only child. Jon Nielsson was a carpenter. Einar's parents were members of the Lutheran Church.

Einar's parents did not live together during most of the first years of his life. Einar stayed with his mother, who was living then in Reykjavik with her parents. Helga Haraldsdottir then worked, and Einar was cared for mainly by Helga's mother and later, during daytimes, in a nursery school. Jon Nielsson appears to have seen little of Einar during these early years and was not an informant for what Einar said about the previous life.

Einar began to speak when he was about a year and a half old. When he was 2 years old, he began to refer to a man on a tractor who had died. He also said that he had another mother, who had died. Gradually, he made further statements about a farm with cows, sheep, and a boat. He described a large farm house with an unusual mountain behind it. He mentioned a fire and an accident to the boat.

Einar's family believed that his statements referred to the life and death of a youth called Harald Olafsson, who had died in a tractor accident a week before Einar's birth.

A correspondent in Reykjavik, Geir Vilhjálmasson, informed me about the case

---

*Icelandic names always include the name of a person's father as an identifier with the use of a suffix, which is sson for males and sdottir for females. Women do not change their names when they marry.

in a letter of March 10, 1973. I sent the information to Dr. Erlendur Haraldsson, who, within a few months, interviewed Helga Haraldsdottir and sent me a report of her statements in November 1973. By this time Einar was 4 years old, and soon afterward he stopped speaking about a previous life. (He did not respond when Erlendur Haraldsson tried to talk with him.)

In 1980 I was in Iceland, and on August 16 I had a long interview with Einar's parents. (Dr. Haraldsson was present, but did not need to interpret.)

In the ensuing years it became increasingly obvious to me that we needed to interview Einar's paternal grandmother, who was also Harald Olafsson's mother. She was Marta Sigurdsdottir, and in 1985 I returned to Iceland in order to interview her. She kindly came from her home in the country to Reykjavik, where I met her on April 11. For this occasion, I needed Dr. Haraldsson as interpreter. Einar and his mother were present during this meeting and contributed some additional information. By this time Einar was almost 16 years old.

Several of Einar's statements referred to the house where Harald had lived and its surroundings. I had not verified these independently and the only way to do so required a journey to Laufas. This involved putting Dr. Haraldsson to the trouble of accompanying me; but he generously agreed to do this. Accordingly, we drove from Reykjavik to Laufas on October 23, 1999. There we had another interview with Marta Sigurdsdottir and also talked with Olaf Petursson, Harald's father, who verified one of Einar's statements. We could also verify by our own inspection Einar's statements about the house where he had lived and its surroundings.

Relevant Information About Einar's Paternal Family

Einar's paternal grandmother, Marta Sigurdsdottir, was married twice. With her first husband, Niels Larusson, she had one son, Jon Nielsson (Einar's father). With her second husband, Olaf Petursson, she had four sons, of whom Harald Olafsson was the second. Harald Olafsson was about 8 years younger than his stepbrother, Jon Nielsson.

Marta Sigurdsdottir and her first husband, Niels Larusson, lived in Reykjavik until Jon Nielsson was about 5 years old. She then moved to a place called Laufas, which is near the town of Akureyri. At Laufas her second husband, Olaf Petursson, had a farm. Her four later-born children were born in that area. Jon Nielsson stayed at Laufas until he was 16–17, when he returned to Reykjavik, presumably for more advanced education. Because Jon Nielsson had lived for 12 years at Laufas, he knew the area well. He had naturally known Harald Olafsson fairly well, even though Harald was about 8 years younger than he was. He left Laufas when Harald was about 9 years old. He was a principal verifier of Einar's statements.

In contrast to Jon Nielsson, Helga Haraldsdottir (his wife and Einar's mother) never knew Harald Olafsson. Moreover, she had never been to Laufas until she took Einar there when he was about 5 years old.

The Life and Death of Harald Olafsson

Harald Olafsson was born at Akureyri on May 22, 1955. His parents were Olaf Petursson and Marta Sigurdsdottir. They had already had one son, and they had two more after Harald's birth.

I learned of only one unusual event in Harald's life until his untimely death when he was about 14 years old. His childhood was apparently that of a normal boy growing up and working on a farm in Iceland.

When he was a boy—I did not learn his age—one of Harald's ankle (Achilles) tendons was cut accidentally and had to be stitched surgically. He limped for a time after this, but the wound eventually healed.

He must have learned to drive a tractor at a young age. On July 18, 1969, he took one of his family's tractors to a neighbor's farm in order to help the neighbor cut grass. He had finished this work and was driving the tractor home when somehow it went off the road and overturned. He was killed instantly. A passerby found his body. It was taken to Akureyri where there was an inquiry into the cause of the accident. Harald's family never learned from it what the doctors thought was the immediate cause of his death, that is, the fatal injury; they assumed he had died of a severe head injury.

Dr. Haraldsson sent me a copy of a brief newspaper report of the accident in which Harald died. This appeared in the leading newspaper of Iceland, *Morgunbladid*, and provided the cause and date of Harald's death.

Statements Made by Einar

In Table 1 I have listed all the statements Helga Haraldsdottir remembered Einar to have made. He made all of them, she said, before he was 4 years old. In 1980 she told me that Einar had referred to the man who limped (item 4 of Table 1) when he was about 7 years old; she had, however, mentioned this statement about a man who had limped to Dr. Haraldsson in 1973, at which time Einar was only just 4 years old.

Einar never mentioned any proper names of persons or places.

We have probably not recorded some statements that Einar made. Dr. Haraldsson noted, in 1973, that, according to Helga Haraldsdottir, Einar "talks about his [Harald's] uncles and aunts and cousins." Yet Helga Haraldsdottir did not mention statements about such persons to me in 1980 or 1985; and I, equally, failed to ask about them.

Among the 16 statements listed in Table 1, 13 are correct for the life and death of Harald Olafsson and 3 are incorrect.

When Einar was 5, Helga Haraldsdottir took him to Laufas, where he spent the summer. I asked her whether he had shown any signs of familiarity with the farm and its area. She said that Einar had not, but that she herself had! This occurred, she thought, because of the accuracy of Einar's description of the large farmhouse and the oddly shaped mountain behind it. Figure 13 shows what she would have seen when she got to Laufas.

Figure 13. View of the farmhouse and unusually shaped mountain behind it at Laufas. The farmhouse is the dark brown building at the far left. (Photograph by Erlendur Haraldsson.)

Einar's Behavior Related to the Previous Life

Circumstances and Manner of Einar's Speaking About the Previous Life. Unlike most subjects of the cases included in this book, Einar never made any direct claim to have lived a previous life. He spoke like an observer watching events that happened to someone else.*

This is not to say, however, that he was not confused about his own identity and the identities of his parents. He rejected his mother and for a time did not even allow her to touch him. He asked to go to his "other mother" and cried because of being thwarted in this request. At the same time he sometimes said that his "other mother" was dead. Once when his mother was taking him home from nursery school, they met a friend of Einar's who asked him if Helga was his mother. Einar replied: "No. This is not my mother. She is dead." At times he would say that his *maternal* grandmother — with whom he and his mother were then living — was his mother; this confusion was not fixed, however, because at other times he said she was *not* his mother.

If Einar's mother asked him questions about details related to some statement he had made, he would never respond. For example, he would not say what color of hair his "other mother" had.

---

*Speaking indirectly about a deceased person, instead of claiming to have been one, is rare among children who seem to remember previous lives, but I have studied several other cases with this feature. I have not yet published reports of these cases.

Table 1. Summary of Statements Made by Einar

Item	Informants	Verification	Comments
1. A tractor turned over and a man died.	Helga Haraldsdottir, Einar's mother	Jon Nielsson, Einar's father Marta Sigurdsdottir, Harald Olafsson's mother *Morgunbladid* of July 22, 1969	This is a correct statement about the death of Harald Olafsson. Einar never stated anything direct like: "I was driving a tractor; it turned over and I died."
2. He had a big brother.	Helga Haraldsdottir	Marta Sigurdsdottir	Harald Olafsson had a brother, Eirikur Olafsson, who was a year older than Harald.
3. He had another mother who was dead.	Helga Haraldsdottir	Incorrect	Marta Sigurdsdottir was still living. When he made this statement, Einar had never met her, so from his perspective she was absent.
4. There was a man who limped.	Helga Haraldsdottir	Marta Sigurdsdottir	Harald's maternal grandfather, Sigurd Stefansson, had stayed with his daughter and her family for about 6 months during the last year of his life. He was then limping. He died in 1958 or 1959. Harald was only 3–4 years old at this time.
5. The farmhouse was large.	Helga Haraldsdottir	Helga Haraldsdottir I visited the farmhouse in 1999.	During my visit in 1999 I compared the farmhouse with other farmhouses in that area of Iceland. It seemed to me not huge, but definitely large.
6. There was a mountain behind the house.	Helga Haraldsdottir	Helga Haraldsdottir Marta Sigurdsdottir I saw and photographed the house and mountain in 1999.	The mountain is directly behind the house.
7. The mountain had an unusual shape.	Helga Haraldsdottir	Helga Haraldsdottir Marta Sigurdsdottir	One side of the mountain was in fact a steep cliff, not a slope. Mountains like this one with a steep cliffside are not uncommon in Iceland. There is even a word —*nupur*— for them in Icelandic. (Einar did not use this word himself.) Unlike most of the mountains in the parts of Iceland that we traversed in 1999, the mountain at Laufas was conical in shape; other mountains usually had flat tops.

No.	Statement			Notes
8.	There were horses there.	Helga Haraldsdottir	Marta Sigurdsdottir	The mountain at Laufas also had clifflike segments on the side behind the farmhouse. Marta Sigurdsdottir said they had one horse, not horses, during Harald's lifetime.
9.	There was a barn.	Helga Haraldsdottir	Jon Nielsson, Einar's father	There were several farm buildings near the farmhouse in 1999, but I believe they dated from after the time of Harald's death.
10.	There was a sheephouse.	Helga Haraldsdottir	Jon Nielsson / Marta Sigurdsdottir	Jon Nielsson, Marta Sigurdsdottir, and Olaf Petursson could not remember any such fire. There *was* a fire not in the out-houses, but in the farmhouse, in 1969; this occurred *after* Harald's death.
11.	There was a cowhouse.	Helga Haraldsdottir	Jon Nielsson	
12.	The cowhouse and sheephouse had burned.	Helga Haraldsdottir	Incorrect	
13.	He had skis.	Helga Haraldsdottir	Incorrect	No one in the family had skis.
14.	He had a bicycle.	Helga Haraldsdottir	Marta Sigurdsdottir	Jon Nielsson did not remember that HaraldOlafsson had a bicycle, but he left Laufas when Harald was 9, and Harald may have obtained a bicycle later.
15.	There was a small boat on the farm.	Helga Haraldsdottir	Marta Sigurdsdottir / Jon Nielsson	The boat was used primarily for fishing. In the autumn it was hauled out of the water and turned over. Jon Nielsson remembered that it had been damaged "a little" during Harald's lifetime. Marta Sigurdsdottir did not remember any damage to the boat during Harald's lifetime.
16.	The boat had become broken.	Helga Haraldsdottir	Jon Nielsson / Olaf Petursson	Olaf Petursson remembered that a boat had been pulled onto the shore and was then caught by a storm and broken. He showed Dr. Haraldsson and me a photograph of the boat. It was destroyed during Harald's lifetime.

Einar tended to be somewhat repetitious. Helga Haraldsdottir told Dr. Haraldsson that he "often talks about his big brother" and "often mentions a big mountain in the countryside."

Einar's Attitude Toward His Parents. I have already mentioned that Einar's wish to go to the "other mother" (even though he said she was dead) included a rejection of his mother. Einar also rejected his father, and at a time when his parents were living apart, Einar did not welcome his father's visits when he came to see him. Helga Haraldsdottir had never heard Einar refer to having two fathers, but she learned that he had been saying this to playmates at his nursery school.

Einar's Statements About Contemporaneous Events on the Farm at Laufas. Einar frequently referred to what was happening on the farm as if he somehow knew about such activity. For example, he would say something like: "Now my grandmother is baking" or "My grandfather is cutting the grass." These statements were never verified.*

Other Relevant Behavior of Einar

Einar had no phobia of tractors or other vehicles.

Einar's Later Development

When I met Einar in 1985 he was 15½ years old. He was then in the ninth grade at school. He said he remembered nothing of a previous life. He had no special inclination either to country or to city life. He wanted to learn more about computers.

Comment

My notes and also my correspondence with Dr. Haraldsson about this case sometimes mention doubts about whether we could regard the case as solved. By this I mean: Do Einar's statements refer to the life and death of Harald Olafsson and no one else? My present answer to this question is a guarded affirmative. Tractor accidents are common on farms; fatal accidents much less so. Many statements Einar made about the farm would be correct for many farms, perhaps for nearly all. Yet only farms near water would have a boat and not many of these would have a man in the house who limped. Also, not many farms would have a mountain of an unusual shape just

---

Several other subjects have shown evidence of paranormal communication with members of the previous personality's family. Subjects of this group include: Shamlinie Prema, Nirankar Bhatnagar, Gnanatilleka Baddewithana, Swarnlata Mishra, and Sunita Khandelwal.

behind them. We cannot attach an estimate of probability to this group of details; but I think most readers will agree with me that we are unlikely to find them all together in farms other than the one where Harald Olafsson lived.

Einar's references to a man who limped is unusual. Harald Olafsson was only 3–4 years old when his maternal grandfather, the man who limped, came to stay for a time in their home. His visit and death later that year, occurred 10 years before Harald's death at the age of 14. In this respect the case, however, is also not unique. Although most of the subjects' memories cluster near the time of the previous personality's death, some few subjects have recalled events from much earlier in the previous life.*

The case is also unusual in the short interval — 7 days — between the previous personality's death and the subject's birth.†

DITTA LARUSDOTTIR

This case is another one with meager data. The scantiness of its data, however, warrants reporting it here as an example to parents of the slight indications of previous lives that some children provide.§

Summary of the Case and Its Investigation

Ditta Larusdottir was born in Reykjavik, Iceland, on January 3, 1967. Her parents were Larus Johansson and Margret Olafsdottir. She was her parents' third child. Larus, a carpenter, was Margret's second husband. Larus and Margret were Lutherans. They separated when Ditta was a young child.

When Ditta's mother, Margret, was pregnant with Ditta, her (Margret's) younger sister Gudrun dreamed about a deceased third sister, Kristin, who implied in the dream that she was being reborn as Margret's daughter.

About 10–14 days after Ditta's birth, Margret noticed a prominent birthmark at the back of Ditta's head (Figure 14).

When Ditta was about 2½ years old, she made two statements that suggested memories of Kristin's life.

Members of the family frequently remarked on the physical similarities between Ditta and her aunt Kristin.

Dr. Erlendur Haraldsson informed me about this case when I was in Iceland in 1981. On March 5, 1981, he and I had a long interview (in Reykjavik) with Margret

---

*Swarnlata Mishra was another subject who remembered an event that occurred long before the death of the previous personality.

†Other cases with an interval of a week or less between the previous personality's death and the subject's birth are those of Cemil Fahrici and Izzat Shuhayyib.

§Other children subjects of these cases who have made only two or three statements about a previous life include Henry Demmert III, Graham Le-Gros, Wilfred Robertson, and Paavo Sorsa.

Olafsdottir. We also met Ditta, who was then 14 years old. I examined, sketched, and photographed her birthmark.

On March 6, Dr. Haraldsson interviewed Ditta's father, Larus Johansson, over the telephone. I was present in Dr. Haraldsson's office then and made notes of the conversation immediately afterwards. Ditta's maternal grandparents had both died before 1981, and Gudrun Olafsdottir, who had dreamed of Kristin before Ditta was born, was then living in Pakistan. Thus Ditta's mother furnished most of the information about the case that I could obtain; but Ditta's father and the police report of Kristin's death provided valuable confirmation of some details.

In October 1999 I was again in Iceland, but it was not feasible for me to meet Ditta and her family again. Dr. Haraldsson obtained a copy of the police report on the fatal accident in which Kristin Olafsdottir had died. He also translated it for me. This thorough report included statements from three persons, including Kristin's husband, who testified to events just before she died.

The Life and Death of Kristin Olafsdottir

In a large family of 15 children Kristin was the third child and third daughter. She was born on November 10, 1925. Her parents were Olaf Loftsson and Elinborg Sigurdsdottir. They later had other daughters of whom Maria, Margret (Ditta's mother), and Gudrun figure in the case. All their children were daughters. They lived in Reykjavik.

When Kristin was about 3 years old, she fell and struck the back of her head. The wound bled. No doctor being available, Olaf Loftsson staunched the bleeding by himself and applied a band-aid to the wound. Afterwards, he forgot about this injury until Margret asked him whether Kristin had ever injured her head.

Before she married, Kristin attended a school of drama and had acted in plays on the radio. She married when she was about 17 years old. Her husband, Einar Grimsson, was opposed to her acting, and she probably had no time for it after she had children. At the time of her death she had a 3-year-old son and 5-month-old daughter. They also lived in Reykjavik.

In the autumn of 1947, Kristin and Einar purchased (with a friend) a new house, the building of which was still incomplete. They nevertheless moved into their new house. The house had a basement, where the central heating and a washing machine were installed. The washing machine was one they had owned and brought with them to the new house. One evening Kristin washed some clothes in a boiling pot and then went to use the mangle of the washing machine. When she touched the machine, she experienced an electric shock, which she mentioned to Einar. They agreed not to use the machine until an electrician had examined it. It was obviously not properly connected and probably ungrounded. Einar then went to visit some neighbors. Kristin remained in the basement. Suddenly, her sister Soffia, who was visiting and upstairs, heard Kristin call out to her. When Soffia went to the basement, she found Kristin held fast to the washing machine by her right arm. She ran to a neighbor for help.

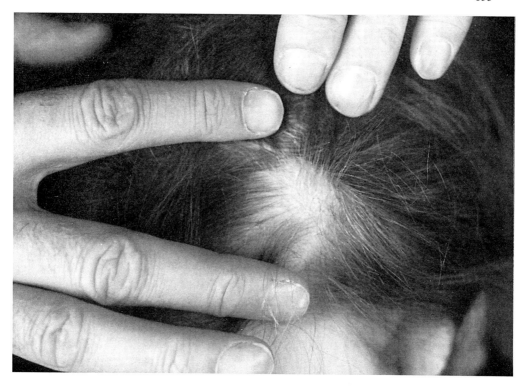

Figure 14. Birthmark on the head of Ditta Larusdottir in March 1981, when she was 14 years old. (Photograph by Ian Stevenson.)

He came quickly and disconnected the electricity in the house. By this time, however, Kristin was dead. She died on November 6, 1947, at the age of 22. Her sister Margret (Ditta's mother) was about 14 years old then.

Kristin was a kind and gentle person. She was Margret's favorite sister among the 14 sisters she had.

Gudrun Olafsdottir's Dream About Kristin

In 1966, when Margret was pregnant with Ditta, her next younger sister, Gudrun, had the following dream.

> Margret and her husband had a newborn baby, and they asked Gudrun to take care of the baby while they went out. They left and Gudrun remained alone with the baby. The baby then sat up and began to talk. She said: "Do you know that I am born again?" Gudrun replied: "No, I did not know that." The baby then said: "Yes, I was here before.... It was very difficult to be born and easy to die." Gudrun asked her to tell how she had died, but the baby would not speak about this. Then Gudrun asked her whether she looked the same. The baby said: "Yes, but I am darker now, darker in complexion and [have] darker hair." Then the baby said that she had a scar. Gudrun asked her whether this had something to do with her death. The baby replied: "No. I

was over 20 when I died, but I got that scar when I was a little girl. It will go away." Then the baby asked Gudrun about Maria [another of the daughters of the family, who had been a baby sitter for Kristin]. Gudrun, on hearing Maria's name spoken by the baby said: "Oh. Did you know us before?" At this the baby lay down again and said: "I do not want to talk about it any more."

(As I mentioned, I could not meet Gudrun and my account of her dream is second-hand, from Margret.)

Gudrun believed that the baby of the dream was Kristin, who was the only daughter of the family who had died. She told Margret about it a day or two after having the dream. Margret paid little attention to it at the time.

Comment. Gudrun's dream occurred before Ditta's birth, and so she could not have known normally about Ditta's birthmark. I cannot, however, be certain that she knew nothing about the injury to Kristin's head, even though this seems unlikely. In 1981 Ditta's father, Larus, knew about Kristin's head injury, but he had never met Kristin. Moreover, Olaf Loftsson seems never to have talked about Kristin's head injury until Margret showed him Ditta's birthmark. Elinborg Jonsdottir (Margret's and Kristin's mother) said her daughters, as children, were always falling and she did not remember a head injury of Kristin.

Statements Made by Ditta

When Ditta was between 2 and 2½, Margret took her to the bathroom. Ditta noticed a ring on Margret's finger. The following conversation (as remembered by Margret in 1981) then took place:

> DITTA: Who gave you that ring?
> MARGRET: My first husband [not Ditta's father].
> DITTA: I had a husband too.
> MARGRET: No. You do not have a husband.
> DITTA: Yes, I do.
> MARGRET: Little girls do not have husbands.
> DITTA: Well, I have one.
> MARGRET: OK. So what is his name?
> DITTA: Einar.
> MARGRET: Do you have children?
> DITTA: No. I have only dolls.

Ditta never alluded verbally to the previous life again. She never spoke of it with her father. She never called herself Kristin, and she never drew attention to the birthmark on her head.

Comment. Einar and Kristin had had two children when Kristin died. As I mentioned, the elder, a boy, was a little over 3 years old, and the younger was an infant girl, just 5 months old. Margret believed that Ditta would never have heard Einar's name mentioned; Einar remarried and became "lost" to Margret's family.

Ditta's Behavior Related to the Previous Life

When Ditta became old enough to have dolls, she named a female doll "Arnheidur." No member of the family had this name. Kristin, however, had had a friend called "Arna," who had subsequently died. Margret did not know whether for this person "Arna" was a short form for Arnheidur, as it often is.

Margret observed Ditta playing at being an actress when she was about 2 years old. When she asked Ditta what she would like to be when she grew up, Ditta said she wanted to be an actress. Later, she changed her mind and said she would like to become a teacher, nurse, or doctor.

Other Relevant Behavior of Ditta

Ditta had no phobia of electrical equipment.

She became able to read before anyone had taught her. At the age of 6 she could read much better than other children who had been taught to read. Ditta herself found it puzzling that she could read without being taught, and she asked her mother how she could do this. Margret said that she did not know.

Margret thought that Ditta had a quicker temper than Kristin had had.

The Attitude of the Adults Concerned Toward Ditta's Memories

As I mentioned, Ditta's parents and grandparents were Lutherans. According to Margret, her sister Gudrun (who dreamed of Kristin before Ditta's birth) believed in reincarnation, but she (Margret) did not. Nevertheless, Margret obviously took our inquiries seriously and showed both patience and interest during our long interview with her.

Margret said that her parents believed in life after death; and she thought it probable that they also believed in reincarnation.

Ditta's Birthmark

Ditta's birthmark was located on the right occipital area of her head above and behind her ear. It was a roundish scarlike hairless area about 1 centimeter in diameter (Figure 14).

Other Physical Resemblances Between Ditta and Kristin

According to Margret, her parents believed that Ditta closely resembled Kristin. "They were always talking," she said, "about how much Ditta looks like Kristin." Both Ditta and Kristin had unusually light blue eyes. Ditta was darker in hair and complexion than Kristin.

Ditta had no birthmark corresponding to the site of the body, presumably her right hand, where Kristin received the electric current that killed her.

Comment

Margret's skepticism about reincarnation makes it unlikely, but far from impossible, that she misremembered the conversation with Ditta that provided the only direct statement about a previous life that anyone attributed to Ditta. Our confidence in the correspondence between Ditta's birthmark and the injury to the back of Kristin's head depends entirely on Margret's memory of her father's memory. (As I mentioned, Margret's mother did not remember any particular injury on Kristin.)

Could there be a normal explanation for Ditta's birthmark? I considered that it might be a pressure necrosis from abrasion of the head during Ditta's passage through the birth canal. This seems improbable because Ditta was Margret's third child. Her labor with Ditta lasted only 3½ hours and was normal. Pressure necrosis during birth occurs most commonly during the prolonged labors of firstborn babies (Hodgman et al., 1971).

Supposing that Ditta's birthmark derives from the scar to the old injury on Kristin's head, the case is unusual but not unique. In at least three other cases, those of Dorabeth Crosby, Jennifer Pollock, and Lekh Pal Jatav a birthmark or birth defect on the subject corresponded to a nonfatal wound on the previous personality.

The interval—almost 19 years—between Kristin's death and Ditta's birth is one of the longest in same-family cases studied at the University of Virginia.

MARJA-LIISA KAARTINEN

Summary of the Case and Its Investigation

Marja-Liisa Kaartinen was born on May 22, 1929, in Helsinki, Finland. Her father died when she was 3 years old, and I never learned his name or occupation. Her mother, Salli Kaartinen, was almost the sole informant for the case.

Marja-Liisa began to speak when she was about a year old. When she was about 2, she began to make statements and show behavior that convinced her mother that she was the reincarnation of an older daughter of the family, Eeva-Maija, who had died 6 months before Marja-Liisa's birth.

Dr. Karl Müller of Zurich, Switzerland, was my informant for the case. He had met Salli Kaartinen in Helsinki in 1959, when she had told him about her daughter's case. Subsequently, she sent him a written account of the case, which he showed me. I went to Helsinki in the autumn of 1963 and on September 3 had a long interview with Salli Kaartinen. She did not speak English, and her daughter Marja-Liisa, who did, acted as our interpreter.*

Salli Kaartinen had kept a written record of Marja-Liisa's statements and behavior, and she consulted this when I interviewed her. Later, I asked to borrow these notes or to be given a translation of them. This was agreed to, but the lending or translation was postponed until eventually the notes became mislaid during a move to a new residence by Salli Kaartinen.

Marja-Liisa had a brother, Anti Kaartinen, who was 7 years older than she, and I thought that he might remember something of Marja-Liisa's statements and unusual behavior as a young child. During my visit to Helsinki in 1963, I had a brief telephone conversation with him. He had no memory then of Marja-Liisa's statements and behavior, although he did remember hearing his mother tell friends about these later.

Later, I corresponded with Salli Kaartinen about some details of the case. Marja-Liisa translated and typed her letters to me. In 1978 I was again in Helsinki and met Marja-Liisa again, but not her mother. I have not met her since.

The Life and Death of Eeva-Maija

Eeva-Maija Kaartinen was born in Oulu, Finland, on August 17, 1923. She was then her mother's only daughter. Three brothers had been born before her.

Eeva-Maija had some distinctive personality traits in which she differed from her brothers. For example, she did not like to eat, and sometimes, in order to avoid eating, she would hide food given to her. She liked fish and fresh milk, but disliked meat and sour milk, which other members of the family enjoyed eating. In fact, she refused to eat meat and sour milk.

She was fond of music and of dancing and learned to dance almost before she could walk. She had been taught the steps of the Charleston (a popular dance of the 1920s).

When she was a little more than 5 years old, Eeva-Maija became seriously ill with what was diagnosed as influenza, and she died in Helsinki on November 24, 1928.

During Eeva-Maija's final illness, Salli Kaartinen promised to buy her a toy baby carriage.

---

*It is certainly undesirable to have one informant for a case — least of all the subject — act as an interpreter for another, and I have been able to avoid this situation in all but a very few instances. After my first visit to Helsinki in 1963, I obtained the assistance of Rita Castrèn, who acted as my interpreter for nearly all my subsequent investigations in Finland, including my later meeting in 1978 with Marja-Liisa.

The close similarity between what I learned about the case in 1963 and what Salli Kaartinen had earlier written for Dr. Müller assured me that Marja-Liisa had not, as she interpreted for me, distorted what her mother was then saying compared with what she had earlier stated.

Salli Kaartinen was grief-stricken when she lost her only daughter, and she longed to have Eeva-Maija return to her. She was at the time already pregnant with Marja-Liisa, who was born almost exactly 6 months after Eeva-Maija's death.

Statements and Recognitions Made by Marja-Liisa

During the period when Marja-Liisa identified herself most strongly with Eeva-Maija, she repeatedly asked to be called Eeva-Maija. At the age of about 2 when she came across photographs of Eeva-Maija, she would take them to other people and say: "These are of me."

When she was about 2 years old and having some difficulty in eating, she said to her mother: "Why don't you say to me what you said to Eeva-Maija: 'Eat, bite, and swallow'"? Salli Kaartinen had in fact used these same words when exhorting Eeva-Maija to eat.

When Marja-Liisa was about 3 years old, her family went for the first time since her birth to a cabin in the country that they owned and used in the summer. It was at Sotkomo. When they arrived there, Marja-Liisa noticed that a servant the family had had was not there and said: "Where is Helim?" Helim had left the family's employ the year before Marja-Liisa was born. This incident occurred before Marja-Liisa's father died, because the cabin was sold after his death. These details show that Marja-Liisa was no more than 3 years old at the time.

At the country cabin in Sotkomo mentioned above, which, as I mentioned, the family visited when Marja-Liisa was about 3 years old, the family had a trunk in which the toys of the family's children had been stored. Some of the toys belonged to the sons, others had been Eeva-Maija's. Marja-Liisa went spontaneously to this trunk and picked out from it the toys that had belonged to Eeva-Maija. It was particularly noticed that she could tell the balls that had belonged to Eeva-Maija from the balls belonging to the boys; all the balls were mixed up in the trunk. One of Marja-Liisa's brothers had a doll in the trunk, but Marja-Liisa ignored it and picked out a doll that had belonged to Eeva-Maija. Salli Kaartinen told me that she had not been present when the trunk of toys was opened and gone through by Marja-Liisa. I presume therefore that she learned of the incident from her husband or from one of her sons, who were all older than Marja-Liisa.

When Marja-Liisa was about 4 years old, she asked her mother "Where were we when Peter Pan flew?" Salli Kaartinen believed this remark alluded to the motion picture based on J. M. Barrie's children's story of Peter Pan, which Eeva-Maija and her mother had seen in 1928, but Marja-Liisa had never seen. (Peter Pan flies in the story and flew in the motion picture.)

Also at the age of about 4, Marja-Liisa asked her mother to give her the baby carriage that she had promised her. As I mentioned, Salli Kaartinen had promised Eeva-Maija when she was ill — terminally as it turned out — that she would buy a baby carriage for her.

I do not know Marja-Liisa's age at the time of the following incident. Salli Kaartinen asked a servant to fetch a coat that had belonged to Eeva-Maija and that had been kept in the attic of their house. When the servant came down from the attic with the coat, Marja-Liisa saw the coat, rushed at the servant, seized the coat to wear it, and said: "My coat, my coat." Salli Kaartinen had been in the kitchen and Marja-Liisa in her room when Salli had asked the servant to bring the coat; she was sure that Marja-Liisa could not have heard her request to the servant.

Marja-Liisa's Behavior Related to the Previous Life

Circumstances and Manner of Marja-Liisa's Speaking About the Previous Life. The incidents I have already described show that Marja-Liisa sometimes spoke spontaneously about the previous life and at other times spoke when some situation familiar to Eeva-Maija seemed to stimulate her memories.

Marja-Liisa initially spoke in an adult manner without going through any phase of "baby talk." Once when Marja-Liisa was about 2, her mother spoke to her in a sort of "baby talk," and Marja-Liisa rebuked her, saying: "Why do you speak like that to me?"

Marja-Liisa's Eating Habits. Marja-Liisa had some difficulty in eating, although not as much as Eeva-Maija had had. She also, but again to a lesser extent, sometimes hid her food in order to avoid eating it. Like Eeva-Maija, Marja-Liisa liked to eat fish and fresh milk, but disliked and refused to eat meat and sour milk. All the other members of the family except the two girls liked to eat meat and sour milk.

Marja-Liisa's Preference for Eeva-Maija's Toys and Clothes. Marja-Liisa preferred to play with the old toys that Eeva-Maija had had instead of playing with new toys bought for her. She particularly liked to play with a toy bed that had belonged to Eeva-Maija.

She also liked to put on Eeva-Maija's clothes. She appears to have recognized some of these clothes besides the coat mentioned above.

Marja-Liisa's Dancing. Marja-Liisa was as fond of music as Eeva-Marja had been. She also learned to dance almost before she learned to walk. When she was still under 4 years old, her mother said she would teach Marja-Liisa some songs and started to play the piano. Marja-Liisa said that she would dance, and she immediately began to dance the Charleston. Eeva-Maija had been taught to dance the Charleston, but Marja-Liisa had not. This incident occurred before Marja-Liisa's father died (therefore when she was no more than 3 years old), and it surprised him.

Marja-Liisa's Identification with Eeva-Maija. I have already mentioned that Marja-Liisa asked to be called Eeva-Maija, and in general she acted as if she were Eeva-Maija reborn. For example, she had an older brother who had been about 1½ years older than Eeva-Maija. (I believe this brother was Anti Kaartinen.) He was therefore about 7 years older than Marja-Liisa. Marja-Liisa, however, regarded him as a peer and expected him to play with her.

There were times, however, when Marja-Liisa referred to Eeva-Maija as if Eeva-Maija were different from her. Sometimes when she put on Eeva-Maija's clothes, she would stand in front of a mirror and say: "Now I want to speak to Eeva-Maija."

At the age of about 5 (the age Eeva-Maija had been when she died), Marja-Liisa had a series of dreams of being buried or of seeing dead bodies. These nightmares receded gradually after Marja-Liisa's mother reassured her (just how, I did not learn).

Salli Kaartinen told me that Marja-Liisa's personality did not seem to resemble Eeva-Maija's fully until she was about 2 years old. It seemed to her that at some time then a marked change occurred in Marja-Liisa, and she became much more like Eeva-Maija than she had earlier seemed to be.

However sudden the change in Marja-Liisa may have been, for Salli Kaartinen it meant the end of her grief over the loss of Eeva-Maija. She wrote (in a letter of October 26, 1967): "Now I did not miss Eeva-Maija any longer, as I knew that I had got her back."

Physical Resemblances Between Marja-Liisa and Eeva-Maija

Eeva-Maija was blond and Marja-Liisa was a brunette. Otherwise, according to Salli Kaartinen, the two girls "resembled each other considerably in physical appearance."

Marja-Liisa was not especially susceptible to respiratory infections.

The Fading of Marja-Liisa's Memories

Salli Kaartinen said that Marja-Liisa's behavior suggesting that of Eeva-Maija began to diminish when she was about 7 years old.

In 1978, when I met Marja-Liisa by herself, she did not say that she remembered anything of the life of Eeva-Maija at that time. (She was then 49½ years old.) She did, however, vividly remember the incident when, at the age of about 3, she had picked out Eeva-Maija's toys from the trunk at Sotkomo. She could still recall the pleasure she felt at having these toys—again, as it seemed to her then. She remembered recognizing a doll, a teddy bear, and a toy perambulator (baby carriage). (The last two items—a teddy bear and perambulator—had not figured in Salli Kaartinen's account of Marja-Liisa's recognitions.) She also recalled recognizing Eeva-Maija's clothes and the pleasure this gave her.

Other Relevant Information

Salli Kaartinen believed in the possibility of reincarnation. Marja-Liisa told me that her mother "was a Theosophist and had studied oriental religions." Salli Kaartinen herself narrated to me (in 1963) three experiences she had had that to her suggested possible previous lives. Two of these were of *déjà vu* and the third was a conviction of having once lived in Scotland. She had no imaged memories related to any of these experiences.

Salli Kaartinen said that she was sure members of the family had not spoken about Eeva-Maija in Marja-Liisa's presence. She said the family purposefully avoided speaking about Eeva-Maija in an effort to forget about her, presumably to ease their grief.

Comment

This case resembles several others I have already described: those of the Pollock twins, Nadège Jegou, and Alfonso Lopes. In each of the cases the death of a child profoundly affected a parent who hoped and sometimes expected that the child would be born again in the same family.

TARU JÄRVI

The subject of this case remembered the life of her mother's second husband. The case therefore has the feature of a difference in sex between the subject and the previous personality.

Summary of the Case and Its Investigation

Taru Järvi was born in Helsinki, Finland, on May 27, 1976. Her parents were Heikki Järvi and his wife, Iris. She was their only child. They were members of the Lutheran Church.

Taru began to speak when she was about 1 year old, and when she was about 1½ she began rejecting her given name and saying that she should be called Jaska. This was the nickname of Iris Järvi's second husband, Jaakko Vuorenlehto, who had been accidentally run over by a bus in 1973. Thereafter, Taru made several statements about the life and death of Jaakko and also showed in various ways that she considered herself a boy. She showed a marked antagonism toward her father, and her attitude toward him generated some alienation between her parents.

Rita Castrén notified me about this case in a letter dated August 28, 1979. I went to Finland in March 1981 and had a long interview with Iris Järvi on March 8. I also talked a little with Taru, who was then just under 5 years old. Rita Castrén was my interpreter. Because she had known Iris Järvi for 12 years, she was also an informant for some of Taru's statements about the previous life. I interviewed one other informant for Taru's statements and behavior. She was Vappu Haanpaa, a friend and fellow-employee of Iris Järvi.

Later in 1981 Rita Castrén translated for me the report by the Helsinki Police Department of the inquest into the death of Jaakko Vuorenlehto.

In correspondence during 1997 Rita Castrén sent me some information about Taru's later development. In September 1999 I was again in Helsinki and had another long interview with Iris Järvi. Unfortunately, I could not meet Taru again, because she was then living away from Helsinki, in Espoo. I was equally disappointed not to be able to meet Taru's father, Heikki Järvi. I had not met him in the 1980s and hoped to learn his views on the early behavior and development of Taru. Unfortunately, in the intervening years he had developed Parkinsonism and had become frail. Iris said it would be inappropriate to try to interview him as he then was.

The Life and Death of Jaakko Vuorenlehto

Jaakko Vuorenlehto was born in Helsinki on November 15, 1929. I learned little about his early life. His childhood was spent close to that of the girl, Iris Sundström, who would later become his wife. Iris was born on September 18, 1935, and was thus 6 years younger than Jaakko. Iris later told me that when she was 12 years old and Jaakko 18, Jaakko said of Iris: "One day I will marry that girl." (Iris learned of this statement later.) She also remembered that at about the same time she herself had said, referring to the house where Jaakko lived: "One day I will live in that house." Although they would then see each other at a distance, Jaakko and Iris did not meet until later.

Iris did not marry Jaakko as her first husband. With that husband she had three daughters. In the meantime, Jaakko grew up. He finished junior high school, but had no further formal education. After a period in the armed services he became employed in a service station. Later, he became the manager of a hardware store. He and Iris became acquainted, and their friendship developed into love, so that in 1970, when Iris was 35 and Jaakko 41, Iris divorced her first husband and married Jaakko.

Their life together was a happy one. Jaakko had become an alcoholic before their marriage, and Iris helped him to drink less alcohol. Jaakko wished for children, but they had none before his untimely death.

On the evening of September 13, 1973, Jaakko was riding a municipal bus in Helsinki, and when it came to his stop he got off the bus. The bus driver, on a signal from the conductor, began driving the bus toward its next stop. Almost immediately, he sensed that the bus had run over something, and he stopped the bus. Jaakko's inert body was found lying under the rear of the bus behind one of the rear wheels. The bus had run over him. His trunk and legs were still under the rear part of the bus, and his head and shoulders were exterior to the bus's frame. The police report stated that: "On leaving the bus at the bus stop Mr. Vuorenlehto apparently stumbled and got under the right back wheel of the bus so that the wheel ran over his chest as well as his throat and the left side of his head."

A physician who came to the scene of the accident declared Jaakko dead, and his body was taken to the Institute of Medical Jurisprudence where a postmortem examination was made. According to the police report, this showed "that death was caused by a fracture of the bottom of the cranium and inner contusions."

The accident occurred shortly after 8:00 P.M. It was then dark in Helsinki, but the street was well illuminated and dry. Jaakko's blood alcohol was not measured, so there was no way of knowing whether alcohol contributed to his death. How and why he stumbled so as to fall under the wheel of the bus remains a mystery. He was 44 years old when he died.

Jaakko was a tall man. Iris Järvi said that he was 1.88 meters in height and weighed 86 kilograms. He was therefore both tall and slim. His movements were slow and clumsy.

Jaakko owned dogs when he was young. He liked nature and flowers, hunting and fishing. He was fond of horses, although he did not own any. He enjoyed driving cars and he played ice hockey. He occupied some of his leisure time with handicrafts. Some of his other activities were ones generally associated with women. For example, he liked to play with dolls, sewed tablecloths, and crocheted. He liked women's clothes and sometimes bought clothes for Iris. She thought that the way he moved was somewhat feminine. Jaakko, however, had never expressed a wish to change sex. He believed in reincarnation.

Events Between Jaakko's Death and Taru's Birth

A little more than a year after Jaakko's death, Iris married her third husband, Heikki Järvi. A year later, that is, in September 1975, Iris visited Jaakko's grave and while there heard his voice saying that he would be reborn as her child on May 27 and this time would be a girl. Iris was not pregnant then, and she did not expect to be, because she was 40 years old. Nevertheless, in October she did become pregnant and gave birth to Taru on May 27, 1976.

Comment. Although Iris did not believe that she would become pregnant again, she was receptive to the idea of reincarnation. She had been brought up in the Lutheran Church, but broke away from it when she was about 25 years old; later, when she married, she rejoined it. She began believing in reincarnation soon after her separation from the church.

Taru's Statements and a Recognition

Taru made few statements that directly expressed memories of Jaakko's life and death. All of her statements of which I learned occurred between the age of 1½ and 5. (As I mentioned, she was not quite 5 years old when I met her in March 1981.)

Her first statement probably occurred soon after she began to speak when she was about 1 year old. She said that she had been run over by a bus. When she was about 1½ years old, she rejected the name Taru and said: "I am not Taru; my name is Jaska." ("Jaska" was Jaakko's nickname.)

When she was about 3½, she said to Iris: "You are not my mother. I was left under a car and died. Don't you know?" A few days later Rita Castrén asked Taru: "Were you a girl or a boy when you died?" Taru replied: "Of course a boy, a big boy." Rita Castrén then asked her: "Was the car big or small?" Taru replied: "It was big. First died the stomach, then the head." On another occasion, Taru said: "I was taken to the hospital, but I was already dead by that time."

Once Taru said: "You do not have to be afraid of dying because I have died many times."* (In support of this last statement Taru once said that she had another mother called Senya in Germany.)

On several occasions Taru said: "I was a big man." Once she said: "Why am I so small? I would like to be bigger." Another time she said: "I was a big man. I have never been a small man."†

At times Taru seemed puzzled by the situation in which she found herself. Once she looked at Iris strangely and said: "Why should I have to choose you as my mother?"

Taru's only recognition of an object that belonged to Jaakko occurred when she said that a large toy car (that had been Jaakko's) was hers. She added: "I have played with it."

She did not say that a photograph of Jaakko was of her; but she did want to keep the photograph by her bed.

Taru's Behavior Related to the Previous Life

Circumstances and Manner of Taru's Speaking About the Previous Life. When I asked Iris whether Taru showed any unusual emotion when she spoke about the previous life, she replied: "She seems to be abstracted, like another person. It is as if she is away."

Taru's Phobia of Large Vehicles. When Taru was just about a year old, she showed a marked fear of buses, large automobiles, and tractors. At the age of (nearly) 5, when I met her, this phobia was persisting. If she was walking with Iris and a bus approached, she would ask Iris to pick her up. She did not react in this way when she saw small vehicles.

Taru's Play. Taru played with dolls, but she also played at games typically preferred by boys. For example, she liked to play with toy soldiers, sometimes wearing

---

*Other children subjects of these cases have reassured adults about the harmlessness of dying. Examples occurred in the cases of Marta Lorenz and Ma Than Than Aye.
†Other children have commented on and sometimes complained about their small physical size or a difference in sex from the life remembered. Examples occurred in the cases of Ramoo and Rajoo Sharma, Helmut Kraus, Muhittin Yılmaz, and Dulcina Karasek.

a helmet and carrying a gun. She played at pretending to drive a car. She asked to be given a gun and a hockey stick.

In playing with other children Taru would never accept a girl's role, saying insistingly: "I am a boy."

Taru's Preference for Clothes. Taru had a strong preference for boys' clothes. In this respect she differed markedly from her three older stepsisters, who had always preferred girls' clothes.

Taru's Preferences for Food. I learned of no unusual preferences for foods that Taru and Jaakko shared, with one possible exception. Jaakko had eaten fish, such as Baltic herring. Up to the age of 3 Taru ate Baltic herring, but then developed an aversion to fish.

Taru's Attitudes Toward Her Parents. Taru sometimes called Iris by her name, that is Iris, and sometimes called her "Mama." She was particularly attached to Iris.

In contrast, Taru had an aversion to her father, Heikki. She never called him "Papa," but only Heikki. Once, referring to Heikki, she told Iris: "He can go away and we can live together without him." Once she said to Heikki: "We do not need you. You should go away." Another time she said to him: "You are only a visitor here." Aware of his coming and going in the house, she still did not understand, even when I met her, that Heikki was a permanent member of the family. She would sometimes say to him: "Heikki, are you coming to us today?"

Physical Resemblances Between Jaakko and Taru

Iris believed that there were close resemblances in the faces and pigmentation of Jaakko and Taru. Jaakko's mother and also Rita Castrén (who had known Jaakko) concurred in this opinion.

According to Iris, Taru was slow and clumsy in her movements as Jaakko had been.

Taru was relatively tall for a woman; she was taller than her father. As I mentioned, Jaakko had been a tall man.

Taru's Later Development

Taru's aversion to Heikki was a significant factor in a partial separation between Iris and Heikki. Her attitude to Heikki had wounded him; she was his only child. He and Iris never formally separated, but found that life was more harmonious if they lived in separate houses during the cold seasons. In the summer, they lived together in a country cottage that they owned.

Taru had little interest in schooling and left school at the age of 15. She never trained for a skilled job. She did, however, train to be a taxi driver, and in 1999 she was working as one. Like Jaakko she was fond of horses, and she owned and managed a stable for boarding horses.

In 1999 Taru was 23 years old. Her mother said that she was "still masculine." As evidence of this Iris mentioned that Taru never wore any makeup and invariably dressed in pants. She had only one skirt. Nevertheless, in 1998 she married and wore a skirt for her wedding. Her husband was a carpenter and interior decorator.

Taru's phobia of vehicles continued until she was about 19 years old, and she then lost it. Iris said that Taru had a superstitious anxiety about the 13th day of the month, which was the day on which Jaakko had been run over and died.

As she grew up, Taru had become reconciled to her father. In fact, her relationship with him was much better than mere harmony; as he became older and frailer, she helped to take care of him as a devoted daughter should.

Comment

This is the third case I have investigated in which a child has claimed to be a deceased spouse of one of its parents. The other cases are those of Ma Tin Tin Myint and Asha Rani. In each case the child has shown a strong attachment to the parent who was the spouse and less attachment, indifference, or even antagonism to the other parent.

Like all same-family cases this one has the weakness that the subject and previous personality were members of the same family. We must also note the further defect of the expectation by the subject's mother that her deceased husband would be reborn as her child. Against this we can balance thoughts about how unusual it would be for a mother to damage her marriage by imposing the personality of a previous husband on the child of that marriage.

I greatly value the opportunities I have had to learn about the later course in life of some subjects I have known as young children. I find Taru's case particularly instructive. In her fondness for horses and her distaste for schooling, she resembled Jaakko. In young adulthood she accepted her anatomical sex and married; and yet she retained residues of masculinity. She overcame an early antagonism to her father and became affectionate toward him. She emerged from a phobia related to Jaakko's accidental death, but retained anxiety about its date in each month.

PAAVO SORSA

This is another case with few details that I have included to illustrate cases that are at the low range for the number of statements the subject made and related behavior that he showed. The subject and previous personality were half-siblings.

Summary of the Case and Its Investigation

Paavo Sorsa was born in Tampere, Finland, on June 24, 1991. His parents were Veikko Sorsa and his wife, Sylvi. Veikko was a mechanic and Sylvi was a part-time masseuse. Veikko and Sylvi later had a daughter, Leea; and Sylvi had had two other children by previous husbands. Of these the important one for this case was Kalevi Paasio, whose father (Risto Paasio) killed him when he was about 2½ years old.

After Kalevi's death Sylvi wished for him to be reborn as her child, although she did not expect this. After she and Veikko became companions, but before they were actually married, she had a vivid dream about Kalevi.

When Paavo was born, he seemed to have an impressive physical resemblance to Kalevi. He had no birthmark. Paavo began to speak clearly at the age of about 2; when he was 3 he made several statements suggesting memories of the life of Kalevi, of whom he would have heard nothing before he made such statements. He showed unusual behavior that also suggested memories of Kalevi's life and death.

Sylvi notified Rita Castrén about the case in late 1998, and Rita Castrén informed me about it soon afterward. On March 8, 1999, Sylvi Sorsa wrote a long letter to Rita Castrén about Paavo's statements and related behavior. Rita Castrén translated this into English and sent it to me.

In September 1999, I returned to Finland, partly to study this case and partly to learn about the further development of the other subjects of the Finnish cases in this volume. On September 22 Rita Castrén and I journeyed from Helsinki to Tampere (by train), and from there we went (by taxi) to the somewhat remote village of Mutala. We spent 4 hours with Sylvi before returning to Helsinki. We met and talked a little with Paavo and saw something of Sylvi's two other children. We did not meet Veikko Sorsa, who was working; and Sylvi remains the sole informant for the case.

The Life and Death of Kalevi Paasio

Kalevi Paasio was born in Tampere on December 11, 1987. His parents were Sylvi and her then husband, Risto Paasio. Kalevi was their only child. They lived in the village of Ylöjärvi, which is about 25 kilometers from Tampere. Risto was given to shouting and also to violence. In quarrels with Sylvi he sometimes beat her to the point where she complained about him to the police.

Kalevi witnessed his father's abuse of his mother. He himself was afraid of his father. This seems to have delayed his speaking. He did not begin speaking until an occasion when Risto was absent for 2 weeks. Kalevi then began to speak, but became silent again when his father returned. He was more than 2 years old by then.

Eventually Sylvi separated from Risto. Risto then obtained some custodial rights with Kalevi, who stayed with him on weekends. On one such weekend Risto took Kalevi with him to his father's home near Kurikka, a town which is about 130 kilometers northwest of Tampere. There he flew into a rage with Kalevi and killed him. There were no witnesses to this dreadful crime, but Risto after his arrest gave a fairly circumstantial account of how he had murdered his son. He first tried to asphyxiate the boy by exposing him to the fumes, laden with carbon monoxide, of the wood stove. Then he tried to prevent the child from breathing by stopping up his nose and mouth. He seems then to have relented for a time. The next day, however, he again tried to asphyxiate the boy and finally struck him on the head four times with a plank of wood. He broke Kalevi's skull, and the boy died of the associated damage to his brain. This tragedy occurred on May 11, 1990.

Risto was arrested and sentenced to prison. He later committed suicide while in prison.

Sylvi's Announcing Dream

A few months after Kalevi's death, but before she became pregnant with Paavo, Sylvi had a vivid dream about Risto and Kalevi. In the dream she heard the doorbell ring. She went to the door, opened it, and found Risto and Kalevi there. Risto disappeared, but Kalevi came in and sat on a window sill. Sylvi tried to touch him and found that her hand went through him.

This dream was so vivid and realistic that Sylvi was unsure whether she was dreaming or seeing discarnate persons while awake. She had never had a similar experience before.

At this time, although she and Veikko were living together, she had not become pregnant. She wanted to have another child and became pregnant with Paavo soon after she and Veikko married. Paavo was born a little more than 13 months after Kalevi's death.

Statements Made by Paavo

As I mentioned, Sylvi had lived with Risto in the village of Ylöjärvi. With Veikko she lived in a different village, Mutala, although this was still in the region of Tampere. The houses were quite different.

When Paavo was about 3, during a winter, he and Sylvi were outside while Paavo played with his sled. When they went back to the house, Paavo refused to go inside. He said that this house was not his and he wanted to go to "his own home." Sylvi tried to persuade him that this one was his home, but he insisted that it was not. The argument continued until Paavo finally became tired, and Sylvi was able to get him into the house, although he was still protesting that it was not his.

Paavo once found a photograph of Sylvi that showed some effects of a beating by Risto. The police had taken it as evidence after she had complained to them of being abused by Risto. When Paavo saw the photograph, he burst into tears and said to his mother: "Nobody will be allowed to beat you." Although the photograph obviously showed injuries to Sylvi's face, she had never spoken to Paavo about her life with Risto and had not mentioned the photograph to him. The facial injuries might have been accidental.

When Paavo saw photographs of Kalevi, he said they were photographs of himself. He could not understand that they were photographs of another child.

Paavo's Behavior Related to the Previous Life

During his first few years, Paavo suffered from frequent nightmares. In his sleep he would yell and seem to be struggling to push other people away from him. Sometimes while he was sleeping the skin around his lips turned blue and white. He never described in words the contents of his nightmares. They had ceased by 1999, when he was sleeping peacefully.

Sylvi had a harmonious relationship with Veikko, who was a quiet person not given to shouting as Risto had been. If, however, he happened to raise his voice a little because of some transient excitement, Paavo would intervene immediately and say: "Nobody shouts to Mom."

Other Relevant Behavior of Paavo

Paavo was strongly attached to his mother and wished to be with her as much as he could. In this respect he differed markedly from his stepsiblings. Rita Castrén and I observed this behavior when we spent 4 hours with Sylvi and Paavo in Mutala. Her other two children were present during part of this time.

Paavo had substantial motor and cognitive deficiencies. He was slow to learn at school and frequently forgot his assignments for homework. Sylvi helped him with this, and the school also arranged for him to have some additional instruction at the school. In September 1999 he was in the second grade of school. Although he was shy, he was not socially withdrawn and in no way troublesome at school. The administrators of the school nevertheless proposed to transfer him to another school, one for disruptive children, which Paavo was not. Sylvi was objecting to such a transfer.

Unlike Kalevi, Paavo had no difficulty in learning to speak. He did, however, show some lack of coordination in such physical activities as drawing, skating, skiing, and throwing a ball.

Paavo's psychological and motor limitations led to his being given some psychological tests by the school. Sylvi never received any formal report about these, but she was told that Paavo did not have dysphasia.

Comment. My observations in other cases of correspondences between wounds on a previous personality and birthmarks or birth defects on the subject led me to conjecture in this case that perhaps Paavo had some cerebral defect corresponding to the fatal brain injuries from which Kalevi had died. (He had no obvious externally visible defect.) This led me to suggest to Sylvi that she ask the responsible medical authorities of the area to arrange for Paavo to have a thorough neurological examination, which might include an examination of his brain with Magnetic Resonance Imagining (MRI). I have not learned whether Sylvi adopted my recommendation.

Physical Similarities Between Kalevi and Paavo

The physical similarities between Kalevi and Paavo stimulated some persons to mistakenly believe that they had the same father; they did not, but they did have the same mother.

Sylvi had brown hair and blue eyes. Both Kalevi and Paavo also had brown hair and blue eyes. Sylvi's other children, whom we met, both had light blond hair.

The Attitude of Sylvi Toward Paavo's Statements and Behavior

Sylvi believed in reincarnation, which is not unusual in Finland, where a survey in the 1990s showed that 34% of the inhabitants believe in reincarnation (Inglehart, Basañez, and Moreno, 1998). She also had a strong interest in alternative medicine and earned some money from medical cupping. Her beliefs made her receptive to the few statements in which Paavo referred to the life of Kalevi; but she gave no signs of embellishing the meager details of the case to make it appear stronger than it is.

SAMUEL HELANDER*

This is another case in which the subject and previous personality belonged to the same immediate family. The subject remembered the life of his mother's stepbrother. The case is unusual among European cases for the abundance of its details—an announcing dream, statements, recognitions, and behavioral memories.

Summary of the Case and Its Investigation

Samuel Helander was born in Helsinki, Finland, on April 15, 1976. His parents were Pentti Helander and his wife, Marja. Samuel was the second of their two children. His sister, Sandra, was 2½ years older. Pentti was a construction worker, who operated a crane. Marja was a member of the Lutheran Church; I did not learn the religious affiliations of other members of the family.

About 10 months before Samuel's birth, Marja's stepbrother, Pertti Häikiö, had died unexpectedly. Marja became pregnant soon afterward and contemplated having an abortion. Then she had a dream in which Pertti came to her and said: "Keep that child." She let the pregnancy continue.†

Samuel began to speak when he was about 1 year old, and when he was about

---

*I published a summary of this case in an earlier book (Stevenson, 1987/2001).

†In two other cases a deceased person whose life the subject remembered communicated to the subject's mother a wish that she not have a contemplated abortion. In the case of Huriye Bugay the communication came during a mediumistic session; in that of Rajani Sukla it came in a dream.

1½ years old, he began to speak about the life of Pertti. His statements were not abundant, and about half of them occurred when a person, photograph, or other object stimulated his memories. He continued to refer to the life of Pertti up to the time of my second meeting with his mother, which occurred in March 1981, when Samuel was 5 years old.

I first learned about this case in September 1978 in a letter from Rita Castrén. Later that year I went to Helsinki and on December 2 had a long interview with Samuel's mother, Marja Helander. I met Samuel, but I have no record that he said anything to me, and I cannot say that I interviewed him. (He was then only 2½ years old.) In 1981 I returned to Helsinki and on March 8 had another interview with Marja Helander. On March 20 I interviewed Marja's (and Pertti's) mother, Anneli Lagerqvist. For my interviews with Marja Helander, Rita Castrén was my interpreter; for that with Anneli Lagerqvist, R. J. Milton interpreted.

I obtained some additional information in correspondence with Rita Castrén and from an interview with Marja Helander conducted by a Finnish journalist, Oskar Reponen.

In September 1984 Rita Castrén obtained and sent me some information about Samuel's development up to that time, when he was 8 years old.

In the autumn of 1999 I was again in Helsinki and had another long interview with Marja Helander. She clarified a few details and gave me information about Samuel's further development. He was then 23 years old. He himself was detained by the need to care for his younger brother, who was ill; thus I did not meet him.

The Life and Death of Pertti Häikiö

Pertti Häikiö was born in Helsinki on June 3, 1957. His parents were Pentti Häikiö and his wife, Anneli. Pertti had two older sisters, Marja (Helander) and Pirjo, and a younger sister, Anne, was born after Pertti. His parents divorced in 1969, and Anneli later married Reiner Lagerqvist.

Pertti seems to have undergone an unusually large number of accidents during his short life. When he was 3, he slipped from his mother's arms and fell into a bathtub full of water, almost drowning. When he was 4, he was standing near some construction when some heavy object fell on him breaking one leg and injuring the other. Following this injury, he spent 5 months in a hospital with casts on his legs, but he eventually recovered completely. A little later, when he was still less than 5 years old, a dog bit him severely. At some time — I did not learn how old he was — he injured his back and had to be admitted to a hospital for its treatment. When he was 15, he fell off a quay on the water at Helsinki. The water was to some extent frozen and he landed on ice; but the ice gave way under his weight, and he almost drowned. He managed to take off some of his clothes and his shoes. He got himself out of the water and returned home in his underclothes. After that he had a phobia of being immersed in water.

Two or three years later he left school and took a job with a company that required medical examinations of its employees. I did not learn the results of this medical examination, but Pertti soon left the company, possibly because he failed the medical examination. He was then observed to be drinking a great deal of water, and after his death it was conjectured that he had developed diabetes mellitus. At this time he was also drinking alcohol excessively. He died quite unexpectedly and suddenly on June 10, 1975. He was 18 years old at the time.

Pertti's mother and stepfather had gone on a cruise just a few days before his death. He had seen them off at the train station. On the day of his death his mother, Anneli Lagerqvist, was lying in her cabin bunk when she suddenly saw before her the figure of her deceased father. The appearing figure did not speak, but nodded. Anneli began to cry and told her husband that the apparition meant that someone in the family had died. Reiner Lagerqvist told her this was nonsense, but he already knew that Pertti had died. A radio communication about Pertti's death had been sent to the ship, but Reiner had not told Anneli because he was afraid she would have a severe reaction to this news, and there was no physician on the ship.

Pertti was musical, and he owned and played a guitar. He was an unusually affectionate person. He was especially attached to his mother and to his older sister, Marja. Although he was younger than Marja, he had to some extent assumed with her the role of a supportive older brother.

Statements and Recognitions Made by Samuel

Samuel's first utterance suggestive of memories of the life of Pertti occurred when he was about 1½ years old and was asked his name. He replied: "Peltti." (He could not pronounce the "r" in Pertti.) Samuel also at times said that he was "Pera," which had been Pertti's nickname.* At this time Samuel called his mother "Marja" and his maternal grandmother (Anneli Lagerqvist) "Mother." He told Marja that she was not his mother. Similarly, he sometimes called Pentti Helander "Pentti" and sometimes called him "Daddy."†

When he was about 2, Samuel saw a photograph taken of Pertti when he was in the hospital after his leg was broken. He said: "That is me when my legs were ill." (He did not say "broken.")

When Samuel was about 2½, he unexpectedly said: "Now Ludi has come to me." He made this statement on the day that Pertti's great aunt Lydia died. ("Ludi" was her short name.) Samuel was aware that Lydia was ill and might have thought she was dying. His remark impressed Marja, however, because Lydia had bought a tomb, intended for herself, shortly before Pertti died, and Pertti had been buried in it as was Lydia herself later.

---

*Examples of other subjects who asked to be called by the previous personality's name occurred in the cases of Ismail Altınkılıç, Cemil Fahrici, and Chaokhun Rajsuthajarn.

†Examples of other subjects of same-family cases who addressed the older members of their family by proper names instead of generic names occurred in the cases of Thiang San Kla, Maung Htay Win, Chaokhun Rajsuthajarn, and Taru Järvi.

When Samuel was between 3 and 4 years old, he was looking through an album of family photographs and came to one of Pertti that was also taken when Pertti was in the hospital. This one showed Pertti in a walker, after the plaster had been taken off his legs. Samuel, speaking to Anneli, said: "Mother, here I am in this picture." Then he said that his legs had both been in plaster and that he had been in the hospital. No one had asked Samuel about this photograph; he had been looking at the album himself, came across this photograph, and then brought the album to Anneli to show her. I believe, but am not certain, that this photograph was different from the one Samuel had recognized when he was 2 years old.

When Samuel was shown photographs of Pertti as he was up to the age of about 10, he would say: "That's me." When he saw photographs of Pertti at ages older than 10, he said nothing. On one occasion when he was looking at the album of photographs, he spontaneously said: "I remember when the dog bit my leg." He also spoke at other times of how the dog had bit him and how much it had hurt.

In about April 1979, when Samuel was barely 3 years old, he said that he had hurt his back and was taken to the hospital in an ambulance.

That same month Samuel made his most detailed statement. He recalled how a long time ago he had gone to a "kiska" (his way of pronouncing "kiosk") with his father. They wore hats, his a blue one, his father's a pale one. They also brought a guitar. One man carried a gun. The house near the kiosk caught on fire and they had to leave. All this, Marja told Rita Castrén, corresponded to an event that took place in 1974, about a year before Pertti's death. A friend had organized a party which was to be held in a small house near a kiosk by the railway. The attic of the house caught fire and the party broke up. (Marja did not say whether Samuel had been correct about the colors of the hats.)

Samuel did not always identify Marja as a sister and Anneli as his mother. On one occasion when he saw a photograph of Pentti Häikiö and Anneli, he said: "There is Daddy and Grandma also." Marja tried to mislead Samuel by saying he was wrong in his identifications, but he repeated what he had said. The important point of this recognition is that Samuel had never seen Pertti's father, Pentti Häikiö.

Looking at a photograph of Pentti Häikiö, Samuel said: "This is my father." Marja and Anneli attached importance to Samuel's recognition of photographs of Pentti Häikiö, because Anneli's second husband, Reiner Lagerqvist, was jealous of Pentti, and Anneli did not openly display photographs of him, where they would trouble Reiner.

Pertti had owned and played a guitar. After his death it had been put in a box that was kept in a cupboard. No one had spoken to Samuel about the guitar, but he looked for it, found it, and said that it was his.

After Pertti's death, all his clothes were destroyed, except for a corduroy jacket, which was kept in a cupboard. One day Anneli and Marja opened the cupboard and discussed (in front of Samuel) giving the jacket away. Samuel, shouting, said it was his and they should not give it away. Because it is possible — although they did not say this — that Anneli and Marja had referred to the jacket as having belonged to Pertti, we should not credit Samuel with having recognized it. We may, however, attach importance to his loud insistence that the jacket was his and should be kept. This incident occurred when Samuel was about 3 years old.

Pertti had owned a watch that was broken and handless. After his death Anneli had put it in a drawer that contained a lot of "junk." One day Anneli opened the drawer while Samuel was with her. He saw the watch, pounced on it, and said it was his. After taking possession of the watch, he kept it either under his pillow or in a drawer beneath his bed.*

Anneli took Samuel with her on a visit to the cemetery where Pertti had been buried. Looking at Pertti's grave, Samuel said, several times: "That is my grave." On another occasion, when Marja was taking Samuel to the cemetery, Samuel said: "Now we are going to my grave."

Samuel's Statements About Events After Pertti's Death and Before His Birth. Samuel commented on how much Pertti's mother (Samuel's maternal grandmother, Anneli) cried for him. (This was a reference to Anneli's grief after Pertti's death.)

Samuel also said that he had been taken to a place where there were a lot of coffins, some of them open. This was correct for Pertti, whose body had been taken to a mortuary after he died suddenly.

Samuel's Behavior Related to the Previous Life

Circumstances and Manner of Samuel's Speaking About the Previous Life. As I mentioned earlier, most of Samuel's statements appeared to be stimulated by some person, photograph, or other object related to Pertti. He did, however, make a number of statements that seemed to be completely spontaneous expressions of memories. They also, however, may have received some stimulus not noticed by Marja or Anneli.

Sometimes Samuel was heard to speak to himself and say: "Oh, that poor fellow who died." Marja assumed that in saying this, Samuel was remembering Pertti's death.

Samuel's Phobia of Water. When he was young, Samuel had a marked phobia of being bathed. Marja described him as becoming "panic-stricken" when he was bathed. He was even afraid of a shower bath.

Samuel's Attitudes Toward His Mother and Grandmother. I have already mentioned Samuel's early tendency to call Marja by her name and to call Anneli "Mother." He was particularly attached to Anneli. On one occasion, when he was about 2 years old and had already been weaned, he sat on Anneli's lap and tried to nurse at her breast. He said: "Mother, give me your breast."

---

*In the case of William George, Jr., a Tlingit of Alaska, the subject recognized a watch that had belonged to the previous personality and showed a possessiveness toward the watch that was similar to Samuel's attitude toward Pertti's watch.

Samuel's Gait and Posture. Pertti had had the habit of standing with one foot forward and often with a hand on his hip. He also walked with his hands behind his back when he was nervous. Samuel was noticed to adopt the same posture and the same way of walking with his hands behind his back. Marja did not have these habits.*

Other Behavior of Samuel Related to the Previous Life. Pertti had an endearing habit at Christmas, when the family were gathered together, of going around the room and kissing each member in turn. At the Christmas of 1978, when Samuel was 2½ years old, he went around the room where the family members were sitting, took each member by the arm, and kissed them on the cheek. This seemed to imitate exactly Pertti's customary behavior at Christmas.

In general, Samuel was an unusually affectionate person, as Pertti had been.

Instances of Apparent Telepathy by Samuel

One day Anneli was looking at photographs of family tombs and weeping. Just then Marja telephoned her and said Samuel had just said to her (Marja): "Little grandmother is weeping. Tell her not to cry." (In this reference Samuel referred to Anneli as "little grandmother," not as "Mother" or "Mummy" as he sometimes did.

On several occasions Samuel was outside playing in the courtyard, when Marja decided to go shopping. Samuel unexpectedly came into the house, apparently wishing to accompany her. Marja believed a telepathic connection had stimulated Samuel to come into the house.

Physical Resemblances Between Samuel and Pertti

Marja believed that Samuel's physique resembled Pertti's and that their smiles were similar. I failed to ask Anneli whether she agreed with Marja in this appraisal. It has, however, little significance because of the possibility of a genetic factor in the resemblance.

Samuel's Later Development

In September 1984 Rita Castrén met again with Marja Helander to learn about Samuel's further development. He was 8 years old and in the second grade of school. Marja thought he still had some memories of the previous life, but they had faded.

In 1999 Samuel was 23 years old. He attended school to the age of 16, but did not go to college. He was working for a moving company. He was in good health.

*In my monograph on cases with birthmarks and birth defects (Stevenson, 1997), I devoted a chapter to "Physiques, Postures, Gestures, and Other Involuntary Movements Related to Previous Lives."

Although unmarried, he had decided to leave his mother's home and live elsewhere in an apartment. (His father, Pentti Helander, had committed suicide in 1986.)

Samuel still had a phobia of water and did not swim. He also had a fear of dying young as Pertti had. This fear came on in "attacks," which passed off and later returned.

Marja said that Samuel never talked about the previous life. She had noticed, however, that when he came to visit her and thought no one was watching him, he would look for a long time at a photograph of Pertti that she had kept in her house.

Comment

I think it important to mention again the weakness of same-family cases in which, with rare exceptions, all the subject's statements refer to events, objects, or persons well known to the family members who are our informants for the cases. The possibility of an unwitting normal transmission of information to the subject becomes increased when someone in the family, Samuel's mother in this case, expects the previous personality to be reborn. The cases of this type do, however, have the advantage that the informants for the subject's behavior can immediately judge its relevance to the life of the previous personality.

Marja acknowledged that she had become convinced Samuel was the reincarnation of Pertti to the point where she sometimes unthinkingly called him "Pertti." (He always responded.) Marja knew that this was perhaps unwise. We should credit her with awareness of the influence of her conviction that Pertti had returned to her as Samuel.

TEUVO KOIVISTO

Summary of the Case and Its Investigation

Teuvo Koivisto was born in Helsinki, Finland, on August 20, 1971. His parents were Jan Koivisto and his wife, Lusa. Teuvo was the youngest of their four children, all boys. Jan Koivisto was a businessman. The recent family ancestry was largely Finnish. More remotely the family had origins in Germany and Hungary. One of Lusa's great-grandmothers had come from Poland. One of Lusa's great-great grandmothers was a Jew.

The Koivistos belonged to the Lutheran Church. Lusa Koivisto had, when she was 16 years old, the experience of seeming to remember a previous life in France at the time of the French Revolution. This had no verifiable elements and neither did another, vaguer apparent memory of a previous life, this one in Tibet. These experiences prepared Lusa to listen attentively when Teuvo spoke about a previous life.

During her pregnancy with Teuvo, Lusa had two dreams at least one of which we could regard as an announcing dream.

Teuvo was healthy when born, but he early showed a phobia of the dark, so that his parents left on a light where he slept at night. He began to speak when he was about 1½ years old. He spoke sentences when he was about 2, but did not speak fluently until he was 3. At about that age he surprised his mother by describing in considerable detail what it was like to be in a concentration camp and put to death with gas there. (Teuvo did not use the phrase "concentration camp," but his statements undoubtedly referred to one.)

At about the time he described the experience of being in a concentration camp, he began to have episodes of difficulty breathing. (Possibly they had occurred earlier, and his mother only noticed them when he was 3 years old.)

Rita Castrén learned of this case in early 1976, when Teuvo was about 4½ years old. She interviewed Lusa Koivisto on February 2, 1976, and sent me notes of the interview. Almost 3 years later I interviewed Lusa on December 1, 1978. Both these interviews took place in Helsinki. I did not meet Jan Koivisto; Lusa said that Teuvo had never spoken to him about his (Teuvo's) memories.

In the autumn of 1999 I visited Finland again. On this occasion I was unable to meet Lusa Koivisto, but Rita Castrén talked with her twice on the telephone and obtained some additional information about Teuvo's childhood and later development. On September 25 I met Teuvo (in Helsinki) and had a long interview with him.

Lusa Koivisto's Dreams During Her Pregnancy with Teuvo

The first of these dreams may have occurred when Lusa was half asleep and half awake. She seemed to be standing in a line of prisoners; the scene suggested some place in the Near East to her. As the line of prisoners was moving forward, someone said to Lusa: "Take shelter under the straw." She then escaped from the line of prisoners and found herself with a man who had a copy of the Cabbala. There were men there who were shooting. One man said: "The baby you are expecting is a Jew, and I will save your life." That experience then ended.

The second dream had less obvious relevance to Teuvo's birth. Lusa found herself in a tent lined with red velvet. In it was a "wise old man" who had a telescope. He pointed out a bright light, which was becoming larger. The old man said the light was bright because of the conjunction of three planets. He pointed to the light and said: "That is your light." (Lusa said that she learned that on the day of Teuvo's birth a conjunction of Mars and Venus had occurred.)

Teuvo's Statements About the Previous Life

In this section I have drawn on Rita Castrén's interview of 1976 and mine of 1978. Lusa's accounts on these two occasions did not differ in essentials, although each included details not mentioned in the other account.

Lusa remembered that Teuvo told her that he had been alive before. Then he referred to "the big furnace." He gave some details about the furnace. He mentioned that the people were piled higgledy-piggledy in layers in the furnace. Some were lying on top of others. He said that he had been taken to the "bathroom." Personal objects were removed from the people in the bathroom, such as their eyeglasses and their golden teeth. Then the people were undressed and put into the furnace. Gas came pouring out of some place in the walls. He could not breathe. Teuvo said that he "knew" that he was going to be put in the furnace, but he did not say that he had actually been put in the furnace. He said that he came to his mother after seeing the others being put there. Teuvo also described an "oven" with children in it.

After Teuvo had made these statements, he added: "Then I came to you. I was given here. Are you happy, Mummy, that I came to you?"

Some time after Teuvo made his first statements about the previous life to his mother, he said: "I was caught by the barbed wire. Come and get me off." He seemed depressed at this time.

Teuvo's Behavior Related to the Previous Life

Circumstances and Manner of Teuvo's Speaking About the Previous Life. Teuvo made his first statements about the previous life one morning after he awakened. Although he was just beginning then — at about the age of 3 — to speak fluently, he surprised his mother by the extent of the vocabulary he used to describe the experience he seemed to remember. Even so, he did not have an adequate vocabulary for what he wished to say, and used his hands to show the shape of the furnaces.

Lusa described Teuvo as "extremely frightened" and "terrified" as he described the experiences he remembered. He was so disturbed that she tried to distract him by telling him a fairy-tale.

In 1976 Lusa told Rita Castrén that Teuvo often repeated his first statements, always when he awoke in the morning. She said he continued to speak about the memories for about half a year. In 1978, Lusa had forgotten the later statements and remembered only Teuvo's first statements when he was about 3 years old. She did not then remember his having repeated his statements or some of them.

Teuvo's Phobia of the Dark. Teuvo remained afraid of being in the dark until he was 7 years old. He then lost the phobia.

Teuvo's Hiding Behavior. As a young child Teuvo often could not be found because he had hidden himself. He sometimes knocked down walls separating rooms. In the house where the family then lived the walls were extremely thin so that an older child could break through them.

Other Relevant Behavior of Teuvo

Teuvo sometimes played at being a soldier. Lusa believed such play imitated that of his next older brother, who was 8 years older than Teuvo.

Up to the age of 2 Teuvo did not wish to wear clothes, even when he went outside in the cold weather.

Unlike David Llewelyn, Teuvo showed no behavior that we might consider typically Jewish.

Teuvo's Difficulty in Breathing

At the time Teuvo first described his memories, he developed difficulty in breathing. He seemed not to inhale comfortably. It seemed painful for him to breathe. The breathing difficulty occurred irregularly, sometimes twice a week and then not again for 3 months. The attacks lasted 10–15 minutes. A physician whom Lusa consulted said Teuvo did not have asthma. This symptom was still present in 1978 at the time I interviewed Lusa.

Apart from his episodic difficulty in breathing, Teuvo had excellent health.

The Possibilities for Teuvo to Have Learned Normally About Concentration Camps

Lusa declared firmly that Teuvo could not have acquired the information he had about German concentration camps normally. He was rarely allowed to watch television and never any program showing violence. His parents and his older brothers never discussed such matters as concentration camps and gas chambers in the presence of Teuvo. At the time Teuvo talked of the previous life the family lived in their own house. They had neighbors, but did not have any social relationships with them. Teuvo was shy then and never talked with the neighbors. No grandparents were living with the immediate family.

Finland's Experience with Germans During World War II

During World War II Finland allied itself with Germany in its war with Russia. The Finnish leaders hoped that a German victory would enable Finland to recover some of the territory it had ceded to Russia at the end of the Finnish-Russian War of 1939-40. At the same time, the Finnish government limited its collaboration with Germany. It did not participate in the German siege of Leningrad (Häikiö, 1992). And it resisted German demands for the return to Germany of Jewish refugees from Nazi persecution. Histories and memoirists later disagreed as to the number of Jewish refugees in Finland that were delivered to the Germans (Lundin, 1957). It was certainly not more than 50 and may have been as few as four; the smaller number were persons who had broken Finnish laws while in Finland. Rautkallio (1987) asserted that no Jewish refugees in Finland had been surrendered to the Germans.

Finland had a small population of Jews who were Finnish citizens, not refugees from Central Europe. In 1941, Reinhard Heydrich, deputy chief of the Nazi Gestapo, developed a list—that can only have been estimates—of the Jews in different European countries. In his "census" Finland had only 2,300 Jews (Gilbert, 1986). The Germans had few troops in Finland and almost certainly removed no Jews other than a small number of refugees. Finnish people who were not Jews could for various reasons be sent to concentration camps. A small number of people from Finland were found still alive at Dachau when it was liberated on April 30, 1945 (Smith, 1995).

Absence of Connections of the Koivistos with Jewish People

The Koivistos had no social connection with Jewish people. During the years of the collaboration of Finland with Germany (1940–44), Lusa's family lived in an apartment building in which there were also some Jewish tenants. Lusa did not know whether the Germans had removed any of these Jewish neighbors and sent them to concentration camps. (From the sources I cited in the preceding section this seems most improbable.)

Correspondences Between Teuvo's Statements and Features of German Concentration Camps

The details that Teuvo mentioned certainly correspond to those of the concentration camps: barbed wire, seizure of personal property, forced undressing of the victims, the pretense by the Germans that the gas chambers were "bathrooms" (even with signs so saying), death from poison gas, and burning of the victim's bodies in furnaces (sometimes open or pit fires).

It is also true that the Germans removed the gold teeth of the killed prisoners. They did this, however, after they had gassed the prisoners and before they burned their bodies in the furnaces or fires. At Treblinka children were sometimes thrown onto fire pits while still alive (Donat, 1979). At Auschwitz also children and sometimes women were thrown alive into fire pits (Kraus and Kulka, 1966).

Teuvo's mention of the difficulty the prisoners had in breathing when they were being gassed receives confirmation from the eyewitness account of Dr. Miklos Nyiszli (Nyiszli, 1960/1993). Dr. Nyiszli, a Jewish physician of Hungary, was arrested in April 1944 and sent to Auschwitz. There, the infamous Dr. Josef Mengele selected him to assist him in his medical experiments. Nyiszli thus became a member of the *Sonderkommando* of the camp, which was comprised of prisoners with education and skills who could be helpful to the *Schutzstaffel* (SS) who controlled the concentration camps. Most members of the *Sonderkommando* were themselves killed (in order to suppress evidence of the crimes), but Nyiszli survived and wrote a detailed account of the procedure of the Germans in killing the prisoners in the concentration camps. The gas used for killing at Auschwitz was a volatile preparation of hydrogen cyanide (Zyklon-B), which killed within 5 to 15 minutes. The prisoners were forced into a room where they were told to undress and leave all their clothing (for later use by the Germans). This room had signs indicating it was a bathroom. They were then crowded into a second room where there were no hangers for clothes or benches, but upright pipes rising from the floor and having holes in their sides. The doors were then closed and the material for the gas was released from containers. It was poured down the pipes to the room below and the gas then escaped through the holes in the upright pipes and quickly began to poison the people in the death chamber. "The gas first inundated the lower layers of air and rose but slowly toward the ceiling. This forced the victims to trample one another in a frantic attempt to escape the gas" (Nyiszli, 1993, p. 52). After the prisoners were all dead, their bodies were hauled out of the death chamber, despoiled of any gold teeth they had, and then pushed into the crematoria whose huge furnaces dispelled through chimneys the smoke and odor of burning flesh.

Nyiszli included in this account graphic details of how the bodies of the prisoners killed with gas were piled on top of each other. Other authors have described the piling up of bodies at other death camps, such as Treblinka (Donat, 1979) and Dachau (Smith, 1995).

Barbed wire encircled the concentration camps. The high outer wire of the camp conducted a lethal electric current of high voltage that immediately killed anyone coming in contact with it. No one could be taken off such barbed wire alive; but this could have happened if someone had become entangled in barbed wire that was not electrified. At a huge camp like that at Auschwitz unelectrified barbed wire separated different sections of the camp. The jackets of three books on the concentration camps have barbed wire on their covers (Donat, 1979; Gill, 1988; Smith, 1995); barbed wire became a symbol for the horror of the camps.

Children arriving at the death camps went straight to the gas chambers or fire pits. Like the old, they were considered unable to work and therefore useless. The age of not being killed for being a child was generally 14 (Gill, 1988).

Teuvo's "hiding behavior" may correspond with conditions in the Warsaw ghetto before the Jewish revolt of 1943. The breaking down of walls featured prominently in the plans of the Jews to be able to move themselves, their possessions, and their supplies according to circumstances as the revolt developed. Donat wrote:

> Besides building shelters, people were also frantically making passageways between rooms, apartments, staircases, cellars, and attics, thereby linking houses until eventually we could move around an entire residential block without once going into the street [p. 96].

Comment. Teuvo's account (or perhaps Lusa's memory of his account) condensed some of the events in the procedure of killing the prisoners. Their personal objects, like spectacles, were taken from them before they were gassed; but they were gassed before their golden teeth were taken. They had usually died before being put in the furnaces. Nevertheless, the details, even though somewhat jumbled, are all remarkably correct.

From the foregoing it does not follow that the life Teuvo seemed to remember had ended in Auschwitz or the adjoining camp at Birkenau. The Germans used similar methods of killing prisoners in other camps, such as at Treblinka and Sobibor (Gill, 1988). Prisoners at these camps were also killed with gas, but not with Zyklon. They were gassed with carbon monoxide in the exhaust fumes of gasoline engines. At Dachau both carbon monoxide and hydrogen cyanide were used for killing prisoners (Smith, 1995).

Teuvo's Later Development

After completing some years of high school, Teuvo attended a business school from which he graduated. For a vocation, however, he chose music, and in 1999 he was working as a professional musician and teaching music.

He said that the difficulty he had in breathing when he was a young child had ceased by the time he began school at about the age of 5.

In 1997 Teuvo married, and by 1999 he and his wife had a 2-year old son.

At the time when I talked with him on September 25, 1999, Teuvo had no imaged memories of the previous life. He did, however, remember his "hiding behavior," which, he said, lasted at least until the age of 13 or 14. He remembered that from his earliest years he always wanted to feel safe. He was dissatisfied with his present residence, because it had no hiding place.

Teuvo said he felt anxiety when he saw Nazi uniforms or the Nazi flag (swastika). He would sometime stand still with fear when he saw these. He had no fear when he saw the flags of Great Britain or France.

Teuvo was much interested in religions, but had no special attraction to Judaism. He believed in reincarnation, but thought it incompatible with Christianity.

Comment

The statements of Teuvo and those of David Llewelyn both described features of German concentration camps; but each remembered different details. They may have remembered lives and deaths at different camps. Alternatively, different features of the same camp may have impressed the minds of the two persons whose memories David and Teuvo later had.

CASE REPORTS: RECURRENT OR VIVID DREAMS

Jenny McLeod

Earlier in this book I described Jenny McLeod's statements about the life of her great-grandmother. These occurred when she was still an infant, barely 2 years old. At a later age, still in childhood, Jenny had a series of recurrent dreams that I now describe and discuss.

Jenny's Recurrent Dreams About the Battle of Culloden

Between the ages of 7 and 8 — which would be in 1956 to 1957 — Jenny began to have the same recurrent dream. The dream never varied in content, but sometimes Jenny would awaken before the dream had reached the final point that occurred in some of the dreams. She did not describe the dream as vivid. The frequency of the dream varied. For some periods she had it as often as every second night for a week and then would not have another dream for months. She continued to have this dream until the age of 13 or 14. When I met her in October 1967, she was not quite 18 years old and said that she had not had the dream for about 4 years.

The following description of the dream derives from the notes I made of what Jenny told me in October 1967, when I met her in Aberdeen. To make for easier reading I have added a few explanatory words and phrases in brackets.

> [I was] lying in a field. At the side [I] could see my body. To my right was a gate, not a modern gate but one made with silver birch trees. It was broken. Various people, not more than four, [were] coming up over a hill and toward me. They were dressed in very dark olive green. [Their] caps were of perhaps the same material. Not clearly seen. They were [all] dressed [in] the same [way]. [Here Jenny interpolated to say that she did not recognize the uniform these men wore.] I thought they were going to do something evil. They came up to me. I pretended to be wounded. Somebody was going to stick a sword into me, but didn't. They left me. As they approached [me], they stopped and hacked at other people. They seemed to have rather short flat swords.
>
> In the dream I was older [than her age when the dreams began]. I was not 7 [then], but seemed to have the mind of a 14-year old. I seemed to have a larger body, but not a full adult's body. I was wearing a red kilt,* but had short hair. [I am] not sure [I] was a girl or a boy. Four or five other people were killed before they got to me.
>
> I waited until they had gone. I got cold and it was getting dark. I was terrified of being left alone. I moved my head [first] and [then] got up. There was some howling —

---

*The Camerons, the Macintoshes, and the Frasers, who had important contingents on the side of the Stuarts at the Battle of Culloden, wore red tartans (Moncreiffe and Hicks, 1967).

people crying. I tried to get through the gate. It would not move. I tried to shut it. I ran in a crouched position. I came to a big wall. I found this was part of the back wall of a house. There was an old lady there. I asked her to help, and she refused — to help me get away. Then I began to run, crying. At that part I normally woke up.

During a further discussion, Jenny added a few more details about the dream. She said that in the dream she felt herself to be running and also saw herself running (as from another viewpoint). She thought the kilt she (the youth of the dream) was wearing was a Stuart* one. As a child she herself had worn kilts. She had a Macpherson one and a Fraser one. The kilt worn in the dream was shorter than the ones she had worn as a child. It was ragged, ripped, and filthy.

Of the scenery in the dream she remembered that there were no trees. The grass was a coarse yellow, not green. There was heather on the hills. "There was one big hill that seemed to be covered with heather with wee ridges of this grass stuff."

Between the ages of 10 and 14 Jenny had another recurrent dream. In that dream she was at the top of a house that was on fire, and she had no way of escape.† She would run from place to place trying to escape and wake up screaming. Jenny had had a fascination with fire when younger, but her mother strictly forbade her to play with matches, and Jenny thought her dream about fire might have derived from her mother's strictness concerning the danger of fire.

Jenny's dreams did not include any direct reference to Culloden. They might have referred to some other battle. In correspondence I asked her when and how she connected her dreams with the Battle of Culloden. She replied (in a letter dated January 23, 1968) as follows:

> The first mention I can recall of Culloden was when I was in Primary [Grade] 7 in school, and then I was only given the bare historical facts of the battle, e.g., who was fighting who and why, by the teacher. Perhaps it was as a result of the proximity of the battlefield and my childish imagination fixed upon its being Culloden. Also, I think it may have been because of the kilts etc. in my dream which induced me to think that it *must* be Culloden. I apologize for not being able to give further information on this matter, but I've considered the question and so far have been unable to find a solution!

Jenny's Normal Knowledge of the Battle of Culloden and Its Aftermath

The Battle of Culloden was fought near Inverness on April 16, 1746. The occasion was the last stand of a small Jacobite Army led by Prince Charles Edward Stuart, the

---

At least one of the Stuart tartans is also red (Moncreiffe and Hicks, 1967).

†Taylor (1965) wrote: "Many of the wounded and fleeing [after the Battle of Culloden] had hidden in turf bothies [huts] or outbuildings on various parts of the moor and its surroundings. One of these is believed to have been the barn outside old Leanach cottage. Over thirty men, who must have broken through the Hanoverian lines during the battle, were found there 48 hours after, on Friday. Instead of merely shooting the survivors out of hand, the soldiers were ordered to barricade up the barn, and set fire to it. The thirty, who included officers and wounded, perished cruelly in the flames" [p. 45].

"Young Pretender" to the throne of Great Britain, and Lord George Murray. They were utterly defeated by a well-trained Hanoverian Army commanded by the Duke of Cumberland.

Margaret McLeod (Jenny's mother) said that she and her husband had an interest in history, but she was certain that there had been no mention of the Battle of Culloden in the family before Jenny began describing her dreams. Jenny herself told the Reverend W. H. S. Muir that she first learned about the battle (normally, that is) when she was about 11 or 12 and in the 7th grade of school. At this time Jenny "knew" (from her recurrent dream) that many people were killed after the battle, although neither the history text nor her teacher mentioned this.* In talking with me a few months after she had talked with the Reverend Muir, Jenny said that she did not learn (normally) about the slaughter after the battle until she was 14 or 15.

Jenny also did not verify another detail of her dream until the same age. This is that youths were engaged in the Jacobite Army. The Scottish History Society published *The Prisoners of the Forty-five,"* which gave the names of 3,300 prisoners, including a large number of youths and even children. I have not examined this work myself, but Col. I. C. Taylor copied out for me a list of 28 such youthful prisoners. Their ages ranged between 8 and 15, but the majority were between 13 and 14 years old (Seton and Arnot, 1928, cited by Taylor in correspondence). Some were pardoned, others transported. I did not ask Jenny and she did not mention how she had learned about the engagement of youths in the Jacobite Army. She had certainly not made any intense effort to study the battle, and up to the time I met her she had not even gone to visit the battlefield.

Jenny had not verified another detail in her dream, even at the time of our meeting in 1967. This is the color of the uniform of the soldiers who were killing the wounded and fleeing Jacobites after the battle. Jenny described their uniforms as "very dark olive green." Although most of the Scottish Highlanders supported the Stuart cause, some did not: "All in all there were actually more Scots in arms on the government side than on the Jacobite side" (Mackie, 1930/1962, p. 248). The Campbells furnished a regiment of militia that fought on the Hanoverian side. Further, as the battle ended, the Campbells climbed a wall on the right flank of the Jacobite Army and attacked them as they retreated. In a letter to me dated December 5, 1967, Col. I. C. Taylor wrote: "It is generally assumed that the early Campbell tartan or, more likely, Argyll district tartan was of sombre hues, i.e., dark blues and greens, and these colours, of course with weathering would turn to a drab olive colour."

---

*Jenny was 11 or 12 in 1960-61. At that time the textbooks of Scottish history used in the primary schools might well have not mentioned the brutalities committed by the Hanoverian Army after the Battle of Culloden. In 1895 Forbes's The Lyon in Mourning had been published in three volumes. It was a compilation of eyewitness and other accounts of the rebellion of 1745, the Battle of Culloden, and its aftermath. This work, however, would not have been much known except to scholars of Scottish history. Probably the atrocities of the Hanoverian Army after the battle did not become generally appreciated until after the publication of the works written for general readers by Prebble (1961), Young and Adair (1964), and Taylor (1965), all of which were published after Jenny began to have her recurrent dreams. This is not to deny that an oral tradition of the atrocities that depended on no written source for its transmission could have persisted in the region of Inverness.

Comment

Although Jenny said that she did not learn about the slaughter of fleeing Jacobites after the battle until long after she had begun having her recurrent dreams, this
is the detail — of the three mentioned above — that she was most likely to have learned
normally. As I mentioned, Jenny's family moved from Kingussie to Tore when she
was about 5 years old, and her dreams of the battle began about a year later. Both
Culloden and Tore are only a few kilometers from Inverness, the largest town of the
Scottish Highlands. The Jacobite Army had been quartered in Inverness before the
battle, and the prisoners were lodged there after it. The killing of Jacobite refugees
after the battle earned the Duke of Cumberland the sobriquet of "Butcher." Apart
from the immediate defeat of the Jacobites and their inhumane treatment by the
Hanoverian victors, the suppression of the Jacobite rebellion led to a complete change
in the way of life in the Highlands. The inhabitants were forbidden to wear the tartan,
the clan chiefs were deprived of their quasi-judicial rights, new roads (suited for military use) were built, and in other respects the Highlands were "pacified." The battle and its sequelae would be matters that even 2 centuries later might be discussed
in the area from time to time, and if Jenny's parents never talked about it, her two
older sisters or other adults might have done so in her presence.

The other two details — youths engaged in the Jacobite Army and dark green
uniforms on the Hanoverian side — are much less likely to have reached Jenny normally before she had her dreams.

Tʜᴏᴍᴀꜱ Eᴠᴀɴꜱ

Summary of the Case and Its Investigation

Thomas J. Evans was born in Cnucke Cilgerran, Cardiganshire, Wales, United
Kingdom, on March 9, 1886. His parents were John Evans and his wife, Emily. John
Evans was a quarryman. Thomas Evans had one older sister and several younger siblings whose sexes I did not learn. When he grew up, he worked as a miner. I do not
know the religion of his parents, but Thomas Evans became interested in spiritualism and eventually considered that his religion was Spiritualism.*

As a young child of perhaps between 4 and 5 years of age, Thomas Evans had
the first of a series of vivid dreams in which he saw himself being hanged with an
angry crowd surrounding him. By 1963, when I met him, he had had about 20 such
dreams. He was then 77 years old.

*A spiritualist believes that it is sometimes possible to receive communications from deceased persons
through specially gifted persons called mediums; communications may also come in dreams or deceased persons many be seen as apparitional figures.

A Spiritualist is a member of a religious group who believes that such communication with discarnate
personalities is ordinarily feasible, and they hold regular religious services to facilitate such communications.

In August 1959, Thomas Evans met Dr. Karl Müller, who was then lecturing in England and Wales. He mentioned his dreams to Dr. Müller, who later asked him to send him an account of them. Dr. Müller later gave me copies of Thomas Evans's first letter in which he described the dreams and some subsequent correspondence about details.

In 1962 I began corresponding with Thomas Evans myself. He answered my questions and agreed to my visiting him in Wales. I met him at his home near New Quay, Wales, on August 8, 1963. Unfortunately, his older sister, who would have been a potential witness to what Thomas Evans said about his dreams when he was a young child, had died less than a year before my visit to New Quay.

Thomas Evans and I exchanged letters once after our meeting. He died on December 4, 1965.

Thomas Evans's Dreams

The dreams in question were invariably similar in all details, but they differed in length. They were in color and seemed intensely realistic. With an exception that I shall mention later, Thomas Evans seemed in the dreams to be reliving the events that occurred. He emphasized the vividness and clarity of these dreams compared with his ordinary ones.

In the first dream, Thomas Evans seemed to relive only the ending of a life in a hanging. In some of the later dreams events that preceded the hanging occurred.

Thomas Evans's First Dream. Thomas Evans described his first dream in a letter to Dr. Karl Müller dated November 9, 1959, from which I cite the following:

> It [the dream] first occurred when I was approximately 8 years of age. I dreamt that I was at the edge of a forest; it appeared to be a large one. Somebody placed a noose around my neck and pulled me up off the ground. There I was left hanging while a crowd of people were laughing and jeering at me. The feeling I had, to be hanged, is that I had been advocating about something of which I could not remember....
>
> The man who placed the noose around my neck was a huge man, who could have been a monk.

In a second letter to Dr. Müller, dated December 25, 1959, Thomas Evans wrote:

> In answer to your question: Yes, it [the dream] did have to do with religion. There was quite a number of monk-like people in the crowd around me. This is the nearest description that I can give you, as they may not have been monks.

An Example of Thomas Evans's Later More Extensive Dreams. Thomas Evans did not have his recurrent dream of being hanged between 1944 and March 4, 1962. He then had another dream that included events preceding the hanging. He described the dream of March 4, 1962, in a letter to me dated June 24, 1962:

I was speaking to a large crowd of people, out in the open, when a large number of the crowd rushed towards me and maltreated me. Then they took me to a dark room. I remained in the room for a long time, and I had no sense of distinguishing between night and day. From the room I was taken to the edge of a forest, where I was hanged watched by a large, jeering crowd.

Variations in the Dreams. In describing this last dream Thomas Evans said that he had it 9 times. When I mentioned to him that he had earlier told Dr. Müller that he had 20 dreams of the same scene, he replied to me, in a letter dated July 21, 1962:

I told Dr. Müller I had dreamt this dream about 20 times. But all these dreams were never completed. Let me explain. Eleven of these dreams, as soon as they commenced have awakened me in a terrible fright. Only 9 have been completed, and this last one, on March 4, 1962, had in addition, the crowd rushing towards me and [my] being in a dark room. These 9 dreams have been vivid and outstanding.

During our interview of August 8, 1963, Thomas Evans mentioned that on two occasions the dream continued after the hanging to the point where after the hanging he saw his body hanging, as from outside it. On all other occasions the dream stopped at the moment of the hanging or he awakened as the dream began.

The dreams were always absolutely identical in their details; on different occasions they differed in length, but never in features.

He could not identify any circumstance in his life that seemed to precipitate one of these dreams; he observed some tendency for them to occur "around the month of March," but offered no explanation for this.

Thomas Evans was convinced that the dreams were memories of a real previous life in which he had been some kind of a prophet or independent thinker and that the events had occurred in Austria.

In the same interview Thomas Evans said he could remember seeing in the dreams bishops and priests watching him being taken to be hanged. The priests had a tuft of hair on the top of their otherwise clean-shaven heads. They wore robes of a "mild chocolate color."

A Waking Vision Repeating the Dreams

In June 1963 Thomas Evans was reading a newspaper. He felt drowsy and the newspaper fell from his hands. He then saw the scenes of his recurrent dream, but this time as an observer watching the events instead of — as in the dreams — seeming to relive them.

This vision began with the scene in the dungeon and ended in the hanging. He saw himself with a long beard and wearing very poor clothing. The vision began with 4 soldiers coming into the dungeon where he was being held. They carried spears and entered in a single file. They led him out to where the crowd was waiting to see him hanged. He sensed that some of the crowd was sympathetic to him, but most were hostile and approved of his being hanged. As he watched the scenes, he felt no fear and was quite detached. When the vision ended, he felt happy and saw the words "The Last." The vision then faded away. He believed that he would not have the dream again. I think this probably the case, because in our subsequent correspondence before his death in 1968 he never mentioned having had the dream again.

Thomas Evans's Attitudes Apparently Related to the Recurrent Dreams

In a letter dated March 14, 1963, he wrote me that he had "always had an intense dislike of monks, priests and anything to do with the Roman Catholic religion. I am a Spiritualist, and I have nothing against other religious faiths."

Thomas Evans wrote in a letter to me dated December 21, 1962: "All my life I have had an aversion for capital punishment. I feel pain when I hear or read of an execution. This fear has been with me ever since the time that I realized what an execution meant."

During our meeting in August 1963, he told me that he had a strong sympathy toward Giordano Bruno and was "impelled" to read a book about Bruno. When he read about Bruno's execution, he felt a great bond of sympathy.*

Thomas Evans wrote me that he liked Austria, although he had never been there.

A Physical Disorder Associated with Thomas Evans's Recurrent Dreams

In 1962 my interest in birthmarks and birth defects possibly derived from previous lives was rudimentary. I did, however, ask Thomas Evans whether he had a birthmark in the area of his neck. In a letter dated June 24, 1962, he replied:

> I have no birthmark, but I have a lump, the size of a small egg, underneath the skin on the nape of my neck. The doctor states this is some kind of a cyst. When I first had this dream I was between 4 and 5 years of age and pain came in the lump which lasted for two or three days. Every time I get this dream I get this pain in the lump and this continues for 2 or more days.

Earlier, Thomas Evans had written to Dr. Müller that he thought he first had the dream when he was about 8 years old. He clarified this discrepancy in a letter to me dated July 21, 1962:

---

*I mentioned Giordano Bruno (1548–1600) in Part I. He was a speculative philosopher whose teachings had more influence after his death than during his life. He taught a kind of pantheism that included the idea of other habitable and inhabited worlds. A Copernican, his concept of the universe as infinite went far beyond that of Copernicus. Bruno also taught metempsychosis, which term (as I explained in Part I) particularly refers to the belief in the reincarnation of humans as humans and also as nonhuman animals. Eventually, Bruno was betrayed to the Inquisition, imprisoned, tortured, and finally tried and sentenced to death. He was not hanged, but was burned at the stake on February 17, 1600 (Singer, 1950).

Since speaking to Dr. Müller, my eldest sister has told me that I could not have been 5 years old when the first dream occurred. My sister, who is 4 years older than I [am], can remember the time better than myself.... As for the lump at the base of the head, I did not know I had it until after the first dream, when I had terrible pains in it which lasted for 2 or 3 days.

At the time of our meeting in August 1963 Thomas Evans gave a further description of the pain associated with the first dream. According to my notes, "for several days afterwards he had severe pain in the neck. He told the family that he was choking and had something tight around his head. He did not on that occasion think of the scene of the dream as representing hanging. This realization came in the later dreams." (From this I infer that the first dream was one from which he awoke just as it began, even though he experienced the severe physical effects he described.) I continue with a further extract (slightly edited for easier reading) from my notes of August 1963:

The lump (cyst) on the back of the neck at the right occipital area was the size of a hazel nut ordinarily, but swelled to the size of an egg for 2–3 days after the dream. Since the last dream [probably that of March 4, 1962] the cyst has gradually decreased in size. Now it is only the size of a pea. The cyst swelled up like a rubber ball after the dreams. The cyst was painful when swollen. It never swelled except after the dreams. He had no pain except at the site of the cyst.

I supposed that the cyst at the nape of Thomas Evans's neck was congenital, and it may have been. There is, however, no evidence on this point. In his letter to me dated December 12, 1962, Thomas Evans wrote: "The first I knew of the cyst was when I had pain in it. My sister knew [it] from that time [only]. So she does not know whether I had it from birth."

Comment

I have reported two other cases (Navalkishore Yadav and U Tint Aung) with death from hanging in which the subjects had physical effects (respectively a birthmark and a birth defect) apparently related to the hanging. These two cases both had verifiable features; that of Thomas Evans does not. Given the vivid realistic nature of the dreams, their exact repetition of details, and the associated physical disorder* and pain of the neck, I do not find it surprising that Thomas Evans believed his dreams derived from a previous life that he had lived.

The details of hanging and of clothing in Thomas Evans's dreams warrant almost

*Other cases have shown the feature of physical symptoms occurring during the recall of events of a previous life. Examples occurred in the cases of Marta Lorenz and Salem Andary. Story (1959/1975) reported the case of a Karen (of Burma), whose arm swelled up and became painful at times when his attention was drawn to substantial congenital indentations of the skin of his hands. The subject of this case, whose statements remain unverified, attributed the indentations to wounds from wire that had been used (by robbers) to bind the deceased person whose life he said he remembered.

no conjecture about the time and place of the occurrence of the events in the dreams, if we interpret them as memories of real events. We can only say that they must have occurred more than 3 centuries ago, if I am correct in believing that religious heretics have not been hanged more recently.

WILLIAM HENS

William Hens was born in London, England, on October 6, 1899. His father was Belgian and his mother English. His mother died in 1907, when he was 8 years old, and he was then sent (with three of his siblings) to an uncle in Brussels. He attended a convent school in Brussels and became converted to the Roman Catholic religion. In 1909 his father remarried and was thus able to have his children return to London. His father was not a Roman Catholic; his stepmother belonged to no formal religion.

I do not know how much formal education William Hens had, but believe it was not extensive. He became a mechanic and worked all his life as one.

He continued a member of the Roman Catholic Church until he was 26 years old and then found that he could no longer accept its teachings and left. In about 1937 he became interested in spiritualism and was so convinced — through some personal experiences — of its value that he could be regarded as a Spiritualist. Around 1940 a medium advised him to study reincarnation, "because it was true."

Sometime during the 1940s — he later did not remember the precise year — William Hens had three dreams that he described as vivid, realistic, and unusually memorable (compared with his ordinary dreams). They all occurred within a period of about a year. He made no record of them at the time, and I believe their first recording did not come until 1967. In that year he learned of my interest in experiences suggestive of reincarnation and wrote to me on January 17, 1967, with an account of these three dreams.

Subsequently, we corresponded about the circumstances and details of the dreams. William Hens answered some of my questions in letters. I decided to meet him and ask further questions. We met in London on February 25, 1970.

I give next William Hens's account of his dreams.

William Hens's Three Dreams

The following accounts are taken from William Hens's letter to me of January 17, 1967. I have edited the account slightly and added some clarifying phrases in brackets to make for easier reading and understanding (but without changing the meaning).

1. I found myself with a companion climbing a long terrace of steps which led to a building with tall columns supporting a large porch. I was dressed in a cotton smock which reached to my thighs and tight trousers which were bound criss-cross with straps.

A belt supported a scabbard with a broad, flat sword, like the Roman type.

As we made our way towards the summit, I knew that we were not supposed to be there — spies, I felt.

On reaching the porch two large metal doors opened and soldiers rushed at us. We turned heel and retreated down the steps at top speed. Coming up to meet us were a number of soldiers. I drew my sword to do combat, but as they fell on me the dream concluded.

I should think the period would be about 500 A.D.

2. The next vivid dream perhaps having a bearing on reincarnation was [of a time] about 1500 A.D.

In this dream I was an attendant to [an] executioner. I was dressed in a leather jacket and tights, a girdle of cord. [I was] age[d] about 17.

The scene opened in a vaultlike dungeon, low arched roof, the executioner standing to one side in the shadows of the dimly lit place.

He was holding the axe head on the floor, which was scattered with straw. By the low block stood two ladies, one [of whom] was in great distress, the other trying to console her. Both were dressed in black as was the executioner also, who wore a mask.

As I stood there my feeling of pity was so great that I went over to her, putting my arm around her shoulder. I said: "Come along, madame. It must be done. It won't hurt." With that I pressed her to her knees and placed her head on the block. I immediately, with a swift action slewed around in front of her and grabbed her hair just under the cap she was wearing and pulled her head hard on the block.

The executioner stepped forward and raised the axe — that was the end of the dream.

In this dream I felt intense pity for the lady, it welled up inside me. Another point [that] struck me was the action of holding the head down by the hair. Now I have never heard or read or seen a picture of this sort of thing, but why shouldn't it be? It wouldn't be hard to imagine the trouble it would cause if anyone raised their head off the block as the blow was struck!

Comment on This Dream. Laurence (1960) reproduced an old German print showing the beheading of a woman in Ratisbon in 1782. An assistant held the victim's head on the block by pulling her hair forward while the executioner prepared to strike the neck with his axe.

3. The next dream [seemed to relate to] the early 1800's. The scene opened with me being taken into an engineering shop.

Underneath a brass oil lamp suspended from a beam was a bench with a man filing a block of steel about three inches square and four inches long. (The vise the man held his steel block in was the type with a long leg stuck in the floor.) He was dressed in a white apron with a bib. He wore side whiskers [and] also a top hat [with] rather a tall crown.

He seemed proud of his filing as he ran his fingers over the smooth surface.

I felt here that I was a young man in my twenties about to start a new job.

The next scene was that I was working on a railway coach — the early type used in the days of George Stephenson. This coach was over a working pit with railway lines along the edge and I was working on the floor, not in the pit. The wheels were of a coach pattern [with] thick forged spokes. I had my head through the wheel tightening up some square type nuts when the coach began to move forward and I felt my head being crushed against the back of the coach body — the dream concluded.

The feelings experienced in this dream were the same as when you start a new job. Also [there was] the terror [of] one's head being caught up.

Additional Information About the Dreams

In the letter from which I have just quoted William Hens's account of his dreams, he also wrote:

These dreams are so real and the details are so vivid and furthermore the retention of them in my mind on awakening so complete without any effort to recall, to me, put them in a different category [from] ordinary dreams.

In our correspondence William Hens told me that each dream had occurred only once; they were not recurrent.

Other Background Information Relevant to the Interpretation of the Dreams

William Hens wrote (in a letter dated February 20, 1967) that he had had no phobias or unusual fears that, if they had occurred in infancy or early childhood, might have derived from previous lives (Stevenson, 1990). Specifically he had not noticed any fear of axes, executions, or railway trains. In a later letter (of March 29, 1967) William Hens wrote that he had not been particularly attracted to any of the historical periods in which the events of his dreams seemed to have occurred.

Two Unusual Experiences of William Hens When Awake

William Hens had other unusual experiences in at least two of which he seemed to be back in some earlier historical time. Both occurred while he was awake. I will cite his accounts of these.

He described the first of these experiences in a letter to me dated February 20, 1967.

While at work during the [Second World] War, at Handley Page, the aircraft firm, a large sheet of aluminum was being turned over and as the reflection caught my eyes, I had a terrible fear grip me and was in a flash thrown back through the ages to, so it seemed to me, the days of Babylon. The fear I experienced was due to a great wall falling on me with other people. The scene was so vivid I could see the terror-stricken people running in confusion. The wall looked like the pictures I have seen of the Hanging Gardens of Babylon. Although this took only a second, I felt I was there. It was real.

William Hens's second experience occurred in the 1960s. He described it in his letter of March 29, 1967. He said that it had occurred "a few years ago."

> I saw clairvoyantly a vision of a Jewish girl, most beautiful. She appeared behind a transparent screen that had "forget-me-not" flowers scattered over its surface. The emotion was such that it took my breath away.

A few weeks later William Hens had a session with a medium who described to him in some detail a previous life she said he had lived in Palestine in the first century A.D. The statements she made, although interesting, contained no verifiable details. She described, however, a woman whose description corresponded to that of the woman in his recent vision. Without telling the medium of his vision, William Hens asked if he had ever seen this woman. The medium replied: "Yes … you have seen her, with her raven black hair and surrounded with the forget-me-nots of spirit."

In reply to a question I put to him, William Hens replied, in a letter dated April 23, 1967, that he had told the medium nothing about his earlier vision. The medium mentioned the forget-me-nots first.

Comment. Assuming William Hens correctly narrated the sequence of events connecting his own vision and the medium's statement about the "forget-me-nots" (which I have no reason to doubt), her statement would seem to be minimally an instance of telepathy between medium and sitter.

WINIFRED WYLIE

Summary of the Case and Its Investigation

Winifred Wylie was born on December 30, 1902, in the village of Fence Houses, County Durham, England. Her parents were Joseph Graham and his wife, Jane. She was their second daughter and second child. Joseph Graham was a store manager. The family were sufficiently well off to send their daughters to a boarding school when Winifred was 10 years old and her sister about 12. Before that they had been taught at home by a governess.

In childhood Winifred had several apparently paranormal experiences, including a recurrent dream about being in a battle. She had this dream for the first time when she was 10 years old. Thereafter it recurred once a year until 1972, when it ceased. When Winifred told her mother about the dream, her mother said that it sounded like an event during the battle of Waterloo (which took place on June 18, 1815).

At the age of 23 Winifred married the Reverend John Wylie, an Anglican clergyman.

Winifred's husband, who was somewhat knowledgeable about history, also believed that her recurrent dream corresponded to an incident during the battle of Waterloo. Accordingly, when her husband retired and had some time for going abroad, they went to the battlefield of Waterloo and examined the building where, they believed, the events of the dream had occurred. This was the chateau of Hougoumont.

Early in 1981 Winifred Wylie responded to a survey concerning paranormal experiences published by *The Times* of London. The survey was published on behalf of the K. I. B. Foundation, whose Executive Secretary, knowing of my interest in experiences suggestive of reincarnation, sent me a copy of Winifred's answers to the survey.

After reading Winifred's account of her recurrent dream, I began corresponding with her. She engaged in this exchange cooperatively, and on April 15, 1982, I went to her home in Penrith, Cumbria, and had a long interview with her. Subsequently, she communicated with the British Broadcasting Corporation, and on April 7, 1983, she was interviewed for its series of radio programs on the subject of reincarnation. The interviewer for the BBC, June Knox-Mawer, sent Winifred a list of questions in advance of the interview, and her answers to these included one of the accounts of the recurrent dream that I give below. This account is not dated but was obviously written early in 1983, probably in February. On April 16, 1983, my colleague Dr. Nicholas McClean-Rice went to Penrith and interviewed Winifred again. At each interview Winifred also gave an account of her recurrent dream. In the end, therefore, from the interviews and her letters we obtained six accounts of the dream.

Winifred Wylie died on July 31, 1985.

The Recurrent Dream

Winifred's first account of her dream, sent in response to the survey in *The Times*, was extremely brief. I omit it here and give the other five accounts of the dream that we obtained.

The following is Winifred's account of her dream given in her letter to me of April 30, 1981.

> 1. I was one of three men trying to close the gate of a walled courtyard against an enemy army. The courtyard was surrounded by a thick stone wall, and on top of the wall leaning over it were swarming fierce-looking men in cocked hats and with long drooping moustaches, shooting at the men behind us. In the corner of the yard to my right was a small barn. On the left were "horse boxes"—stables whose doors open in two parts so that horses can look out. Behind, at some distance, was the farmhouse. I and my two companions struggled with all our might to close the gate. I felt such a surge of relief when the bar fell into the socket and the gate was barred. The men knocked out by the firing from the wall were carried into the horse boxes by their comrades.

Variant Accounts of the Dream. In succeeding interviews and correspondence Winifred gave additional details of the dream and sometimes variant ones.

In my interview with her on April 1982, she said:

> 2. In the dream I am pressing against the gate. A voice is shouting "Shut the gate." There were men on a high wall, taking shots at the men inside. The wounded men were taken into a stone barn.... The men who were shooting had long moustaches

and (? three) cornered hats with a point in front. There was a noise of the bombardment.

Winifred wrote the next account early in 1983 (probably in February) in response to questions from June Knox-Mawer, who wished to prepare for the planned interview on a BBC radio program.

> 3. I was one of a crowd of soldiers, immediately behind some of them who were trying to shut a large rough wooden gate. I was pressing against them to help with my weight. A voice behind shouted "Shut the gate, shut the gate!" On a high wall, which continued from the gate to the right, were foreign-looking soldiers—they had long drooping moustaches and black hats, and they were firing at random into the courtyard. The wounded were picked up by some of the soldiers behind me and carried into horse boxes behind us to the left.
>
> The wall continued to the right of the gate for a few yards and joined another wall with trees visible near it. In the corner formed by the two walls was a small stone hut (? a pig house). It looked rather dilapidated. One of the thick stone tiles was slipping.
>
> The gate was fastened by means of a thick wooden bar, which dropped into a slot in the gatepost. When it 'clunked' shut, I woke up.

In her interview for the radio program of the BBC on April 7, 1983, Winifred gave the following oral account of the dream. In speaking during the broadcast, possibly because she was slightly nervous, she omitted some words—or they were missed by the transcriber; I have supplied these, enclosed in brackets.

> 4. I am in a farmyard with a very high wall on two side[s of a gate] and loose boxes, horse boxes at the other side, and I am one of a group of soldiers. I have been [sent] to shut a gate. There is a voice behind [that] says "Shut the gate, shut the gate." And I think five or … five men pressing against this gate. And I don't actually touch the gate, but I am pressing against the back of the man who is, you see, to help him, and the gate is a rough wooden one. I can feel it. I did feel the end of it and finally, before—this comes before—the … on the wall were soldiers with long droopy moustaches, firing into our soldiers, and they fire rather at random, and it's a very high wall, and I think by the way they have fired they were holding on with this [one] arm and firing with the other. They were standing on the backs of other men. They couldn't actually get into the place because it was such a high wall.
>
> [They were wearing] three cornered black hats and they were firing at random into the … and of course men were falling, either killed or wounded, and they were being carried into the horse boxes by some of our companions behind and this went on for some time, the shooting and the sound of a cannonade in the distance, some distance, the other side of the wall. And when finally the gate—it was shut in a sense, but it wasn't locked, it was locked by this bar falling into—what do you call [it]? A socket. And when it fell it made a sort of clunking noise and I woke up.

Later in the interview for the BBC the following exchange occurred:

JUNE KNOX-MAWER: Did you see wounded being carried off?
WINIFRED: Yes—Yes and put into those horse boxes.

June Knox-Mawer: When you say horse boxes, do you mean more like stables? Were they stone?

Winifred: Well, it was a stone building, but it was divided into smaller compartments to take a horse, and a horse box.... You're not a country woman, are you?

June Knox-Mawer: At the beginning, but not now....

Winifred: It has a double door, you see. The top opens. You can open the top so the horse can put its head out, but they can't get out. That's a horse box.

June Knox-Mawer: I see.

Winifred: And when both the gates were open, both the top and bottom gate were open in this case, you could see they were horse boxes, you could see there were two doors.

June Knox-Mawer: And this is where they were taking the....

Winifred: They were taking the wounded and the dead. Yes.

On April 16, 1983, Winifred gave the following account to Nicholas McClean-Rice.

5. I am standing with shoulder pressed against a gate. Men are trying to shut the gate from the other side,* shouting "Shut it." I can only see part of the gate. There is a wall [on] either side of the gate. On the wall are soldiers with three-pointed hats on. They are shooting at the troops in the yard where I am. I am in the yard but very close to the wall. There is a dilapidated hut in the courtyard with trees behind it. From outside, farther up, there is the sound of a lot of firing. We are trying to keep these other men out by pushing the gate. Finally the gate shuts as a bar goes clunk and I wake. I always wake then.

Comment. In talking with me on April 15, 1982, Winifred said that the dream "was always exactly the same." In her interview for the BBC radio program June Knox-Mawer asked Winifred: "Was it the same dream each time?" Winifred replied: "Exactly." To Nicholas McClean-Rice Winifred said that the dreams were "absolutely identical." We have seen, however, that her descriptions of it were not always exactly the same. Nevertheless, the principal features of her accounts remained stable, despite variations in details. The variations in the details were not discrepant except for her statement about the number of men involved in trying to shut the gate and whether the soldier she dreamed herself to be was next to the gate or only behind another man who was next to it.

The Quality and Associated Emotions of the Dream. In her letter to me of April 30, 1981, Winifred wrote: "It was an extremely vivid and terrifying dream ... I felt the mixture of fury, exhilaration and terror which I suppose men feel in battle." In answer to the questions posed by June Knox-Mawer (before the interview for the BBC)

*By "other side" Winifred here meant the other panel of the two-part gate, which would meet (in the middle) the panel on which she saw herself pushing.

Different accounts, and sometimes my own phrases, variously refer to "a gate" and "gates." The chateau had a south gate, which was effectively shut and never crossed by the attacking French soldiers. The north gate — with which we are here concerned — had two panels or sections, which met in the middle. The panels are sometimes referred to as gates and sometimes as part of a gate.

she wrote, regarding the effect the dream had on her: "I enjoyed it. It was exciting and exhilarating, terrifying and above all puzzling." In her interview with Nicholas McClean-Rice on April 16, 1983, she said: "What I can't describe is that it [the dream] is so real. It's as if I was there. It's not like a dream."

Circumstances and Frequency of the Recurrence of the Dream. The dream first occurred on Winifred's first night at the boarding school to which she went at the age of 10. Although her older sister went with her to the school at the same time, the sister was in a different dormitory. Thus Winifred was away from home and among strange people for the first time in her life. She told June Knox-Mawer, during the interview for the BBC, that the bed was cold and uncomfortable. She said: "I had to crawl in the top [of the bed] and I felt absolutely miserable, and I lay awake for hours. Then when I went to sleep, I had this dream for the first time." She thought these circumstances had somehow precipitated the first occurrence of the dream.

She did not identify any factor that seemed to stimulate the later occurrences of the dream. They occurred about once a year.

The later occurrences of the dream were not unpleasant. She told me that when she awoke after having the dream she felt "exhilarated."

The dreams ceased in 1972 or 1973, after she had visited the site of the battle of Waterloo. (On one occasion she said they had ceased around 1943, but usually she gave 1972 or 1973 as the year of the last occurrence.)

The Defense of Hougoumont During the Battle of Waterloo

When the battle of Waterloo began, in the late morning of June 18, 1815, the chateau of Hougoumont was nearly at the extreme right of the mixed army (of British, Dutch, and German troops) that the Duke of Wellington commanded. Because the chateau and its surrounding buildings and walls were solidly built of brick and stone, they provided a substantial obstacle to the left wing of the French army that Napoleon commanded. He therefore opened the battle with an attempt to capture the chateau. At first the French succeeded in driving back the chateau's defenders who had been deployed in the surrounding woods and orchards. This enabled them to approach the walls of the chateau with a view to gaining entrance to its courtyard and thus capturing it.

The allied soldiers withdrew into the chateau and closed its gates, north and south. The north gate, however, remained vulnerable. It consisted of two heavy wooden panels which could be firmly closed with a bar of wood socketed in the walls at the sides of the gate. The French, led by a giant lieutenant wielding an axe, managed to push open the gate. A small group of French soldiers then rushed into the courtyard. The British commander of the forces within the fortress, Lieutenant-Colonel James Macdonell, sensing the danger, shouted to other officers to join him and rushed to the gate. Some other soldiers joined them,* and between them they slowly

---

Paget and Saunders (1992) gave the names of nine British soldiers, additional to Colonel Macdonell, who pushed on the two parts of the gate to close them.

Figure 15. Painting by Robert Gibb (in the middle of the 19th century) representing the closing of the north gate at Hougoumont during the battle of Waterloo. Lieutenant-Colonel James Macdonnell is shown, sword in hand, pushing on the left panel of the gate. (Courtesy National Museums of Scotland.)

pushed back the panels, overcoming the pressure of the French soldiers who were trying to push the gate open. (Figure 15 shows a painter's representation of this scene.) They replaced the bar in its sockets and then piled heavy materials on the inside of the gate as a further barrier to the French, who continued trying to break it open. The 20 or so French soldiers who had entered the courtyard were then rounded up and killed. (Only a drummer boy was spared.) The chateau's garrison was then reinforced, and for the remainder of the battle Hougoumont remained in British hands.

Perhaps more has been written about the battle of Waterloo than about any other single battle. All accounts of the battle emphasize the importance of the defense of Hougoumont to its outcome, and some devote large sections or a whole chapter to it (Chalfont, 1979; Hamilton-Williams, 1993). The most authoritative account of this phase of the battle fills an entire book (Paget and Saunders, 1992). All the accounts of the fighting around and for Hougoumont emphasize the crucial importance of the closing of the north gate. The Duke of Wellington himself afterwards wrote: "The success of the battle of Waterloo turned upon the closing of the gates of Hougoumont" (Macbride, 1911, p. 123).

The celebrity and widespread knowledge about Hougoumont among the English people have an obvious bearing on the question of whether Winifred's dream derived from normally acquired information.

Winifred's Visit to Hougoumont

In about 1972 (it might have been 1973) Winifred and her husband, who had recently retired, visited the site of the battle including the chateau of Hougoumont. This is what Winifred told June Knox-Mawer during her interview for the BBC on April 7, 1983:

> ...we went inside the farmyard and my first feeling was one of disappointment because the gate was absolutely different, but obviously hadn't been there more than about 20 years at the outside. Looking around there was no little hut ... the farmer's wife was showing us around and I said: "This is a new gate." She said: "Yes, madam, the other was so worn out." I said I thought there was a little stone pigsty or barn there. She gave me a rather peculiar look and she said: "Madam has been here before?" It was there but it was falling to pieces and was removed.

Concerning another detail, Winifred Wylie said in two of her accounts that she had shown her husband where the "horse boxes" were still in the farmyard.

In a letter Winifred wrote to me on June 16, 1983 — her last as it happened — she wrote: "My visit to Hougoumont in 1972 was not, I felt, a visit to a strange farmyard in a foreign country, but more like revisiting a place I had known in my youth."

My Visit to Hougoumont

Despite extensive reading about the battle of Waterloo, I thought I could appraise Winifred's dream better if I visited Hougoumont myself. Accordingly, I went there on November 11, 1997. I walked around three sides of the chateau and also went inside the courtyard. I took the photographs of Figures 16 and 17. The chateau and many of the other buildings had been irreparably damaged during the battle and were not replaced. Paget and Saunders (1992) provide two sketches showing the extent of the buildings in 1815 and in the 1990s. The chapel and a farmer's house remained, and the chapel can be seen in Figure 17. I did not identify any buildings that I consider horse boxes, that is, stalls with doors divided in two so that the upper part can be opened while the lower part remains closed. A building where farm machinery was kept appeared comparatively new, and it may have replaced the buildings that Winifred called "horse boxes."

I could see that there were no small buildings, whether a pigsty or for other purposes, adjoining the north wall. Sketches and diagrams of the layout of the chateau's grounds in 1815 show that there was then a building where Winifred said the pigsty or small barn had been (Paget and Saunders, 1992; Hamilton-Williams, 1993.) Figures 16 and 17 show that there were no buildings adjacent to the north wall on either side of the north gate in 1997.

Top: Figure 16. View from the distance of the buildings at Hougoumont in November 1997. Note the absence of buildings adjacent to the gate or near the north wall. (Photograph by Ian Stevenson.) *Bottom:* Figure 17. The north gate at Hougoumont as it appeared in November 1997. Note the absence of buildings near the gate. (Photograph by Ian Stevenson.)

Winifred's Other Apparently Paranormal Experiences

Before describing Winifred's preferred explanation of her recurrent dream and my own interpretation of it, I will briefly describe other unusual experiences that she had.

She said that in her early childhood she had the experience of floating bodily from the top of a flight of stairs to its bottom. She insisted that this was not an out-of-the-body experience; her whole body seemed to move without effort on her part. She thought this natural and never told anyone else about it.

Winifred was much attached to her paternal grandfather, and she thought that she was probably his favorite grandchild. One day in February 1913, when she was a little more than 10 years old she went to visit him at his home, which was about 3 kilometers from where her family lived. Her grandfather, who was 67 years old, seemed in good health and spirits. Nevertheless, that night, back home and in bed, Winifred woke up and told her sister that their grandfather had just died. A little later, her father's brother came to the house, and she overheard him tell her father that her grandfather had just died.

In her late teens, during a migraine attack, she had the experience of seeming to be above her body on a bed and looking down on it from near the ceiling.

In September 1927, when Winifred was 24 and married, her mother asked her to come to the family home and look after it while she (her mother) went to help her other daughter, who had an infant daughter and was then engaged in moving from one house to another. Winifred agreed and returned to the family home. Almost as soon as she reached the house she began to have intense abdominal pain. Her mother had already left to go to her other daughter. Winifred felt so ill that she thought she was dying. She began to think about her mother and wished silently to herself that her mother would return.

An hour or so later her mother returned in her car. She had become so certain that Winifred needed her that she had not taken time to telephone to verify her impression, but had turned around and gone directly back to her house and daughter.* Her mother immediately took Winifred to a physician who found that she had developed a fulminating peritonitis. She was operated on the next day and recovered.

The last experience she related to us occurred early in 1983. She was ill with pneumonia and had been given some medicine by her doctor, but in the evening she felt "dreadful, tearful, and miserable." She then became aware of two vague outlines, forms like humans, that she could not recognize. She heard voices, however. One voice said: "I wish we could tell her that we are thinking about her." The other voice said: "Oh, but I am sure she knows." She recognized the first voice as that of her mother and the second as that of her husband. (They were both deceased.)

---

*"Telepathic impressions," as I call them, and actions taken in response to them, seem to occur frequently, although we have no precise knowledge of their incidence (Prince, 1931; Stevenson, 1970a). In this example, Winifred was the presumed sender or agent, her mother the percipient.

Winifred's Explanation of Her Recurrent Dream

A remote uncle of Winifred's mother, with the family name of Twitty, had fought at the battle of Waterloo. Winifred's mother was not a descendant of this uncle, and she did not even know his first name. A genealogical searching service (Debrett Ancestry Service) found that a Thomas Twitty was on the Waterloo Medal Roll. (Winifred let me have copies of the relevant correspondence with Debrett.) Thomas Twitty, however, had been in the Grenadier Guards, which were not involved in the defense of Hougoumont. (The Coldstream Guards and the Third Guards were.) Also, the name of Twitty does not appear among the list of 10 soldiers (from the Coldstream Guards and the Third Guards) who pushed the north gates closed (Paget and Saunders, 1992).

Nevertheless, Winifred's own interpretation of her recurrent dream was that the remote uncle who fought at Waterloo was somehow communicating with her and imposing his memories on her. She imagined the uncle as wanting to share his experience with a member of the family and chose Winifred, because of her soldierly qualities, to be the recipient. After she went to Hougoumont, Winifred believed, the discarnate uncle was satisfied that he had adequately communicated what he wanted to have known, and the dreams ceased. Winifred rejected the suggestion that the dream might have derived from a previous life and told me: "I do not want to believe in reincarnation." She wrote to June Knox-Mawer that [Dr Stevenson] "took my account of the dream seriously and tried to get me to agree to his suggestion of reincarnation." (I comment on this below.)

Comment

Given that Winifred had an uncle who—family legend said—had fought at Waterloo, we should expect that Winifred would have known something, if not much, about Waterloo before her dreams began when she was 10. She denied this. She said her mother never talked about the battle and that indeed she (Winifred) had never heard of the battle itself before her mother suggested that her dream might refer to it. As a source of information about the battle Winifred dismissed the teaching from a governess that she had had at home before she went to boarding school at the age of 10; she said that the governess never taught her any serious history.

I need here to emphasize that no written record of Winifred's dream was made until she was nearly 80 years old. It seems to me possible that she had originally had a somewhat different dream from the one narrated to us. Certainly she had in her later years read much about Waterloo, and her husband, who had studied history at Cambridge University, was specially knowledgeable about Wellington's campaigns. Two of the books that I consulted in preparation for writing this report reproduce a well-known painting that depicts the scene of closing the gates at Hougoumont. The painting is by Robert Gibb, a Scottish artist, and it was painted in the latter half of the 19th century (Figure 15). The exact date of its painting is unknown and unimportant.

It hangs in the Scottish United Services Museum at the Castle in Edinburgh.* In view of Winifred's later normally acquired knowledge of the battle, it seems difficult to exclude the possibility that the memory of a dream she had about a battle, one involving a fortress with gates to be closed, had become transmogrified into the accounts that she gave us in the 1980s. I certainly cannot refute this interpretation.

Nevertheless, obstacles to its acceptance remain. First, it requires us to suppose that an intelligent woman — as I judge Winifred to have been — had misled herself in saying first that the dream, in its principal features, had not changed since she was 10 years old and second, that she knew nothing about the battle of Waterloo before she began having the dream. Also, the details of the dream contain three items — two of them verified — that I think Winifred Wylie unlikely to have learned normally. These are the following:

1. French soldiers shooting from over the walls at the British soldiers inside the courtyard of the chateau. Howarth's book on Waterloo reproduces a photograph of a painting of a scene at Hougoumont in which one can see a soldier shooting over the wall (Howarth, 1968). Winifred had a copy of this book. She did not, however, have it until it was published, in 1968.

Paget and Saunders (1992) describe how a French Grenadier stood on the shoulders of a comrade and took aim from the top of the courtyard wall at Lieutenant-Colonel Henry Wyndham, who was one of the officers active in shutting the gate. A British soldier shot and killed the Frenchman before he could aim properly.

2. The small buildings mentioned by Winifred that were near the walls adjoining the north gate were not mentioned or shown in texts about the battle, so far as I know, until the detailed publications of the 1990s (Paget and Saunders, 1992; Hamilton-Williams, 1993). I could see myself that these buildings, known to have existed earlier, were no longer present in 1997, and presumably they were not present in 1972, as Winifred said.

3. Finally, there is the detail of the "horse boxes" with doors in two halves where the wounded were cared for. I have not found this description of the place where the wounded were taken. Paget and Saunders (1992) refer to the wounded as being in "the stables," but they give no particulars about doors such as Winifred described. She said that she showed these doors, still extant in 1972, to her husband; but I could not verify this independently.

Winifred grumbled (to June Knox-Mawer of the BBC) that I had tried to impose the interpretation of reincarnation on her. I deny that I have ever tried to press this interpretation on her, or on anyone else. I did, however, mention it to Winifred as a possible interpretation of her dreams, which she rejected.

I also posed some questions to her that seem relevant to the difference in sex between the soldier she thought she was in the dream and her sex in this life. From

---

*This and other paintings of the battle around Hougoumont were made long after the battle. They were more or less romanticized, and we should not regard them as evidence.

these the only item that seems in any way concordant with reincarnation was her statement that she was, for a woman, unusually brave and had a sort of manlike courage. In illustration of this quality, she mentioned an episode when a drunken villager tried to break into her family's house. She, then a young girl, took a gun, opened the door, and frightened the intruder into precipitate flight. In recounting this episode Winifred said that she "often behaved like a man." As another instance of unusual courage she described how she had once seen a dog who had gone onto some railroad tracks and remained there as a train approached; she had run to the dog and snatched it from the rails just before the train reached it.

John East

I have rarely published a report of a case for which I have never met the subject. This book contains five such exceptions, and this is one of them. Yet I could almost believe that I had met John East, because during the last year of his life we exchanged frequent letters — many of them several pages in length — about his experiences. He diligently answered questions that I put to him concerning details of three vivid dreams that he had had. I had made plans to meet him in 1962, when I learned of his death. He had been ill — he had told me in some letters — but his death, for me, was quite unexpected, because the last letter I received from him was written 4 days before he died and showed no evidence of his ill health.

Summary of the Case and Its Investigation

John East was born in the United Kingdom on October 4, 1883. His family was wealthy, and he was free to pursue his own interests. After education at Eton College he went to Oxford for a year, but found the university life boring. He wished to enter the Army, but was rejected because of poor eyesight. He spent the next 3 years hunting big game in three continents. He then returned to England and from 1912 to 1927 — with the exception of 3 years service in the Army during World War I — he lived on a large country estate, engaged in farming, and hunted 4 days a week. In the autumn, he often went deer stalking and grouse shooting in Scotland. In 1927, when he was 44 years old he decided to start a business, but nothing came of that, and he resumed his life as a country gentleman-farmer. He married three times. His third marriage was especially happy; his wife predeceased him. He himself died in 1962 at the age of 79.

In 1927 John East had two dreams on successive nights. They were so realistic that he decided to make notes about them, which he did in the middle of the night (following the second dream). The next morning he made a sketch of a house seen in the second dream. In 1950 he had a third dream that related to the first two. It seemed to take place in the house seen in the second dream of 1927.

In 1954 an English illustrated weekly published photographs and a plan of a substantial country mansion, Shredfield Hall in Staffordshire; and John East instantly "recognized" the house as that of his dreams.

Apart from the notes made in the middle of the night, John East made no written record of his dreams until 1949. In 1950 he added to his record additional information after the third dream of that year. He made further additions to his account after seeing the photographs in the illustrated weekly. Finally, in a book published in 1960, he included an account of the dreams and his efforts at verification (East, 1960a). A friend of mine reviewed the book in the *Journal of the Society for Psychical Research* (Heywood, 1960). I asked my friend to forward a letter from me to John East and thus began the extensive correspondence that we maintained until his death early in 1962.

During our correspondence John East sent me his rough notes made after the second of his three dreams, the draft account he had made of his dreams prior to his publishing this account, and some relevant correspondence. I made copies of these and returned them to him. He gave me permission to publish whatever I wished provided I concealed the identities of persons concerned. (The name "John East" is itself a pseudonym that he adopted, but he used his real name in correspondence.)

Before the publication of his book John East had made some inquiries about the possible place and period of the action in his dreams, which he firmly believed derived from a previous life. He concluded that they referred to the life of a young English officer who had participated in a war between Great Britain and Burma, later known as the First Burmese War, which lasted from March 1824 to February 1826. After John East's death I continued inquiries with a view to obtaining further confirmation. I defer an account of these until after describing the dreams. For these I give first a transcript of the rough notes that John East made immediately after the second dream in 1927 and then the much more detailed account that he later wrote.

John East's Rough Notes Made Immediately After Awaking from the Second Dream

> The white trooper with semi-naval officers.
> ? studying a lot of maps and charts.
> A sort of naval discipline. (Indian Marine ?).
> Very hot and damp. living on barge on a river.
> Only one mess and ante room.
> The awful loneliness and horror. The sickness.
> The game of sliding over the deck boards.
> The dance in the shore bungalow. bamboo chairs.
> ? half-caste girls.* Dark girl with red ? camellias.
> No! you dance this with me, of course. It is the last time.

*John East added the following note to the transcript of the notes that he made in May 1961: "Burmese are not very dark, they are pale coffee color. They might appear half-caste." By the time of this note he had learned that the details of his dreams corresponded to events in Burma.

What? going home?
Thoughts of the house.

Comment. The notes are obviously fragmentary, and their principal value is that of showing the importance that John East attached to the dreams. He stated that he had the dreams during a period when he was reading a popular book on precognition, *An Experiment with Time*, which was first published in March 1927 (Dunne, 1927). The dating of these two dreams is further fixed by the stationery on which John East wrote his notes. He moved from the house of this stationery soon afterwards and had different stationery printed with the address of his new house.

John East's Detailed Account of His Dreams

The following is taken from the draft account of his dreams that John East wrote first in 1949 and subsequently revised and expanded after the third dream in 1950. I omit a few interpretive comments made by John East in order for readers to study the dream report without interruption.

For clarity of explanation we will call the dreamer A and the chief actor in the dream B. There were then two definite consciousnesses, A and B; A, while always observing B, as it seemed ever from a little behind B and somewhat to his right, being perfectly aware of what was passing in B's mind, as if A were B as well as being the observer.

The dream opens with the dreamer, A, being aware of B coming up the broad companionway of a ship to the open deck. There were no risers to the treads; as B came up he could see between the treads to the deck below. As he reached the deck, it seemed to be somewhere amidships, he had a feeling of most welcome freshness, of sea air and of light almost blinding after semi-darkness, relieving the sensation of having been confined for days in a dark evil smelling cabin of far too small proportions; a feeling of rapidly returning strength after days of illness, of calm after storm.

A, through B, was aware first of all of whiteness, an expanse of white deck, high bulwarks with a long line of whiteness along the top above which glimpses of a blue sea, white topped, were disclosed by the gentle movement of the ship. Above towered layer upon layer of white canvas in such vast array that it almost blotted out a blue sky lightly covered with white clouds. The impression gained was that the ship did not belong to the navy and that the uniforms of the officers were not naval uniforms but were of a similar type,...

A was also aware of, and noted, B's costume, a tight fitting waist length scarlet tunic with two rows of gilt buttons and short tails behind, with white trousers. The facings or cuffs, were yellow. A noted that the cloth was of a coarser, thinner material than that used for the modern full dress uniform; the surface was rougher and not so smooth. He noted the high collar or stock and had the sensation of it confining his own neck.

As he left the broad companionway he saw facing him an officer, clad like himself, a youth much shorter than himself with fair almost yellow hair and the beginnings of whiskers and a moustache, who said, smiling, "Ah! so you are well again, we shall be glad to have you back."

A experienced a feeling of superiority in B, a sensation of condescension in dealing with someone of a lower social status, of having agreed, as it were, for a time to play a part. Something of this attitude of B's mind seemed to be present throughout. While this was perfectly natural to B, it struck A with a sense of peculiarity, that B did not in fact always behave with very good taste.

As B began to speak the scene faded, as if it were a vignette with the sides closing in on the picture.

There was then another scene apparently many days later. There was an impression of a big low ceilinged cabin, looking out through the stern windows of the ship, with senior officers standing round two or three seated at a table, where were spread many maps and charts. B, though junior in years, seemed to hold a senior rank and was consulted equally with the others.... One chart particularly noticed was of the course of a river.

The next scene followed at once. A sensation of intense heat, oppression and moisture, of depression and weariness with existing conditions. It was a large, boarded and somewhat bare looking room, low ceilinged, through the open doors and windows of which could be seen a narrow gallery or length of deck and beyond this an expanse of water dully glistening in the night through patches of dark vegetation. A big barge, almost all deck house, moored to an overgrown bank, sweltering, clammy, insect ridden; a sense of weariness, of delay and frustration. Above all there was heat. A scene of gloomy senior officers, mostly weak with illness and grown listless with a sense of having been forgotten; a knowledge of thinned ranks of weary men, of a campaign terminated and now waiting on someone's forgetfulness for a recall.

A knew all this from his instant knowledge of what was in B's mind. He was also now aware of B's appearance, tall, broad shouldered, muscular beyond the average, dark haired and aggressive by nature.

B now seemed to be the chief actor in the scene, although officers senior in age stood apart. He appeared to be the only one still full of energy, trying to overcome the listlessness of others by urging them to a new game, a kind of human shove-halfpenny. In spite of the room being moderately crowded, a space had been cleared. One took a short run to a mark on the floor and tried to slide as far as possible across the boards, the termination of each man's slide being marked in chalk. Certainly it served to increase the almost intolerable damp heat, but it was a new game, a relief from boredom for a time, while the excuse for fairly heavy betting helped to remove one's mind from the ever present thought, When will they recall us? When are we going home? And always there was the damp heat, the insects, the high tight collars, the feeling of having been forgotten, near hopelessness.

The next scene came the following night. A room in a big shore bungalow on the edge of the water. Night again, but this time there had been a dinner somewhat more impressive than usual; a good deal of wine. There appeared to be bamboo chairs. Still there was the heat and the feeling of having been forgotten. In this scene there were two or three native women present, small and faintly dark, in short jackets and tight skirts; the older officers somewhat aloof from noisy juniors, of whom the noisiest was B. Somewhere there was a band. Clinging to B and urging him to dance was one of the native women, with red flowers in her hair, holding to his left arm, pleading in bad English, "You not go home, you never leave me, you stay." B, intent on something else not clear to A, trying to shake himself free, replied in an annoyed tone, "No! I will never leave you, I will never go. Oh! bother the woman."

At that moment through the door hurried an officer with a beaming face, holding aloft a long paper, calling out above the noise in the room, "Orders at last! We are going home!" B, half turning towards him, feeling a sudden uplift, a swelling of joy and relief all through, cried out, "What, going home?"

These three words struck the dreamer as a shout, so as almost to waken him, like a mental blow that could never be forgotten. At the same time he sensed B's quick thought, My God! What have I said? A, entirely powerless, saw the woman who was now behind B in his effort to shake her off, with a look of hatred and determination on her face, obviously realizing the import of B's words, quickly draw a long knife from her girdle and with all her force strike it to the hilt into the hollow on the left side of B's neck, between the shoulder and the collar bone, striking downwards.

As she struck A had the sensation of becoming B wholly and entirely. It was on his own shoulder that he felt the blow, just the blow, a sharp pain and little more. There was a weakness at the knees, his legs gave way under him and the people in the room seemed to rise towards the ceiling. Someone tried to hold him under the arms, he felt his jaw sagging and there was a mist gathering. He heard a voice, "Hold her! Hold her! Don't let her go!" There was no observer now, only one consciousness, slowly ebbing. In the moments of that ebbing, in the realization that he would now never go home, a scene rose before his mind, as if he were again experiencing it. Himself on a big black horse in black riding clothes; a black swallow tail coat and polished black boots, cantering across a big level park under old oak trees through which he could see the house that he was approaching.

It seemed to be a long low, white house of little more than two floors. He approached it through the trees from the right front of the house and could see two big bow windows, rising the height of the two floors at each end of the front of the house with pillared portico that faced, down a few shallow steps a driveway that led through the park into the distance. On each side of the porch the house stretched with a long unbroken front.

Full of the joy of life and the knowledge that few but himself could manage the big horse, his mind was full of his mission, to tell Her who waited for him in the white house that he was at last going to do something with his time that was worth while, he had his commission and was sailing almost at once for the new war. He knew that she would be proud of what he had done and that she would wait for him. Then, vaguely conscious that his head had fallen forward as someone tried to raise him, life faded into blackness and the dreamer woke.

Added in June 1950.

In June 1950 there occurred a further dream, short, almost momentary but as clear and precise in its nature as the former scenes with the same unforgettable quality. It was inspired, no doubt, by the fact that not long before the above account had been re-written from the notes and the whole occurrence had been vividly brought back to the mind.

A, the dreamer, was conscious of a big bedroom, one side of which was largely taken up by a big bow window, very wide with sashes of the early Georgian type. There was a light wall paper with a faint pattern. The fireplace was in the center of the right hand wall as you faced the window and there was a small door in the same wall between it and the window. The bed, a four poster, stood in the center of the wall facing the window with the door into the room in the corner on its left. A mahogany wardrobe or tallboy stood in the middle of the left hand wall. There seemed to be a dressing table in the center of the window with a small basin stand on its right.

Between fireplace and bow window stood B in the same dark riding clothes, having evidently only just arrived. A had the feeling that he was awaiting his baggage to arrive by chaise. He was looking round the room with intense pleasure and A, as before experienced his thought. How pleasant to be here again, it will be a long time before I come back. She would be downstairs waiting for B for it was Her home, the long white house in the park and he had come to say goodbye.

All this took place in that momentary glimpse, the awareness of the room, its furnishings, the house and the park and what was passing in B's mind. One important fact, behind B, in the fireplace wall between bow window and fireplace was a door which A knew through B's mind, gave into a small room or closet. This struck A as odd, because this wall should have been the end wall of the house and there should have been no place for a room here.

This dream was but a momentary glimpse, but was clear as crystal and its connection with the former dreams quite unmistakable. In this dream A seemed to be standing just inside the door of the room.

Three Comments to the Dreams Added by John East

1. One point has occurred to me since writing the above. I have always been puzzled by the fact that B, the actual personality to whom these events occurred and the same as the re-incarnated A who experienced the dreams, should, being so very junior in age, have been present in the ship's after cabin at a conference of senior officers immediately before the landing. There is also the impression of his authority in the scenes on the barge and on the final evening. This would be amply accounted for by B's having purchased his commission, a senior one, or even the command of a regiment. In those times [first half of the 19th century] this did occur.... Regiments were normally commanded by quite young men of title and wealth.

2. It will be seen that the final dream, of B in the bedroom with the big bow window, occurred in 1950 and was immediately recorded the following day.

3. Every incident, every thought, every sensation have always remained clearly fixed in the dreamer's mind since those two nights. The dream was entirely reasonable and coherent throughout. There was nothing that could not have happened exactly as it was dreamt. The sequence of events was perfect.

Comment. Throughout the dreams John East as A seems mostly to have been a spectator of B and B's actions. This separation of A and B is particularly clear in the third dream when B stood between the fireplace and the small door near the bow window that led to the small adjoining room. A was at the other side of the room, near the door to the room from the hallway. The room had only these two doors.

John East's Inquiries Toward Confirmation
of Details in the Dreams

Some time between the first two dreams and the third one, John East asked a friend who was an authority on army uniforms and military history whether there had ever been a military campaign in a very hot damp climate, where the troops wore uniforms such as he saw in his dreams, lived on barges and waited a long time before being ordered home. His friend immediately suggested that all these details fitted the First Burmese War of 1824–26 (Doveton, 1852; Laurie, 1880; Trant, 1827).

John East's inquiries led him to additional sources that confirmed the plausibility and even the accuracy of details in his dreams. For example, in his report of the first dream he stated that he gained the impression that "the ship [troop transport] did not belong to the navy and that the uniforms of the officers were not naval uniforms but were of a similar type." In fact, the troops participating in the First Burmese War were transported in ships of the East India Company (Laurie, 1880). Their officers wore uniforms that were somewhat similar to naval uniforms, but not exactly the same (Chatterton, 1914).

Even more impressive to John East was his recognition in an illustrated weekly of the house, Shredfield Hall, toward which B rode in the second dream (after he was stabbed) and where he saw himself standing in a room in the third dream. The illustrated weekly published in the 1950s several photographs showing views of Shredfield Hall and also a diagram of the rooms of the first floor.* Shredfield Hall was a long white house with a columned portico at its front. Near each end of the house there was a prominent bow window. The central part of the house has three stories, not two as B seemed to remember. John East thought that trees to the south of the house in the photographs published in the illustrated weekly seemed not as they were when B (the dreamer) rode to the house. He consulted a book describing and illustrating the country seats of notable persons in the early 19th century (Neale, 1821). A view of Shredfield Hall in that book showed that a spinney of trees at the south end of the house figuring in photographs of the illustrated weekly were not there in 1820; this detail corresponded to B's view of the trees near the house as he rode on his horse toward its southeast corner.

For John East his most impressive confirmation derived from the diagram of the rooms on the ground floor of Shredfield Hall that was published in the illustrated weekly. This shows at the south end of the house, a large room with a bow window and a door next to the window leading to an adjoining smaller room. The illustrated weekly stated that this end of the house had been altered in the second half of the 18th century in order to provide smaller bedrooms for the owners. The room with the large bow window is markedly asymmetrical because of the apparent later partition to make two smaller rooms from one larger one. The corresponding room with a bow window at the north end of the house is exactly the size of the two smaller rooms at the south end. John East believed that the room in which B stood in his third dream is of such an unusual shape (because of its being made from the division of a larger room) as to be unique. He was convinced that Shredfield Hall was the house that figures in the second of his dreams of 1927 and in the dream of 1950.

The owners of Shredfield Hall are listed in directories of British titled families.

---

*Respect for the privacy of the present owners of Shredfield Hall requires me not to publish any details of the articles in the illustrated weekly that could identify the house.

From one of these, *Burke's Peerage, Baronetage, and Knightage* (Townend, 1826/1963) and correspondence with the editor of the *Peerage* he learned that the owner of Shredfield Hall in the 1820s had two unmarried sisters, Wilhelmina and Helen, who must have been living with him. He conjectured that these sisters, who were born in 1807 and 1808, would have been too young to marry in 1824. Therefore, he thought that B had fallen in love with one of them and had decided to fill in the time of waiting for her to become older by buying a commission in the army and going off to the war in Burma. The scenes of riding on horseback to the house and waiting in the unusual room with the bow window occurred when he went to say goodbye to the girl to whom he was attached.

During his correspondence with me in 1960–62, John East expressed complete confidence that his dreams derived from real memories of a previous life. He had not, however, solved the case by learning of a young man the events of whose life corresponded to those of B in the dreams.

Later Inquiries Toward Confirming Details of the Dreams

In my correspondence with John East I asked him some questions about details. For example, he had described the room with the bow window where B stood in the third dream as on the second floor of the house. He referred to the girl he had come to meet as waiting for him "downstairs." I wrote him that the diagram of the rooms published in the illustrated weekly showed the division of the rooms on the first or ground floor, not those of the second floor. To my query about this John East replied that he had made a mistake and should have said that B was waiting in the room with a bow window on the first floor.

In the second dream B had a Burmese mistress who killed him when he exulted over the news of going home. In the more detailed account of his second dream John East remembered B as waiting for news of orders to go home. In the notes written immediately after the second dream the Burmese mistress refers to the next dance as the "last time," which suggests some intimation of B's departure. John East explained this possible discrepancy by pointing out that the officers and soldiers were certainly expecting to be ordered home soon and it would be reasonable for them — and their mistresses — to think that any dance might be "the last one."

In addition to examining the photographs and text of the articles about Shredfield Hall in the illustrated weekly, I confirmed the accuracy of John East's description of the uniforms worn by the British Army in the period of the First Burmese War. I also confirmed what John East had learned about the use of ships of the East India Company to transport troops to south Asia and about the uniforms of the ships' officers (Chatterton, 1914). I examined the engraving of Shredfield Hall in Neale (1821) and noted some difference in the trees at the southeastern side of the mansion between what Neale showed and the photographs of the 1950s. (I do not consider this difference significant.)

Efforts to Identify a Person Corresponding to B of the Dreams

Shredfield Hall is in Staffordshire, and it is reasonable to suppose that a man like B riding a horse to visit a girl at Shredfield Hall would be living in Staffordshire and, when joining the army, likely to join a Staffordshire Regiment. I was fortunate in being able to enlist the help of the late Guy Lambert in this case. He was a former senior official in the War Department of the British government as well as a former President of the Society for Psychical Research.

He searched the records of British regiments for those that had yellow facings on their uniforms and found that 31 (out of nearly 100) had such facings. Then he searched for those who had "Ava" (the ancient capital of Burma) among their battle honors. This would indicate participation by the regiment in the First Burmese War. He found that 10 regiments had been authorized to include "Ava" in their battle honors. Of the group, however, only two regiments had both yellow facings on their uniforms and "Ava" included in their battle honors. Of these, one was the 38th Regiment from Staffordshire. In fact, the Commander of the British Army during the First Burmese War, Major General Sir Archibald Campbell, was an officer of the 38th Regiment.

It then seemed plausible to think that B had been a junior officer of the 38th Regiment serving in Burma during the First Burmese War. Sir Archibald Campbell's own son, Lieutenant John Campbell, was serving as an aide-de-camp to his father during the war. He, however, survived the war, had a successful later military career, and was killed during the Crimean War.

In 1970 Dr. Alan Gauld drew my attention to *History of the South Staffordshire Regiment* (Vale, 1969). I began to correspond with its author, Colonel W. L. Vale. He in turn became interested in the case and was able to tell me that during the First Burmese War the 38th Regiment lost two officers who were killed, one who died of wounds, and nine others who died from disease. Understandably, no officer would be listed as "killed by his Burmese mistress." Any officer murdered as B seemed to have been would have his death attributed to disease.

We cannot be certain that B died of the stabbing wound he received, although I think this likely. The area of the neck into which the Burmese woman thrust her knife has numerous large blood vessels and the severing of one of these — at least in Burma in 1826 — would be fatal within a few minutes. As B was losing consciousness, he had a memory flashing back to the time when he rode to say goodbye to his girlfriend at Shredfield Hall. This might be regarded as a fragment of a life review of the kind that occurs in about 13% of the cases of persons who come close to death and recover (Stevenson and Cook, 1995). Such life reviews can also occur in persons who die, so its occurrence in John East's case has no weight in deciding whether B survived his wound or died from it.

Equally unhelpful in this respect is the absence of a birthmark on John East. (In our correspondence he told me that he had no birthmark at the site of B's wound.) Although many subjects who claim to remember a previous life that ended violently have related birthmarks, many others do not (Stevenson, 1997).

Could the Life of B Have Occurred During the Second Burmese War?

John East's report of his second dream emphasizes the tedium and the length of waiting for orders to go home after the war had concluded. The First Burmese War ended with the Treaty of Yandaboo on February 24, 1826. Colonel Vale learned from the records of the Staffordshire (38th) Regiment that it was transferred to India beginning in March with some units not leaving until April. Six weeks does not seem to me a long time of waiting; but it may have seemed unbearably long to a man eager to return to his girlfriend.

Many of the details of the dreams could fit equally well the circumstances of the Second Burmese War (1852–53). Another Staffordshire (80th) Regiment participated in it. The uniforms were much the same (including the high collars or stocks and yellow facings), the troops were still transported by ships of the East India Company, and officers still bought their commissions. This time, however, the waiting for orders to go home was markedly longer than it had been after the First Burmese War. This war lasted from April 5, 1852 until January 20, 1853; but the 38th Regiment waited 10 months before being ordered home.

The Second Burmese War does not suit so well as the First with regard to a young unmarried girl waiting for B to return from the war. The owner of Shredfield Hall at that time (1852) had one unmarried daughter who was then 15 years old. Perhaps this was not too young an age for her to become attached to a young man like B. If so, we are unable to decide whether the First or the Second Burmese War best fits all the relevant details of B's dreams.

Similarities Between the Personalities of B and John East

John East saw important similarities between the personality of B (so far as the dreams revealed it) and his own character. B, he could assume, must have belonged to one of the "county families." He was a skillful horseman, with some interest in military affairs, and was presumably wealthy enough to buy a commission in the army. Before joining the army he had not done anything "worth while" with his life.

The brief autobiography that John East wrote for me shows that in his early life, indeed up until the middle years of his life, he lived and liked the life of a country gentleman who enjoyed hunting and shooting. He disliked academic life and would have developed a military career if poor eyesight had not prevented this.

It must be added that some other elements emerged in John East's character following and perhaps because of his first two dreams. He became profoundly interested in quantum physics and had read and assimilated Heisenberg's *Physics and Philosophy*. He read the works of W. Y. Evans-Wentz, who was one of the most important scholars of Tibetan Buddhism of his period. He corresponded with Evans-Wentz, who wrote a Foreword to a second book that John East published before his death (East, 1960b).

John East's Interpretation of His Dreams

The plenitude of details in his dreams, about the First Burmese War (as John East believed it was) and the unusual floor plan of Shredfield Hall convinced John East that his dreams derived from memories of a previous life in Staffordshire in the first quarter of the 19th century. In one of his accounts of the dreams he wrote: "The architectural plan of the bedroom and the little room adjoining is certainly asymmetrical and unusual, and I very much doubt if it exists in any other house." As is the case with other dreamers of vivid dreams the realism of his dreams and their ineradicability from his memory added to his conviction about their origin in events that he (as B) had experienced.

Comment

John East's conclusions seem reasonable to me. We cannot exclude the possibility that, given his education and wide reading, he had acquired some knowledge of the First Burmese War before he had his dreams. That he would have known details of the uniforms worn by ship's officers and soldiers seems doubtful. Even more doubtful would be normal knowledge of the participation of a Staffordshire regiment in this particular war. It is moreover quite certain that he could never have seen a plan of the rooms of Shredfield Hall before the publication of a plan in the 1950s. We may discount individual details, but not readily disregard the sum of them found together.

TRAUDE VON HUTTEN

Summary of the Case and Its Investigation

Traude von Hutten was born in Dresden, Germany, on January 7, 1905. Her father was a Lutheran minister. Traude was the youngest child of a large family. (I did not learn how many siblings she had.)

When Traude was 5 years old, she had a dream in which she seemed to be living in a castle during the Middle Ages. In the dream she experienced the deaths of both her parents in accidents and then the loss of her husband, who failed to return from a Crusade. She had exactly the same dream when she was 8 years old and again when she was 13.

At the age of 17 she was invited to a dinner where she sat opposite a woman she had never met before. The woman stared at her fixedly for a time and then suddenly said: "Do you know that you have lived before on this earth?" Before Traude, astonished, could reply, the woman continued, and told her that she (Traude) had had a recurrent dream about a previous life. She then went on to mention details of this life that corresponded with extraordinary exactitude to Traude's dream. Traude had not previously been exposed to the idea of reincarnation. She later learned that this woman was a much respected clairvoyant.

In adulthood Traude married twice and was twice widowed. Her second husband died when serving with the German Army at the siege of Leningrad during World War II. After the war, she lived first in Mannheim and then in Munich. She worked as an interpreter for the American Army in Germany until 1952, when she qualified for a pension as a war widow and retired from employment. During these years she had no further significant dreams and no suggestions that the dreams she had had in childhood were verifiable.

In childhood Traude had a keen interest in the Middle Ages. Although she later remembered that her childhood had been happy, she had preferred being alone and daydreaming over playing. She would like to climb the sloping trunk of a walnut tree in the compound of her family's home and sit in a hollow of the tree. She said she did this "daily." There, images of being a woman in the Middle Ages would come to her as daydreams. (Presumably she would not have done this before the age of 5 by which time, according to her later memory, she had had the "castle dream" for the first time.)

She never visited medieval castles until she was 15 years old. At that time her parents took her on a tour of castles in Thuringia. Thereafter, she often visited other castles, but none evoked in her any sense of familiarity until she went to the castle of Trifels in the Palatinate of Germany, now in the state of Rheinland-Pfalz.

On May 6, 1956, she visited the castle of Trifels with a friend, Clara Holzer, and immediately identified it as the castle of her recurrent dream. Looking at the castle on the top of a steep incline, Traude explained to Clara that here her parents of the previous life had both died accidentally. As soon as she said this, an old-timer appeared, as if from nowhere. He warned Traude and Clara about the dangers of the steep incline and went on to tell them that a prince who held the castle as a fief from the Emperor had died on this steep hill accidentally, as had his wife. This seemed to confirm the details of Traude's recurrent dream.

In 1956 the German newspaper *Das Neue Blatt* invited its readers to submit accounts of memories of previous lives.* Traude sent the newspaper an account of her dream, and *Das Neue Blatt* published it on May 24, 1956. The newspaper account does not mention Traude's visit to Trifels, because she submitted it before she went there and its publication was delayed.

Subsequently, at least one other German publication printed an account of Traude's dream, and this came to the attention of Dr. Heinrich Wendt.† He showed an interest in the dream and made a suggestion about a medieval prince to whom it might refer. He referred Traude to me, and she sent me an account of her dream in

---

*Ruprecht Schulz also responded to this newspaper's invitation. So far as I know, his case and that of Traude von Hutten were the only reports the newspaper published.

†Dr. Wendt, a retired judge, had a considerable knowledge of paranormal phenomena. I visited him several times in Mannheim, where he lived. He translated my first book of reports of cases of the reincarnation type into German.

a letter of January 2, 1968. During the next 2 years I corresponded with her about the details of her dream and possible relevant circumstances of her life. She answered all my questions carefully. She also sent me a statement from her friend Clara Holzer, which corroborated Traude's claim to have recognized Trifels as the castle of her dream.

Because Traude had identified Trifels as the castle of her dream, I sought and obtained the assistance of Dr. Günter Stein, the Assistant Director of the *Historisches Museum der Pfalz*, which is in Speyer am Rhein. Trifels is about 35 kilometers southwest of Speyer, close to the small town of Annweiler. Dr. Stein was the coauthor of the official guidebook to Trifels, and it is unlikely that anyone knew more about the castle than he did. Like Dr. Wendt he became interested in the case and corresponded with me about the possibilities for verifying it.

On March 4, 1970, I met and interviewed Traude at her home in Munich. A few days later, on March 9, she and I went to Speyer, where we met Dr. Stein in his office at the museum. Dr. Stein and I asked Traude to describe what she remembered of the castle as from her dream, and I made a sketch according to her indications. The next day, we all went to Trifels. A few weeks later, in April 1970, Dr. Stein sent me a detailed report of our visit to Trifels and his opinion of its correspondence (as it was in the time of the Crusades) to the details of Traude's dream. Also on March 10 I was able to meet Clara Holzer, who lived in the area of Trifels. Dr. Stein later allowed me to borrow and copy pages from a register of documents that mentioned Trifels.

Traude von Hutten died in Bad Gastein on December 8, 1970.

Traude von Hutten's Dream

The dream has three parts. It begins with a scene of inconsolable loneliness. Then follows a scene in which the dreamer explains her unhappiness by recounting the accidental death of her parents. In the third part of the dream she is an older woman awaiting the return of her husband from a Crusade; but he does not return with his companions, and the dreamer is again left alone.

I have translated an account of the dream that Traude sent me with her first letter to me, dated January 2, 1968. I have separated the three parts of the dream.

> I see my physical form and feel myself embodied. I am aware of how the folds of my long dress fall on my legs as I walk. I hear myself walking over the creaking wooden floorboards of the long hall…. Loneliness engulfs me, comfortless loneliness.

> The last faint rays of the setting sun are coming through Gothic windows. I go over to an open window and look out. The black fir trees, which are half as high as the mountain, surround it thickly and have a gloomy, almost sinister effect. Stretching away in front of me, as far as the horizon, the land is green except for a few small castles. I stare fixedly downwards. Yes, down below where I am, occurred the horrible event that in one blow changed my whole world. In a single day I lost both my parents in accidents.

That autumn day remained as clearly in my memory as if it had been only yesterday. I could see my slender, beautiful mother, full of the joy of life. She climbed elegantly onto her white horse, turned smiling toward me, and making a gesture with her riding crop, she galloped off downwards. A little later a thunderstorm begins. My father comes home early from hunting. When he learns that his wife is still away, he turns his horse around and races down the mountain. I hear the sound of his horse's hooves on the planks of the wooden drawbridge. When after some hours my parents have not returned, I send servants out to search the forest with torches. Around midnight they bring my parents into the castle on makeshift litters—both dead. The rain had washed the mountain path and my mother's horse had slipped and then rolled over several times down the steep slope with my mother under him. The broken bushes immediately showed my father—searching for my mother—where the accident had occurred; but then the very same accident happened to him.

I feel the misery of being alone in the huge castle. I look at the only people around me, a pair of old servants. I am afraid. I have a tormenting uncertainty about what has happened to my husband, who joined a Crusade and has now been gone a long time. Every day I climb to the battlements of the castle to look for a sign of his return. Yet every day that passed lessened my hopes. One bright day in June I noticed a cloud of dust in the distance. It came closer and closer. Then I could see the reflection of the sun on armor. I gave a jubilant shout: "They are coming! They are coming!" I broke into tears, and they ran down my face that had become thin. I see myself running down the stairs, grabbing a scarf and racing down the mountain. Then I am standing, breathless, in the middle of the villagers. My eyes are fixed on the cavalcade that comes nearer and nearer. With banners waving, armor shining, and visors half-opened the riders came on, greeted joyfully by the crowd. Soon one of them jumped down from his horse and hugged his wife, then his mother. I hear myself whispering: "My darling must be arriving next." As if spellbound I look at every single rider. Suddenly one of them leaves the group and turns his horse toward me. I get ready to stretch out my arms. Then I become aware that this man has light gray eyes. I think: "No. He cannot be my husband. My husband has blue eyes." Silently I look at these strange eyes and I become serious again. Then I suddenly face the truth. "My husband is not with the group. He will never return. He is dead." The people around me seem to become enshrouded in a fog. The sunshine had gone. I begin to feel faint, as if slowly my life is being drained from my body. The dream ends.

Circumstances and Features of the Dream

Traude described the dream as vivid. For her the dream experience had the quality of a reliving, quite unlike her usual dreams. Each later repetition of the dream was identical in every detail to its first occurrence. She knew of no circumstance that acted as a stimulus to this particular dream. The occurrences were spontaneous. Later in life, she sometimes wished to have the dream again, but it did not occur.

When she had the dream for the first time, at age 5, she awoke crying. Her mother came to her, and she told her mother that she was not her "real mother." On this and the second occasion of having the dream she described it to her mother; she did not tell her mother about the third occurrence, when she was 13 years old.

Unlike Traude's memories of ordinary dreams, that of the castle underwent no fading as she became older.

. **Comment.** Traude's report of her dream differs in style from the reports of most other dreams that the dreamer later describes as a reliving of a previous life. It begins with a description of the deep depression that the events later narrated induced. Within the second and third parts of the dream Traude varied the tense; sometimes she used the present tense, at other times the past tense. In addition to these features, the report contains an incongruous detail: that of the dreamer's father recognizing where his wife had been killed when her horse slipped. He himself died soon after his wife, and no one could know how he recognized the site of his wife's death.

Every report of a dream attempts to translate images, usually pictorial, into words. Almost inevitably, condensations, omissions, and distortions occur. Traude's dream perhaps contains more of these modifications than most reports of dreams.

Details Added Later by Traude

In our correspondence and when we met in Munich and Speyer, Traude added some details to the account of her dream. She mentioned that her mother rode the horse with a side-saddle and on her head had a long cone-shaped hat. Her own hair, in the second part of the dream, was arranged in two pigtails; in the third part of the dream, when she seemed to be an adult, her hair was gathered at the top of her head. In that part of the dream she experienced herself as being in a physical body larger than the child's body she then had.

Her description of the plan of Trifels from which I made a sketch included additional details, such as the location of the main entrance to the castle and the story where the great hall had been located.

Corroboration Concerning Traude's First Visit to Trifels

In November 1957 Clara Holzer wrote a short statement in which she corroborated Traude's report of how she had recognized Trifels and said she had lived there before. I quote the following from her statement:

> At the beginning of the road up the mountain [to the castle] Traude said spontaneously to me: "I know all this. I lived here once before." As we arrived at the top in front of the castle, Traude pointed to a level area on the left and said: "Here earlier were the servants quarters and over there was a lodging for horsemen and yonder there had been a drawbridge." Just then the caretaker emerged and came toward us. Having overheard what Traude had been saying, he remarked: "You know everything already. I do not need to show you around." As we entered the interior of the castle, Traude said: "The stairs are on the right; previously they were on the left." The caretaker confirmed this. When we reached the upper level, Traude said that previously there had been a larger hall there. The caretaker confirmed this also.

Clara Holzer's statement made no reference to the old-timer who had described how at Trifels a prince and his wife had both been killed accidentally. When I met her in 1970, it had been almost 14 years since she and Traude had visited Trifels. Clara Holzer had been seriously ill in the meantime, and she said that this had impaired her memory. She could recall nothing about the old-timer and his narration.

Failed Efforts to Verify the Dream

In the 12th to 14th centuries Trifels was an important castle during the Holy Roman Empire (Sprater and Stein, 1971). As a *Kaiserburg* (imperial fortress) it had military importance. The imperial insignia were kept there and so were many political prisoners of the intermittent wars. Of these prisoners, King Richard I of England, who was lodged there in 1193, was the most notable. With the decline of the medieval German Empire, Trifels lost its previous importance. Despite some attempts at repair and even restoration, the castle deteriorated structurally and was finally abandoned in the 17th century. Thereafter, the people of the surrounding area plundered it for building materials. In the 19th century a new interest among Germans in the history of their country included research into places of previous importance, such as Trifels. The government of Bavaria, in whose territory the castle then was, stopped it from being used as a quarry. In 1938, the German government (of the Nazis) initiated a program of restoration. This continued, with interruptions, until 1954. The restoration, however, was not a rebuilding of the castle as it had been during the Middle Ages. This is why Dr. Stein could write me in his letter of January 13, 1970:

> If your correspondent [meaning Traude] visited Trifels after 1954, she would presumably have been impressed by the newly built section of the castle; unfortunately, this does not in any way correspond to the previous structure of the building; on the contrary, it was based on the fantasies sketched by the architect Professor Esterer.

Despite this difficulty, Dr. Stein took Traude's dream with sufficient seriousness to listen to her description of the castle and visit it with us. From this it became clear that in one respect Traude was clearly wrong. She placed the principal entrance on the northern side of the castle, whereas it had been on the northeastern side. The northern side overlooked a steep, almost clifflike incline, quite unsuitable for any road of access to the castle. The stairs to the main part of the castle were "rebuilt" on the west side. They could not have been on that side earlier, but no one knows on which side they were. (The caretaker who assured Traude that she was right about the place where the stairs had been could not have had any certain knowledge of their previous location.) In some respects, however, Traude's description of the castle as it had been could be correct. In Dr. Stein's opinion most of Traude's details about the building were possibly correct but could not be shown to be so. He wrote, in his report of April 1970:

> I have to say that I cannot definitely identify Trifels as the site of [Traude's] dream, although there is much to support this interpretation and not much against it.

The inconclusiveness of the comparison between Traude's description of how she seemed to remember Trifels in her dream and the best information we have about how the building formerly was does not end the difficulty in identifying Trifels as the site of the dream. The importance of Trifels during the height of the German medieval empire resulted in, for that time, fairly ample records of its owners or holders (as well as its prisoners). These show no instance of any holder of the castle dying accidentally, with or without his wife dying at the same time.

Dr. Stein had never heard of any history or legend about a holder of the castle dying accidentally as Traude's dream suggested. Not trusting his own knowledge, Dr. Stein consulted Viktor Carl, a folklorist who had conducted research on the legends of the region; he had never heard of any episode corresponding to the second part of Traude's dream.

Traude's dream might correspond not to a holder of the castle of Trifels, but to some other castellan of the region or, for that matter, one of a different region in Germany. The detail of going on a Crusade imposes a temporal bracket, that of the dates of the first five Crusades (in which Germans participated), which means 1096 to 1229. A further constraint comes from the inheritance, according to Traude's dream, of the castle by a daughter. During the high Middle Ages castles were primarily, almost exclusively, of military importance; a woman by herself could not become the holder of one. Dr. Stein assured me that there exist no records of such an inheritance in Germany during the 12th and 13th centuries.

Dr. Wendt and Dr. Stein both suggested the candidature of Marquard von Annweiler, who was a prominent nobleman in the late 12th century. He was a close associate of the Emperor Henry VI, who appointed him Governor of Ancona (in Italy) and Duke of Ravenna. His name occurs in a list of documents that mention Trifels (Biundo, 1940). He must certainly have been at Trifels, and probably often, but he is nowhere identified as "from Trifels." Moreover, although he participated in the Third Crusade, he returned safely from it and later died in Sicily.

Dr. Stein suggested another candidate to have been the dream person's husband: Ludwig IV, Landgrave of Thuringia. His castle at Wartburg is not far from Dresden, where Traude had grown up, and she had visited it on the tour of castles with her parents when she was 15 years old. Ludwig set out on the Sixth Crusade and did not return from it. Instead, he died on the way, in Otranto, Italy, on September 11, 1227. His widow did not have to wait long — about two months — before learning of his death. Moreover, Ludwig inherited his dominions from his father, not through his wife, who was Elisabeth, a princess of Hungary, later canonized as Saint Elisabeth (Ancelet-Hustache, 1963; Lemmer, 1981).

I do not believe we can identify a medieval German nobleman satisfying the criteria I have mentioned: inheritance of a great castle by a daughter with a husband who left on a Crusade and did not return. If we could do this, one further detail would remain incongruous. Long conical hats were worn by women in the late 15th century, but not earlier. Such hats, however, have often been anachronistically associated with the earlier Middle Ages. A cartoon in *The New Yorker* (July 11, 1970) depicts a woman dressed in medieval clothes wearing such a hat and arguing with her husband, who is in heavy armor and about to set out on a Crusade.

Comment

This case is unsolved, and I do not believe that it ever will be solved. I consider it another lesson in the importance of independently verifying a subject's statements.

We may nevertheless ask ourselves about the origin of the dream or, perhaps I should say, the report of the dream to me and to other persons who took it seriously. At one time I thought that Traude might have contrived a hoax. That would mean, however, that she had missed having a great career as an actress; she gave no hint of anything but complete sincerity during our correspondence and the time we spent together — about 2½ days altogether.

A more likely explanation supposes that Traude misremembered her age when she had the "castle dream" for the first time. If she first had the dream not at 5, but at a later age, say after the age of 8, she might well have absorbed enough of German history — with abundant mention of castles—for the main ingredients of her dream. By this time, she was climbing the walnut tree and preferring daydreams of the Middle Ages to playing with other children.

Traude was no more immune than the rest of us to the influence of current stimuli on her dreams. On March 11, 1970, as we were taking leave of each other, she told me that during the night before, sleeping in the hotel in Mannheim, she had dreamed that "all the people of Trifels" (dressed in medieval clothing) had come to her and assured her that the former entrance to the castle was indeed on its northern side. This dream denied the evidence we had seen the day before: that the clifflike slope of the northern side made any entrance there infeasible, if not impossible.

The case has other perplexities. For example, how are we to understand the episode of the old-timer who turned up in a timely way and claimed to verify Traude's dream? He might have been imagined by Traude later; Clara Holzer's failure to remember him suggests this. He might also have been a friendly villager who, happening to overhear what Traude had been saying to Clara, obligingly furnished a confirmation.

We need also to understand the correspondence between the details of Traude's dream and those mentioned by the woman — then a complete stranger to her — whom she met at a reception when Traude was 17 years old. I have no reason to believe that Traude imagined this woman, although I cannot exclude this possibility; another is that the woman was, as Traude said she later learned, extraordinarily gifted at telepathy and "read" the dream in Traude's mind.

It remains to consider the explanation that Traude's dream contained some ingredients of memories of a previous life that unconscious mental processes had elaborated into what she remembered and reported many years later. I cannot leave this case without raising the question of why a young child would be as preoccupied with the Middle Ages in Germany as Traude said she had been. There are, after all, many other epochs and places from which a child may derive its fantasies. A real previous life might have influenced the selection of the country and period for the elaboration of the fantasies.

Luigi Gioberti

The subject of this case had a recurrent dream accompanied by strong emotion. He later had other dreams and waking images that he believed were memories of a previous life. None of the dreams or waking images has been verified, and one has been proved wrong.

Summary of the Case and Its Investigation

Luigi Gioberti was born in Venice on October 12, 1958. He was the third child and only son of his parents, Andrea Gioberti and his wife, Monica. He had two older sisters. Andrea Gioberti was an officer in the Italian Air Force. He died in 1977 at the age of 60. He had fought in World War II. The family were formally Roman Catholics. Monica Gioberti, however, believed in reincarnation. Her mother had some reputation for precognizing unexpected deaths. In the 1970s the family lived in Florence.

I learned of little remarkable about Luigi's early childhood except for an illness described by his mother as enterocolitis. According to her, Luigi nearly died during this illness. When he was 2 years old, he was vaccinated against poliomyelitis. Soon thereafter he was found to have impaired vision and from the age of 3 he wore glasses.

In these years he said that he wished to be an aviator, as his father was. He was much interested in airplanes and drew sketches of them. His mother said that he had been an introspective child, more serious than other children of his age. Teachers at school said that he seemed in his behavior older than other children of his age. He did not express any memories of a previous life in early childhood.

When he was about 11 years old, he had a nightmarish dream of being in a military airplane that was shot down and crashed. The dream recurred, perhaps a dozen times, within a few months. He had some other unusual dreams and also waking images that, put together, provided a coherent narrative of events preceding the shooting down of the airplane. He believed that he had been a British military pilot shot down by German antiaircraft guns during the Battle of Monte Cassino in 1943-44. He thought his name had been John Graham.

Luigi's experiences came to the attention of a friend of mine, Zoe Alacevich, who also lived in Florence. She and her husband were Italians, and her husband's Slavonic name derived from Dalmatian ancestry. Zoe Alacevich was a spiritualist and like most continental spiritualists she believed in reincarnation. She sent me a summary of the case in a letter dated January 15, 1978. The case seemed potentially important because the subject included in his statements the proper name of the aviator about whom he had dreamed. I therefore wrote to Luigi and asked him to send me a full account of his dream and related experiences. He replied with a long letter dated March 16, 1978. (He wrote in English, showing a completely adequate although imperfect knowledge of the language.) Some further correspondence between us followed. Later in 1978 I was able to go to Florence, and on December 3 I had a long interview with Luigi and his mother. During this, Luigi himself spoke little (from shyness perhaps) and in English. His mother spoke Italian, which Zoe Alacevich (in whose apartment we met) translated into French for me.

At the time of my interview with Luigi and his mother he was 19 years old. He was then a student of astrophysics at a college near Florence. His poor eyesight had thwarted his wish to become an aviator.

In 1979 I had some further correspondence with Luigi, mainly in an effort on my part to distinguish elements of Luigi's images that had occurred to him in dreams from those that he experienced in a waking state.

Because Luigi had given first and last names for the British military aviator, I thought it would be possible to verify these details from the records of the British Ministry of Defense. Accordingly, I wrote the Ministry of Defense, but the staff there were unable to confirm that a person corresponding to Luigi's statements had ever existed. I thought it incumbent on me to communicate this negative result to Luigi, and did so. Thereafter, I received some friendly letters from him, but we have not communicated since late 1979.

Luigi's Primary and Recurrent Dream

The following is the first account of the dream that Luigi wrote for me, in his letter of March 16, 1978:

> I was piloting a damaged airplane which crashed at last down to earth. Before I could get out of the cockpit, the main tank of the plane exploded and the burning fuel reached my face.... I woke with a start and I was quite upset.

The dream recurred about nine or ten times over the next 3 months. Luigi was about 11 years old at the time. After that he did not have the dream again until October or November 1978, when he had it again. I did not learn why it occurred at that time after a long interval.

Qualitative Features of the Primary Dream. For Luigi the dream was an experience lived or, as he later thought about it, relived. In a letter of March 25, 1979, he wrote: "I was watching the scene by [through] the eyes of the pilot. I was not observing the pilot as an external observer." In the same letter he wrote that after the airplane crashed: "I clearly felt the heat and the fuel smell, something like kerosene and petrol. I did not see only. I felt everything there was to feel, and maybe this is the most unpleasant side of the matter.... I feel uneasy [now] when I remember these things."

Supplementary Images Experienced by Luigi After the Primary Dream

In his letter of March 16, 1978, Luigi, after describing what I have called his primary dream, continued as follows:

> Later I come "to see" pictures of the life of this pilot; it was as [if] I saw a film in which the main actor was this young Englishman.... It was like a radio interference during a magnetic tempest. While I was thinking of something completely far from this story [the airplane crashing] a sequence suddenly passed in my brain and I was not able to think [of] anything else. Furthermore, I did not see the sequences of facts as you have read [them]. I remembered untied episodes, and I had to work hard to link all [the] episodes in one story. This phenomenon has been diminishing since one year, maybe because my studies make me busy far more than in the past times.... I must remark that most of what you have read has been remembered when I was wide awake.

The phrase "you have read," which occurred in two places in the letter, refers to material, indicated by the ellipses, of images that occurred to Luigi after he had the primary dream. As he wrote, he tied these together in the following history from which I have omitted some of the less important details.

He was a Scot called John Graham, born in Glasgow about 1920. When he grew up he became an aviator. He married a Scottish girl called Ann Irvine (or Irving) who had been a waitress at a pub near his airbase. They went to London where they lived near Victoria Station. They had a child. As a fighter pilot he participated in the Battle of Britain (August to October, 1940). His airplane was a Spitfire with the letters YLZ on the fuselage. Ann and their child were killed when a German bomb hit and destroyed the building where they lived and hoped to be sheltered. This angered him so much that following a battle in the air with German airplanes he deliberately strafed a ship (possibly German) that was rescuing persons in the water [perhaps the English channel]. For this misconduct he was tried by a court martial, but acquitted or exonerated because of his bravery earlier in the war. He was sent to the campaign against the Germans in Italy. At the battle around Monte Cassino in 1943-44 he was in a Spitfire airplane assigned to destroy German antiaircraft guns. His airplane was hit by a shell from a German antiaircraft gun and he crashed. As he went down, he was able to communicate by radio with his commanding officer.

As with the primary dream, the experiences of the later images included strong emotions. He wrote (June 7, 1978): "...when I see the episodes, I am not a neutral observer.... If I see a dangerous action or a special fight I realize that my heart beat accelerates, my fists are clenched and the muscles of my back get stiff."

Luigi referred, in his letter of March 25, 1979, to having had more than one dream, although the first dream (of crashing in his airplane) was by far the most significant.

I believe most of the later images came to him, as he wrote himself, when he was awake. Two, however, occurred in dreams. He said that images of how his wife and child were killed when a German bomb struck the building where they lived occurred in a dream. He also had dreams of air fights with German airplanes and noted that details of these varied in different dreams.

Normal Sources of Information Available to Luigi and Consulted by Him

The occupation of Luigi's father, a military aviator who had served in the Italian Air Force throughout World War II, provided an abundant normal source of information for Luigi about that war and some of its major events, such as the Battle of Britain, the bombing of London, and the battle around Monte Cassino. I am not asking my readers to think that such topics were never mentioned in Luigi's presence when he was a child. The family must also have had some books about the war and perhaps mementos of it.

In addition to these sources, Luigi acknowledged that he had tried to verify some details of his dreams and waking images. I did not learn when he began these efforts at verification. He was certainly active in this in the years before we began our correspondence. In 1977 he believed he knew (without conscious knowledge of a source) the colors of the Scottish clan Graham, and he drew a colored sketch of them. He then checked the correctness of his sketch in a book that he described as an "encyclopedia."*

In June 1978, Luigi bought an Italian magazine "*Storia della Aviazione*, No. 67," which was largely devoted to military aircraft of World War II. It gave detailed information about the British Spitfire airplane, which Luigi believed he, as John Graham, had piloted and crashed.

Luigi was somewhat aware — although I think not fully so — of the likelihood of normal knowledge contaminating his reports of his dreams and waking images. In his letter of March 25, 1978, he wrote: "I had tried to separate what I felt from what I thought later as for interpreting the dream." (This refers to his account of the primary dream.)

Corroborations by Monica Gioberti

Monica Gioberti remembered that Luigi had told her about his dreams soon after he had them. She said he was 10 or 11 years old at the time. She particularly recalled the strong emotion he showed in narrating the dream in which he seemed to crash in his airplane. He was between 10 and 11 years old when he had this dream.

*Compared with the example of the Graham tartan given in Moncreiffe and Hicks (1967) the colors of Luigi's design and of that published in the "encyclopedia"—predominately green and blue with black and white—are correct, but the designs are both wrong.

Monica also remembered Luigi telling her about how, in the previous life, he had a wife and child and that both had been killed in London "by the Germans." She remembered his narration of how, in the previous life, he had fired at rescuers on a ship who were trying to save wounded Germans who were in the water.

When Luigi was about 11, he and his mother passed near Cassino, and Luigi remarked: "There is where I died."

Independent Verifications of Details in Luigi's Experiences

In the summer of 1978 I wrote to the office (in Gloucester, England) of the Ministry of Defense concerned with officers' records of the Royal Air Force and asked whether they could verify the existence of John Graham. I mentioned some of the details in Luigi's dreams and waking images. A search of the records was made and no evidence of John Graham found. It seemed to me that the search might have been less than thorough, and so Emily Kelly (then working as my Research Assistant) asked for a further search. She added the detail that the John Graham of interest to us had been shot down in Italy near Monte Cassino and might have been buried there. A second search was then made and included ranks other than officers. Our correspondent at the Ministry of Defence also inquired about John Graham at the Commonwealth War Graves Commission. Both of these later searches revealed no trace of John Graham.

Comment

One cannot often prove that a named previous personality could not have existed; but I think I have done that in this case. There was no pilot in the Royal Air Force of World War II called John Graham.

I cannot avoid concluding that a large part of Luigi's images about John Graham came from normal sources and fantasies. Perhaps, however, the primary dream had some other source, even one in a previous life. Without verification we can only conjecture such an origin. It seems, however, legitimate to consider this possibility. If we reject it, the question remains of why a 10-year-old boy would suddenly have a series of nightmarish dreams about being a fighter pilot shot down during a battle.

CASE REPORTS: MISCELLANEOUS

RUPRECHT SCHULZ

This case has two unusual features. First, correspondence from which I will quote provides a written record of the subject's memories that he made before he tried to verify them. Second, the subject was born about 5 weeks before the previous personality died.

Summary of the Case and Its Investigation

Ruprecht Schulz was born in Berlin, Germany, on October 19, 1887. His father was a Roman Catholic, but his mother belonged to the Protestant (Evangelical) Church. They must, however, have been receptive to the idea of reincarnation. When he was 10, his older sister Rosa died. A few months later, his mother gave birth to twins who were markedly dissimilar. One of the twins so much resembled the deceased older sister — physically and temperamentally — that they named her Rosa.*

Ruprecht Schulz had little interest in book learning; and when he was 18 years old he left school and went into business for himself. By the time he was 20, he had more than twenty employees. He later said that he was the first person to provide a laundry rental service; his was especially successful with mothers of infants who eagerly welcomed the delivery of fresh diapers. His company ultimately had 200 employees. He and his wife owned some six pieces of real estate, and a villa also. They had a chauffeur. In brief, they were rich. Ruprecht Schulz was also active in the affairs of his community. He became a member of the Council of the Chamber of Commerce and a representative to the municipal council of his district of Berlin.

Then World War II began, in 1939. During the war, the Allied bombing of Berlin damaged or destroyed much of his property. After the war, the division of Berlin into eastern and western sectors affected him even more. His remaining property was plundered. Before the war, Ruprecht Schulz had been ardently fond of Berlin, but afterward he came to dislike its isolation. At the age of 68, he retired from what little remained of his business and moved with his wife to Frankfurt (am Main), where he died in 1967, at the age of nearly 80.

In his childhood Ruprecht Schulz had a habit, when he was scolded, of gesturing with his hand as if he were going to shoot himself. I shall say more about this later.

This is an example of the persistent belief among some Europeans that a deceased child (or other member) of a family may be reborn in it (Bergunder, 1994). The case of Alessandrina Samonà (Part II of this work) provides another example of this belief and some evidence for it.

The success of his business enterprises enabled him to travel widely between the two world wars. He visited Italy and Turkey, where he had experiences of déjà vu accompanied by vague, unverifiable memories of previous lives in some of the cities he explored.

More distinct memories did not come to him until the early 1940s, when he was in his fifties. Their essentials were: that he had been a businessman concerned with ships; that he saw himself in a dark office building looking at account books which he took from an old safe; and that he found that he was financially ruined and shot himself. The memories seemed to include verifiable details. He noted down some of them in a diary that he kept. He also dictated an account of them to his secretary, Ingrid Wollensach, who encouraged, even urged him to try to verify them. Although he thought this might be possible, the war and its aftermath made any effort at verification impossible until the 1950s.

Finally, in May and June of 1952, he used the free time of a vacation to begin inquiries. Believing that the previous life he seemed to remember had been passed in a small seaport town of northern Germany, he wrote to the municipal officials of half a dozen towns of that description. He at first excluded Hamburg, Bremen, and Kiel as being too large. That left as possibilities more than half a dozen other, smaller seaports, namely Lubeck, Emden, Flensburg, Bremerhaven, Wilhelmshaven, Rostock, and Wismar. Of these, he thought Wilhelmshaven was probably the correct place; but he wrote to all of them, and, for good measure, to Bremen, Hamburg, and Kiel also. Affecting to be searching his family's history for an ancestor, he asked for information about a man who had lived and died in the 1880s of whom he furnished the main particulars that had figured in his memories. All but one of the towns replied negatively to his inquiries. From Wilhelmshaven, however, he received a letter (dated July 24, 1952) that briefly mentioned the life and suicide (in 1890) of a ship-broker and timber merchant who might have been the person Ruprecht Schulz hoped to find.

The first letter from Wilhelmshaven gave the family name of the putative previous personality as "Kohl." Ruprecht Schulz immediately knew that the name "Kohl" was slightly off, and a later letter (dated September 11, 1952) from Wilhelmshaven corrected the name to "Kohler." In this letter the municipality also gave him the name and address of Helmut Kohler's still living son, Ludwig Kohler.

Almost immediately after receiving the name and address of Ludwig Kohler, Ruprecht Schulz wrote to him, on September 17, 1952. After first apologizing for intruding into the family life of a stranger, he described his memories and asked Ludwig Kohler whether they matched events in his father's life and death. Fortunately, Ludwig Kohler responded cordially, and in a letter (dated September 21, 1952) he acknowledged that Ruprecht Schulz's memories corresponded to events leading up to the death of his father. This man, Helmut Kohler, had been a timber merchant, ship-broker and sawmill operator. He imported timber, which he then processed in his sawmill and sold. In 1887 he gambled on a rise in the price of lumber, miscalculated, and stood to lose a great deal of money. He then conspired with his accountant to falsify their records, but the accountant panicked and fled with the available cash. Helmut Kohler then lost his nerve and shot himself.

Ruprecht Schulz and Ludwig Kohler exchanged several further letters in the autumn of 1952. They did not meet, however, until October 1956, when Ruprecht Schulz went to Wilhelmshaven for the first time in his life. Earlier in 1956, the case of "The Search for Bridey Murphy" (Bernstein, 1956/1965) received sensational publicity in Germany (as well as elsewhere). As I mentioned in the report of Traude von Hutten's case, a German newspaper, *Das Neue Blatt*, invited its readers to submit personal accounts of seeming memories of previous lives. It received "hundreds of submissions," but the editors judged those of Traude von Hutten and Ruprecht Schulz the only ones worthy of publication; and they decided to publish an account of Ruprecht Schulz's case only after they had sent one reporter to interview Ruprecht Schulz in Frankfurt and another to interview Ludwig Kohler in Wilhelmshaven.

The report in *Das Neue Blatt* came to the attention of Dr. Hans Bender, the Director of the Institut für Grenzgebiete der Psychologie und Psychohygiene in Freiburg. In August 1960, he met and interviewed Ruprecht Schulz. He borrowed and copied various documents, such as letters and notes, that Ruprecht Schulz had preserved. He passed these to me, and I made copies of them. In 1960, Dr. Karl Müller interviewed Ruprecht Schulz and also obtained copies of some of the pertinent documents. Dr. Müller informed me about the case in 1962. He made available to me copies of some documents of which he had copies.

I went to Frankfurt on May 2, 1964, and had a long interview with Ruprecht Schulz and his wife, Emma. After that I corresponded with him until he died.

Subsequently, on December 8, 1970, I met Emma Schulz again, in Bonn, to which she had moved to be near her daughter, whom I also interviewed, briefly. Emma Schulz allowed me to examine some of the original documents that she had retained so that I could compare them with copies that I had. She also gave me the address of the Kohler family in Wilhelmshaven.

In the meantime, Ludwig Kohler had died, but in the hope of obtaining some further relevant information I wrote to his son, Ernst Kohler. He replied amiably, and after some further correspondence I arranged to meet him and his older sister, Gertrud. This meeting took place on October 15, 1971, at the home of Gertrud and her husband, which was in Emden. Gertrud was born in 1910 and Ernst in 1915. Not surprisingly they could contribute little further information to the case. Some of their statements disagreed with earlier ones of their father, and I shall discuss these discrepancies later.

The dates of Helmut Kohler's death and Ruprecht Schulz's birth have particular significance in this case, which is one of what we call "anomalous dates." In order to be certain that I had learned the correct dates, I corresponded with the municipal registries in Wilhelmshaven and Berlin. Ruprecht Schulz was born in the part of Berlin that, in the 1970s, was known as East Berlin. I enlisted the help of officials in West Berlin, and they obligingly pursued the matter with their counterparts in East Berlin. They finally obtained for me a copy of Ruprecht Schulz's birth certificate.

Two other contributing items deserve mention here. The first is an exchange of letters between Dr. Müller and Ingrid Wollensach, who, as I mentioned, had been Ruprecht Schulz's secretary during the 1940s, when he recovered his memories. (His diary had been lost during the wartime bombing of Berlin.) The second, a document dated August 1, 1952, is an account of his memories that Ruprecht Schulz wrote after he had begun writing to the seaports, had received a first reply from Wilhelmshaven, but had not yet corresponded with Ludwig Kohler.

The Circumstances of the Recovery
of Ruprecht Schulz's Memories

Ruprecht Schulz gave the following (tape-recorded) statement to Dr. Bender in August 1960.

> It [the memories] happened to me at the time of the bombing attacks on Berlin during the war [World War II; Ruprecht Schulz elsewhere mentioned the years as 1942-43]. We had 700 siren alarms; not all were followed by air attacks, but many were. We were on duty every night [to raise an alarm in case of fire]. I was keeping a diary, even though this was forbidden. The duty watch was rotated, and because I had been accustomed to working on Saturdays at my own business, I took the duty watch from Saturday evening to Monday morning. My place of business was in Breitenstrasse, opposite the old Berlin palace. The house was built at the time of the Thirty Years War and was registered as an historical monument. I could lie down on a couch, but had to remain fully dressed and alert. (This was not a responsibility that could be assigned to just anyone.) At these times [of being on duty] I would catch up with the work of my business that had been left over from the week.... As I mentioned, the building was an old romantic one; and the safe was an ancient one, which for reasons of security was not in an open place, but instead was sort of hidden in a kind of corridor, which was only dimly lit. And I used to go to this safe and take out [and examine] the account books. That is how it all began. The thought came to me that the account books were showing how our affairs were. Then every time I went to the safe and brought out the account books I would think: "You were in this situation once before. So what *was* that [previous] situation?" The feeling grew stronger and then — not in a trance or sleepy state — almost like something I could see before my eyes, I could see how I looked then. I was wearing a high collar and formal clothing. I had come from a ceremony on a special day. My business was finished. An employee had run off with the money — embezzled it and absconded. So I sat down with the account books and could see that there was no future. It was all over. Then I was in a room by myself and put a bullet into my head at the right temple. You would call these images clairvoyance, but for me they are memories.

In another statement (dated June 8, 1960) Ruprecht Schulz emphasized the similarities between his situation in 1942-43 and that in the previous life. He wrote:

> The setting of the previous time was similar to the one I was in then. The safe was in a similar location and the account books were also similar.

On May 2, 1964, I made the following notes during my meeting in Frankfurt with Ruprecht and Emma Schulz:

When RS first began to have his memories they were vague and unclear; but over the ensuing weeks they became clearer and clearer. He never had them except when he was in the office on watch duty on Sundays. He was completely awake at these times. He experienced again the emotions of the situation remembered. He saw the memories as an inner image, not as a projected vision.

Evidence of Written and Other Statements by Ruprecht Schulz Made Before Their Verification

As I mentioned earlier, Ruprecht Schulz used the leisure of a vacation in the spring of 1952 to write letters of inquiry to seaports of northern Germany. The first written record we possess of his memories occurred in these letters in which he pretended to be searching for the details of an ancestor whose name he did not know. The letter to the municipality of Wilhelmshaven (dated May 30, 1952) contained the following:

> In the hope of improving my family history I am trying to learn more about an ancestor or perhaps a relative of my family.... He would have died between 1870, perhaps earlier, and 1885. He lived in a German seaport and had something to do with shipping, freight, or something similar. He was about 40 years old. On returning from some celebration he shot himself because of financial troubles.

The first reply from Wilhelmshaven said that the man Ruprecht Schulz was trying to trace might be a ship-broker and lumber merchant named Kohl (*sic*) who had killed himself in 1890.

Ruprecht Schulz wrote back to Wilhelmshaven and asked for further details about the lumber merchant Kohl. Before he received a reply, he wrote out, on August 1, 1952, an account of his memories. Because this contained few details additional to those I have already listed I will not quote it here. It did, however, give more details about the formal clothing, such as a frock coat and stiff, white collar that the man he believed himself to have been had worn when he killed himself. It also stated that he thought the previous life had been lived in a small seaport, not a large one. (By the date of this statement, we should note, he had already learned that a ship-broker of Wilhelmshaven had killed himself in the late 19th century.)

The next letter from the municipality at Wilhelmshaven (dated September 11, 1952) gave the full name of the lumberman: Helmut Kohler. It also gave the name and address of Helmut Kohler's still living son, Ludwig.

Ruprecht Schulz almost immediately wrote to Ludwig Kohler. His letter of September 17, 1952, included the following:

> Since my earliest years I have had a distinct impression, with various details that I was [in a previous life] somehow connected with shipbuilding or shipping and that I shot myself. I was in the prime of life. For the place [of this life] I knew that it occurred in an old small or middle-sized seaport; and it seemed to me later and more clearly that this seaport was Wilhelmshaven. Further, the man [I was] seemed to be in an

ancient house. In this there was a small room with a chest or a kind of safe or filing cabinet in which important papers, account books and probably also some cash were kept. The person [I was] wore dark clothes of the style of that period, as if he had come from some important session or unusually important event. As for the date of these events—the suicide of the person [I was]—it has seemed to me that it would have been around 1885.

In 1960 Dr. Müller wrote to Ruprecht Schulz's former secretary, Ingrid Wollensach, who was still living in Berlin. He received from her two letters, dated September 24 and September 30, 1960. Ingrid Wollensach's first letter included the following:

> …I am happy to tell you what I still remember about the experience mentioned in your letter.
>
> I recall that Mr. Schulz said the events [of his memories] occurred in a small seaport, like Wilhelmshaven.* It definitely was not in a big seaport like Hamburg.
>
> I also remember the idea of a holiday, because in this connection we spoke about the clothes worn on such an occasion.
>
> Having noticed that in the statement of August 1, 1952, Mr. Schulz said that in the previous life he was alone in his office, I would like to mention that Mr. Schulz has the habit of working alone in his office — after everyone else has gone home — including Sundays and Holidays.

The second letter included the following:

> Regarding your letter about the memories of Mr. Ruprecht Schulz, I have thought about the matter again. Here are the further details that I remember.
>
> There was a reference to being concerned with a business handling wood. The person [of the memories] on a day of some special holiday, was alone in his office, examined his account books, and discovered that an untrustworthy employee had cheated him; consequently he was faced with bankruptcy. If I remember correctly, a revolver, which was kept in a desk, was also mentioned and that was the weapon used in the suicide.
>
> You may well ask yourself how it is possible for me to remember these details after so many years. With Mr. Schulz, however, he did not just dictate to me after which I typed out what he had said. In this case Mr. Schulz had spoken with me about the matter earlier, and we also spoke about it together later.

The Verification of Ruprecht Schulz's Statements

The first reply from the municipality of Wilhelmshaven to Ruprecht Schulz's letter of inquiry was dated July 24, 1952. It suggested the man about whom Ruprecht Schulz was inquiring might be "the ship-broker and lumber merchant Kohl, who committed suicide in 1890."

The second letter from Wilhelmshaven was dated September 11, 1952, and it gave

---

*Dr. Müller, in his letter of inquiry, had asked Ingrid Wollensach whether Ruprecht Schulz had mentioned the port of Wilhelmshaven by name.

some correct and more specific information. It gave the full name of Helmut Kohler, described him as a lumber merchant and sawmill operator, and said that he shot himself at the age of 54 on December 23, 1887. (This date was incorrect also.) This was the letter that gave the name and address in Wilhelmshaven of Helmut Kohler's son Ludwig.

With this information Ruprecht Schulz wrote to Ludwig Kohler on September 17, 1952. I cited earlier relevant passages from this letter. Ludwig Kohler replied immediately to Ruprecht Schulz's letter, on September 21. After first stating that he found it painful to share details of his family's life, he explained that he knew the matter was important to Ruprecht Schulz and would therefore oblige him with an answer to his questions. He also explained that he himself was only a child at the time of the events to which Ruprecht Schulz referred. (Ludwig Kohler was born in 1875, and so was 12 years old when his father killed himself.) His letter continues:

> My father, Helmut Kohler, had a substantial business in Wilhelmshaven that included trading in timber and also a sawmill. Our residence was in 25 Friedrichstrasse, and right next to it was a one-story building that was used for the offices. This building faced north, and it had only small windows, so that it was always dark in there. In a corner of one of the rooms there was a somewhat antiquated safe, which you have mentioned. In it money, account books, and also a cash box and important papers were kept. My father ordinarily wore dark clothing, and whenever he went out he wore a top hat on his head.
>
> He imported wood by ship from Danzig, Konigsberg, and Memel, but particularly from Norway, Sweden, Finland, Russia, and America. In 1888* he mistakenly believed that the customs duty would increase, and he purchased from abroad an unusually large amount of timber. Unfortunately, this was a faulty speculation, because the price of timber fell and much more than the customs duty rose. He then had difficulty paying the invoices. In order to get through the crisis he arranged with his accountant, who had been his "right hand" and enjoyed his complete trust, to falsify the records of their foreign exchange transactions. The two of them thought that they would extricate themselves when the exchange rate fell. This did not happen. The accountant became afraid that he would be arrested, and he fled to America taking with him a substantial amount of the company's available funds. My father now got into a complete panic and shot himself on the Day of Prayer and Repentance.† The company had to declare bankruptcy, although this was in fact unnecessary. Even though the buildings, the sawmill, and the lumber on hand were all sold in a forced auction, all the creditors were paid off.

In Ruprecht Schulz's letter of September 26, 1952, in which he thanked Ludwig Kohler for his helpful reply of September 21, he asked Ludwig Kohler whether Ludwig's father had shot himself "in the right temple or in the heart." In a reply, dated September 30, Ludwig Kohler wrote that he knew only that his father had shot himself in the head.

Table 2 furnishes a summary of all the verified items for which we have evidence

---

*Ludwig Kohler was a year off in the year of his father's death.

†In German this holiday is Buss- und Bettag, *the day of repentance and prayer. It always falls on a Wednesday in November. In 1887 it was on November 16.*

that Ruprecht Schulz wrote them down himself or stated them to his secretary before they were verified.

Ruprecht Schulz's Visit to the Kohlers in Wilhelmshaven

In October 1956 Ruprecht and Emma Schulz went to Wilhelmshaven where they met Ludwig Kohler. Wilhelmshaven had been much damaged by bombing during the then recent war. Ruprecht Schulz believed that he had recognized the Town Hall and an old archway. He noted that he could recognize photographs of Helmut Kohler's sons taken with a large group of schoolchildren, but he failed to recognize his daughters. We have no corroboration for any of the recognitions Ruprecht Schulz believed he had made.

Ruprecht Schulz's Prior Ignorance of Wilhelmshaven

In his letter to Ludwig Kohler of September 17, 1952, Ruprecht Schulz stated:

> I have never been in Wilhelmshaven. I have and have had neither relatives nor other connections with it. Despite my interest in doing so, I have never gone there because of the pressure of my business as well as the difficulties of traveling during Hitler's time and later.

The "interest" Ruprecht Schulz had in going to Wilhelmshaven derived solely from the conviction he had of having lived and died there; otherwise he had no interest in the city, which is about 370 kilometers northwest of Berlin on an inlet of the North Sea.

Additional Biographical Information About Helmut Kohler

In the course of my interviews and from reading documents made available to me, I learned a few details of the life of Helmut Kohler additional to those mentioned in the letters I have cited that Ludwig Kohler wrote to Ruprecht Schulz.

Helmut Kohler was born in Wilhelmshaven on January 7, 1834. He married a cousin, and they had at least three children, two sons and a daughter. Ludwig Kohler, the second son, was born, also in Wilhelmshaven, on May 9, 1875.

In 1887 Wilhelmshaven had only one newspaper, the *Wilhelmshaven Zeitung*. On November 24, 1887, it printed a brief notice of the death of Helmut Kohler describing it as "sudden and unexpected," but giving no details of the cause of death.

After returning for his first (and I think only) visit to Wilhelmshaven, Ruprecht Schulz wrote an account of what he had learned during the visit. He was told, presumably by Ludwig Kohler, "that on the day of Buss- und Bettag the entire family had

Table 2. Summary of Details in Memories of Ruprecht Schulz

Item	Written or Other Early Record	Verification	Comments
1. His business had something to do with ships.	Letter from R. Schulz to L. Kohler of September 17, 1952 Letter of May 30, 1952 from R. Schulz to Municipal Office of Wilhelmshaven	Letter from Municipal Office of Wilhelmshaven of July 24, 1952 Letter from L. Kohler to R. Schulz of September 21, 1952	
2. His business had something to do with wood.	Letter from I. Wollensach to K. Müller of September 30, 1960	Letter from I. Kohler to R. Schulz of September 21, 1952	
3. He lived in a small or medium-sized seaport town, most probably it was Wilhelmshaven.	Letter from R. Schulz to L. Kohler of September 17, 1952 Letter from I. Wollensach to K. Müller of September 24, 1960	Letter from I. Kohler to R. Schulz of September 21, 1951	R. Schulz had already learned from a letter from Wilhelmshaven of July 24, 1952, that a man called Kohl (sic) who lived in Wilhelmshaven had a business trading in wood and had committed suicide. R. Schulz's letter of May 30, 1952 to the Municipal Office of Wilhelmshaven referred to a German seaport without mentioning its size.
4. He had an old-fashioned house.	Letter from R. Schulz to L. Kohler of September 17, 1952	See comment	Ernst Kohler told me that the residential house itself was of modern construction (in 1887), but was surrounded by much older buildings. The smaller building attached to the house, which served as an office, and where the safe was, must have been of old construction because Ludwig Kohler said its windows were small and it was dark inside.
5. He had an antique safe.	R. Schulz's notes of August 1, 1952	Letter from L. Kohler to R. Schulz of September 21, 1952	
6. He kept documents, account books and money in the safe.	Letter from R. Schulz to L. Kohler of September 17, 1952	Letter from L. Kohler to R. Schulz of September 21, 1952	
7. The safe was kept in a small room which was rather dark.	Letter from R. Schulz to L. Kohler of September 17, 1952	Letter from L. Kohler to R. Schulz of September 21, 1952	The safe was kept in a corner of a dark room.
8. He had gone to the safe, taken out account books, and from	R. Schulz's notes of August 1, 1952	Not specifically verified, but can be inferred from the letter of	R. Schulz's first letter to the Municipal Office of Wilhelmshaven mentioned only "financial difficulties."

Item	Source	Verification	Comment
examining them learned that he was ruined.		L. Kohler to R. Schulz of September 21, 1952	
9. He was betrayed by an untrustworthy employee who forced him into bankruptcy.	Letter from I. Wollensach to K. Müller of September 24, 1960	Letter of L. Kohler to R. Schulz of September 21, 1952	
10. He shot himself in the right temple.	Notes by R. Schulz of August 1, 1952	Partly correct; letter from L. Kohler to R. Schulz of September 30, 1952	Ludwig Kohler knew only that his father shot himself in the head, not in what part of the head.
11. On the day he shot himself he had attended some important ceremony.	Letter from R. Schulz to L. Kohler of September 17, 1952 Letter of May 30, 1952 from R. Schulz to the Municipal Office of Wilhelmshaven Letter from I. Wollensach to K. Müller of September 30, 1960	Letter from L. Kohler to R. Schulz of September 21, 1952	The day was that of "Repentance and Prayer."
12. When he shot himself, he was still dressed in the clothes appropriate for the formal occasion he had attended. He had on a dress coat, and a stiff white collar.	Notes by R. Schulz written on August 1, 1952	Probable, but not independently verified; see comment	In a photograph that I have of Helmut Kohler, he is seen wearing a stiff white collar and a formal black coat. Ruprecht Schulz said that Ludwig Kohler had verified this to him when they met in Wilhelmshaven.
13. He was wearing dark clothing.	Letter from R. Schulz to L. Kohler of September 17, 1960	Letter from L. Kohler to R. Schulz of September 21, 1952	
14. The suicide occurred about 1885.	Letter from R. Schulz to L. Kohler of September 17, 1952	H. Kohler died on November 23, 1887 He lived for about a week after shooting himself	In his letter dated May 30, 1952 to the municipality of Wilhelmshaven, R. Schulz had given a range of dates between 1870 and 1885. By the time of writing to L. Kohler on September 17 he learned from Wilhelmshaven that the year of death was 1887.
15. He had been in the prime of life, perhaps about 40 years old.	Letter from R. Schulz to L. Kohler of September 17, 1952 R. Schulz's notes of August 1, 1952	See comment	The death certificate of Helmut Kohler stated that he was 53 years old when he died.

gone to the (Evangelical) church. They then gathered together at home for lunch. Suddenly Helmut Kohler stood up, went into his office and shot himself. This was between 2 and 3 P.M."

Discrepant Testimony from Helmut Kohler's Grandchildren

Helmut Kohler's grandchildren, Gertrud Kohler Schmidt and Ernst Kohler, were born respectively, in 1910 and 1915. They disagreed with their father's statements in his correspondence with Ruprecht Schulz on two points.

First, they said the house figuring in the death of Helmut Kohler was not old-fashioned, but modern, although it was surrounded by old buildings. I think, however, that the smaller attached building used as an office, where Helmut Kohler kept his safe, must have been old, because Ludwig Kohler described it as having small windows and always being dark inside.

Second, these later informants denied that their grandfather had engaged in any falsification of records. Gertrud Kohler Schmidt said that the suicide of her grandfather had been a scandal in the family, and she only learned about her grandfather's death from her aunt when she (Gertrud) was about 20 years old. This would have been more than 40 years after her grandfather's death.

Comment. Ludwig Kohler had no need to invent a story about his father's attempted dishonesty if it were untrue. I believe therefore that his sister (Gertrud's aunt) concealed from Gertrud the shameful fact of her grandfather's dishonesty.

The Dates of Birth and Death

Ruprecht Schulz said that he was born in Berlin on October 19, 1887. I obtained a copy of his birth certificate.

I also obtained a copy of the death certificate of Helmut Kohler, who died in Wilhelmshaven on November 23, 1887. I confirmed the correctness of this date from a copy of the death notice published in the *Wilhelmshaven Zeitung* of November 24, 1887. It said that the death had occurred "suddenly and unexpectedly yesterday."

Helmut Kohler must have lived for about a week after shooting himself. In 1887 Buss- und Bettag occurred on Wednesday, November 16.

The interval between Ruprecht Schulz's birth and Helmut Kohler's death was therefore about 5 weeks.*

Information About Ruprecht Schulz's Behavior

Ruprecht Schulz's Behavior Related to the Previous Life. Ruprecht Schulz remembered that as a child, whenever he was depressed or scolded, he would mold

---

Subjects of other cases with anomalous dates include: Jasbir Singh, Chaokhun Rajsuthajarn, Smriti Kana Kunda, Sudhir Rastogi, Sumitra Singh, and Manju Bhargava.

his hand into the shape of a gun with forefinger extended. He would hold the finger to his temple and say "I shoot myself." He did this so often that his mother became annoyed and alarmed. She considered it a bad omen of some future calamity and forbade him to continue the habit.

From his youth revolvers fascinated Ruprecht Schulz. He had much more interest in them than in other weapons. Nevertheless, he found that actually handling a revolver was unpleasant for him.

Ruprecht Schulz also described having had, from early life, a keen interest in ships and shipping. He collected models and pictures of ships. This interest could have had no obvious stimulus from the activities of Berlin, an inland city with only a small river running through it.

Ruprecht Schulz wrote (in a letter to me of May 26, 1964) that in financial matters he was extremely cautious and avoided any involvement that seemed to carry a risk of loss. Among his relatives and circle of friends he was known as "security conscious." He attributed this trait to the financial disaster of the previous life when he took a risk and miscalculated.

Ruprecht Schulz's Attitude Toward Suicide

Regarding the suicide of the previous life Ruprecht Schulz had neither regrets about it nor approval of it. He believed, however, that in some circumstances of life suicide offers a rational solution. He mentioned the appalling conditions in Germany during World War II as sometimes warranting suicide. It would be a means of escaping from an intolerable situation.

The Attitudes of the Adults Concerned in the Case

Ruprecht Schulz understood and agreed to Ludwig Kohler's request, stated early in their correspondence, that the details of the affairs of the Kohler family should not be made public. Ludwig Kohler was therefore annoyed when Ruprecht Schulz, answering the appeal of *Das Neue Blatt*, wrote to the newspaper and narrated his experience. The newspaper published the Kohlers' name with a pseudonym (not the one I have adopted), but this did not nullify the Kohlers' annoyance. Ruprecht Schulz was himself somewhat annoyed over the tendency of the media to sensationalize his experience. In addition to *Das Neue Blatt*, at least one other newspaper and a national illustrated magazine published accounts of the case.

Ruprecht Schulz himself made no attempt to exploit his experiences. He answered correspondents who read about the case in *Das Neue Blatt*, or otherwise learned about it; he gave one or two public lectures; and he cooperated with serious investigators like Professor Hans Bender, Dr. Karl Müller, and myself. To the best of my knowledge, he obtained no financial gain and only the most transitory public attention from the publication in the media of his experience.

Ruprecht Schulz's Formula for Remembering a Previous Life

In a letter to Dr. Müller, dated June 24, 1959, Ruprecht Schulz outlined a sort of formula for remembering a previous life. It requires, he wrote, the concatenation of three elements, as follows:

a) A person must be unusually sensitive, somewhat like a seismograph; but he or she must not be too easily disturbed, like "a bundle of nerves."

b) In the previous life there must have been some unusual event that left a deep effect on the "inner self."

c) The person must happen to encounter in the present life some place, objects, or events that release the memories of the previous life.

Comment

This case has the weakness that, unlike with many of the stronger cases in Asia, I could assemble no platoon of informants who would corroborate the subject's statements. Ruprecht Schulz remains almost the sole informant for his statements before they were verified. Yet we have no reason to doubt the authenticity of the exchange of letters between him and Ludwig Kohler which led to the verification of these statements. Ruprecht Schulz's letter of September 17, 1952, provides as good a record of the essential statements as we could wish.

Can we say, however, that we have solved a case when the subject has stated no personal name and, somewhat unsurely, the name of one seaport?* In answering this question we must acknowledge that many of Ruprecht Schulz's statements could apply to numerous businessmen in north German seaports. How many could, however, apply *collectively* to any person other than Helmut Kohler? No doubt some other German businessmen in financial difficulties shot themselves in despair over financial ruin. How many of these, however, lived in smaller north seaports and committed suicide on a special day of a religious ceremony? How many kept their documents in an old-fashioned safe that lay in a corner of a small dark room? We cannot exclude the possibility of some other person's death matching that of Helmut Kohler, but the probability of finding such a person seems to me extremely small.

Equally small seems the likelihood that Ruprecht Schulz could have had any normal knowledge of the business affairs and culminating suicide of Helmut Kohler, who lived in a seaport (Wilhelmshaven) 370 kilometers from Berlin, where Ruprecht Schulz lived all his life until he moved to Frankfurt.

For these several reasons I consider this case one of the stronger ones that I have investigated.

The case of Indika Guneratne included similarly few proper names: those of a city and a servant. Indika stated no names of family members, but he furnished enough other details to warrant my believing that they corresponded to the life of a particular person who lived in the city he named.

Edward Ryall

In 1974 the subject of this case, Edward Ryall, published in book form a long account of what he believed were memories of a previous life in 17th-century England (Ryall, 1974). I had encouraged the writing of the book and contributed a long Introduction and an Appendix of verifications of some of the details included in Edward Ryall's account.

The publication of Ryall's book would ordinarily make it inappropriate to include a report of this case in the present work. Two reasons justify making an exception. First, I have considerably expanded my own investigations of the case and had the benefit of consultations with experts in the history of Somerset, the county of England in which Edward Ryall believed he had lived before. Second, through these consultations I have come to modify my own appraisal of the case and owe it to my readers to acknowledge this.

Summary of the Case and Its Investigation

Edward Ryall was born at Sheoburyness, Essex, England, on June 21, 1902. His parents were George Ryall and his wife, Annie. Annie Ryall died when Edward was 3 years old, and until his father remarried, when Edward was 6, he was raised by his maternal grandmother. George Ryall was a laborer. Edward Ryall attended local primary and secondary schools. He obtained the Cambridge Leaving Secondary School Certificate. Thereafter, except for service in the Army during World War II, he worked at a variety of jobs, principally clerical ones. He married at the age of 22, in 1924.

Edward Ryall wrote that when he was still a young child, he became aware of images in his mind — pictures and also unusual words — that seemed to derive from some other time and place. It seemed to him that he had lived before. Sometimes he blurted out something about his apparent memories. He recalled that he sometimes used words unknown in Essex, such as the word *rhine* for a drainage ditch. (In Essex, such a ditch would be called a dyke.) His grandmother found such usages strange, and she also objected to Edward Ryall's telling her that he had no "granma." Nevertheless, he made no attempt to give a systematic account of his memories to anyone else; nor did anyone ask him to do so. This was hardly surprising, as an incident that occurred in 1910 when he was about 8 years old showed. His father took him into the garden of their house and showed him Halley's comet, that was then bright in the sky on its reappearance after over 75 years. Edward Ryall unthinkingly told his father that he seen it before and had shown it to "his" sons. His father sternly rebuked him for making such a preposterous remark and warned him against the dire consequences — he specified consignment to a mental hospital as a most likely possibility — if he went on talking such nonsense. Edward Ryall was an apt pupil for such admonishment, and he said nothing further about his memories of a previous life for many years. Even his wife knew nothing about them until 1970. George Ryall's suppression of his son's statements deprived them of their possible corroboration by persons older than Edward Ryall or even his contemporaries, who knew nothing about them until he published an account of them at the age of 68.

His father's suppression of the telling of Edward Ryall's memories had not, however, erased them, or prevented him from recovering others. He stored them all in a remarkably retentive mind and did not commit any of them to paper until he was in his late 60s in 1970. He said later that his first memories of a previous life occurred in childhood and they developed in more detail during his teens. They remained, however, without a venue, until 1962. At that time he and his wife took a bus journey to Devon and toured through parts of Somerset, without stopping there. In Somerset he suddenly realized that the previous life had taken place in that county.* In 1970 he read an appeal by the (London) *Daily Express* for readers to send in accounts of memories of previous lives. He decided to break his silence and sent the newspaper a summary of his own case. The *Daily Express* published an article about his claims on May 4, 1970. Friends in England sent me clippings of it. It impressed me favorably, and I began corresponding with Edward Ryall. Subsequently, I met him on several occasions at his home in Hadleigh, Essex. I encouraged him to set down as many details as he could still recall about the previous life that he seemed to remember. Later, I suggested to him that he write a book about his experiences, and when he did so, I helped him find a publisher and contributed an Introduction to the book, which he entitled *Second Time Round*. In the meantime, I had begun to verify the existence of the persons figuring in his narration and to check the correctness of the abundant details included in it. My verifications and the sources I used formed an Appendix to *Second Time Round*.

I continued to investigate the case after Edward Ryall's death. Shortly before his death I learned that searches of parish records had failed to find any evidence of the existence of the nearly two dozen persons whom Edward Ryall had named as members of John Fletcher's family and circle of friends. He died before I could discuss this failure with him. He died quite unexpectedly at his home on February 4, 1978.

I will next give a brief summary of the main events narrated in *Second Time Round*.

Principal Events Narrated in Second Time Round

Edward Ryall wrote that he remembered the life of a yeoman farmer called John Fletcher who was born in 1645 and died in 1685. John Fletcher lived, as he died, in Somerset on the other side of England from Essex, where Edward Ryall was born and lived. (Edmund Halley observed the comet later named after him at its visit to the

---

He may have earlier had some sense that the images in his mind derived from Somerset. His son Raymond told me in 1980 that as a youth of 17 he had made a bicycle tour that took him through Somerset. When he returned home, his father asked him whether he had been to Weston Zoyland. (He had been through it.) Edward Ryall explained his question by saying that, he had met someone from Weston Zoyland. Raymond Ryall and his mother, who corroborated Raymond's account, then conjectured that Edward Ryall was thinking about someone he had met during his service in the army.

earth's sphere in 1682, that is, within the designated period of John Fletcher's life.) Edward Ryall wrote that he remembered numerous events from different periods of Fletcher's life. An incomplete list of such events includes the following: the death of John Fletcher's father, Martin Fletcher, after he was gored by a bull; the love affair of John Fletcher with Melanie Poulett, member of a prominent Somerset family; a trip to the Mendips with John Fletcher's close friend, Jeremy Bragg, which ended when John Fletcher accidentally fell through a hole in the ground and landed in the shaft of a lead mine; the courtship and marriage of John Fletcher; his purchase at Axmouth of an unusually fast horse from a Spanish ship captain; the rescue of Joseph Alleine, an ejected clergyman, from constables searching for him; adulterous relations, sanctioned by Somerset custom at the time, on the part of John Fletcher and Jeremy Bragg; and finally, the part played by John Fletcher as a guide for the Duke of Monmouth's rebel army during its night march to surprise the troops of King James II encamped near Weston Zoyland. (Edward Ryall located John Fletcher's house and farm at the edge of Weston Zoyland.) The narration of these and other events, however, occupies only a part — perhaps the smaller portion — of Edward Ryall's book. He devotes much of it to quite detailed descriptions of the daily life of a farmer and his friends in 17th-century Somerset.

The Three Kinds of Information
Stated by Edward Ryall

For the purposes of analysis with regard to evidence of paranormal processes, we may appropriately divide these seeming memories into three groups. The first group consists of events concerned with persons who figured prominently in the history of the last half of 17th-century England. In particular, Edward Ryall recalled considerable detail about the events of the Duke of Monmouth's rebellion against King James II. Monmouth, an illegitimate son of Charles II, challenged his uncle's right to the throne of England. After a series of mishaps and mistakes Monmouth's rebellion fizzled and was finally crushed at the Battle of Sedgemoor at which John Fletcher lost his life. Edward Ryall's account of these events is in the main accurate so far as we can check it against contemporary sources. Its most important aberrant detail is the claim that John Fletcher acted, for at least part of the way, as a guide across the moors when the Duke of Monmouth attempted a surprise attack by night on the Royalist troops sent to suppress the rebellion. Most contemporary sources (and later writers) state or imply that Monmouth's army was guided by a man called Godfrey. Godfrey is a somewhat elusive figure, however, and it is conceivable that Monmouth's officers had supplementary guides; but this is not to say that Edward Ryall's John Fletcher was one of them.

This first group of memories holds nothing of interest for students of paranormal phenomena. All the events and the persons concerned in it are either well known to general readers or information about them is readily available and might almost be considered part of the stock of information of even half-educated Englishmen.

Edward Ryall denies that he ever read anything about the Duke of Monmouth and his rebellion beyond a brief summary in a school textbook. He was, however, a person of wide-ranging interests, and he had an enviably adhesive memory. So I think we should assume that he might have obtained in a normal manner all the accurate information about the main events known to historians that are included in his book.

A second kind of information in the memories concerns events happening to persons not mentioned in histories—even the most specialized ones—of the period in question. Edward Ryall mentioned the names of about twenty persons who were members of John Fletcher's circle of family and friends. Most of these persons were unlikely to have been known outside their county, or even beyond the boundaries of their parishes. And yet within their parishes they were, as described by Edward Ryall, persons of some local importance whose existence one would expect the local registers to have recorded. Their names should have figured in records of births, baptisms, marriages, and deaths. With the help of correspondents in England, I had numerous parish and county records examined for traces of the various persons mentioned by Edward Ryall. The searches failed completely with regard to John Fletcher and all the members of his family as well as that of Jeremy Fuller whose daughter, Cecily, John Fletcher was said by Edward Ryall to have married. Nor could any trace be found of Jeremy Bragg and his wife, Catherine. We did verify the names and some of the details Edward Ryall gave about the rectors of several parishes and about Andrew Newman, a smithy. Yet some information about all of these persons was printed and, in principle, available to an earnest inquirer.

The failure of the first searches through the records surprised me so much that I arranged for a repeated search for records of twelve of the more significant persons mentioned in *Second Time Round*. This also failed.

Why have we not found evidence of John Fletcher or the other persons Edward Ryall mentioned as figuring in the domestic and social life of John Fletcher? Several possible explanations for this failure occur to me. First, the registers of the late 17th century in England have many imperfections. During the political tumults of the time, numerous clergymen were ejected from their parishes, and those that remained must often have given their attention to matters that seemed more urgent than keeping records. In addition to these gaps in recording, some records have been lost through fire, damp, and misplacement. The handwriting in the extant registers is at best difficult to read, and in places illegible. (I saw this for myself when I examined some records at the church in Weston Zoyland.) We are not, however, necessarily warranted to account for all disappointments by attributing them to faulty or missing records.

The third type of information figuring in Edward Ryall's memories are those concerned with daily life in Somerset during the late 17th century. *Second Time Round* contains many allusions to foods, clothes, house furnishings, customs, festivals, coins, newspapers, medicines, and other aspects of the life of that period. In addition to what I can fairly describe as a mass of detail about such matters that Edward Ryall included in his book, he also had a reserve fund of information that he deployed in correspondence with me and other persons, but which he never used in his book. This supplemental material is, on the whole, concerned with details just as recondite as many mentioned in *Second Time Round*, and it also is in the main quite accurate. Ordinarily educated persons might know or conjecture some of these details. Others, however, required much labor — for me, at least — to verify. Readers have challenged some of them, either in reviews of the book or correspondence with me. This sometimes sent me back, or back again, to check on the verifications.

Omissions and Mistakes in Edward Ryall's Statements

Some readers of *Second Time Round* have found its style a somewhat artificial "olde englishe," and I agree with that criticism. It has the form of a historical novel. I think, however, that Edward Ryall's errors of fact are more important than the manner of his presenting them.

He used several words anachronistically. For example, the word *lugger* (describing a small sailing ship) was not used until the 18th century. The word *stiff*, an adjective for strong alcoholic drinks, did not come into use until the 19th century. The word *goodies* for sweetmeats was anachronistic for the 17th century; it was not so used until the 18th century. The phrase *of that ilk* (meaning of the same name or place) is appropriate only in Scotland. Edward Ryall cited a prayer in modern Italian as if it were Latin. He described the location of a farm near Lyme Regis in Dorset that was owned, he wrote, by John Fletcher's brother, Matthew; but records show that the farm of the location given was owned in the period of John Fletcher by a family called Jones. Edward Ryall described a Spanish ship as docking at Axmouth (on the coast of Dorset) to which John Fletcher had gone in order to fetch shingle for Bridgwater; but an encroaching bar had closed the harbor at Axmouth by the time of John Fletcher. Also, shingle was available at places far closer to Bridgwater than Axmouth. The Pouletts of Hinton St. George are a well-known family of Somerset, but their pedigrees contain no indication of a daughter named Melanie, who, Edward Ryall said, was the child of the second Baron Poulett. Edward Ryall wrote that because Melanie's promiscuity had disgraced the family her father had sent her to relatives in Basing (Hampshire) and struck her name out of the family rolls; the Pouletts had had a branch at Basing, but their residence there had become a Royalist fortress during the Civil War of the 1640s, and Cromwell's forces had utterly destroyed it. Edward Ryall correctly described the Rev. Thomas Holt as the Vicar of Weston Zoyland during John Fletcher's time; but he wrote as if Holt had remained Vicar throughout Fletcher's life, whereas he was ejected by Parliament in the 1640s and only restored to his living at Weston Zoyland in 1660.

The errors I have mentioned seem serious, but we should weigh them against a far greater number of details, often of obscure objects or customs in which no critic has questioned Edward Ryall's accuracy or in which the critic was wrong and Edward Ryall right. Examples of the second group occurred in Ryall's use of the words *leman* (lover), *shaker* (a person whose religious ardor showed in bodily movements), and *vastly* (meaning greatly).* Edward Ryall's claim that John Fletcher's farm was located on the western edge of Weston Zoyland stimulated one critic to expostulate that land at the location indicated had not been enclosed in the period of John Fletcher. Dr. Robert Dunning, an editor of the *Victoria History of Somerset,* told me (when I met him in Taunton on September 19, 1988) that an enclosed farm might well have existed in the 17th century at the place indicated by Edward Ryall for John Fletcher's farm.

Second Time Round contains abundant and often detailed descriptions of the sexual practices in Somerset in the late 17th century. Some critics challenged Ryall's description of consensual "wife-swapping" in Somerset, but Quaife (1979) confirmed the existence of the practice.

To show the diversity of Edward Ryall's references to places and objects of his time and location, I will mention: the correct location of three windmills in the region of Weston Zoyland; the M.D. degree earned by the second Lord Poulett; a gravity clock made by Hubrecht (or Habrecht); a Royalist coin issued at Pontefract Castle in 1649 after the execution of King Charles I; a line of a poem (slightly misquoted) by Phineas Fletcher, said to be a relative of John Fletcher; the northern lights (aurora borealis) visible on the night before the Battle of Sedgemoor; and keyhole horseshoes. We could not verify these items if they did not exist in published sources; I list them only to show that if Edward Ryall derived them from such sources, he must have read much more widely than he admitted. I think it important to note also that he did not have to dredge slowly in his mind to use his extensive knowledge of Somerset in the late 17th century. He answered a multitude of questions put to him by interviewers (of the media, for example) with speed as well as accuracy.

Edward Ryall said that before the development of his memories he had never undertaken any research into the social history of Somerset in the late 17th century. Since he grew up in Essex, far removed from Somerset, he would not have soaked up specialized information about that county from the elders and playmates of his childhood. To be sure, Essex and Somerset are both counties of England, and they had much in common in the 17th century, as they have now. They also had, and have, important differences with which Edward Ryall seems to have been familiar, as familiar indeed as we should expect a farmer of Somerset, or a social historian, to be. Or was he? I consulted four authorities on the social history of Somerset and Dorset about the accuracy of the details in *Second Time Round.* They were Peter Earle, author of a history of the Monmouth Rebellion (Earle, 1977), W. McDonald Wigfield, author and editor of two books on the Monmouth Rebellion (Wigfield 1980, 1985), Robert Dunning, one of the editors of the *Victoria History of Somerset* (1974) and author of a book on the Monmouth rebellion (Dunning, 1984), and John Fowles, formerly Curator of the Museum at Lyme Regis, Dorset. Two of these experts condemned *Second Time Round* for serious inaccuracies, one judging it to be a hoax. In contrast, two others endorsed the book, one asserting that "I think there are fewer

---

I have used the Oxford English Dictionary *in determining the occurrence of words and phrases in 17th-century England.*

mistakes in this book than in any other that I have read about Monmouth and his rebellion."*

Relevant Information About Edward Ryall's Personality

During my meetings with Edward Ryall in Hadleigh, his wife, Winifred, had been in the house but, apart from serving tea, she remained inconspicuous. After Edward Ryall's death I visited her twice in 1980 and 1981, and she gave me some relevant information about her husband as she saw him, especially in their later years together.

Although on their journey through Somerset in 1962 he had experienced strong emotion and for the first time, he later said, he had located the images he was having, she knew nothing about his claim to remember a previous life until 1970, when the London *Daily Express* published his first account of his memories. She herself did not believe in reincarnation and had no interest in it. She paid little attention to her husband's writing.

Winifred Ryall said that her husband owned few books, and she showed me the few that were in the house; she had disposed of none since her husband's death. He did, however, read a great deal, and he frequently borrowed books from the Hadleigh Library. He borrowed one, two, or three at a time. Sometimes he asked her to return them before he had finished reading them. He did not borrow more books during the period (1971–74) when he was writing *Second Time Round*. Nor had he ever been away on long trips without her. (This eliminated the possibility that he had surreptitiously used the British Library or the Cambridge University Library.) I inquired about Edward Ryall's possible use of the interlibrary loan service at the Hadleigh Public Library, but was unable to learn whether he had or had not used this service. Before 1974, he had never gone to Somerset without her. She never saw him making notes when they were in Somerset, although he did make some when they returned from one trip there.

Winifred Ryall said that at times her husband's behavior changed after he retired. He began to feel that other members of his family and persons outside the family "were opposed to him." She thought this unwarranted because he enjoyed the affection of his children. Nevertheless, he would get into "moods" and would leave the house for a few hours. Then he would return in better spirits.

Winifred Ryall did not think her husband's book was a hoax, but she could not deny (or affirm) that it contained ingredients from his imagination.

I also met the Ryalls' daughter, Iris Driver, in 1981. She confirmed what her mother had said about her father's withdrawal from the family after he retired. He would "sit and think"; one or two persons suggested that he had a "double personality." She did not think *Second Time Round* was a hoax.

In addition to the foregoing interviews, I corresponded with a friend of Edward

---

*I have not identified the authors of these diverging judgments. I learned of one during an interview, and the others occurred in correspondence. I obtained permission to quote from only one of the historians whom I consulted.

Ryall and with his supervisor at his last position. Both of them affirmed his reputation for honesty, but they could say little about the possible normal sources for the details in *Second Time Round*.

Comment

In the Introduction that I wrote for *Second Time Round*, I discussed various interpretations for Edward Ryall's apparent memories, including a hoax and source amnesia (cryptomnesia) (Stevenson, 1983). Having considered the various possible interpretations that occurred to me I went on to say that as of that time I believed reincarnation to be the best explanation of Edward Ryall's case (Stevenson, 1974c). I reserved the right, however, to alter my opinion of the case, and I have since done so.

I can no longer believe that *all* of Edward Ryall's apparent memories derive from a previous life, because some of his details are clearly wrong. Furthermore, the search for verifications of the persons who had no historical importance (those belonging to the second group of information that I described earlier) was continued after Edward Ryall's death and, as I mentioned, proved unsuccessful. If we had found a trace of any one of these persons, I could have rationalized our failure to find records of the others by reference to the deficiencies of the registers that certainly exist. These deficiencies *may* account for the failure to verify the names Edward Ryall gave for John Fletcher's family and friends. I do not, however, like to cover cracks in the plaster with paper, and we must consider other possibilities.

One of these is that Edward Ryall misremembered names or even filled in some from his imagination. The family names he gave were common enough in John Fletcher's part of Somerset during the 17th century, and if Edward Ryall remembered these, but could not get the first names right, he might have put in wrong first names. This would account for the failure to verify the existence of persons with these names. He may have added names that occurred to him without realizing they were wrong, or he may have imagined names that he thought appropriate to fill in gaps of which he became aware. I find this explanation less than satisfactory, because it supposes that John Fletcher had fixed better in his memory the names of persons well known in contemporary affairs than those of the members of his family and circle of friends. Is this plausible? If I survive death, am I likely to remember the name of, say, President Jimmy Carter and forget those of my wives? And if I do forget their names or my own, am I more likely to say "I do not remember," or to insert (with the best intention) a false name that seems right? The answers to questions of this sort will no doubt vary with the person about whom they are asked and with the person asking them.

In the meantime, however, I will state my present judgment of the case. I still believe that Edward Ryall was not lying when he said that he had read almost nothing about 17th-century Somerset and had never — until he had his memories — done any research into that period of history. This leads me to believe that he had some paranormal knowledge of 17th-century Somerset, which might have derived from a life he had lived then and there. In his later years he became intensely absorbed in his apparent memories. He thought about them much of the time, and he seems to have brooded about them in a rather solitary way. (His conviction about the factuality of his memories led him to "recognize" a young woman who had married into his family as the reincarnation of Cecily Fletcher.) What may finally have emerged as the content of *Second Time Round* could have been an historical novel — part derived from normal sources he no longer remembered, part paranormally derived and correct, and part imagined and wrong. I suggested earlier that we might consider an interpretation of this type for rare results in hypnotic regression to ostensible previous lives (Stevenson, 1987/2001).* Edward Ryall may have entered a condition related to that of some hypnotized persons and some meditators. In such a state real memories and other images may mingle freely and remain undiscriminated.

We might also explain paranormal elements in the case by the concept of retrocognition. Does the past continue to exist somewhere? If so, can human beings sometimes read it and tell us about it? It seems that some can. Some persons have given credible accounts of having glimpses, visions we might say, of past events (Ellwood, 1971; Spears, 1967). Some experimental investigations have also revealed an ability to read the past (Geley, 1927; Osty, 1923). I do not, however, believe that retrocognition fits Edward Ryall's case —for explaining paranormal elements— as well as memories of a previous life. Retrocognitions known to me are either brief visions, for example of a battle, or developed during clairvoyance. If we believe Edward Ryall, as I do, he had some apparent memories when he was under 8 years old, and thereafter he added to them in other ways until he published his book at the age of 72, in 1974.

PETER AVERY

Surveys have shown that the majority of persons have had at one time or another the experience of unexpected familiarity with a place or an event. For example, among 182 students at Aberdeen University 115 (63%) reported this kind of experience (McKellar, 1957).† Psychologists and psychiatrists have proposed several interpretations for these experiences, which are commonly called ones of *déjà vu* (Hermann,

---

*Although the procedure of hypnotic regression may have some nonspecific therapeutic value, improvement in a patient's condition does not authenticate the technique (Stevenson, 1994). Most "previous personalities" evoked during hypnotic regression are fantasies, worthless as evidence for any paranormal process. Experiments have shown that suggestions explicit or more subtle can easily influence the features of the evoked "previous personality" (Baker, 1982; Spanos et al., 1991; Spanos, 1996). Other experiments have traced the content and even small details of the "previous personality" to printed or oral sources available to the subject (Björkhem, 1961; Harris, 1986; Kampman, 1973, 1976; Kampman and Hirvenoja, 1978; Venn, 1986; Wilson, 1981; Zolik, 1958, 1962).

†Palmer (1979) found an even higher incidence (76%) of reports of this experience in a survey of students and townspeople in a university city of the United States. Neppe (1983) and Sno and Linszen (1990) summarized results from several other surveys in all of which the reported incidence of the experience was 25% or higher.

1960; Neppe, 1983). The details of the experiences subsumed under the common phrase déjà vu vary in different reports, and it seems unlikely that any single interpretation of them can explain all.

Sno and Linszen (1990) summarized a variety of psychological and neurological explanations that different authors have suggested for this kind of experience. They included a claimed memory of a previous life in their list. Some otherwise sensible persons have offered this interpretation of their own experiences of déjà vu. For example, Charles Dickens (1877) wrote of an experience he had in Italy:

> At sunset, when I was walking on alone, while the horses rested, I arrived upon a little scene, which, by one of those singular mental operations of which we are all conscious, seemed perfectly familiar to me, and which I see distinctly now. There was not much in it. In the blood-red light, there was a mournful sheet of water, just stirred by the evening wind; upon its margin a few trees. In the foreground (of a view of Ferrara) was a group of silent peasant girls leaning over the parapet of a little bridge, looking now up at the sky, now down into the water. In the distance a deep dell; the shadow of approaching night on everything. If I had been murdered there in some former life I could not have seemed to remember the place more thoroughly or with more emphatic chilling of the blood; and the real remembrance of it acquired in that minute is so strengthened by the imaginary recollection, that I hardly think I could forget it [p. 37].

The writer and statesman John Buchan described in his autobiography (Buchan, 1940) more than one experience of déjà vu that he interpreted as memories of previous lives. He wrote:

> I find myself in some scene which I cannot have visited before and which is yet perfectly familiar. I know that it was the stage of an action in which I once took part and am about to take part again [p. 122].

Neither of the persons whose experiences I have just cited provided any evidence of specific memories of a previous life; nor did they claim to have had such memories. Some persons who have had such memories, including verified ones, have sometimes shown familiarity with places where they believed they lived in a previous life. They have commented on changes in the buildings or acted as if buildings were as they had been during the life they said they remembered.*

Case Report

The subject of this case, Peter Avery, was born on May 15, 1923, in Derby, England. After completing secondary school, he entered Liverpool University. Service in the merchant marine and army during World War II interrupted his studies, which he resumed after the war at the University of London's School of Oriental and African

---

*Subjects of this group, those who had claimed memories of a previous life that were verified and who showed familiarity with the places they believed they had previously lived, include: Swarnlata Mishra, Prakash Varshnay, Parmod Sharma, Rabih Elawar, Chaokhun Rajsuthajarn, and Savitri Devi Pathak.

Studies. He graduated from there in 1949. He had learned Arabic and Persian, and his knowledge of these languages led to his appointment as a senior teacher of them with the Anglo-Iranian Oil Company. His first assignment was at Abadan in southwestern Iran. He had his first experience of déjà vu while working at Abadan. In 1951 the government of Iran nationalized the oil industry, at which time Peter Avery moved to Baghdad, where he taught English, first at the Iraqi Staff and Military College and then at the Baghdad College of Arts and Sciences. In 1952 he published (with John Heath-Stubbs) translations of the Persian poet Háfiz. In 1955 he returned to Iran, where he was employed by a company of civil engineers engaged in road construction.

In 1958 he was appointed University Lecturer in Persian Studies at the University of Cambridge. He remained in this position until 1990, when he retired from the Lectureship but continued his research and writing as a Fellow of King's College, Cambridge, to which position he had been appointed when he first went to Cambridge. Justifiably renowned as a scholar of Persian, Peter Avery is best known to general readers for his translations of classical Persian poets, such as Háfiz and Omar Khayyam. He has also written extensively on the history of Iran from its earliest origins to the present time.

I first met Peter Avery in September 1992 at a friend's house in Cambridge, where I was spending that month. He narrated two experiences of déjà vu that he had many years earlier, in Iran and in Pakistan. Subsequently, I asked him to describe the experiences in writing, and I am able to quote the accounts he sent me in a letter dated January 14, 1993. In his statement he described the second and more moving experience before the first one:

> 1. My companion in Isfahan in the winter of 1949-50, the Training Manager of the Anglo-Iranian Oil Company was Mr. John Evans. After graduating in Persian and Arabic in 1949 I went to Iran as a Training Officer. Some six months later, I was allowed to go to Isfahan* from Abadan with the [Training] Manager on a visit from the London office. I had never left Abadan and the southern oilfields since arrival and hence had no direct knowledge of central Iran; my selection as Mr. Evans's cicerone on the trip to Tehran and Isfahan was, in addition to [my] ability to speak Persian, due to my eagerness, to which my superiors responded sympathetically, to leave the oil industry's enclave and see something of the country that was the subject of my studies.
>
> We arrived at Isfahan in the evening. Over breakfast the next day I told Mr. Evans the route we would take from the hotel to the Maidan-i Shah and the bazaar. He expressed surprise at my knowing it so precisely in a manner I found too natural to need explanation. We set out and everything fell into place as I had foreseen. Our last sight that morning, on the way back to the hotel, was the blue-domed mosque situated in the garden of the Madrasseh Madar-i Shah Sultan Husain, the School of the Mother of Shah Sultan Husain, [who was] the Safavid Shah put to death after the Afghan

---

*Isfahan (sometimes spelled Esfahan) is in central Iran, about halfway between Abadan and Teheran. It is on the Zayandeh River. Successively conquered by the Arabs, the Turks, and the Mongols, it was regained by the Persians and reached a zenith of political and cultural importance under the Safavid dynasty (1502–1736). Shah Abbas I (the Great) (1587–1629) made it the capital of Persia in 1598. In 1722 the Afghans conquered Isfahan and initiated its decline. The capital of Persia was transferred to Teheran at the end of the 18th century. Under Shah Abbas I, Isfahan was greatly embellished by magnificent palaces, gardens, and avenues (Lockhart, 1960).

invasion in 1722.* After a morning sight-seeing, I might have been tired, and exploring Isfahan for the first time had certainly been an exciting experience. Although aware, as most of us are, of its beauty, I, who seldom look at guide-books until *after* looking at what they refer to, and Isfahan was no exception (in fact I have never read a guide-book on Isfahan), was of course spell-bound by all that we had seen; but the breakdown occurred only in the Madrasseh, and as soon as we entered its courtyard-garden.

I burst into uncontrollable sobbing under an overwhelming impression that I had somehow at last come *home*. I sat on the parapet of a pond. Mr. Evans very tactfully walked away. He said afterwards that this seemed the best he could do, until I could dry my eyes and rejoin him. Little passed between us about the episode which, in front of one of my employers, embarrassed me, although he showed no sign of disapprobation and seemed quietly understanding. Thus culminated a morning throughout which I had all the time felt a strange familiarity with a city I had never visited before, and of the geography of which I had had no former conscious knowledge.

2. My first and until today only other experience of what an aunt of mine used to refer to as "the spirit of place", but of such a spirit in a very personal way, (one is often aware of it in a less personal way), was in, I suppose, 1944, in Lahore,† again on a first visit to an ancient city. I was an officer in the Royal Indian Navy, aged twenty-one or going into twenty-two.... A fellow officer, an Indian whose father was a distinguished Orientalist, the (late) Khan Bahadur Muhammad Shafi, Principal of the Punjab School of Oriental Studies, invited me to go and stay with his father, for he knew of my already burgeoning interest in Islamic literature and history. His father was marvelous and showed me wonderful Persian manuscripts with miniatures; books he had purchased after the fall of Amanullah of Afghanistan when, he said, treasures from the royal library in Kabul came through the Khyber Pass into northern India.

Early one morning, before the day's heat grew too intense, we drove in tongas, horse-drawn traps in which the passenger sits back-to-back to the driver, to the Shalimar Bagh, a splendid garden laid out by the Mughal emperors to be a halting place on their annual trek to Kashmir from Delhi.§ It is situated a little outside Lahore. Subsequently I read the Khan Bahadur's article on it in a learned journal, but on the morning of our visit I was uninformed. The purpose of the visit was that he should explain its history to me, but when we alighted and entered by an insignificant doorway in a wall, I said that this had not always been the entrance: it used to be in the wall at the other end of the enclosure. He agreed. Inside, I asked if I might be allowed to walk about alone, to which he readily concurred, saying "You seem to know the place already." When I rejoined him later, I commented that the pavilion in the centre did not belong to the garden. It did not, he said. It had been a *shami-ana*, a summer house, on the roof of an emperor's tomb on the other extremity of Lahore, overlooking the river Ravi. Ranjit Singh, the Sikh ruler, had had it brought into the garden. Lord Curzon, when Viceroy, had noticed that it was in the wrong place and instructed the Department of Antiquities to restore it to where it belonged, but this had not been done.

Although not as shatteringly moved as I was to be in Isfahan by my sense of *déjà vu*, in the Shalimar Bagh in Lahore I certainly had a similar feeling of having been there

---

*Shah Sultan Husain's pious mother erected this school (Madrasa) and an adjoining caravanserai between 1706/7 and 1714/15 (Lockhart, 1958).

†Lahore is now the capital of the province of Punjab in Pakistan. It achieved great importance during the Mughal Empire in India and under the kingdom of the Sikhs. The British conquered it in 1849.

§These gardens were laid out in 1637 by order of the Mughal emperor Shah Jehan.

before: of knowing the place intimately; of returning, as it were, home, to somewhere where I had once been "at home," but this feeling in the Madrasseh in Isfahan was more penetrating than that in Lahore, where it was confined to the garden and did not extend to the whole environment.

In 1992-93, when Peter Avery described his experiences to me, no possibility existed for an independent corroboration of his statement that he had had knowledge of Isfahan and Lahore that he had not acquired normally. I subsequently met him several times during later stays in Cambridge. He reiterated that he had never read any guidebooks or other works that could have given him the information he had about Isfahan and Lahore when he first went to these cities.

Peter Avery's statements show that he favored previous lives as the origin of the unusual knowledge he believed he had. To this interpretation, however, he showed no zealous attachment. As an alternative interpretation he considered some kind of inherited memory plausible. One of his direct ancestors was a famous pirate in the 17th century who preyed upon shipping in the Indian Ocean. His accomplishments included capturing a ship that was carrying a Mughal princess on her way to Mecca. Peter Avery's father once expressed the thought that his son's great interest in the Islamic East might have derived from a child Captain Avery had had with his captive princess; but there is no evidence of such an offspring. Peter Avery's mention of the possibility demonstrated his ability to weigh alternative interpretations of his experiences.

HENRIETTE ROOS

The subject of this case, Henriette Roos, never had any imaged memories of a previous life. I include the case in this volume because a small series of experiences suggest that she had been in a previous life Rosario (or Rosarito) Weiss, the daughter of Leocadia Weiss, who was the mistress and devoted friend of the Spanish painter, Francisco Goya (1746–1828).

Summary of the Case and Its Investigation

Henriette Roos was born in Amsterdam, The Netherlands, in 1903. I did not learn the names of her parents. Her father was a diamond merchant of moderate means.

Early in life Henriette showed superior talents both for pictorial art and for music. At the age of 22 she married a Hungarian pianist called Weisz. When she was about 30, she divorced Weisz, but instead of reverting to her maiden name, she continued to use the name Weisz, which seemed to have a special attraction for her.

In the meantime, she had decided on a career as a painter instead of that of a musician. She won a scholarship that permitted her to study in Paris and went there

Figure 18. Painting made by Henriette Roos in 1936, rapidly and in the dark. (Courtesy of Henriette Roos.)

in 1934 when she was about 31 years old. While in Paris, perhaps 2 years after she had gone there, she one night felt an impulsion, almost like a command, to get up and paint during the night. She did so and went to her easel in the dark, painted for a time, and then went back to bed. In the morning she found that she had painted the head of a beautiful girl (Figure 18).

She showed the portrait to a close friend and told her how she had painted it during the night. The friend suggested that they take it to a clairvoyant in whom she had confidence. Henriette reluctantly agreed. At the clairvoyant's session Henriette put the portrait on a table where were arranged other psychometric objects* brought by other persons attending the session. The clairvoyant picked up the portrait and then said that a name — *GOYA* — was being spelled out before her. Goya then seemed to communicate and said that he was grateful to Henriette because she had made a home for him in southern France when he had been forced to leave Spain.

Despite her studies of art, Henriette knew almost nothing about the private life of Goya and what the clairvoyant said to her made no sense. She happened, however, on the same day to be invited to the home of a musician who owned a biography of Goya. Henriette borrowed the biography, and when she got home immediately began to read it. She was astonished to learn that a woman called Leocadia Weiss (with her daughter Rosario) had made a home for Goya in Bordeaux when he voluntarily exiled himself from Spain at the end of his life.

Henriette never made her experience public until 1958. In that year an acquaintance to whom she described her experience advised her to write out a full account and send it to the American Society for Psychical Research. She did this, and the Editor at that time, Laura Dale, sent her account to me. (I shall quote from this account below.)

I began a correspondence with Henriette concerning details of her experience and, with her permission, included a brief account of the case in my first paper on cases suggestive of reincarnation (Stevenson, 1960). In 1960 I met Henriette in New York City, where she was then living. After that I met her on numerous occasions when

---

*Many clairvoyants and mediums believe that touching and handling an object that belonged to a deceased person facilitates their getting into contact with that person, after the person's death. Osty (1923) described examples of the use of psychometric objects by French mediums.

I was in New York. I have notes of seven meetings between 1961 and 1976. After the latter year we rarely met, but we continued to exchange Christmas cards and notes of news almost every year until her death in New York City on May 1, 1992.

Henriette's experience had occurred more than 20 years before she wrote her account of it and I learned about it. By 1958 there was no longer any possibility of corroborating any of her statements about her experiences. There was still, however, an opportunity to investigate two aspects of the case. These are first, whether Henriette Roos had had any similar trance-like experiences in which she seemed to paint under an extraneous influence; and second, which of the two women who lived with Goya in Bordeaux—Leocadia Weiss or her daughter, Rosarito—is more likely to have been the person of whom, if the clairvoyant was correct, Henriette Roos was the reincarnation.

Before coming to these questions, I will give more information about Henriette Roos's early life up to the time of her unusual experience in Paris; and then I will cite the account of the experience that she wrote in 1958.

The Early Life of Henriette Roos

Henriette Roos showed unusual skill at painting even before she had had any lessons. At the age of 5 she drew a good likeness of her father with crayon. At 12 she accomplished an oil painting of two birds. (I saw this in her studio and would have judged it the work or a much older, or at least much more experienced, artist.) At 16 she became interested in painting miniatures and would have continued at this had she not been afraid of weakening her eyes with such work. At 18 she painted a portrait of her mother.

As a child, Henriette Roos was quiet and preferred to stay at home painting or reading. Her mother pushed her to go out socially, but she resisted this. She wanted to study art, but her parents considered this an unsuitable vocation for a respectable young lady in Amsterdam and would not permit it.

As I mentioned earlier, at the age of 22 she married a Hungarian pianist, Franz Weisz.* She thought later she had been more attracted to his name than to his personal qualities. Her marriage did free her from parental control, however, so that at the age of 24 she began taking instruction in painting at the (Dutch) Royal Academy of Art. At about the age of 30 she divorced Weisz and shortly thereafter went to France, a country to which she quickly became attached. Although as a schoolchild she had had some difficulty in learning French, once in France she picked up the language quickly and was speaking fluently within several months. She lived in France, first in Paris and then on the Riviera, for about 20 years, earning her living by her painting. Although she was a skillful original painter, she had a strong interest in copying and at one time was an official copyist in the Louvre.

*The spelling Weisz is a Hungarian variant of the name Weiss, which is found in Germany and France. Most biographies of Goya and articles about him spell the name Weiss, but some use Weis.

In about 1954 Henriette emigrated to the United States, where she lived until her death.

Henriette Roos's Unusual Experiences
While an Artist in Paris

Although doing so will entail some repetition of what I have already said, it will be best for me to cite next Henriette Roos's written statement about her experiences, which she wrote on January 10, 1958:

My studies at the Royal Academy of Amsterdam had brought me a Royal Award (a personal gift from Queen Wilhelmina) for three years in succession, which I used to go and work abroad in Paris. The means were small, and I stayed in a small hotel room. I had a French girlfriend, whom I liked very much. The only thing which disturbed me was her belief, her conviction in occultism. I found it hysterical and full of exaltation. I didn't believe in those things at all! I had been married for some years to a great Hungarian pianist called ... Weisz. This marriage failed. We divorced. It was I who didn't love him the way I hoped I would ... but strange enough, I still wanted to be called Mrs. Weisz for years. My mother used to say: "Why do you still carry that name, once you're divorced you take back your maiden name" (in Holland it's that way). And my answer was always the same: "I don't know, it is a strange feeling. I can't explain, that name somehow suits me. I feel *one* with it, it is more *me* than my own name Roos. Each time I call myself that way I have the feeling I'm talking about someone else." So I decided to be Mrs. ... Weisz-Roos.

This introduction was necessary and is of the highest importance for what follows.

It all happened before the war.* One evening in my Paris hotel room, after a day's work at a portrait, I felt miserable — sick — with terrible headaches, heartbeatings, short of breath — and I went to bed at 9 P.M., trying to recover by a good sleep. Suddenly I hear (I don't think I really heard it with my *ears* — but somewhere at my forehead, between the eyes) a voice, saying: "Don't be so lazy, get up and work." I didn't pay any attention first and turned around, trying to fall asleep ... until a second time the same words were said. I began to wonder, but still remained in bed and desperately tried to sleep — but a third time — and this time very distinctively and energetically: "Don't be so lazy, get up and work" was heard. This time I got up, as I couldn't sleep anyway, and I asked myself: "Am I crazy? What the h... am I going to work at at night!?" But in spite of all, I did take my easel, wanted to push it under the tiny electric bulb at the ceiling (typical of all cheap Paris hotel rooms) but a force came within me to turn the whole thing into the darkest corner of the room and *away* from the light, with the result that *I couldn't see anything*. My palette, still full of paints, was on the table, also a little canvas-board. This I took — and I started to paint, hardly knowing what I was doing, in a feverish haste, for 45 minutes, when suddenly I felt my right arm becoming immensely heavy. I had to put down my brushes. Realizing that I felt fine, without any headache, free from all my discomforts, I went back to bed and fell asleep almost immediately. When I awoke from a sound sleep at 6 A.M. next morning, I suddenly remembered ... was it a dream? ...or did I really paint something? ... I jumped out of

*This refers to the Second World War. Henriette Roos later dated the experience to (probably) 1936.

bed and there it was. A beautiful little portrait of a young woman ... the eyes looking far away at something unreal, unseen. I shivered. What was that? How to explain this phenomenon!?

I decided to go to my girl friend, who lived only one block away. I could hardly wait until 9 A.M. After having told her what happened, she of course wanted to come home with me right away. When she saw it, she nearly burst out into tears, saying: "Oh Henriette, oh dear, this is wonderful, this is great! You know what we're going to do? We'll take it to a meeting for psychic research. Every Thursday afternoon they have a clairvoyant, extraordinarily gifted, and you take your little canvas along." "Oh no," I said, "nothing of this humbug, I don't believe in it!" But she insisted so much that I finally gave in and I thought, well, let's have the fun.

So we went. No use telling that no one knew me there! A crowded room, in the middle of which an old and extremely simple and poor looking woman was seated. Near her was a small table on which anyone could place an object about which he or she wanted to know something. So I deposited my picture amongst at least a dozen of other objects already there, and took a seat somewhere hidden. New people still come in. I was talking to my friend. The place was far from silent yet ... but the old woman had already grabbed my picture — and fell "in trance." Her face lifted — eyes closed — very pale — her lips trembling — slowly — very slowly first — she started —

And here is what she said. "I see very large golden letters — a name is spelled to me. G—O—Y—A .. now he speaks to me. He says: He was a great Spanish painter. He had to fly from his country from his enemies, and it was you who received him in your home in a big southern city in France — until the end of his life. He still is so thankful for this that he wants to guide you — but he is not satisfied, you resist too much, you are too much tied up in your academic education* — you never relax and let him guide you, you make it very difficult for him — he therefore made you paint in the dark, so that you couldn't see what you're doing. He says: "You have good effects with simple means. Your colors are warm, etc., etc."

Well, the woman must have talked for at least 15 minutes in this style — I gazed at her in perplexity first — but when my friend and I finally left — I was considerably cooled off. My friend of course was terribly excited. Sure of her triumph she said: "Well, what do you say now!" But my answer was: "I don't know — it all is very strange. I do believe in telepathy alright — and I think this is the explanation. *I* know that I am the artist — *I* know that I did it in the dark — *I* know that I have an academic education — *I* know that I use simple means — and so did you — She must have read our thoughts. Only one thing puzzles me ... the Goya in the story. I do not know anything about his life. (It happened that at that time I had never read anything about him, nor had my friend, who was a business woman). Well, that ended the afternoon. I was still full of disbelief.

That *same evening*, however, I was invited for the first time at the home of a famous French musician, and as soon as I entered the room, my attention was drawn to a bookshelf. And what was the book-title I saw first? *La vie de Goya* (the life of Goya). I told the hostess what had happened to me that afternoon, and that I would be most anxious to read this book. She let me take it home, and as soon as I entered my room I

This attitude of opposition to the rigidities of academic teaching of painting was typical of Goya. Hull (1987) wrote: "Goya sought to free young artists from straight-jacketing formulas as taught in academies, to encourage them to discover divine nature in all its manifestations. This appeal for artist's freedom was spelled out in a report he gave to the [Royal] Academy [of San Fernando] on October 14, 1792 [Goya, 1981, pp. 310–312]. And he meant every word he said" [p. 77].

opened it somewhere in the middle and what I saw gave me such a shock, that I couldn't believe my own eyes!

What I saw — was

My own name: Weisz.

Weisz — spelled the same way — with a first name Leocadia.* Leocadia Weisz was Goya's friend in Bordeaux (the big southern city in France, that woman [the clairvoyant] had told about) who kept him in her home until his death.

There was finally the explanation for my wanting to keep the name, because once before I had carried it! This convinced me. It was as if someone had said: So you still did not want to believe — here, *here* is your proof.

Henriette Roos's Loss of Attachment to the Name "Weisz"

Following her unusual experiences in Paris, which occurred in 1936 (approximately), Henriette Roos felt that the strong grip on her of the name "Weisz" ceased almost immediately. She then had no difficulty in giving up the name and had since signed her paintings simply "Roos" instead of "Weisz-Roos" as she had been doing from the time of her marriage, including the 3 years between her divorce and the experiences in Paris.

Henriette Roos's Later Experiences of Painting Unusually Rapidly

Following the first experience in Paris of painting rapidly and, on that occasion, in the dark, Henriette had four other rather similar experiences in which she painted with unusual speed, ease, and skill.

The most notable of these experiences occurred in 1953 when Henriette was living in Nice and making a rather precarious living as a portrait painter. She had been commissioned to paint the portrait of an elderly and wealthy man who did not want to have his portrait painted, but reluctantly agreed to have it painted at the request of his daughter. When Henriette went to his home, a large villa on the Riviera, she found not only the reluctant sitter but his entire family with their children and pets all assembled in the room where she was to paint. They stood around her, and the atmosphere became oppressive. In addition, she had been working hard and was tired and fatigued. Under these circumstance she thought it would be impossible to paint a portrait. She set up her easel and paints, but felt overcome by despair and fatigue. At this point she made a strong mental plea to Goya to help her. Almost immediately she found herself able to paint and within a brief time had put on the canvas an astonishing likeness of the sitter. The family was delighted with what she did within

*When I first met Henriette, she remembered the title (in French) of the book she had borrowed and read. It was La vie de Goya. She could not then remember the name of the author. In 1966, however, she was sure that the book was the biography with that title by Eugenio d'Ors (1928). In the French translation of this work the surname of Leocadia and Rosario is spelled Weiss.

a few minutes, and the sitter's attitude became transformed so that he thereafter became fully cooperative. The portrait became one of her most successful. This portrait was not painted in the dark.

Henriette had a second experience (also in France) in which she seemed to paint automatically and as if in a kind of semi-trance. By the time I talked with her about this, in 1960, she had forgotten the details of the circumstances in which it had occurred. She did recall that there was again some unusual pressure on her to paint a portrait under circumstances somewhat similar to those of the episode in Nice in 1953. The ensuing portrait was that of a small, rather emaciated girl.

A third occasion of this type occurred in 1960 when Henriette (then living in the United States) received a commission for a portrait to be painted from photographs. She found herself delayed in starting and then suddenly began and finished very quickly. She described the experience to me in an interview and also in a letter dated January 30, 1961, from which I quote the following description:

> I had been wanting to paint this portrait many times in the past. The moment I wanted to start it something kept me from doing so, and each time I put down my brushes before even starting the first lines. This time I was not even *thinking* of doing it—and suddenly (it was a matter of seconds!) I was in front of my easel and did the portrait in a day and a half. Everything around me vanished. The whole world could have changed. I even forgot to eat. When my phone sometimes rang, I answered that I couldn't talk. It was the same furious drive as I had felt when doing the ... "girl's face." [Henriette here meant the portrait painted in Paris about 1936.] And another strange feeling is that now I've done it, I am constantly wondering how I did it!

At the end of this letter Henriette commented on the success of this portrait, which she and other persons considered one of her best. In the same letter she also answered a question I had put to her asking whether she had on this occasion tried to invoke the help of Goya by conscious supplication. She replied: "I did *not* call [for] Goya's assistance this time because there was not any impossible situation as there had been in Nice."

The fourth occasion of this type occurred in 1965. Henriette again had a commission for a portrait, this time rather an important one since its success might lead to other commissions. There was not, however, the sense of desperate pressure which characterized the situation she was in at Nice in 1953. I will again quote her own description of the experience in a letter to me dated January 28, 1966:

> The fact is that quite differently from my usual procedures in painting from photographs, I started it immediately, feeling a tremendous urge to do so. Generally I have to keep a photo about a week with me, getting the feeling of the person as far as that is possible, studying it daily, before starting anything on canvas. This time I just seemed to *know*. I knew also how her [the person whose portrait she was to paint] bone structure was, and what she used to wear. In fact when her son-in-law warned me that she never wore black (as the photo suggested) but always blue, I had already done it. Blue it was. Usually I am afraid to show portraits to the family, not knowing what their reaction would be ... after all, they knew her so closely. This time, no fear at all! I just

knew, it was her all over all right! And the fact that it came so easily, so quickly, without any effort. It all seems quite puzzling.... The *urge* was unusual. Doing portraits from photos does not generally excite me too much.

Henriette Roos painted this portrait in 2 days and therefore quite rapidly.

Occasions such as the four just mentioned and the first one in Paris in about 1936 were exceptional in Henriette Roos' experience with painting. They were spread over almost 30 years. She made no claim to be regularly under the influence of Goya in her day-to-day painting. For that matter, she made no dogmatic assertion about a Goya influence even on these five special occasions. She only insisted that they had had certain features in common and contrasted with her usual experience in painting. On these particular occasions, she was usually tired or for some other reason reluctant to paint. Then rather suddenly she "found herself," so to speak, able to paint with much more speed, skill, ease, and sureness than she ordinarily felt. She was never aware of any "presence," by which I mean, any sensing of the characteristics of another personality, at these times. Only on the first occasion (in Paris) had she painted in the darkness during these episodes.

Comment. Goya often painted very fast (Hull, 1987), a fact that deserves noting in connection with Henriette Roos's unusual speed of painting during the occasions when she believed that she might have had the assistance of the discarnate Goya.

Henriette Roos's Knowledge of Goya Before 1936

Henriette had known a little about Goya as an artist, but she was quite certain that she had learned nothing about his personal life, much less that he had been in exile in Bordeaux. During her training at the Royal Academy of Art in Amsterdam, she had taken no course in the history of art.

The Identification of the Most Probable Previous Personality

As Henriette learned, Goya had lived in Bordeaux with Leocadia Weiss. It seemed natural to assume that if this case is best explained by reincarnation and temporary possession, then Leocadia Weiss would have been the related previous personality of Henriette. But was she? Henriette herself first raised doubts about this point during one of our meetings, in 1966. She had acquired a copy of *La vie de Goya* by d'Ors (1928), the biography she had read in Paris in 1936. She had read again the passages dealing with Leocadia Weiss. There was no reference to Leocadia ever having painted; but she had a daughter, Rosario, often called Rosarito, who *did* paint. Henriette suggested that perhaps the previous life in question for her might have been that of Rosarito, not Leocadia.

This suggestion stimulated me to examine information about the lives of Leocadia and Rosarito with a view to learning whether Rosarito had other traits in common with Henriette, additional to their skill in painting. Accordingly, I studied other biographies of Goya and some articles describing his last years in France. Equipped with the information thus obtained, I questioned Henriette (during an interview in 1968) about her interests, likes, dislikes, and other relevant aspects of her life. I phrased my questions so that she could not tell what answers I expected; I was not sure anyway what answers I should expect. Henriette Roos was already acquainted with some facts in the life of Goya (and the lives of the Weisses), because she had read d'Ors's biography, although she denied that she had read any other.

I will next give brief biographies of Leocadia Weiss and her daughter, Rosario.* After these I will summarize the relevant correspondences between their lives and that of Henriette.

Leocadia Weiss. After the restoration of the Bourbon King Ferdinand VII to the throne of Spain in 1814, Goya felt himself increasingly uncomfortable in Madrid. He himself was pardoned for his flirtations with the French regime during the usurpation of Joseph Bonaparte, and he was appointed Court Painter once more. Nevertheless, the tyrannical regime of King Ferdinand repelled him more and more. In 1819 he withdrew from Madrid to a place outside the city. To the house he bought in the country there came as half-mistress, half-housekeeper Goya's relative (a second cousin probably), Leocadia Weiss. Leocadia Zorilla, to give her maiden name, was born in 1790 and was therefore more than 40 years younger than Goya. She had been married to a German, Isidro Weiss, by whom she had had two children, Guillermo and Maria del Rosario, whose pet name was Rosarito. The daughter, Rosario, was born in 1814. Sometime between then and 1819 Isidro Weiss deserted Leocadia, but she continued to use his name as hers.

Goya and Leocadia lived together near Madrid until 1824. At this time Goya felt so alienated from the government of Spain, which had recently suppressed a liberal movement with French troops, that he resolved to quit the country. He applied for permission to travel to France for his health and received it. He then moved to Bordeaux, and there Leocadia again kept house for him. Rosario was there also. Goya returned to Spain briefly on two occasions after 1824, but in effect he lived in exile in France (mostly in Bordeaux) until his death in 1828.

Leocadia was much interested in politics on the liberal side and seems to have made some effort to arouse Goya's interest in politics. (He tended to look upon politicians of all factions as equally unworthy of his interest and approval.) She was a person of hot temper and contemporaries recorded stormy quarrels (and following peaces)

---

*As sources of secondary information for Leocadia and Rosarito Weiss, I have used the books and articles by Baticle (1986), Hull (1987), Lafond (1907), Sánchez Cantón (1951), and Stokes (1914). Fauqué and Etcheverria (1982) provide a valuable compilation of information about Goya's life in Bordeaux. The primary sources I have examined are the letters of Goya himself (Goya, 1981), of the liberal poet Leandro Fernandez de Moratín (in exile in Bordeaux himself) (Moratín, 1929), and of Leocadia Weiss (Bordona, 1924). The work by d'Ors (1928), which I have already cited, is not always accurate, written in an almost fictional style of narrative, and totally without references.

between her and Goya. She was a restless, gregarious person who loved to get out of the house and walk around the city. She particularly enjoyed circuses and fairs and often more or less dragged the aged and deaf Goya to such entertainments in Bordeaux. She did not paint and seems to have had little interest in art, but no one has doubted her devotion to Goya as a person.

In Bordeaux Goya continued to paint and to sketch. Moreover, Ferdinand VII continued his salary as Court Painter and in the end assured Goya of its continuance during his lifetime. Thus so long as Goya lived, he, Leocadia, and Rosario had comfortable circumstances.

In the spring of 1828 Goya, who was born on March 30, 1746, was just 82 years old. On April 2, he suffered a stroke and became bedridden. He apparently realized that he had made no provision for Leocadia and Rosario after his death, and he somehow gestured or mumbled that he wished to make a will for their benefit. His daughter-in-law, who was present then, told him that he had already made a will. (This was true; he had made a will that amply provided for his son Javier, in 1811; but this will said nothing about Leocadia, who had not then entered his life.) As a result, he made no new will, and when he died on April 16, 1828, Leocadia and Rosario became almost destitute. Leocadia appealed to friends for help and eventually to the French Minister of the Interior. She and Rosario returned to Madrid, where Rosario had some success as an artist.

Leocadia Weiss died in 1856. She was then about 70 years old.

Rosario Weiss. Rosario Weiss was born in 1814, probably in Madrid. Her father deserted not long after her birth, and she was barely five in 1819 when her mother and Goya established housekeeping together. From then until Goya's death she lived almost continuously with him, first in Spain and then in Bordeaux.

All contemporary witnesses testify to Goya's warm attachment to Rosario and to her affection for him. One biographer hints that Leocadia Weiss had a "special hold" over Goya through the gay, attractive child (d'Ors, 1928). Goya sometimes referred to her as his "daughter," but we should take this as an indication of their attachment to each other, not of his paternity.

When the three reached Bordeaux, Rosario was 10 years old. She had already shown a precocious ability in art and wished to become a painter. Goya sought to encourage this in every way he could. He spent much time in teaching her himself, but was no longer effective as a teacher. He arranged for her to study under other artists in Bordeaux. He wrote and spoke to others enthusiastically about her talents. In one letter he wrote: "This amazing child wishes to do miniatures, and I wish it too; for it is perhaps the greatest phenomenon in the world to do what she does at her age" (Lafond, 1907, p. 124; my translation). He wanted to send her to study in Paris, but this plan did not materialize.*

As I mentioned, Goya had some intention of providing for Rosario (and Leocadia)

---

*Two of Goya's biographers have conjectured that Rosario was the model for one of Goya's last paintings, The Milkmaid of Bordeaux, which he painted in 1827 (Baticle, 1986; d'Ors, 1928). Rosario was 13 years old in 1827.

in a revised will, but he never did this. After Rosario and her mother returned to Madrid, she became established as a faithful copyist of the paintings in the Prado. She also became a lithographer. In 1840 she was appointed Professor of Drawing to Queen Isabella II, the daughter of Ferdinand VII, who was still a child. Not long after this, she was caught in a riot on her way to the palace, and the severe fright of this experience led to a high fever and her death on July 31, 1840, at the age of 26 (Lafond, 1907).*

Rosario was extremely fond of animals, if we may judge from the numerous drawings of animals evidently made by Goya for her when she was a child. It would seem, however, that Leocadia Weiss was also fond of animals as her fondness for circuses suggest. Rosario seems to have been an affectionate child free of her mother's bitterness and emotional storms. Her brightness and gaiety gave much joy to the exiled Goya.

In addition to her skill as an artist, Rosario had an interest in music and began to learn to play the piano as a child. When, after Goya's death, Leocadia had to let the piano go, for the money it could bring, Rosario was much disappointed (Bordona, 1924).

Relevant Features of the Life and Personality of Henriette Roos. I have already described Henriette's precocious ability as an artist, her interest in miniatures, and her skill as a copyist. I shall now describe some features of her personality that we may compare with those of Leocadia and Rosario Weiss.

Henriette was almost as gifted musically as she was in painting. She became an accomplished pianist and might, if she had wished, have become a professional one.

Henriette told me that she had been fond of animals all her life. She had no interest in politics whatever. She preferred to lead a quiet life and had little interest in social occasions or other outside activities. Whenever she could, she avoided crowds of all kinds such as one finds in subways, concerts, theaters, circuses, and other public places. Although she was fond of music, she said that she would not attend a concert at the large Lewisohn Stadium in New York even if she were offered $1,000; and she once left an opera at the end of the first act because she was so uncomfortable in the crowd of the audience. When she went to movies, she paid close attention to the location of the exits. The word *phobia* does not seem too strong an expression for describing her dislike of crowds.

When she was a child and young adult, Henriette was restrained and inclined to timidity. Later she learned to express assertive and aggressive impulses more easily.

As a child (or adult) Henriette had no special interest or attraction for Spain. She never tried to learn the Spanish language. She likewise when young had no special interest in France, although when she lived there in her adulthood she became much attached to it.

In her painting Henriette tended to emulate the style of the 17th-and-18th century masters. She did not care for that of the Impressionists and equally avoided the "photographic" precision of some portrait painters. She took pride in her refusal to

---

*Bordona (1924) stated that Rosario died in 1843, 3 years later than the date given by Lafond. Hull (1987) and Stokes (1914) accepted the date of 1840.

flatter sitters, trying to paint their characters as they seemed to her, not as they might have wished to be represented. (In this respect she resembled Goya, who was celebrated for the frankness of his portraits.) She was equally willing, however, to portray favorable qualities of character when she discerned them.

In Table 3 I have listed the various experiences and character traits for the three personalities that I have identified from the available information. I have indicated with an asterisk those items described in d'Ors's life of Goya, which Henriette had already read at the time of my questioning her about her own traits and experiences. Her knowledge of some details of the life of Rosario and Leocadia could have influenced her responses to my questions about herself.

Comment. This last possibility may weaken, but I do not think it nullifies, the preponderating evidence of correspondences between Rosario and Henriette compared with those between Leocadia and Henriette. I believe that Henriette was indifferent, at least consciously, to the question whether she might be the reincarnation of Leocadia or that of Rosario.

Table 3. Summary of Experiences and Traits of Leocadia Weiss, Rosario Weiss, and Henriette Roos

Experience or Trait	Leocadia Weiss	Rosario Weiss	Henriette Roos
Precocious skill in painting*	Not a painter	Yes	Yes
Interest and skill in copying	Not a painter	Yes	Yes
Interest in painting miniatures*	Not a painter	Yes	Yes
Love of animals	Yes	Yes	Yes
Piano playing	No information	Yes	Yes
Ill-tempered*	Yes	No	No
Fear of crowds	No	Unknown, but died following fright of being in a rioting crowd	Yes
Interest in politics*	Yes	No information	No
Liking for circuses, fairs, horse races, etc.*	Yes	No information	No, except for the animal acts of circuses
Love of social and other activities outside the home	Yes	No information	No

Items identified thus are given in d'Ors's (1928) life of Goya and therefore were normally known to Henriette Roos before she answered questions about herself.

Two Somewhat Similar Older Cases

An important weakness of this case is its complete dependence on the uncorroborated memory of Henriette Roos. The stability of her descriptions of her experiences during the 30 years that I knew her somewhat mitigates this weakness without removing it.

If we accept reincarnation as the best explanation for the case, it becomes one of the few in which we have evidence of the carry-over from one life to another of a skill — that for painting; and both Rosario Weiss and Henriette showed this skill when they were still children.

I know of only two other cases in which artists have claimed to paint when under the influence of a discarnate personality: Frederic Thompson and Augustin Lesage.

The case of Frederic Thompson was carefully studied by J. H. Hyslop, who published an exhaustive report (1909) about it, as well as a shorter summary (1919). The subject was an American engraver with little interest or aptitude for painting, and no training for it. Nevertheless, in 1905 he unexpectedly began to feel strong impulses to paint. It seemed to him that these impulses came from Robert Swain Gifford, an artist of some distinction. Thompson had known Gifford very slightly, but was unaware that he had died some 6 months before his own impulses to paint began.

Under the influence of the "Gifford impulses," Thompson began to paint with a remarkable skill which surprised him and other persons also. He made some sketches and paintings entirely from visions of rural scenes. The impulses also led him to distant parts of New England where he painted various scenes that, so he learned later, Gifford had been fond of painting. Thompson's pictures of these scenes bore a close resemblance to Gifford's, and yet he disclaimed any prior normal knowledge of them or any possibility of having acquired it. After prolonged study, Hyslop concluded that the case minimally provided evidence of paranormal communication from somewhere to Thompson, and that communication from the deceased Gifford was as plausible an explanation of the facts as any other.

No fair judgment can be made of this case without a study of Hyslop's copious records. Here I wish merely to draw attention to the *form* of some of Thompson's experiences. Eventually he had definite imaged auditory hallucinations, but at first he experienced simple impressions and impulses only. In an autobiographical account Thompson wrote:

> …during the time I was sketching I remember having the impression that I was Mr. Gifford himself, and I would tell myself before starting out that Mr. Gifford wanted to go sketching, although I did not know at that time that he had died early in the year [Hyslop, 1909, p. 32].

Thompson's descriptions of his impulses to paint closely resemble those reported by some subjects of cases of telepathic impressions (Stevenson, 1970a). They often describe what amounts to a compulsion to return towards some person or place, sensing that some distressing event is occurring there. Thompson's experiences differed from these in that he attributed them to a deceased personality, even though, as he said, when they started he did not know that Gifford had died. Thompson's compulsion to paint continued over several years also, in contrast to the much shorter duration of the impulses to action found in the cases of telepathic impressions with living agents.

Augustin Lesage was a French miner who (in 1911) at the age of 35 suddenly took up painting, an activity in which he had had no interest before and for which he had no training whatever (Bondon, 1947; Dubuffet, 1965; Osty, 1928). He painted with oils, usually on very large canvases. Initially he painted only designs of a rather unusual type with much small detail and no identifiable persons or objects. Later he introduced persons, animals, and objects into his paintings which, at about the same time, suggested an ancient Egyptian, or other oriental, style and themes. Although Lesage's paintings *suggested* oriental motifs, they were not in fact true representations of any identified style of art, oriental or Western. Some of his later paintings included Egyptian hieroglyphic symbols. Most of these were accurately reproduced as individual symbols, but they were not arranged in a meaningful way, and so they had evidently been reproduced without comprehension from memory traces in Lesage's mind. Although Lesage's painting received some favorable attention from art critics in France during the period between 1920 and 1940, they can only be regarded as examples of crude or primitive art. I only mention them here because Lesage claimed to be a painting medium and believed that his paintings were influenced by discarnate persons. His case, however, unlike those of Frederic Thompson and of Henriette Roos, contains no suggestion of paranormal processes.

Comment

In reports of other cases I have frequently drawn attention to some emotion shown by the subject of a case that was appropriate to the circumstances, especially the mode of death, of the deceased person whose life the subject remembers. The most common emotions of this type are vengefulness (toward the persons held responsible for the death in the previous life) and fear, as in phobias of the instrument or place of the death (Stevenson, 1990). This case—that of Henriette Roos—includes evidence of a phobia perhaps attributable to a previous life.

More importantly perhaps, the case provides evidence of the persistence of a different emotion: gratitude. If the case is best interpreted as showing evidence that Henriette Roos was the reincarnation of Rosario Weiss, it also shows evidence of gratitude on the part of Goya (presumably surviving death) that persisted for more than a century. (He died in 1828, and Henriette's experience in Paris occurred in [about] 1936.) As we have seen, Goya was grateful to Leocadia and Rosario Weiss during his lifetime; and as he was dying, he seemed to want to make some provision for them in a new will, but was dissuaded from doing so. Thus he probably died with a sense of gratitude and also one of unrequited indebtedness.

Part IV

General Discussion

No reader of this book will deny that cases suggestive of reincarnation occur in Europe. I wish we knew the incidence of such cases, but we do not. We can surmise that parents suppress some cases because, from their traditional religious beliefs, they think a previous life impossible. They therefore believe that a child speaking about a previous life must be lying or expressing wild fantasies. In other instances a child may suppress itself because its parents have given it no context in which to place and therefore understand images of events in a previous life. The cases of Giuseppe Costa and Georg Neidhart illustrate the bafflement of young children who have such images. Other cases are lost to investigation because the persons concerned have no knowledge, let alone the addresses, of responsible investigators. Among the 32 investigated cases of this book, I learned of only 7 from the subject or a subject's parent.

The three causes just mentioned — parental suppression, self-suppression, and ignorance of potentially interested investigators — bear on the reporting of cases; they tell us nothing, however, about their real incidence. I do not believe that the losses to reporting can explain the paucity of cases we learn about. In Part 1 I cited surveys of the 1990s showing that in several European countries more than 25% of respondents believed in reincarnation. Parents in this group would probably provide an attentive audience for any child who tried to talk about a previous life. As for the other 75% of parents, we may note that measures of suppression are often applied in India, but apparently have no effect on a child's wish to describe memories of a previous life (Stevenson and Chadha, 1990). I conclude, therefore that the real incidence of cases in Europe is low and probably much lower than that in India and some other countries. If I am right on this point, I have no explanation for the difference in incidences between Europe and, say, India. In an earlier book, I conjectured that the difference might derive from deep and still poorly understood differences in the cultures of the two regions (Stevenson, 1987/2001).

Leaving this presently intractable problem, I turn to the similarities and differences in the features of European cases and those of other countries. Almost 20 years ago my colleagues and I examined the principal features of 856 cases from six different countries: Burma (now Myanmar), India, Lebanon, Sri Lanka, Thailand, and the United States. (The series included no European cases.) We found that four features occurred in the cases of all six cultures: an early age (usually between 2 and 4 years) of a subject's first speaking about a previous life; a slightly older age (usually between 5 and 7 years) when the subject stopped speaking spontaneously about a previous life; a high incidence of violent death in the previous life; and frequent mention of the mode of death in the child's statements (Cook et al., 1983). These features occurred so regularly in the cases of different cultures that I have sometimes referred to them as "universal features." The incidence of other features varies widely in different cultures. Examples of such cultural variation in incidence occur in cases with a claim of sex change from one life to another and in cases in which subject and previous personality belong to the same family. Nevertheless, the phrase "universal features" showed excessive confidence on my part because we had examined the cases of only a few countries. We needed to study cases in other cultures. Having the European cases before us, even though they are few, permits an opportunity for such comparisons.

Table 4 provides the data of 22 European children's cases compared with 668 cases from India, Lebanon, the United States (nontribal cases), and Canada.* For each feature of the cases some data were missing, but sufficient were available for valid comparisons.

Table 4. Comparison of Four Features of European Cases and Those of Four Other Countries (India, Lebanon, United States, and Canada)

	Other Countries N=668	Europe N=22
Mean age of first speaking (months)	36.4 (n 571)	35.9 (n 21)
Mean age of ceasing to speak spontaneously (months)	85.6 (n 222)†	97.1 (n 15)
Mention of mode of death by subject (percent)	76.2 (n 581)	84.6 (n 13)
Violent mode of death in previous life (percent)	68.8 (n 545)	73.7 (n 19)

NOTE: Figures indicated by *n* show the number of cases that include reliable data for each feature.

*These countries were selected because the data of all the cases from them in our files have been coded and are available for the comparisons.
†Another 105 subjects were still speaking of the previous life at the time of the last interview.

From studying the figures of Table 4, readers will surely agree that the European cases show prominently the four features that we have commonly found in the cases of other cultures.

The European cases also sometimes have several other features frequently observed in the cases of other cultures. Five of the children had phobias corresponding to events of the claimed previous life. Six of them showed unusual play similarly corresponding to the child's statements. In four cases the child spoke about a previous life as a member of the opposite sex; two of these subjects were males and two females. In five cases a dream and in one an auditory communication seemed to foretell the subject's birth. In six cases informants reported that the subject showed some unlearned skill or other unexpected knowledge. Three subjects had congenital abnormalities that may have derived from the life to which the subject referred. In sum, the European cases appear to be of the same general type as those of other cultures where my colleagues and I have studied such cases.

We must next consider the extent to which the European cases show evidence of some paranormal process. If we base our appraisal solely on the children's statements, we cannot avoid disappointment. Among the 22 cases 7 are unsolved; and among the remaining 15 cases all but three (Gladys Deacon, Wolfgang Neurath, and Helmut Kraus) are same-family cases. In same-family cases we can never achieve a desirable assurance that the subject received no normal communication of information about the concerned deceased family member. We could say this also of the case of Wolfgang Neurath, in which the two families concerned were near neighbors. I never obtained an independent verification for the otherwise impressive case of Gladys Deacon. Eliminating it, we have the case of Helmut Kraus as the only solved and independently verified case (among the cases beginning in early childhood) in which the families concerned had no connection with each other. To it we can perhaps add the case of Ruprecht Schulz, which had a slight beginning in early childhood.

In addition to the mentioned weaknesses in the evidence, we need to remember that the adult informants may have incorrectly remembered or misinterpreted what the child said. The parents of a deceased child have a special vulnerability to such errors. In seven cases we can recognize the possible influence of such longing for a return of a deceased family member. In contrast to these cases, however, we can count seven other cases in which the child's statements surprised and nonplused its parents. I see no reason to think that they encouraged such statements let alone that they instigated them.

We could not avoid disappointment in the European cases if we counted as favorable to the interpretation of a paranormal process only statements that were both verified and outside the child's capacity for receiving a normal communication about the concerned deceased person. We are, however, not so restricted. Our appraisal of the cases should include the behavior of the children that is both unusual in the child's family and that accords with what the child says about a previous life. If we count phobias, philias, unlearned skills, and other unlearned knowledge, 16 of the 22 children showed such unusual behavior. As I have continued in these investigations, I have come to think that the unusual behavior shown by the majority of these children should count for as much in the appraisal of paranormality as a child's statements and any birthmarks or birth defects it may have. In some of the European cases, for example in those of Carl Edon, David Llewelyn, Taru Järvi, Gedeon Haich, and Teuvo Koivisto, the child's unusual behavior seemed more prominent than the statements the children made. It was sometimes totally foreign to the expectations and values of the child's family. I do not think we can explain such behavior either by genetics or the influence of the child's family.

Nevertheless, the European cases are, on the whole, much weaker in evidence of a paranormal process than the stronger cases found in Asia, especially in India and Sri Lanka. Tucker (2000) developed a Strength of Case Scale (SOCS) that assigns or denies points according to the various features of the case that contribute to a judgment of a paranormal process. He examined 799 cases from six different countries (three quarters of the cases coming from India, Turkey, and the United States). The scores ranged between a low of -3 and a high of 49. The overall mean was 10.4 and the median was 8. The mean score for European cases (22 children's cases and that of Ruprecht Schulz) was only 6.4 and the median was 5. Only 5 of the 23 European cases had a score above 10 (the mean for cases of other countries). The case of Ruprecht Schulz, quite exceptionally for the European cases, received a score of 23.

Before concluding I will comment on the cases with vivid and recurring dreams. Dreams give us involuntary pictorial images while we sleep; they seldom have any verbal content. The attempt we sometimes make to describe the scenes of a dream in words can rarely provide complete accuracy. We should not express surprise therefore when a dreamer's accounts of a recurrent dream vary from one narration to another.

We also should attach little importance to adjectives the narrator of dreams may use, such as "vivid" and "realistic." I once conducted an informal analysis of 125 dreams that counted as precognitive (Stevenson, 1970b). In 45% of these cases the dreamer had used words like "vivid" and "realistic" in describing the dreams. Such words may therefore furnish indicators of a paranormal process, but no affirmation of it. That can only come when the dream includes verified information of which the dreamer had no normal knowledge. Few vivid or realistic dreams qualify in this respect. Of the seven dreams I have included in this work, two—those of Traude von Hutten and Luigi Gioberti—proved almost valueless when fully probed. The dreams of two other subjects—those of Thomas Evans and William Hens—were unverifiable. The remaining three dreamers, however, left me convinced that their dreams included some paranormal process. These are those of Jenny McLeod, Winifred Wylie, and John East. They might have remembered a previous life during dreams. At least 13 subjects of cases in Asia have had verified memories of a previous life when awake and also dreams or nightmares that included some of the contents of the waking memories.* We can therefore believe that some persons may have dreams about a previous life without having any waking memories.

I have used the phrase "paranormal process" repeatedly, and I should now say

---

I have given elsewhere a partial list of these subjects (Stevenson, 1997, pp. 1386–87).

what kind of process I favor for cases suggestive of reincarnation. One alternative to reincarnation is a clairvoyant perception of information available to living persons. This supposes powers of paranormal perception that the children of these cases do not show in any context apart from their statements and unusual behavior suggesting a previous life. It also fails to account for the near universal amnesia for the apparent memories that sets in during later childhood. Paranormal perception also does not explain the children's impersonation of someone else in their behavior.

A second possible paranormal interpretation is "possession" of the subject by a person who has died and can influence living persons from a discarnate realm. I am convinced that cases best interpreted as instances of possession have occasionally occurred. I favor that interpretation for Henriette Roos's painting reproduced in Figure 18. Other examples occurred in the cases of Jasbir Singh and Sumitra Singh. Such cases differ markedly, however, in their features from the cases of young children who seem to remember previous lives. The concept of possession does not explain the amnesia of later childhood that the cases of children claiming to remember past lives almost invariably show. It also does not explain congenital anomalies corresponding to wounds or other marks in the previous life. (The cases of this work have admittedly few of these.)

The European cases of children who seem to remember a previous life clearly do not provide the strongest evidence of reincarnation that we have. I nevertheless conclude that for some of them reincarnation is the best interpretation, albeit not the only one.

Appendix

List of Reports of Cases Mentioned in This Book

The cases are listed in alphabetical order (by letter, not by word) of the subjects' first or given names. Honorifics sometimes used in the text, especially with names of Burmese persons, are not used in this list, except in a few instances where an honorific has been added in parentheses to aid in identifying the subject of a case.

The following abbreviations are used for published works I have written:

R and B = *Reincarnation and Biology: A Contribution to the Etiology of Birthmarks and Birth Defects.* Two volumes. Westport, CT: Praeger, 1997.

Synopsis = *Where Reincarnation and Biology Intersect.* (This short book contains brief reports of many cases described in more detail in *R and B.*) Westport, CT: Praeger, 1997.

Twenty Cases = *Twenty Cases Suggestive of Reincarnation* 2nd ed. Charlottesville: University Press of Virginia, 1974.

CORT (followed by an Arabic numeral) = *Cases of the Reincarnation Type,* Volumes 1–4. Charlottesville: University Press of Virginia, 1975–83.

CWRPLS = *Children Who Remember Previous Lives.* (This book provides information about some cases, but not detailed case reports) rev. ed. Jefferson, NC: McFarland and Co, 2001.

For page numbers of case reports consult the indexes of the books.

Asha Rani	Not published in detail
Bajrang Bahadur (B. B.) Saxena	*R and B*; *Synopsis*
Bir Sahai	*R and B*; *Synopsis*
Bongkuch Promsin	*CORT 4*
Cemil Fahrici	*R and B*; *Synopsis*
Chanai Choomalaiwong	*R and B*; *Synopsis*

Chaokhun Rajsuthajarn: *see* Rajsuthajarn (Ven. Chaokhun)	
Dolon Champa Mitra	*CORT 1*
Dorabeth Crosby	*R and B*
Dulcina Karasek	*R and B*; *Synopsis*
Erkan Kılıç	*CORT 3*
Gnanatilleka Baddewithana	*Twenty Cases*
Henry Demmert III	*R and B*; *Synopsis*
Htay Win (Maung)	*R and B*; *Synopsis*
Htwe Win (Ma)	*R and B*; *Synopsis*
Htwe Yin (Ma)	*R and B*
Huriye Bugay	*R and B*
Indika and Kakshappa Ishwara	*R and B*; *Synopsis*
Indika Guneratne	*CORT 2*
İsmail Altınkılıç	*CORT 3*
Izzat Shuhayyib	Not published in detail
Jasbir Singh	*Twenty Cases*
Kumkum Verma	*CORT 1*
Lalitha Abeyawardena	*CORT 2*
Lekh Pal Jatav	*R and B*; *Synopsis*
Mallika Aroumougam	*Twenty Cases*
Manju Bhargava	Not published in detail
Marta Lorenz	*Twenty Cases*
Mary Magruder	*CWRPLS*
Mounzer Haïdar	*CORT 3*
Muhittin Yılmaz	*R and B*; *Synopsis*
Myint Myint Zaw (Ma)	*R and B*; *Synopsis*
Myint Thein (Ma)	*R and B*; *Synopsis*
Nasır Toksöz	*CORT 3*
Navalkishore Yadav	*R and B*
Nirankar Bhatnagar	*R and B*; *Synopsis*
Norman Despers	*Twenty Cases*
Par (Ma)	*R and B*
Parmod Sharma	*Twenty Cases*
Prakash Varshnay	*Twenty Cases*
Rabih Elawar	*CORT 3*
Rajani Sukla	*R and B*
Rajsuthajarn (Ven. Chaokhun)	*CORT 4*
Ramoo and Rajoo Sharma	*CORT 1*
Rani Saxena	*CWRPLS* (not published in detail)
Ravi Shankar Gupta	*Twenty Cases*
Salem Andary	*CORT 3*
Sanjeev Sharma	*R and B*
Savitri Devi Pathak	*R and B*; *Synopsis*

Semih Tutuşmuş	*R and B*; *Synopsis*
Shamlinie Prema	*CORT 2*
Smriti Kana Kunda	Not published in detail
Sudhir Rastogi	Not published in detail
Sujith Lakmal Jayaratne	*CORT 2*
Suleyman Andary	*CORT 3*
Sumitra Singh	Stevenson, Pasricha, and McClean-Rice, 1989
Sunita Khandelwal	*R and B*; *Synopsis*
Suzanne Ghanem	Not published in detail
Swarnlata Mishra	*Twenty Cases*
Than Than Aye (Ma)	Not published in detail
Thiang San Kla	*R and B*; *Synopsis*
Tint Aung (U)	*R and B*
Tin Tin Myint (Ma)	*CORT 4*
Tin Yee (Ma)	*R and B*
William George, Jr.	*Twenty Cases*
Zaw Win Aung (U)	*R and B*; *Synopsis*

Bibliography

Almeder, R. 1992. *Death and personal survival: The evidence for life after death.* Lanham, MD: Rowman and Littlefield.

_____. 1997. A critique of arguments offered against reincarnation. *Journal of Scientific Exploration* 11: 499–526.

Ancelet-Hustache, J. 1963. *God tried by fire: St. Elizabeth of Hungary.* Translated by P. J. Oligny and V. O'Donnell. Chicago: Franciscan Herald Press.

Archbold, R. 1994. *Hindenburg: An illustrated history.* New York: Warner/Madison Press.

Arnold, E. 1911. *The light of Asia.* London: Kegan Paul, Trench, Trübner & Co. Ltd. (First published in 1879.)

Baker, R. A. 1982. The effect of suggestion on past-lives regression. *American Journal of Clinical Hypnosis* 25: 71–76.

Barker, D. R., and Pasricha, S. 1979. Reincarnation cases in Fatehabad: A systematic survey in North India. *Journal of Asian and African Studies* 14: 231–40.

Baticle, J. 1986. *Goya d'or et de sang.* Paris: Gallimard.

Battista, F. 1911. Un caso di reincarnazione? *Ultra* 5: 585–86.

Bergunder, M. 1994. *Wiedergeburt der Ahnen: Eine religionsethnographische und religionsphänomenologische Untersuchung zur Reinkarnationsvorstellung.* Münster: Lit Verlag.

Bernstein, M. 1965. *The search for Bridey Murphy.* New York: Doubleday. (First published in 1956.)

Bible. Authorized King James Version. New York: Thomas Nelson. (First published in 1611.)

Bigg, C. 1913. *The Christian Platonists of Alexandria.* Oxford: Clarendon Press.

Biundo, G. 1940. *Regesten der Reichsfeste Trifels.* Kaiserslauten: Saarpfälzisches Institut für Landes-und Volkforschung.

Björkhem, J. 1961. Hypnosis and personality change. In *Knut Lundmark and man's march into space: A memorial volume,* edited by M. Johnson. Gothenburg: Värld och Vetande.

Bochinger, C. 1996. Reinkarnationsidee und "New Age." In *Die Idee der Reinkarnation in Ost und West,* edited by P. Schmidt-Leukel, pp. 115–30. Munich: Eugen Diedericks Verlag.

Bondon, G. 1947. *Augustin Lesage, le peintre mineur: Sa vie et sa mission.* Ans: Imprimerie Masset. (Pamphlet privately printed.)

Bordona, J. D. 1924. Los ultimos momentos de Goya. *Revista de la Biblioteca, Archivo y Museo.* 1: 397–400.

Bozzano, E. 1940. *Indagini sulle manifestazioni supernormali.* Serie VI. Città della Pieve: Tipografia Dante. (Reprinted with the title "Reminiscenze di una vita anteriore" in *Luce e Ombra* 94: 314–27, 1994.)

Brazzini, P. 1952. *Dopo la Morte si Rinasce?* Milan: Fratelli Bocca Editori.

Broad, C. D. 1962. *Lectures on psychical research*. London: Routledge & Kegan Paul.

Browning, R. 1971. *Justinian and Theodora*. London: Weidenfeld and Nicolson.

Buchan, J. 1940. *Memory hold-the-door*. London: Hodder and Stoughton.

Burkert, W. 1972. *Lore and science in ancient Pythagoreanism*. Cambridge, MA: Harvard University Press.

Burton, R. F. 1987. *The book of the sword*. New York: Dover Publications. (First published in 1884.)

Butterworth, G. W. 1973. *Introduction. In On first principles* by Origen. Gloucester, MA: Peter Smith.

Caesar, Julius. 1917. *The Gallic war*. Translated by H. J. Edwards. London: William Heinemann.

Carbonelli, G. 1912. *Gli Ultimi Giorni del Conte Rosso e i Processi per la sua Morte*. Pavia: Pinerolo.

Catéchisme de l'église Catholique. 1992. Paris: Mame-Librairie Editrice Vaticane. (English language edition. *Catechism of the Catholic Church*. 2d ed. Washington, DC: United States Catholic Conference, 1997.)

Chalfont, Lord. ed. 1979. *Waterloo: Battle of three armies*. London: Sidgwick and Jackson.

Chatterton, E. K. 1914. *The old East Indiamen*. London: T. Werner Lauri.

Cognasso, F. 1926. *Il Conte Verde*. Turin: G. B. Paravia.

———. 1931. *Il Conte Rosso*. Turin: G. B. Paravia.

Cook, E., Pasricha, S., Samararatne, G., Maung, W., and Stevenson, I. 1983. A review and analysis of "unsolved" cases of the reincarnation type: II. Comparisons of features of solved and unsolved cases. *Journal of the American Society for Psychical Research* 77: 115–35.

Cook, E. W., Greyson, B., and Stevenson, I. 1998. Do any near-death experiences provide evidence for the survival of human personality after death? Relevant features and illustrative case reports. *Journal of Scientific Exploration* 12: 377–406.

Corson, E. F. 1934. Naevus flammeus nuchae; its occurrence and abnormalities. *American Journal of the Medical Sciences* 187: 121–24.

Costa, G. 1923. *Di là dalla vita*. Turin: S. Lattes.

Cox, E. L. 1967. *The Green Count of Savoy: Amadeus VI and Transalpine Savoy in the fourteenth century*. Princeton: Princeton University Press.

Crehan, J. 1978. Reincarnation. London: Catholic Truth Society.

Daniélou, J. 1955. *Origen*. Translated by Walter Mitchell. New York: Sheed and Ward.

Davidson, H. R. E. 1964. *Gods and myths of Northern Europe*. Harmondsworth, Middlesex: Penguin.

Davie, G. 1990. Believing without belonging: Is this the future of religion in Britain? *Social Compass* 37: 455–69.

Delanne, G. 1924. *Documents pour servir à l'étude de la réincarnation*. Paris: Éditions de la B. P. S.

Delarrey, M. 1955. Une réincarnation annoncée et vérifiée. *Revue métapsychique* 1(2): 41–44.

Dickens, C. 1877. *Pictures from Italy, Sketches by Boz, and American Notes*. New York: Harper and Brothers.

Diogenes Laertius. 1925. *Lives of eminent philosophers*. Vol. 2. Translated by R. D. Hicks. Cambridge, MA: Harvard University Press. (First published in c. 250.)

Dodds, E. R. 1951. *The Greeks and the irrational*. Berkeley: University of California Press.

Donat, A. 1963. *The Holocaust kingdom*. Washington, DC: Holocaust Library.

———. ed. 1979. *The death camp Treblinka: A documentary*. New York: Holocaust Library.

d'Ors, E. 1928. *La vie de Goya*. Translated by Marcel Carayon. Paris: Gallimard.

Doveton, F. B. 1852. *Reminiscences of the Burmese War in 1824-5-6*. London: Allen.

Dubuffet, J. ed. 1965. *Publications de la Compagnie de l'art brut. Fascicule 3. Le Mineur Lesage*. Paris: Compagnie de l'Art brut.

Ducasse, C. J. 1961. *A critical examination of the belief in a life after death*. Springfield, IL: Charles C Thomas.

Dunne, J. W. 1927. *An experiment with time*. London: Faber and Faber.

Dunning, R. W. ed. 1974. *A history of the County of Somerset*. Vol 3. Published for the Institute of Historical Research. Oxford: Oxford University Press.

_____. 1984. *The Monmouth rebellion: A complete guide to the rebellion and bloody Assizes*. Wimborne: Dovecote Press.

Earle, P. 1977. *Monmouth's rebels: The road to Sedgemoor 1685*. London: Weidenfeld and Nicolson.

East, J. N. 1960a. *Eternal quest*. London: The Psychic Press.

_____. 1960b. *Man the immortal*. London: The Psychic Press.

Eliade, M. 1982. *A history of religious ideas. Volume 2. From Gautama Buddha to the triumph of Christianity*. Translated by W. R. Trask. Chicago: University of Chicago Press.

Ellwood, G. F. 1971. *Psychic visits to the past*. New York: New American Library.

Evans-Wentz, W. Y. 1911. *The fairy-faith in Celtic countries*. New York: Oxford University Press.

Fauqué, J., and Etcheverria, R. V. 1982. *Goya y Burdeos*. Zaragoza: Ediciones Oroel.

Flournoy, T. 1899. *Des Indes à la planète Mars. Étude sur un cas de somnambulisme avec glossolalie*. Paris: Lib. Fischbacher, 4th ed. (New American edition with introduction and concluding chapter by C. T. K. Chari. New Hyde Park, NY: University Books, Inc., 1963.)

Forbes, R. 1975. *The Lyon in Mourning or a collection of speeches letters journals etc. relative to the affairs of Prince Charles Edward Stuart*. 3 vols. Edited by Henry Paton. Edinburgh: Scottish Academic Press. (First published in 1895.)

Frankl, V. E. 1947. *Ein Psycholog erlebt das Konzentrationslager. 2d ed*. Vienna: Verlag für Jugend und Volk.

Fraser, J. 1905. *Chronicles of the Frasers (The Wardlaw manuscript)*. Edinburgh: Scottish History Society.

Freeman, J. 1996. *Job: The story of a Holocaust survivor*. Westport, CT: Praeger.

Gallup Opinion Index. 1969. *Special report on religion*. Princeton, NJ: American Institute of Public Opinion.

Geley, G. 1927. *Clairvoyance and materialisation*. Translated by S. de Barth. New York: George H. Doran Company.

George, M. I. 1996. Aquinas on reincarnation. *The Thomist* 60: 33–52.

Gilbert, M. 1986. *The Holocaust: A history of the Jews of Europe during the Second World War*. New York: Holt, Reinhart, and Winston.

Gill, A. 1988. *The journey back from Hell: An oral history. Conversations with concentration camp survivors*. New York: William Morrow.

Goya, F. de. 1981. *Diplomatorio*. Edited by A. C. Lopez. Zaragoza: Librería General.

Grant, J. 1939. *Winged pharaoh*. London: Methuen.

Hackl, N. 1950. *Die Geschichte der Burgruine Weissenstein bei Regen*. Regen: Verlag Waldvereinsektion Regen.

Haich, E. 1960. *Einweihung*. Thielle: Verlag Eduard Fankhauser. (English edition: *Initiation*. London: George Allen and Unwin, 1965.)

Häikiö, W. 1992. *A brief history of modern Finland*. Lahti: University of Helsinki.

Hamilton-Williams, D. 1993. *Waterloo: New perspectives*. London: Arms and Armour Press.

Harding, S., Phillips, D., and Fogarty, M. 1986. *Contrasting values in Western Europe*. London: Macmillan.

Harris, M. 1986. *Investigating the unexplained*. Buffalo, NY: Prometheus Books.

Hawkes, J. 1981. *A quest of love*. New York: George Braziller.

Head, J., and Cranston, S. L. eds. 1977. *Reincarnation: The Phoenix fire mystery*. New York: Crown Publishers.

Hermann, T. 1960. Das déjà vu Erlebnis. *Psyche* 9: 60–76.

Heywood, R. 1960. Review of *Eternal quest* by J. N. East. *Journal of the Society for Psychical Research* 40: 370–71.

Hodgman, J. E., Freeman, R. I., and Levan, N. E. 1971. Neonatal dermatology. *Medical Clinics of North America* 18: 725–33.

Hodgson, F. C. 1910. *Venice in the thirteenth and fourteenth centuries*. London: George Allen.

Hornsby-Smith, M. P., and Lee, R. M. 1979. *Roman Catholic opinion: A study of Roman Catholics in England and Wales in the 1970s*. Guildford: University of Surrey.

Howarth, D. 1968. *Waterloo: Day of battle*. New York: Atheneum.

Hull, A. H. 1987. *Goya: Man among kings*. New York: Hamilton Press.

Huxley, T. H. 1905. *Evolution and ethics and other essays*. New York: D. Appleton.

Hyslop, J. H. 1909. A case of veridical hallucinations. *Proceedings of the American Society for Psychical Research*. 3: 1–469.

———. 1919. *Contact with the other world*. New York: The Century Co.

Iamblichus. 1965. *Life of Pythagoras*. Translated by Thomas Taylor. London: John M. Watkins. (First published in c. 310.)

Inge, W. R. 1941. *The philosophy of Plotinus*. 3d ed. 2 vols. London: Longmans, Green and Co.

Inglehart, R., Basañez, M., and Moreno, A. 1998. *Human values and beliefs: A cross-cultural sourcebook*. Ann Arbor: University of Michigan Press.

Johnson, P. 1976. *A history of Christianity*. Harmondsworth, Middlesex: Penguin.

Kampman, R. 1973. Hypnotically induced multiple personality: An experimental study. *Acta Universitatis Ouluensis*, series D, Medica no. 6. Psychiatrica no. 3, pp. 7–116.

———. 1975. The dynamic relation of the secondary personality induced by hypnosis to the present personality. *Psychiatria Fennica* (1975): 169–72.

———. 1976. Hypnotically induced multiple personality: An experimental study. *International Journal of Clinical and Experimental Hypnosis* 24: 215–27.

———, and Hirvenoja, R. 1978. Dynamic relation of the secondary personality induced by hypnosis to the present personality. In *Hypnosis at its bicentennial*, edited by F. H. Frankel and H. S. Zamansky. New York: Plenum Press.

Kaspar, W. 1990. Réincarnation et christianisme. *La documentation catholique*. Number 2005, May 6, 1990, 453–55.

Keltie, J. S., ed. 1875. *A history of the Scottish highlands, highland clans and highland regiments*. Edinburgh: A. Fullerton.

Ker, W. P. 1904. *The dark ages*. New York: Charles Scribner's Sons.

Kraus, O., and Kulka, E. 1966. *The death factory: Document on Auschwitz*. Oxford: Pergamon Press.

Krüger, M. 1996. *Ichgeburt: Origenes und die Entstehung der christlichen Idee der Wiederverkörperung in der Denkbewegung von Pythagoras bis Lessing*. Hildesheim: Georg Olms Verlag.

Lafond, P. 1907. Les dernières années de Goya en France. *Gazette des beaux arts*. 1: 114–31 and 241–57.

Lambert, Y. 1994. La religion: Un paysage en profonde évolution. In *Les valeurs des français*, edited by H. Riffault. Paris: Presses Universitaires de France.

Lancelin, C. c. 1922. *La vie posthume*. Paris: Henri Durville.

Laurence, J. 1960. *A history of capital punishment*. New York: The Citadel Press.

Laurie, W. F. B. 1880. *Our Burmese wars and relations with Burma, being an abstract of military and political operations, 1824-25-26 and 1852–53*. London: W. H. Allen.

Leasor, J. 1957. *The millionth chance: The story of the R 101*. New York: Reynal and Company.

Lemmer, M., trans. and ed. 1981. *Das Leben der heiligen Elisabeth*. Vienna: Verlag Styria.

Lengyel, O. 1947. *Five chimneys: The story of Auschwitz*. Chicago: Ziff-Davis.

Le Roy Ladurie, E. 1975. *Montaillou, village occitan de 1294 à 1324*. Paris: Éditions Gallimard. (American edition: *Montaillou: The promised land of error*. Translated by Barbara Bray. New York: George Braziller, 1978.)

Lockhart, L. 1958. *The fall of the Safavi dynasty and the Afghan occupation of Persia.* Cambridge: Cambridge University Press.

_____. 1960. *Persian cities.* London: Luzac and Company.

Lund, D. H. 1985. *Death and consciousness.* Jefferson, NC: McFarland and Company.

Lundin, C. L. 1957. *Finland in the Second World War.* Bloomington: Indiana University Press.

Macbride, M. ed. 1911. *With Napoleon at Waterloo.* London: G. Bell and Sons.

Macdonald, A. 1934. *The old Lords of Lovat and Beaufort.* Inverness: The Northern Counties Newspaper and Printing and Publishing Company.

MacGregor, G. 1978. *Reincarnation in Christianity.* Wheaton, IL: The Theosophical Publishing House.

McKellar, P. 1957. *Imagination and thinking.* New York: Basic Books.

Mackenzie, A. 1896. *A history of the Frasers of Lovat.* Inverness: A. and W. Mackenzie.

Mackie, R. L. 1962. *A short history of Scotland.* Edinburgh: Oliver and Boyd. (First published in 1930.)

McTaggart, J. M. E. 1906. *Some dogmas of religion.* London: Edward Arnold.

Madaule, J. 1961. *Le drame albigeois et le destin français.* Paris: Bernard Grasset.

Mass-Observation. 1947. *Puzzled people: A study in popular attitudes to religion, ethics, progress and politics in a London Borough.* London: Victor Gollancz.

Mead, G. R. S. ed. 1921. *Pistis Sophia: A gnostic miscellany.* 2d ed. London: John M. Watkins.

Mesquita, D. M. B. de. 1941. *Giangaleazzo Visconti.* Cambridge: Cambridge University Press.

Moncreiffe, I., and Hicks, D. 1967. *The highland clans.* London: Barrie and Rockliff.

Monumenta Boica. 1765. Munich: Edidit Academia Scientiarum Maximilianea. (Cited by G. Oswald in a letter to G. Neidhart of June 28, 1956.)

Mooney, M. M. 1972. *The Hindenburg.* New York: Dodd, Mead.

Moratín, L. F. de. 1929. *Epistolario de Leandro Fernandez de Moratín.* Madrid: Compania Ibero-Americano de Publicaciones.

Murphy, F.-X., and Sherwood, P. 1973. *Histoire des Conciles Oecuméniques: Constantinople II and Constantinople III.* Paris: Éditions de l'Orante.

Neale, J. P. 1821. *Views of the seats of noblemen and gentlemen in England, Wales, Scotland and Ireland.* London: Sherwood, Neely and Jones. Vol. iv.

Neidhart, G. 1957. *Werden Wir Wiedergeboren?* Munich: Gesellschaft für religiöse und geistige Erneurung.

Neppe, V. 1983. *The psychology of déjà vu*: Have I been here before? Johannesburg: Witwatersrand University Press.

Norwich, J. J. 1982. *A history of Venice.* New York: Alfred A. Knopf.

Nyiszli, M. 1993. *Auschwitz: A doctor's eyewitness account.* Translated by T. Kremer and R. Seaver. New York: Arcade Publishing. (First published in 1960.)

Origen. 1973. *On first principles.* Translated by G. W. Butterworth. Gloucester, MA: Peter Smith.

Orne, M. T. 1951. The mechanisms of hypnotic age regression: An experimental study. *Journal of Abnormal and Social Psychology* 46: 213–25.

Osty, E. 1923. *La connaissance supra-normale*: Étude expérimentale. Paris: Félix Alcan. (English edition: *Supernormal faculties in man.* Translated by S. de Brath. London: Methuen and Company, 1923.)

_____. 1928. Augustin Lesage. Peintre sans avoir appris. *Revue métapsychique,* Jan-fév 1–35.

Oswald, G. 1952. *Die Geschichte der Stadt Regen.* Regen: Verlag Wilhelm Dirmaier.

Paget, J. and Saunders, D. 1992. *Hougoumont: The key to victory at Waterloo.* London: Leo Cooper.

Palmer, J. 1979. A community mail survey of psychic experiences. *Journal of the American Society for Psychical Research* 73: 221–51.

Paterson, R. W. K. 1995. Philosophy and the belief in a life after death. London: Macmillan.

Philostratus. 1912. *The life of Apollonius of Tyana.* Translated by F. D. Conybeare. London: William Heinemann.

Plato. 1935. *The Republic*. Translated by A. D. Lindsay. London: J. M. Dent.

_____. 1936. *Five Dialogues*. Translated by P. B. Shelley, F. Sydenham, H. Cary, and J. Wright. London: J. M. Dent.

Plotinus. 1909. *Select works of Plotinus*. Translated by T. Taylor. London: George Bell and Sons.

Prat, F. 1907. *Origène: Le théologien et l'exégète*. Paris: Librairie Bloud.

Prebble, J. 1961. *Culloden*. London: Secker and Warburg.

Prince, W. F. 1931. Human experiences: Being a report on the results of a questionnaire and a discussion of them. *Bulletin of the Boston Society for Psychic Research*, 14, 1–331.

Quaife, G. R. 1979. *Wanton wenches and wayward wives: Peasants and illicit sex in early seventeenth century Somerset*. London: Croom Helm.

Rautkallio, H. 1987. *Finland and the Holocaust: The rescue of Finland's Jews*. New York: The Holocaust Library.

Rivas, T. 1991. Alfred Peacock? Reincarnation fantasies about the *Titanic*. *Journal of the Society for Psychical Research* 58: 10–15.

Rochas, A. de. 1924. *Les vies successives*. Paris: Chacornac frères. (First published in 1911.)

Ruhe, B. 1982. *Boomerang*. Washington, DC: Minner Press.

Runciman, S. 1965. *The fall of Constantinople 1453*. Cambridge: Cambridge University Press.

_____. 1969. *The medieval Manichee: A study of the Christian dualist heresy*. Cambridge: Cambridge University Press.

Ryall, E. W. 1974. *Second time round*. Jersey: Neville Spearman. (American edition published in 1974 under the title of *Born Twice*. New York: Harper and Row.)

Samonà, C. 1911. Un caso di rincarnazione? *Filosofia della scienza* 3: 1–3.

_____. 1913a. Un caso di rincarnazione? *Filosofia della scienza* 5: 30–33.

_____. 1913b. Ancora della critica del Dottor Fugairon. *Filosofia della scienza* 4: 230–33.

_____. 1914. Una breva risposta al professor Morselli del Dottor Carmelo Samonà. *Filosofia della Scienza* 6: 163–64.

Sánchez Cantón, F. J. 1951. *Vida y obras de Goya*. Madrid: Editorial Peninsular.

Savoia, M. J. di. 1956. *Amedeo VI e Amedeo VII di Savoia*. Milan: Arnoldo Monadori Editore.

Scheffczyk, L. 1985. *Der Reinkarnationsgedanke in der altchristlichen Literatur*. Munich: Verlag der Bayerischen Akademie der Wissenschaften.

Schönborn, C. 1990. La réponse chrétienne au défi de la réincarnation. *La documentation cathologue*. Number 2005, May 6, 1990, 456–58.

Schopenhauer, A. 1891. *Parerga und Paralipomena*. In *Arthur Schopenhauers sämmtliche Werke*. Vol. 2. Leipzig: F. U. Brockhaus. (First published in 1851.)

Secrest, M. 1986. *Salvador Dalí*. New York: E. P. Dutton.

Segal, N. 1999. *Entwined lives: Twins and what they tell us about human behavior*. New York: Dutton.

Seton, B. G., and Arnot, J. G. 1928. *The prisoners of the 'Forty-five.'* Edinburgh: Scottish History Society. (Cited by I. C. Taylor in letter of December 5, 1967.)

Singer, D. W. 1950. *Giordano Bruno: His life and thought*. New York: Henry Schuman.

Smith, M. J. 1995. *Dachau: The harrowing of Hell*. Albany, NY: State University of New York Press.

Sno, H. N., and Linszen, D. H. 1990. The déjà vu experience: Remembrance of things past? *American Journal of Psychiatry* 147: 1587–95.

Spanos, N. 1996. *Multiple identities and false memories: A sociocognitive perspective*. Washington: American Psychological Association.

Spanos, N. P., Menary, E., Gabora, N. J., DuBreuil, S. C., and Dewhirst, B. 1991. Secondary identity enactments during hypnotic past-life regression: A sociocognitive perspective. *Journal of Personality and Social Psychology* 61: 308–20.

Spears, E. 1967. *The picnic basket*. London: Secker and Warburg.

Sprater, F., and Stein, G. 1971. *Der Trifels*. Speyer am Rhein: Verlag des historischen Museums der Pfalz.

Stanley, M. P. 1989. *Christianisme et réincarnation: Vers la réconciliation.* Saint-Martin-le-Vinoux: L'or du Temps.

_____. 1998. *Réincarnation: La nouvelle affaire Galilée.?* Paris: Éditions Lanore.

Stevens, J. E. ed. 1986. *Coke's first 100 years.* Shepherdsville, KY: Keller International Publishing Corporation.

Stevenson, I. 1960. The evidence for survival from claimed memories of former incarnations. *Journal of the American Society for Psychical Research* 54: 51–71 and 95–117.

_____. 1970a. *Telepathic impressions: A review and report of thirty-five new cases.* Charlottesville: University Press of Virginia. (Also published as Volume 29 of the *Proceedings of the American Society for Psychical Research.*)

_____. 1970b. Precognition of disasters. *Journal of the American Society for Psychical Research* 64: 187–210.

_____. 1974a. Some questions related to cases of the reincarnation type. *Journal of the American Society for Psychical Research* 68: 395–416.

_____. 1974b. *Xenoglossy: A review and report of a case.* Charlottesville: University Press of Virginia. (Also published as Volume 31 of the *Proceedings of the American Society for Psychical Research.*)

_____. 1974c. Introduction to *Second Time Round* by E. W. Ryall. Jersey: Neville Spearman.

_____. 1983. Cryptomnesia and parapsychology. *Journal of the Society for Psychical Research* 52: 1–30.

_____. 1984. *Unlearned language: New studies in xenoglossy.* Charlottesville: University Press of Virginia.

_____. 1990. Phobias in children who claim to remember previous lives. *Journal of Scientific Exploration* 4: 243–54.

_____. 1992. A new look at maternal impressions: An analysis of 50 published cases and reports of two recent examples. *Journal of Scientific Exploration* 6: 353–73.

_____. 1994. A case of the psychotherapist's fallacy: Hypnotic regression to "previous lives." *American Journal of Clinical Hypnosis* 36: 188–93.

_____. 1997. *Reincarnation and biology: A contribution to the etiology of birthmarks and birth defects.* 2 vols. Westport, CT: Praeger.

_____. 2001. *Children who remember previous lives: A question of reincarnation.* rev. ed. Jefferson, NC: McFarland & Company, Inc. (First published in 1987; Charlottesville: University Press of Virginia.)

_____, and Chadha, N. K. 1990. Can children be stopped from speaking about previous lives? Some further analyses of features in cases of the reincarnation type. *Journal of the Society for Psychical Research* 56: 82–90.

_____, and Cook, E. W. 1995. Involuntary memories during severe physical illness or injury. *Journal of Nervous and Mental Disease* 183: 452–58.

_____, and Keil, J. 2000. The stability of assessments of paranormal connections in reincarnation-type cases. *Journal of Scientific Exploration* 14(3): 365–82.

_____, Pasricha, S., and McClean-Rice, N. 1989. A case of the possession type in India with evidence of paranormal knowledge. *Journal of Scientific Exploration* 3: 81–101.

Stokes, H. 1914. *Francisco Goya.* New York: G. P. Putnam's Sons.

Story, F. 1975. *Rebirth as doctrine and experience.* Kandy, Sri Lanka: Buddhist Publication Society. (First published in 1959.)

Taylor, I. C. 1965. *Culloden: A guidebook to the battlefield with the story of the battle, the events leading to it and the aftermath.* Edinburgh: The National Trust for Scotland.

Tertullian. Apological Works. 1950. Translated by E. A. Quain. New York: Fathers of the Church.

Thomas Aquinas (Saint). 1984. *Questions on the soul.* Translated by J. R. Robb. Milwaukee, WI: Marquette University Press. (First published c. 1269.)

Thomas, J. 1991. *The boomerangs of a pharaoh.* Paris: Privately published.

Toland, J. 1972. *The great dirigibles: Their triumphs and disasters.* New York: Dover Publications.

Townend, P. 1963. *Burke's peerage, baronetage, and knightage.* 103d ed. London: Burke's Peerage Limited. (First published in 1826.)

Trant, T. A. 1827. *Two years in Ava from May 1824 to May 1826.* London: John Murray.

Tucker, J. B. 2000. A scale to measure the strength of children's claims of previous lives: Methodology and initial findings. *Journal of Scientific Exploration* 14: 571–81.

United States Government Printing Office. 1945. *Handbook on German military forces.* War Department Technical Manual TM-E 30–451 March 15, 1945.

Vaccarone, L. 1893. *I Challant e loro Questioni per la Successione ai Feudi dal XII al XIX Secolo.* Turin: F. Casanova Editore.

Vale, W. L. 1969. *History of the South Staffordshire Regiment.* Aldershot: Gale and Polden.

Venn, J. 1986. Hypnosis and the reincarnation hypothesis: A critical review and intensive case study. *Journal of the American Society for Psychical Research* 80: 409–25.

Von Müller, F. 1924. *Das Land der Abtei im alten Fürstentum Passau.* Landshut: Sonderabdruck aus den Verhandlungen des historischen Vereins für Niederbayern.

Wallis, R. T. 1972. *Neoplatonism.* London: Duckworth.

Walter, T., and Waterhouse, H. 1999. A very private belief: Reincarnation in contemporary England. *Sociology of Religion* 60: 187–97.

Waterhouse, H. 1999. Reincarnation belief in Britain: New age orientation or mainstream option? *Journal of Contemporary Religion* 14: 97–109.

Watters, P. 1978. *Coca-Cola: An illustrated history.* Garden City, NY: Doubleday and Company.

Wells, G. L., and Murray, D. M. 1984. Eyewitness confidence. In *Eyewitness testimony, edited by* G. L. Wells and E. F. Loftus. Cambridge: Cambridge University Press.

Wigfield, W. M. 1980. *The Monmouth rebellion: A social history.* Bradford-on-Avon: Moonraker Press.

_____. (Compiler). 1985. *The Monmouth rebels 1685.* Gloucester: Alan Sutton.

Wilson, I. 1981. *Mind out of time?* London: Victor Gollancz.

Young, P., and Adair, J. 1964. *Hastings to Culloden.* London: G. Bell and Sons.

Zolik, E. S. 1958. An experimental investigation of the psychodynamic implications of the hypnotic "previous existence" fantasy. *Journal of Clinical Psychology* 14: 179–83. (Also unpublished case reports presented at the meeting of the American Psychological Association, 1958.)

_____. 1962. "Reincarnation" phenomena in hypnotic states. *International Journal of Parapsychology* 4(3): 66–78.

Index

Honorifics are omitted with Burmese names.